AFRO ASIA

AFRO

Revolutionary Political and
Cultural Connections

ASIA

between African Americans
and Asian Americans

EDITED BY FRED HO AND BILL V. MULLEN

DUKE UNIVERSITY PRESS
Durham and London 2008

Printed in
the United States
of America
on acid-free paper ∞

Designed
by Jennifer Hill
Typeset
in Scala
by Keystone
Typesetting, Inc.

Library of Congress
Cataloging-in-Publication
Data appear
on the last printed page
of this book.

"Is Kung Fu Racist?"
by Ron Wheeler
with David Kaufman,
originally appeared
in *Kungfu*,
April/May 1997.

CONTENTS

ACKNOWLEDGMENTS

We are indebted to the many contributors in this volume, and we also extend our gratitude to Reynolds Smith of the Duke University Press. The minute we described this anthology project to him, he "got it."

From Fred Ho: For giving me the time to finish this book I would like to extend my deepest appreciation and thanks to the Djerassi Resident Artists Program where I was the 2004 recipient of the Gerald Oshita Memorial Fellowship. My thanks also to Fred Yuen Lee, yellow soul-brother, who gave me many e-mail current events on anti-Asian racism; and to the following people who in my life journey have furthered Afro/Asian solidarity and support: Max Roach, Sonia Sanchez, Archie Shepp, Kalamu Ya Salaam, Andrea Lockett, Jayne Cortez, the late saxophonist and friend Sam Furnace, Wesley Brown, Marilyn Lewis, Amiri and Amina Baraka, Peggy Choy, Diane Fujino and Matef Harmachis (and their Afro Asian sons Kano and Seku), David Bindman, Jennifer Feil, Richard Hamasaki, Ricardo Gomes, Charli Persip, Richard Aoki, Janice Mirikitani, Genny Lim, Ishmael Reed, Quincy and Margaret Porter Troupe, Roger Buckley, Angela Rola, Fe de los Santos, Ann T. Greene, Jamala Rogers, Baraka Sele, Colleen Jennings-Roggensack, Yuri Kochiyama, Greg Morozumi, Ricardo Gomes, Robin D. G. Kelley, Salim Washington, the late Sun Ra, the late John Coltrane, the late Thad Jones, the late Charles Mingus, Ngugi wa Thiong'o, the late Huey P. Newton, the late Fela Kuti, the late Malcolm X, the late Kenneth Noel, Frederick Tillis, Jacob Epstein, royal hartigan, Giovanni Bonandrini, Norman Riley, the late Cal Massey, the late Charles Majeed Greenlee, Hafez Modirzadeh, Tchaiko and Eusi Kwayana (for contributing an essay that, regrettably, we were not able to publish in this anthology), Jose Figueroa, Ron Wheeler, Ruth Margraff, Melanie West . . .

From Bill V. Mullen: All great and just things begin with Tithi Bhatta-charya, my comrade, partner, and life source. Meye—you are mine. Love me (no commas).

This book as always is for Max. I love you.

In solidarity I also celebrate Zhu Ying, Xiao Xiao Yu, Chen Chuoa Chen, Julian Madison, Grace Lee Boggs, Margaret Burroughs, Byron Harlan, Richie Wong, Homer Warren, Mike, Marlene, Steven, Claire, and Audrey Mergenthaler, Mark Dery, Margot Mifflin, Thea, friends, and family.

Fred Ho and Bill V. Mullen

Introduction

B ill Mullen writes: I first saw Fred Ho perform live in November 1997 at the Brooklyn Academy of Music, where the Monkey Orchestra delivered a revisionist performance of the classic Chinese novel *Journey to the West.* At this time I was preparing to teach African American literature in China, and thus I was beginning my research into the long history of connection between African Americans and Asian Americans. The Monkey Orchestra performance blew me away. The band was hot, the martial arts choreography scintillating, the words and ideas in the text radical. Fred was retooling China's most longstanding and cherished popular story of Monkey, the consummate trickster hero in Asian literature, into a smashing allegory of people's liberation.

Fred and I later talked on the phone about his work. It was out of our discussions that the idea for this anthology was born. It was our shared assessment that no single book had yet to capture the full range of important historical, political, and cultural connections between Asian Americans and African Americans. Indeed, at the time of our early conversations on the topic, blacks and Asians were typically being pitted against one another in mass media narratives or rolled together in popular films that pretended that one good martial arts scene could stand in for a long and complex process of historical exchange. Fred's own term for this distinctly American process, "chop-sueyism," speaks to the difficulties in producing a book like the one we envisioned: a book that would pay tribute to work by writers, scholars, and cultural workers with long roots in Afro Asian struggle; with deep commitments to forms of cultural and political practice; and with bold and original insights into what we could both see was quickly becoming a fairly trendy area of academic inquiry. In short, we wanted to do a book that would include some of the best new thinking on Afro Asia by people who had paid long and hard dues in the struggle to bring truth, justice, and light to their ancient history of cooperation, sacrifice, and work.

It was this tendency in Fred's own life and work that drew me to him in 1997. Fred's own musical and political education in Afro Asia is an outgrowth of his long-standing cultural and political activity as a leader in Afro Asian unity building. Fred is most well known as the founder and leader of the Afro Asian Music Ensemble, which started in 1982. The ensemble merges traditional "jazz" instrumentations and idioms with classical Asian musical motifs, genres, sounds, and themes.

Fred himself came of age during the late 1960s and early 1970s, and he claims that his identity as Asian/Chinese American was ignited by the upsurge of the Black Power movement in the United States. It was reading Malcolm X's *Autobiography* while being singled out for racial harassment in public school that forged his own sense of mutually shared oppressions. Like many other United States activists of color, Ho first came to an affirmation of ethnic identity from the inspiration and impact of radical and revolutionary African American politics and culture. This discovery brought with it, however, a far larger challenge: namely, a way to enact, analyze, and catalyze a radical and revolutionary political and cultural stance grounded in anti-imperialism and anti-oppression and devoid of Eurocentric and white supremacist reference and ideals. For Ho, and for other authors in this book, Afro Asia is a strategic intersection for thinking through an internationalist, global paradigm that joins the world's two largest continents and populations, as well as an anti-imperialist, insurgent identity that is no longer majority white in orientation. Afro Asia, that is, is the imperative to imagine a "new world" grounded upon two great ancient worlds as well as a radical and revolutionary anti-imperialist tradition.

It is a tradition with long roots, one that includes and links W. E. B. Du Bois, Ho Chi Minh, Mao Zedong, Malcolm X, Robert F. Williams, the Black Panthers, the Asian Pacific American movement, Yuri Kochiyama, Ishmael Reed, Frank Chin, and Maxine Hong Kingston, to name just a few. These figures give a name and voice to their international counterparts in the black and Asiatic worlds, and they have for two centuries sustained a tradition of collaborative radical political and cultural connections heretofore undocumented in the literature of the West. From the earliest days of the United States, Africans and Asians in the Americas have been linked in a shared tradition of resistance to class and racial exploitation and oppression. With the formal abolition of African slavery arose the Asiatic "coolie" (or contract labor) trade that brought Asian laborers, often on the very same ships that transported captured Africans, to the very same plantation societies in the West. In this common and often overlapping diasporic experience, shared traditions of resistance and struggle have developed for liberation and equality. African Americans and Asian Americans have mutually influenced, borrowed from, and jointly innovated new forms in culture (from music to cuisine to clothing) and politics (from shared movement ideologies to organizations).

This intersecting ground of cultural borrowing and exchange has been partly documented by classicists engaged by questions of the relationship between Greek and Rome on the one hand, and the larger realm of the contemporary Middle East, from North Africa to the Mediterranean, on the other. Among the early pioneers in this work was the African American classicist Frank Snowden. His books, *Before Color Prejudice: The Ancient View of Blacks and Blacks in Antiquity* and *Ethiopians in the Greco-Roman Experience*, describe the influences on Western art, literature, and design of North African societies in particular. Snowden's work sits squarely in the tradition of the Classics. Martin Bernal's influential multivolume book *Black Athena* provides a polemical cultural studies framework for understanding the influence of North African and Mediterranean influence on Greco-Roman culture as a story of racist historiography extending to eighteenth- and nineteenth-century European scholars' efforts to downplay or eradicate the Afro Asian role in the production of Western culture. Wilson Moses, in his book *Afrotopia*, provides his own historiography for this debate, noting that nineteenth-century Afrocentrists and Egyptocentrists in the United States likewise struggled to make visible the influences of African thought and culture on antiquity debates. Later, G. M. James's *Stolen Legacy* gave a name to the accusations of cultural "pirating" described by Bernal, an argument that W. E. B. Du Bois also made vigorously in his chapter "Asia in Africa" in the expanded edition of his book *The World and Africa,* first published in 1946. Du Bois's own large body of writing on Asian politics and history is perhaps the most overlooked legacy of his capacious intellectual career and a sign of the ethnocentrism that has constrained the analysis of Afro Asian exchange. Indeed, the publication of Vijay Prashad's two important books *The Karma of Brown Folk* and *Everybody Was Kung-Fu Fighting* helped to reanimate attention to Afro Asian intersections. Prashad used the term "polyculturalism" to characterize the long, repressed but vital tradition of Afro Asian encounter and exchange, particularly among the working classes.[1]

While the focus of this anthology is likewise on shared and common struggles as well as the linkages, connections, cross-cultural borrowing, and mutual solidarity, it is important to recognize the complexities, contradictions, and conflicts between black and Asian peoples in the United States. It is also important to provide a proper framework and analysis of the systemic causes for such complexities as well as the political function served by the manipulation of race, the promotion of nationalist divisions and rivalries, and the inculcation of mutually pervasive stereotypes and racial jealousies. Indeed, Du Bois himself was perhaps the first to recognize the nefariousness of these divisions and misunderstandings. For example, in his 1935 essay "Indians and American Negroes" Du Bois complained that black Americans were provided almost no information on Asia, especially India, and thus had no context for seeing their own racial struggles in the necessary context of anticolonialism. Likewise, South Asians, fed a steady Western diet of imperialist rhetoric, were absent a positive understanding of African Americans and Africans. Du Bois's ability to recognize this dual orientalism capable of dismantling and forestalling Afro Asian unity also illuminates the work done by the scholars Reginald Kearney and Mark Gallichio.[2] They note that during the 1930s and 1940s subgroups of black Americans, primarily from the working classes, were drawn to Afro Asian solidarity and even infatuation with Japanese imperialism as an imaginative means of cross-racial alliance. Gerald Horne, in his impressive book *Race War! White Supremacy and the Japanese Attack on the British Empire*, situates these desires and at times misunderstandings within the broad context of white supremacy.[3] Horne argues that the importation of British and U.S. forms of racial supremacy across the Pan-Pacific region came home to roost both in the racial supremacist rhetoric undergirding Japanese imperialism during the 1930s as well as in the various nationalist, cross-nationalist, and otherwise anti-racist Afro Asian dreams of alliance. Put simply, race, racism, and capitalism have conspired, according to Horne, to both produce and manipulate the black world's understanding of Asia and the Asian world's understanding of the black "West."

And yet the dominant form of black-Asian alliance across the twentieth century is a carefully considered strategic anti-essentialism rooted in analysis of political, economic, and racial conditions across the colored world produced under white supremacy. This is the clear legacy of the so-called Bandung era of 1955 to 1973 that arguably countered and corrected many of the advances made in the Afro Asian solidarity movements of the 1930s by linking them to emergent anticolonial struggles around the world. Richard Wright understood this movement well when he traveled from Paris to Bandung, Indonesia, in 1955 to attend the Afro Asian meeting of twenty-nine decolonizing heads of state. His book on the event, *The Color Curtain*, is itself a contradictory example of Afro Asia's themes: a vigorous support for anticolonial solidarity, an indictment of white supremacy, a cry to the wretched of the earth, and yet an oddly anti-Communist and at times orientalist rendering of his own dislocation from both the "Eastern" and "Western" worlds during his American exile. Bandung informs and haunts any and all efforts to theorize Afro Asia. It is both the watershed and high-water mark of black-Asian affiliation and the unfinished and imperfect dream of a road still being pursued and paved by the authors represented in this book.

Afro Asia and Black Power

Fred Ho writes: The Black Power era in U.S. social history (circa the late 1960s) included many other social movements—queer liberation, the Asian movement, the Chicano movement, and the women's liberation movement, among others—that asserted the principles, so powerfully articulated and advocated by Malcolm X, of self-respect, self-defense, and self-determination. While these movements asserted particularistic demands and self-aware pride and the assertion of autonomous identities, the dominant leaders of these groups were radical and revolutionary and, therefore, targeted "the system" and promoted unity and alliances among oppressed peoples rather than isolationism, protectionism, and narrow chauvinism. While efforts to unite and develop a concerted revolutionary Left united front were many and sincere, they were short-lived, limited, and fraught with conflicts, contradictions, and failures. This was especially true in the case of the New Communist movement when organizations that came out of the black, Asian, Puerto Rican, Chicano, and white Left merged and united into "multinational" organizations, with many either falling apart due to internecine splits or fading away due to their inability to sink roots and expand.[4] While it is neither the focus nor role of this anthology to analyze the rise and fall of the United States New Left, it is important to recognize that by the Reagan-Bush years of the 1980s and early 1990s, many of the radical and revolutionary initiatives had imploded, disappeared, and become marginalized due to a combination of internal errors and failures as well as the overall right-wing onslaught to retake the political, social, and cultural initiative that the Left had briefly seized. The U.S. elites, perhaps in learning more from the sixties and early-seventies experience than did the U.S. Left, quickly deployed an array of strategies and tactics that combined the "stick" and the "carrot" to repress, crush, and co-opt the energies that had erupted.

The documentation of the violent repression, military assault, and incarceration of radicals is well assembled in accounts about the FBI's COINTELPRO (Counter-Intelligence Program) as well as in the counter-insurgency and destablization programs of the CIA in other countries.[5] Less documented and analyzed are how the various movements and their leaders were co-opted, tempted, and seduced by reformism, careerism, and a host of distractions, eviscerations, and compromises and dilutions. The tactics of co-optation and containment employed domestically have included divide and conquer, the promotion of neoconservative ideologues, and the general discrediting and disappearing of social consciousness for a cultural conditioning that promotes hyperindividualism, consumerism, and instant gratification.

The African American radical and revolutionary movement has, since its explosion, suffered assassination, incarceration, and calumny. The expansion of the black middle class has been one of the most significant gains won from the hard-fought civil rights and Black Power struggles. As concessions and response to revolutionary demands for full equality and empowerment, federal government–instituted policies and programs such as affirmative action recruitment and hiring were instituted. The expansion of a black elite beholden to government and corporate admittance has spawned a reformist and neoconservative black leadership, often in direct consequence and designed to supplant the black Left. The appointment of Clarence Thomas to the U.S. Supreme Court, and the rise of neoconservative black ideologues such as Thomas Sowell, Shelby Steele, Clarence Pendleton, Stanley Crouch, Alan Keyes, and others, reflect a new generation of media pundits who support the neoconservative agenda of minimizing or erasing racism and the saliency of race by attacking special programs and supporting the overall drumbeat of U.S. imperialism. Along with the rise of black neoconservatives, which is the direct political and intellectual wing of black franchise capitalism, is the rise of an essentialist black fundamentalism, articulated in part as Afrocentrism and represented by Louis Farrakhan and Molefi Asante. Another very influential sector, based primarily in academia and in intellectual power, is an integrationist celebrity strata with well-known and well-paid intellectuals. Many of the neoconservatives, along with their counterparts in the Afrocentrist sphere, have promoted an attitude of black protectionism for the small gains secured by these middle classes. A "black versus other minorities" endgame has been constructed in the competition for status, resources, and token power, reflected in debates and divisions between Afrocentrism versus multiculturalism and between the black community as consumer versus the Korean or Asian merchant as outside parasites. What is also noteworthy is that within the African American community, cleavages, fault lines, contradictions, and conflicts are also promulgated and fanned by both neoconservatives and black essentialist-fundamentalists—namely, black men versus black feminism and self-responsibility versus blaming the system and racism, as well as the rise of variants of black masculinist capitalism.

In the maintenance of ruling power, the tactic of divide and conquer has been very effective especially in conditions of limited and narrow political consciousness on the part of the oppressed. Between Africans and Asians in the United States, divisions are accentuated through competition over resources and positioning vis-à-vis the institutional funding troughs in vastly dissimilar terrains ranging from colleges and universities to inner-city ghettos. The concessions such as ethnic studies programs or minority affairs offices or student cultural centers are increasingly embracing isolationism and protectionism in a defensive circle-the-wagons mentality for the small, hard-won gains on college campuses. The dramatic increases in the Latino and Asian/Pacific student presence has intensified competition over limited student government and administration funds and support for these programs. Pressure to reallocate funds, once perceived as black entitlements and preserves, to be shared with "other" minorities has fueled resentment and suspicion on the part of African Americans. The history of collaboration and common struggle that brought about these concessions in the first place is often "lost" or "forgotten" as demagogues from both black and other minorities vie for most-favored minority status with the dominant administration.

In inner-city ghettos, as skyrocketing real estate pressures force newer immigrants into cheaper real estate markets within black and Latino neighborhoods, the presence of seemingly prosperous Asian small businesses has instilled bitterness and resentment on the part of black communities in the context of widening black inequality and increasing black poverty. Combined with these new immigrants' own racism, ignorance of American race relations, and petty capitalist greed, misunderstandings and indignities have ignited bitter and violent clashes between Asian merchants and black consumers.

During the early 1990s, headlines and television news stories focused on conflicts that erupted in predominantly black inner-city communities toward Korean greengrocers. On Church Avenue in Brooklyn, New York, two Korean convenience stores became the target of a major boycott for disrespecting African American customers. In Los Angeles, Korean merchants were also the target of boycotts for disrespectful treatment of their black customers as well as for the case of the Korean store owner Soon Ja Du's killing of a black girl, Latasha Harlins, for shoplifting. Furthermore, during the 1992 riots following the aftermath of the first verdict that exonerated the police officers in the beating of Rodney King, Koreatown businesses were especially targeted for vandalism and looting, with entire buildings destroyed and set aflame. Other such incidents and eruptions that had African Americans in conflict with Asian merchants included a boycott called by black businesses and community members against the competition of faux-African textiles manufactured in Taiwan and sold by Asian merchants.

In part, the mass media has exploited and sensationalized these conflicts. Some critics would argue that the corporate mass media has actually created a conflict when there really is none. The so-called "black-Korean" or "black-Asian" conflict seems no more or no less a phenomenon than the ongoing, historical "black-white" conflict or the "black-brown" conflict. The special attention given to the black-Asian conflict seems to serve the purpose of victims blaming victims and letting white supremacy off the hook. The issues of bank redlining, the maldistribution of social services and resources, police brutality, narcotics trafficking, and impoverished education are conveniently deferred for sensationalistic headlines about black-Asian violence and altercations.

However, the social context for such conflicts are a result of the greater inequality and impoverishment contributed by federal and state government policies that have ushered in a major withdrawal and abandonment of support services and funding to the inner city, the elimination and rescinding of welfare benefits, and the shrinking investments into urban improvement—all of which are born most unduly and harshly by African Americans as well as Latinos. Beginning with the withdrawal of U.S. forces in Southeast Asia, U.S. government policies favored the repatriation of powerful and wealthy anti-Communist allies in Asia. Additionally, Pacific Rim overseas capital investments drastically increased in inner-city areas along with the particular phenomenon of newer Asian immigrants investing their entire family savings into small businesses, most commonly liquor stores, greengrocers, cleaners, and other mercantile enterprises. The long-standing obstacles and difficulties to African American capital expansion are well documented, ranging from practices and policies of bank redlining (i.e., not granting capital loans), to corporate franchise monopolization (e.g., a big corporate chain muscling out smaller local businesses), and lack of adequate financial and managerial services. Certain African Americans resent and are angry at perceived Asian economic success. "They just come in, start up their businesses, take our money, and give nothing back except disrespect" is the all-too-common attitude in the black community toward the Asian "outsiders." The Asian new immigrant entrepreneurs sometimes have an attitude of indifference and harshness toward their low-income black clientele, along with a limited English-language ability and a lack of historical understanding of U.S. racism. To their credit, certain black nationalist protestors (such as those in the December 12th movement) have distinguished between specifically criticizing Korean capitalists and have opposed a general anti-Asian position. And there is no doubt that some newer Asian immigrants (not just the merchants) hold racist attitudes that are greatly influenced by overall U.S. white racism and stereotypes toward black people.

Whatever the racist incident, by an Asian committed upon Africans or by an African committed upon Asians, media attention never focuses on collaborative attempts to protest and condemn the racism. Given the "low and narrow" consciousness between blacks and Asians as a reflection of the weakness and ebb of the black liberation movement and the Asian movement respectively, increasing incidents, conflicts, and flare-ups will occur.

In such a climate, it is no surprise that a patently racist and offensive game such as Ghettopoly could be introduced. Created by the Taiwanese American David Chang, Urban Outfitters and other distributors and marketers of the game were forced to pull it due to massive protests and outrage from both mainstream black organizations such as the NAACP as well as mainstream Asian American civil rights groups such as the Organization of Chinese Americans. While Chang tried to defend his creation as simply "a game" (echoing justifications of racist films as simply "entertainment" or "only a movie") as well as draping his intentions as wanting to "bring people together," his contribution to the litany of American racist popular cultural projects deserved widespread condemnation, and certainly it was heartening to see black and Asian collaboration in the protests and objections. Ghettopoly mimics Monopoly, except that the game pieces include a machine gun, marijuana leaf, crack rock, and a forty-ounce bottle of malt liquor. Properties are crack houses and housing projects instead of houses and hotels. Players draw "Hustle" and "Ghetto Stash" cards reading "Police Shakedown!!! Pay $150" or "Carjacked!!! Pay $80." Ghettopoly joins the ranks of popular cultural projections of buck-toothed, fortune-cookie-spouting, pigtailed "heathen Chinee" as well as pimp-strutting hustlers and booty-shakin' hos. The fact that Asian and African individuals perpetuate racist, demeaning, and degrading stereotypes doesn't lessen or mitigate or excuse them. Rather, it simply spreads the shame and blame and confirms that oppressed people often ape and mimic their oppressors and the stereotypes foisted upon them.

While Ghettopoly was met with combined black and Asian protest and denunciation, the recent racist mutterings by the basketball superstar Shaquille O'Neal toward rival NBA center Yao Ming—poking "fun" at the Chinese center's name in an infantile "ching-chong" style of name calling—was met with a firestorm of protests by Asian Americans nationwide. Although O'Neal quickly apologized, what was conspicuously absent was the protest and condemnation from African Americans. Chinese names are considered "foreign" and "strange" while African American adoptions of Islamic or Swahili sobriquets are not. Anti-racism and anti-oppression needs common solidarity and support by all "people of color" and justice-minded whites.

African Americans through their hard-fought struggles have earned a somewhat central focus in the mainstream of American "racial sensitivity" quotients. Successful athletes and entertainers may be granted status as media darlings and celebrities. Colin Powell and Condoleeza Rice have been prominently featured in the Bush cabinet media and photo ops. It is unthinkable in Hollywood sensibilities to offend blacks by the once-common practice of blackfacing. However, "yellowfacing" (as well as "redfacing" and "brownfacing") are still common practices in Hollywood. One need only point to the implausibly ludicrous example of the return of David Carradine in an updated remake of the 1970s "Kung Fu" television series to see the odious continuation of yellowfacing. Or, as in the case of the pop camp and highly racist *Kill Bill* films by Quentin Tarantino, the "covering" of Asian martial artists by white actors who defeat hordes of Asian martial artists including Gordon Liu, one of the martial arts film cult stars from the 1970s. Asians have not had the patronizing racist good fortune of being classified as "hip" or "cool" while blackness and Latinness conjure sexual potency and trendiness. Blackness has in turn been partially commodified in mass market advertising and in popular culture promotion globally and has become manipulated as the biggest billboard for American consumerism and prosperity.

A complication to blackfacing is now rampant in Japan with the *ganguro* subculture of Japanese teenage girls wearing cornrows, adorning themselves in bling-bling ostentatious jewelry, and mimicking black hip hop stars such as Missy Elliott and Lil' Kim.[6] The exportation of hip hop is the Yankeeification of black American culture as commodity spectacle, a case of race without the resistance, a fashion, a posture of hipness and coolness without the substance of struggle and self-respect—it is blackfacing not done by whites but by Asians. Though, in the analysis of the money trail, certainly white-dominated corporations (from merchandisers to Madison

Avenue marketers), with residuals paid to certain black individual celebrities, are the primary profiteers. Individual black success stories who pimp and push stereotyped portrayals are rarely condemned but more commonly lauded and promoted by mainstream African American media (from *Jet* to *Ebony* to *Vibe*, BET, etc.). Rarely are such celebrities criticized for their low social consciousness or lack of it, for their subservience to corporate interests, and for their nauseous superpatriotism. The era of a superstar black athlete such as Muhammad Ali refusing to join the U.S. military for both personal religious beliefs as well as political principle ("No Vietcong ever called me nigger") is passé. Individual black superstar athletes at times lucratively benefit from endorsement deals with athletic shoe companies with sweatshops in the Pacific Rim.

During the 1968 student strike at San Francisco State University led by the Third World coalition—the longest campus student strike in U.S. history, which eventually led to the creation of the first Ethnic Studies Department in the United States—then-president of San Francisco State, the Japanese Canadian S. I. Hayakawa, in an effort to divide the Third World students and pit them against each other, pointed to the Asian students as an example of a "model minority" that the blacks and Latinos needed to emulate. Hiyakawa became infamous for employing this divide-and-conquer ploy by promoting Asians as an example of quiet, passive, and hard-working minority members who had pulled themselves up by the bootstraps and thus served as examples that the loud and protesting blacks and Latinos should follow. Given the heightened political consciousness of the student leadership of the Third World coalition, many of whom had associations with the new revolutionary organizations in the Bay Area (such as the Black Panther Party and the Red Guards of San Francisco's Chinatown-Manilatown), Hiyakawa was denounced by Asians, along with others, as a "banana" (the metaphor for being yellow on the outside and white on the inside). As tokenism and the co-optation of individual Third World leaders were employed by policymakers and institutions, such terms as "coconut" (brown on the outside, white on the inside), "apple" (red on the outside, white on the inside), and "oreo" (black on the outside, white on the inside) became popular political signifiers for Latino, Native American, and black sellouts, respectively. The "model minority" stereotype affixed to Asian and Pacific Islander Americans (API), while challenged strongly by the Asian movement, nonetheless continues today with efficacy and currency. Some special programs for minorities have omitted APIS, deeming them too "successful" or "overrepresented." Statistical deception has been used to reduce oppression to a matter of numerical representation rather than degree of political, economic, and social power, as well as quality and control of representation (media and academic inclusion as well as image type). The main site of struggle over API "overrepresentation" has been in college and university admissions. At many elite schools, APIS are present in greater percentages than their proportion in the U.S. population as a whole. While on the surface this appears to be true, critics point out that qualified Asians apply in greater proportion to their admissions; that the concentration of elite schools tends to be in major urban centers where API population percentages are far greater than in the overall U.S. population; and that API income analyzed on a per capita basis instead of as a family unit reveals a disturbing trend of larger numbers of income earners and therefore a lesser per capita income.

The urgency for greater Afro Asia solidarity and the general elevation of radical, anti-imperialist leadership and political consciousness has become dire with the escalating tragedy of sensationalized racist violence between Asians and blacks. In recent years in New York City, there has been a series of killings of Chinese restaurant takeout-delivery workers—all with alleged and arrested black perpetrators. Four Chinese delivery workers in the last five years have been brutally murdered, all in predominantly black areas. The killings include Jian Lin Chun, killed in the lobby of a Bedford-Stuyvesant building on October 15, 2002; Golden Wok restaurant owner Jin-Sheng Liu, killed on Sept. 1, 2000, in St. Albans while making a delivery; Ng Cheung Cheung, beaten to death by a baseball bat in Jamaica on June 23, 1999; Li-Rong Lin, repeatedly stabbed to death on December 10, 1998, in Hollis while delivering from the China Buffet restaurant; and, most recently, Huang Chen, killed in South Jamaica on April 30, 2004, where an investigation resulted in the arrest of two African American teens. In the last example, the *New York Post* reported the incident as an example of "Chink-bashing" and characterized such violence as a new "urban sport" of premeditated assaults committed largely by black youth upon Chinese delivery "boys" (though in typical *New York Post* racism the majority of these "boys" are men over the age of forty, as Chinese men are still desexualized and belittled as perpetual adolescents incapable of being "real men" as compared to white men).[7]

This condition of narrowed and lowered consciousness has allowed for the rise of narrow nationalism and ethnic economic protectionism, paralleling the rise of religious fundamentalism and extreme protonationalism from the destruction and subversion by the United States of independent democratic and leftist movements and governments globally. The rise of black neoconservativism, masculinist black capitalism, black petty-bourgeois protectionism, etc. could only occur with the suppression and dismantling of the radical and revolutionary forces that emerged and held dominance during the late 1960s and early 1970s as well as U.S. governmental, corporate, and academic promotion of a reformist and reactionary elite. Gone are mass slogans and popular cultural concepts such as anti-imperialist Third World unity. Instead, pro-blackness has increasingly taken on a form of essentialist, narrow, reformist black capitalism that reflects the general nihilism, cynicism, self-gratification, and solipsism of the pro-Yankee imperialist New World Order and Mass Consumer Plantation culture and society.

This anthology seeks to fight, counter, resist, and attack this condition by illuminating a tradition of creative political and cultural resistance grounded in Afro-Asian collaboration and connectivity. We, the editors of this anthology, have created a hybrid collection of scholarly and testimonial essays along with creative writings, and we hope to bridge academic and scholarly interest with a popular readership—in other words, to provide a tool that can be useful for and supportive of building Afro Asian unity, solidarity, and common struggle. In doing so we extend the work of scholars whose writing has focused important attention to the dynamics of Afro Asian exchange. This work includes the aforementioned important books *The Karma of Brown Folk* and *Everybody Was Kung Fu Fighting* by Vijay Prashad; Mark Gallichio's *The African American Encounter with Japan and China: Black Internationalism in Asia, 1895–1945;* Martin Bernal's *Black Athena*; Gerald Horne's *Race War!*; and Viet Thanh Nguyen's *Race and Resistance: Literature and Politics in Asian America* as well as essays and articles by a number of scholars, some of which are included in this book.[8]

The area of African American and Asian American intersections is wide and expanding and we welcome contributions to the topic. There remain certain topics that have not been explored or need further investigation and discussion, including black and Asian intersections in cuisine, clothing, lifestyle (child rearing, marriage), social life (dating, friendships, daily inter-

actions), and more. There are also a number of social and historical interactions that need further research and analysis, including common experiences and interactions among the plantation societies throughout the
nineteenth-century Americas; black American responses to the anti-Asian
movements that pervaded from the anti-Chinese agitation of the nineteenth
century to the modern civil rights movement; Asian American responses to
black American oppression prior to the 1960s; and African American response to U.S. imperialism in Asia.

On the latter issue, a strong, militant, anti-imperialist tradition of African
American opposition to U.S. imperialism in Asia has existed since the
Spanish-American War of 1898, beginning with African American news-
papers' opposition to American colonization of the Philippines.[9] W. E. B.
Du Bois and Paul Robeson fiercely denounced U.S. intervention in Korea.
And the U.S. anti-Vietnam War movement included a broad African American involvement, including not only radical anti-imperialist leaders and
organizations of the black Left but also mainstream civil rights leaders
and organizations such as Ralph Abernathy, Dick Gregory, and Dr. Martin
Luther King Jr., who in April of 1967 declared his total opposition to the war
in Southeast Asia, supported draft resistance, and targeted the U.S. government as "the greatest purveyor of violence in the world today."

African American opposition to the U.S. war in Southeast Asia moved
the "peace" movement to a position of anti-imperialism as the Student
Nonviolent Coordinating Committee (SNCC) was led by Stokely Carmichael
in a chant of "Hell no, we won't go!" at a United Nations demonstration in
1967. African Americans were at the forefront of the early antiwar movement. The activist-attorney Conrad Lynn was the leading advisor and counsel to youth fighting induction into the U.S. army. "In 1965, the Mississippi Freedom Democratic Party issued the first organizational opposition
to President Johnson's escalation of the war, rejecting 'fighting in Vietnam
for the White Man's Freedom' and urging black men 'to not honor the draft
here in Mississippi.'" In 1966, SNCC became the first national U.S. organization to come out against the war. "For endorsing this stand, Julian Bond,
duly elected to the Georgia legislature, was denied his seat (later restored by
the Supreme Court). Also in 1965, *Freedomways,* the first national magazine
to denounce the war, editorially labeling it 'racist' in origin and intent,
became the fountainhead of a black anti-war position."[10]

By 1969, massive African American opposition to the war was reflected in the pronouncement by every major civil rights organization of the time (with the notable exception of the NAACP) that American policy in Asia was a reflection and continuation of American racism at home. African American opposition to U.S. Asian policy was highly dramatized by the slogan "No Vietnamese ever called me nigger," with its most dramatic adoption by world heavyweight boxing champion Muhammad Ali in his refusal to be drafted. Ali announced his refusal to be drafted into the army of a country that "continue[s] the domination of white slavemasters over the dark people the world over." A 1967 film produced/directed by David Loeb Weiss, entitled *No Vietnamese Ever Called Me Nigger*, documented growing black urban community opposition toward the U.S. war in Southeast Asia.

Clearly, in all social struggles in the United States, African American leaders and organizations have played a vanguard role and have provided a radical and anti-imperialist influence and impact. Less recognized and examined has been the influence and impact of Asian cultural and political traditions, forms, and experiences upon African American developments.

In our focus upon interconnectivity, collaboration, mutual influences, and inspirations, we assert and establish an alternative tradition of cross-cultural unity among oppressed peoples in the United States (and in the Western Hemisphere). We consider our anthology to be a beginning contribution to survey the political and cultural connections developed by peoples in the African and Asian diasporas in confronting white supremacy and national oppression.

Notes

1   See Frank Snowden, *Before Color Prejudice: The Ancient View of Blacks* (Cambridge, Mass.: Harvard University Press, 1983); Martin Bernal, *Black Athena: The Afroasiatic Roots of Classical Civilization*, vols. 1 and 2 (New Brunswick, N.J.: Rutgers University Press, 1987); Wilson Moses, *Afrotopia* (Cambridge: Cambridge University Press, 1998); G. M. James, *Stolen Legacy: The Greeks Were Not the Authors of Greek Philosophy, but the People of North Africa Commonly Called the Egyptians* (New York: Philosophical Society, 1954); W. E. B. Du Bois, *The World and Africa* (New York: International Publishers, 1965); Vijay Prashad, *The Karma of Brown Folk* (Minneapolis: University of Minnesota Press, 2000), and *Everybody Was Kung Fu Fighting: Afro-Asia and the Myth of Cultural Purity* (Boston: Beacon Press, 2001).

2   See Reginald Kearney, *African Americans Views of the Japanese: Solidarity or*

Sedition (Albany: State University of New York Press, 1998); and Marc Gallic-chio, *The African American Encounter with Japan and China: Black International-ism in Asia, 1895–1945* (Chapel Hill: University of North Carolina Press, 2000).

3   Gerald Horne, *Race War! White Supremacy and the Japanese Attack on the British Empire* (New York: New York University Press, 2004).

4   It is only recently that testimonial and scholarly books have begun to be pub-lished on the New Communist movement that emerged in the late 1960s and early 1970s in the United States; two recommended works are Ho et al., *Legacy to Liberation: Politics and Culture of Revolutionary Asian Pacific America* (Oak-land, Calif.: AK Press, 2000); and Max Elbaum, *Revolution in the Air: Sixties Radicals Turn to Lenin, Mao, Che* (London: Verso, 2002).

5   See Samuel Yette, *The Choice* (Silver Spring, MD: Cottage Books, 1982); and Ward Churchill and Jim Vander Wall, *Agents of Repression: The FBI's Secret Wars against the Black Panther Party and the American Indian Movement* (Boston: South End Press, 1980).

6   Clark Buckner, "Bling BlAsian Bling," *San Francisco Bay Guardian*, April 28, 2004, 72.

7   For reports on the murders of Chinese delivery workers, see Andrew Popper, "P.C. Media Ignores Racist Murder," FrontPageMagazine.com, March 1, 2004: www.frontpagemag.com/Articles/ReadArticle.asp?ID=12392; Alex Ginsburg, " 'Monster' Jailed for 'Too Chinese' Slaying," *New York Post*, November 25, 2005, p. 30; and Bryan Virasami, "Leaders Decry Deliveryman Murder," *New York Newsday*, February 16, 2004.

8   Viet Thanh Nguyen, *Race and Resistance: Literature and Politics in Asian America* (Oxford: Oxford University Press, 2002).

9   See George P. Marks III, "Opposition of Negro Newspapers to American Philippine Policy, 1899–1900," *Midwest Journal* 4 (winter 1951–1952): 1–25. This essay was later published as *The Black Press Views American Imperialism* (New York: Arno Press, 1971).

10 William Loren Katz, "The Afro-American's Response to U.S. Imperialism," *Freedomways* 11, no. 3 (1971): 285–90.

PART I

THE AFRICAN AND ASIAN DIASPORAS
IN THE WEST: 1800–1950

Part I introduces the dominant historical relationships between peoples of African and Asian descent. Fred Ho's "Nobody Knows the Trouble I've Seen," an essay published in the late 1980s by the now-defunct Brooklyn-based black community weekly newspaper the *City Sun*, provides a framework for viewing black and Asian relations in the United States's framework that affirms common oppression and struggle while acknowledging difference. Lisa Yun discusses the parallel courses of Afro-Asian diaspora in her "Chinese Freedom Fighters in Cuba," and in so doing she demonstrates the mutual exploitation of black and Asian labor during the years of the slave trade. Daniel Widener's essay "Seoul City Sue and the Bugout Blues" speaks to the place of African American soldiers in the so-called Korean conflict. Widener's essay closes part I by suggesting how the long arc of justice and the long arc of imperialism have struggled for primacy in Afro-Asia.

Fred Ho

Nobody Knows the Trouble I've Seen:
The Roots to the Black-Asian Conflict

hen my Afro Asian Music Ensemble's debut Soul-note recording was released in late 1985–early 1986, Martin Johnson, a young African American journalist, wrote a feature on me in the *City Sun.* After the feature was published, a reader named Yusef Salaam wrote a letter to the paper noting the political comments I had made about "jazz"; he took exception, however, to my use of the term "Afro" in the title of my band.[1] To him, an "Afro" was a hairdo; he preferred that I use the phrase "African-Asian."

It was not until much later, in a 1990 feature on me by Esther Iverem, an African American arts writer for *New York Newsday,* that I publicly clarified my use of the term "Afro Asian" as inspired by and taken from the "Afro Asian Unity Conference" of Bandung of the mid-1950s. This was the initial summit meeting of leaders from the newly in-dependent nation-states and anticolonial movements of Africa and Asia that included Julius Nyerere, Chou En-lai, Kwame Nkrumah, and Nehru, among others. The conference gave birth to the Non-Aligned Movement or "Third World" (not "third" as in lesser than first or second, but as an alternative to the two major power blocs of the West/Europe–United States and the East/Soviet bloc).

I had begun my ensemble to express musically a vision of unity between the cultural-socio-political struggles of African Americans (the originators and innovators of "jazz") and Asian Americans. Since my teen-age years, the Black Power movement (particularly the leading ideas of Malcolm X) and the Black Arts movement (especially the poetry of Baraka, Sanchez, Scott-Heron, and the Last Poets, and the music of Mingus, Coltrane, Shepp, Parker, Ellington, and Cal Massey) greatly inspired my social consciousness and identity as a Chinese American (to understand that I, as an Asian in America, suffered as a victim of white racism and the need to wage a comprehensive struggle to end this systematic oppression).

Because I did not grow up in a community with many other Chinese Asian Americans, I looked to the revolutionary thought and cultural expression of members of the growing community of African American intellectuals and artists who came to teach in the colleges of the Amherst, Massachusetts, area in the early and mid-1970s (including Max Roach, Archie Shepp, Sonia Sanchez, Reggie Workman, and others). I immersed myself in the music, literature, and political activism of Black Power, finding analogous conditions and perspectives in the struggles of Asian Americans. Since those days, and having embarked on a career as a composer, a baritone saxophonist, and a bandleader, I have sought through the use of music to promote the solidarity of Asian Americans and African Americans, by forging what I have termed "an Afro Asian New American Multicultural Music."

The highly media-sensationalized "Black-Korean" conflict of Brooklyn and other altercations between Asian small-business owners and African Americans in recent years have raised the question of how united are people of color. To the more politically conscious, the media preoccupation with conflicts and divisions among people of color seemed to exacerbate disunity rather than offer a perspective regarding the source of the problems. In these incidents, the media seemed to revel in pointing out that people of color could be racist toward one another without the active presence of white people. In *Do the Right Thing*, Spike Lee seemed to suggest that the Korean grocer would be the next target of the African American community's anger and frustration. While Korean merchants had given hefty financial contributions to the electoral campaigns of Jesse Jackson and the successful mayoral bid of David Dinkins, African American political leadership in unifying and "healing" the conflicts has been minimal at best.

In my view, neither Asian Americans nor African Americans are to blame for the prejudices, ignorance, misunderstanding, and racism held against the other.[2] In a white-racist, oppressive society, the victims of that racism and oppression can be expected to harbor the racist attitudes, xenophobia, and even self-hatred fostered by the segregation, Eurocentric education, and endemic powerlessness that fuel frustration, fear, and mistrust. What is needed from educators, activists, and intellectuals is dialogue and knowledge about each other's experience and social history of oppression and struggle rather than convenient, evasive explanations of "cultural differences." (The "cultural differences" thesis presumes that what is needed is greater "cultural sensitivity" and not political consciousness and organizing around common interests as peoples of color.)

The primary difference between people of African and Asian heritage in the United States is that the experience and historical process of slavery forged African Americans into a distinct nationality while Asian Americans are a composite of diverse minority nationalities: Chinese American, Japanese American, Korean American, Filipino American, Asian Indian, Cambodian, Hmong, Vietnamese, etc.[3] Generations of slavery fused the diverse West African peoples brought to the Americas into one common people who no longer trace their ancestral origin to a specific West African people; the varying languages of Yoruba, Ibo, Wolof, etc. were replaced by the language of the slave master (English in the British colonies). Their identity, religion, music, and history were no longer any specific African tradition but became definitively *African American.* Thus, some contemporary African Americans, endeavoring to reclaim their African heritage, divest themselves of "slave names" such as Smith, Jones, Johnson, Washington, etc. for a range of self-identifications such as Xs to Islamic and other non-European adoptions.

Asian Americans are a plurality of nationalities that retain their ancestral family names and specific national cultural heritages including language, customs and traditions, as well as national histories. Chinese Americans are quite different from Japanese Americans, who are also quite different from the more than a dozen varying Asian/Pacific Islander minority nationalities in the United States. They are Wongs, Chins, Yamaguchis, Salvadores, Parks, etc. Obviously, the first generation of Asian peoples in America retain more of their ancestral identity, while subsequent generations growing up in the United States experience identity crises and cultural confusion.

Under slavery, African Americans held no illusions about their status in U.S. society. They were simply property, a condition maintained by total force for virtually two and a half centuries prior to the mid-nineteenth century. Asian immigration into the United States began in the mid-1800s and was the result of a combination of what social historians term "push/pull" factors: "pushed" by the devastation of their ancestral homelands from crushing poverty, semicolonial penetration, government and social corruption, and varying types of cheap-labor recruitment (a semislavery or indentured servitude); "pulled" by hyped promises of America as the "Mountain of Gold" (the Chinese expression for the United States was literally that) and promises for opportunities to make a new and better life. Because of this combination of ambivalent, contradictory impulses, between the sojourner (who came to work with the idea of returning to Asia) and the immigrant (who came to stay) Asian Americans reflect ambivalent responses to their conditions in America, rooted to the question: Is America home? Immigration has prefigured as a critical and dominant characteristic in the Asian American experience.

In U.S. society, an individual is either white, black, or foreign. American racism has lumped its Latino, Asian, and even Native American groups into "other." Even fourth-generation Asian Americans still face this condition of subtle racism when told to "go back to where you came from" or that they "speak good English," as well as the not-so-subtle racism of being a target of racist violence.

Prior to the twentieth century, the concentration of African Americans was in the "black belt" region of the South. For Asian Americans (mostly Chinese until the 1900s), it was on the West Coast and in Hawaii. Even well into the twentieth century, there was little social intercourse or contact between these peoples, except for a small population of resettled Chinese laborers in the South that occurred as a short-lived experiment to replace slave labor. Two significant contrasts between African Americans and Asian Americans were evident in late-nineteenth-century U.S. society: the failure of Reconstruction for African Americans and the period of exclusion for the Chinese in America, which eventually extended to all Asian immigrants until well into the second half of this century.

The smashing of Reconstruction by what Du Bois noted as an alliance between northern finance capital and southern agrarian interests thwarted the possibility of genuine emancipation for the African American people. Furthermore, without "40 acres and a mule"—the granting to African Americans basic capital through ownership of land and basic means of production—African American economic (as well as political) empowerment was restricted and suffocated. While a tiny African American middle class (petite bourgeoisie) did emerge under segregation, it was not until the great migrations of World Wars I and II to northern industrial urban centers did African Americans achieve some measure of social mobility and economic advancement. Indeed, the proletarianization of the African American masses, with increasing presence and activity in the burgeoning labor movements and trade unions, was probably the chief means of economic advancement. African Americans joined the ranks of trade union workers in steel, auto, municipal, and public-sector employment. African American economic life, though having a distinct segregated market, increasingly became part and parcel of the general functioning of the U.S. capitalist, industrial, and urban economy.

This was not the case for Asian Americans. The anti-Asian and "Yellow Peril" racist movements of the late nineteenth century were in large part led by the white labor movement, culminating in the series of Exclusion Acts passed by Congress that halted Asian immigration to the United States with the exception of members of the merchant class and students. Heretofore, the majority of Asian laborers were unmarried young men. The few Chinese women in the mainland United States invariably were prostitutes. The halting of immigration made it impossible for the wives or families of these male laborers to join them. Thus, these single Chinese male workers were condemned to an enforced existence as a bachelor society, unable to find love and to procreate. Such a move was tantamount to genocide, and as a consequence the Chinese population in the United States severely declined from 1890 until the mid-1960s.

The ghettoization of the Chinese, from a rural/farming-based existence to Chinatown's urban, isolated communities, led to the formation of the ubiquitous Chinese restaurant and laundry trade—employment in which the Chinese would not find themselves in competition with hostile white labor. The Chinese and other Asian laborers were effectively denied proletarianization in being confined to marginal small business economic activity and dispersed to West Coast cities such as San Francisco (which were not industrial centers). Since their days as workers on the transcontinental railroad, the Chinese have tried their hand at every possible kind of work, only to be scapegoated and targeted by hostile white labor. They were eventually excluded from virtually all forms of economic activity except for a small handful of occupations. By World War II, however, African Americans had become a significant presence in key industries and unions.

As noted above, the merchant class of Asian immigrants was one that was not excluded. Trade between Asia and the United States made for the presence of a merchant entrepreneurial class in the various Asian communities scattered across America. These merchants ran the social-political-economic life of these communities through clan-based merchant associations. The Asian continent was penetrated by European colonization to varying extents (from total colonization as in the case of India to total independence as in Japan, which made for Japan's undisturbed development into an independent industrial capitalist power by the twentieth century, whereas most of the non-European world had its economic course of history dominated and disrupted by the West). Africa, in contrast, was thoroughly colonized; its very borders were redrawn and parceled out to European powers. Asian merchants, on the one hand, serviced a unique Asian American market in these ghetto, urban, isolated communities (the demand for Asian foods and other cultural-based products; sharing a common language); on the other hand, import-export trade influenced relations with mainstream American economic and political life—the silk trade, for example, was big business until the development of nylon.

African Americans had no African merchant class that maintained a distinctive connection to Africa. Both African Americans and Asian Americans have been greatly influenced by the geo-political changes in Africa and Asia, respectively. As Malcolm X so forcefully made the connection: "There was a time in this country when they used to use the expression about Chinese, 'He doesn't have a Chinaman's chance.' . . . You don't hear that saying nowadays . . . Just as a strong China has produced a respected Chinaman, a strong Africa will produce a respected Black man anywhere that Black man goes on this earth."[4] Middle-class Asian Americans grew in part due to the influx of merchants and educated classes. African American mobility was largely a result of unionism and industrial urban concentration.

The greatest changes and progress for both groups occurred during the 1960s. Asian immigration restrictions were finally removed in 1965 by the liberalization of the Immigration and Naturalizations Quota, restoring Asian entries to the same number as other groups. Much of this change occurred in the context of the civil rights movement, led by African Americans. The byproducts of the African American civil rights and Black Power movements benefited most of America. A college-educated, professional African American middle class grew dramatically. Asian families could now immigrate to the United States. They brought a lifetime of savings as start-up investment capital, though most continued to labor in Asian ghetto-based industries such as restaurant, garment, and service occupations.

In the past decade, Asian immigration to the United States has been the largest of any group—doubling the Asian American population. Much of this immigration has been to the urban centers, with an extensive diversity of economic and educational backgrounds, national origins, notably including large numbers of Filipinos (the fast-growing Asian/Pacific group), other Southeast Asians, and Koreans). These new immigrants commonly settle in areas bordering on longtime African American or Latino ghettos. Many use their savings to start small businesses because they are unable to find jobs commensurate with their education or training. Thus, it is not uncommon to find Korean engineers and technicians who, unable to find work in these areas, invest a pool of savings in order to start a grocery or dry-cleaning business, in which they work long hours and employ several family members.

A large part of the xenophobia against these recent Asian immigrants stems in part from the prevailing model minority myth or stereotype that Asians are innately driven toward superachievement. Some Asians themselves buy into this myth, attributing it to "cultural values" such as Confucianism, the education ethic, respect for family, etc. Educational achievement and attainment is often viewed as a means to economic advancement, and on a limited level it works. But education and income are not a measure of real economic and political power. The presence of successful Asian Americans does not equate with power on the level of the monopoly bourgeoisie, which is still white.

Black success stories are also not a measure of the overall condition for the masses of African Americans. The number of black millionaires is about one hundred thousand—most of whom are athletes and entertainers. The presence of a Bill Cosby, Eddie Murphy, or Kareem Abdul Jabbar represents only individual wealth, not corporate monopoly power. Neither the Asian American nor the African American wealthy represent any real power or competition to U.S. corporate capitalism. Just to demonstrate the fallacy of equating educational attainment and economic power, according to the 1980 census Chinese American males were the second most highly educated group (after Asian Indians) in terms of years of education, but they also ranked at least-paid for that level. (Interestingly, the highest-paid group in years of education was black women Ph.D's.)

Despite the relatively significant growth of a black middle class since the integration and affirmative action programs of the 1960s, the gap between the masses of African Americans and whites has widened rather than lessened. Nearly one out of every four African American males is in jail or on parole or probation. African American unemployment is double to quadruple the percentage of white unemployment. Among African Americans, 33 percent live in poverty compared to 10 percent of whites. While African Americans comprise 12 percent to 15 percent of the U.S. population, they make up only 2 percent of the elected and appointed government officials (albeit this does show progress from ten years ago when the figure was less than 1 percent). The deterioration of social conditions in the United States generally (homelessness, crime, cuts in education and social programs) combined with government weakening of affirmative action and civil rights has meant even harder times for African Americans. "Last hired, first fired" remains the situation for the vast majority of African Americans.

The media-hyped "success" of Asian Americans (the model minority myth) points to the relatively higher proportion of Asians in elite institutions of higher education. The jokes are that MIT stands for Made in Taiwan and UCLA is University of Caucasians Living among Asians. It's cited that Asians are 20 percent of the student body at UC Berkeley (but not mentioned that Asian/Pacific Islanders are about 40 percent of parts of the Bay Area). While Asians form a higher percentage of the student body at Harvard or Brown than is reflected in their overall percentage of the U.S. population, it is not examined that Asians are not admitted to the proportion of their applications; that is, even more Asians do better than whites on standardized tests than are admitted to these schools. Asian Americans have charged that there is a ceiling quota that penalizes them for "outperforming" whites. Some Asian Americans are doing well, but the majority are not well off, notably the numbers made up of Southeast Asian refugees living below the poverty line, working at jobs below their skills, and facing language and cultural barriers and discrimination. In a study of attitudes toward race and affirmative action at San Jose State University it was found that the greatest support for special programs for minorities was among Southeast Asian Americans. Any careful examination of the socio-economic realities for Asian/Pacific Islander Americans reveals a diversity and complexity in class bipolarity.

Finally, Asian Americans have experienced not only every form of oppression suffered by African Americans (including anti-miscegenation laws, denial of land ownership, school segregation, lynching, racist legislation), but also forms specific only to them—for example, the racist Cubic Air laws that restricted how much air they could breathe; laws that prevented them from carrying poles, as this was a common form of work; and laws that restricted the length of their hair. Unlike white, European immigrants who undeniably faced discrimination and xenophobia, people of color had their oppression codified in law—that is, institutionalized. But it is pointless to debate the degree of severity of oppression between peoples of color. As Malcolm X pointed out, it is not whether the knife stuck in you is six inches or three inches; the point is that you've been stabbed and have wounds that need to heal.

Certain forms of racism persist for Asian Americans that African Americans no longer encounter. The Hollywood racist practice of blackface (in which whites wear black makeup to caricature African Americans) has ceased, but it persists for Asians in the form of "yellowface" or "Scotch-tape orientals"—for example, the Charlie Chan revivals, David Carradine in *Kung Fu*, the opera *Nixon in China*, and the objection to Broadway's *Miss Saigon*. Also in media entertainment, the interracial sex/love taboo still holds between Asian men and white women, but in the 1960s this taboo was broken between black men and white women. In the film *100 Rifles*, Jim Brown made love to Raquel Welch, who in fact is of mixed Latino/white heritage but has always masqueraded as a white sex symbol. In television, William Shatner/Captain Kirk, albeit forced and against his will by cruel aliens, kissed Nichelle Nichols/Lt. Uhura in an episode of *Star Trek*.

African Americans and Asian Americans exhibit common symptoms of their oppression: self-hatred with their physical features, weak cultural identity and infatuation with things European, ignorance about their own respective histories and struggles, disunity and jealousies, etc. The struggle to unite oppressed peoples must proceed from an informed consciousness first as victims of oppression, and subsequently with clarity about the target of the struggle: the system of colonialism, white supremacy, and monopoly capitalist imperialism.

Notes

An earlier version of this essay was published as "Political Détente through the Medium of Jazz: Notes from a Work in Progress," *City Sun,* June 19–25, 1991.

1 The word "jazz" is problematic in the same manner as the words "Oriental," "Negro," etc.—that is, as appellations that the dominant Euro-American society has put on oppressed nationalities ("people of color"). "Jazz" comes from either the word "jizz" or "jass," which referred to semen, as the music was originally common to houses of prostitution. Another explanation is that "jazz" comes from the French verb *jasser,* which means to "chatter nonsensically"—as New Orleans, the birthplace of the music, was a French colonial territory. In either case, the word "jazz" has a pejorative context, as do many terms from the legacy of colonialism and oppression. If one objects to "Afro-," does that objection apply to such a term as Afrocentric?

2 Some would contend that "racism" implies institutional power to oppress groups of people; since by definition oppressed people don't have such power they therefore can't be "racist." However, I believe that oppressed peoples can hold "racist" ideals and thereby perpetuate their own disunity and continued victimization.

3 The U.S. census allows for well over a dozen entries for "Asian/Pacific Islander American."

4 *Malcolm X: By Any Means Necessary* (New York: Pathfinder Press, 1970, 136).

Lisa Yun

Chinese Freedom Fighters in Cuba:
From Bondage to Liberation, 1847–1898

T he most enduring words about the Chinese freedom fighters of Cuba were written by the Cuban
patriot Gonzalo de Quesada, who recalled that there
was never a traitor or a deserter among them: "No hubo un
chino cubano traidor; no hubo un chino cubano desertor."[1]
In Havana his words are inscribed on a black marble
monument—a dark obelisk that is distinctive yet mysteri-
ous. Little is known about these Chinese freedom fighters:
What were their names; where did they come from; what
was their experience? The Chinese participation in the wars
for liberation spanned a remarkably long period of thirty
years, with their presence in the very beginning of *la Guerra
de los Diez Anos* (Ten Years War of 1868–1878) through *la
Guerra Chiquita* (Little War of 1878–1879) to the end of
la Guerra de Independencia (War of Independence, 1895–
1898). Testimonies from commanders and comrades, interviews with survivors, memoirs by Cuban insurgents, and

newspaper accounts of the period all help to reconstruct what amounted to the extraordinary history of Asians who took up arms in a prolonged battle to overthrow a colonial and slavery system of the Americas. For the Chinese, the struggle for Cuban liberation was the struggle for freedom from slavery, and their stake in it was on patriotic grounds linked most of all to emancipation. In 1870, the Cuban rebel government promised liberty to any *chinos* and *negros* who joined the insurrection against Spain. Before the 1870 declaration, however, both coolies and slaves already were escaping the plantations to join in force. Despite the *ranchadores*, the ubiquitous man-hunters whose job was to capture runaways, *los chinos* responded to the call for insurrection within the first days of the conflict.[2] Little is known about their ages, names, and which plantations they came from. Moreover, the story of Asian rebellions in the Americas has been overshadowed by narrative conventions, as histories of emancipation have been preserved and most often told on the Atlantic template of white and black, metropole and colony. Added to this was the nature of rebel participation, as fugitive runaways in an insurrection against their colonial masters hardly revealed their names for posterity. Although there are recountings that are documented, in those instances, we do not know the rebel Chinese names but rather only their Spanish names, and even then, perhaps just their first names. This is the case, for example, of one Chinese corporal known as "José," who as a member of general Antonio Maceo's personal escort made a reputation for bravery as well as for his sardonic statements in battle.[3] The Chinese, as one Cuban commander put it succinctly, were sacrificed on the front lines and never complained about it.[4] Charged with breaking open the Spanish lines, we can infer the rate of losses to be extremely high among the Chinese fighters.[5] Accounts describe encounters with Chinese troops in formations of hundreds and thousands. Among many examples, one Chinese sergeant, Crispin Rico, described his battalion of four hundred Chinese troops by characterizing them as indentured laborers who were fighting for a Cuban "motherland."[6] The Chinese captain Bartolo Fernandez recounted being among five hundred Chinese troops in battle.[7] Fernandez was keen to point out that Chinese forces served across the board, with some being brought under now-legendary generals of Cuban independence. He also makes note of Chinese troops under General Napoleón Arango, General Maximiliano Ramos, and General Calixto García.[8] The Chinese captain José Tolon and his forces, along with four to five thousand Chinese, made their critical appearance in Oriente, a pivotal region in the launching of insurrection.[9] In addition, the Chinese served in key roles as leaders and strategists, such as the captain José Bu who was personally entrusted with crucial decisions by the famed General Maximo Gomez.[10] The Chinese served in all capacities, including soldiers, corporals, sergeants, lieutenants, captains, and commanders. Others were active recruiters who risked going into plantations to enlist coolies and slaves into rebel forces.[11] Though there were thousands of *mambises chinos* whose names would never be recorded, scores led and distinguished themselves in decisive battles, such as Antonio Moreno, José Tolon, José Bu, and Sebastián Sian, among many others. Some served in all three wars. In a sustained fashion, the Chinese chose to join anticolonial forces. Yet if the Chinese had sided with their masters and colonial authorities in the same sustained manner, the representation of Cuban anticolonial, multiracial struggle would be fundamentally different today. As men with nothing to lose—most without families, completely severed from their birthland, and trapped in a corrupt system of indenture that had become melded into slavery—the Chinese became *cimarrones* and *mambises* in a venture that offered no guarantee of survival. While the freedom fighters undertook the ultimate sacrifices for independence, 1898 would mark the end of one era and the beginning of another—the American occupation of Cuba. Indeed, the next century would bring other struggles for the Chinese of Cuba,[12] with their rise and fall in fortunes contingent upon immigration laws, transnational ties, world wars and revolutions, strategic alliances, and the sweeping changes of the Castro era. The coolies thus were the first wave, the predecessors who established the groundwork for freedom from colonial bondage but who endured a tortuous history of "coolie slavery," in which most did not survive to see the day of liberation.

Coolie Labor in the Americas

In 1874, a *New York Herald* correspondent in Cuba, James O'Kelly, observed that a Chinese coolie "contrary to the representations made about the traffic in Asiatics was treated in every respect the same way as his sable companions in misfortune."[13] O'Kelly was one of many observers of that period who recorded similar assessments; later, Cuban historians came to the same conclusion. Authoritative scholars of Chinese labor in Cuba, such as Juan Pérez de la Riva and Juan Jiménez Pastrana, substantiated the horrific conditions of Chinese coolies in Cuba and unreservedly stated that coolies were slaves in all but name. What were the conditions of Chinese coolie labor in Cuba and how is this related to our present understanding of labor's legacy in Asian American and disapora studies? Such questions become critical as we assess our present narratives of human experience, with the "coolie" having become a major figure in the study of Asian migration to the Americas. The coolie has figured into our diasporic history, literary narratives, ethnographic studies, and perhaps most importantly in communal memories and constructions of ancestral heritage.

How we understand the "coolie" era of the 1800s as well as shape its narratives has profound significance. In Cuba, the Chinese coolie occupied a role of exploited laborer who transformed into the freedom fighter as viewed in the nationalist history and memory of war. The Cuban poet and literary critic Nancy Morejón wrote that "the Chinese, brought to the New World in a supposedly 'new' coolie concept of slavery, soon felt the opprobrium of slave exploitation.[14] The Chinese were honored as freedom fighters in the independence struggle. As noted above, a marble monument to their struggle stands in Havana. In Asian American historiography, the coolie is a distant figure of indentured labor shadowed by historical debate over the connotations of "coolie"—coolie labor's existence and its disputed legality or illegality. However, a revisiting and excavation of "coolie" historiography in all its forms may be relevant for the ways in which we imagine labor formations and narratives today. There are scholars who have laid groundwork for the study of coolies in Latin America and the Caribbean, including Evelyn Hu-DeHart, Walton Look Lai, and Denise Helly. In this essay, I address the particular questions of colonial political economy and the "new coolie slavery."

When O'Kelly made his observation in 1874, Chinese coolie traffic to Cuba was being curtailed by a weak but indignant Chinese government after it received an official document, The Cuba Commission Report, that related accounts of Chinese being tricked or kidnapped to Cuba against their will and their subsequent inhumane treatment in Cuba. The exhaustive report was submitted to the government with supporting documents and over a thousand depositions to support its conclusions. In a report from 1899, Robert Porter, special commissioner for the United States to Cuba, wrote, "[The Chinese] were virtually slaves until the Chinese government intervened on their behalf."[15] The conditions of coolie labor in nearby Jamaica or in Guyana, however, were not necessarily the same. What emerges from the nineteenth century is a widely varied picture of what "coolie" and "coolie history" mean. The history of the Americas, with its Spanish, English, French, and American colonial legacies, cannot be homogenized. Likewise, the role and condition of Asian coolie labor in the Americas—both Indian and Chinese—cannot be oversimplified. The definition of "coolie" and the contexts and consequences of coolie labor varied widely—as a term, it generalizes Asian laborers in a wide spectrum of ethnic histories, material conditions, and political contexts. The terms "coolie" or "indentured laborer" are generic assignations that classify the economic utility of coolies. However, these terms obfuscate the very political and experiential nature of coolies. Coolie labor was utilized in Cuba, Peru, Guyana, Trinidad, Jamaica, Panama, Mexico, Brazil, and Costa Rica, among other places in the Americas. The legacy of Asian coolies continues to bear weight on profound sociopolitical struggles in several countries, such as Guyana and Trinidad.

In the case of Cuba, the history of Chinese coolies stands out much unlike its counterparts. For the purposes of this article, I focus on the Chinese coolies of Cuba because they constitute a unique history of coolies being injected (beginning in 1847) into foreign terrain during a time when the system of slavery was in full force (slavery did not expire until 1886 in Cuba, over forty years after the arrival of Chinese coolies in Cuba). Elsewhere, for example in Jamaica and Trinidad, coolies arrived after slavery had been abolished.[16] The fact that Chinese coolies arrived in the midst of an entrenched slave system greatly affected their lived experience in terms of the formation of class consciousness, and it motivated their considerable role in the Cuban war for independence. The Chinese coolie in Cuba functioned within a predominantly black "context," constituting a minority labor group working in close proximity among African people. In the case of Cuba, Chinese coolies arrived when the politics of economy and labor and the politics of class and race converged during a critical period of history: the overlapping and then final dismantling of African slavery, the war for independence, and the beginnings of a Cuban nation.

Coolies to the Americas:
Early Nineteenth Century

The use and exploitation of coolie labor was by no means a new concept. During the 1620s Jan Pieterzoon Coen, governor of the Dutch East Indies (now Indonesia), considered acquiring Chinese laborers to work the region: "No people in the world can do us better service than the Chinese. It is requisite by this present monsoon to send another fleet to visit the coast of China and take prisoners as many men, women, and children as possible."[17] Later, the Dutch joined the British as one of many colonial powers to profit from the massive coolie trade. It was during the 1800s that large numbers of Chinese and Indian coolies were transported to the Americas and to Africa. Early on, the Chinese were considered as a source of labor for the Caribbean. Walton Look Lai records the figure as 192 Chinese taken to Trinidad in 1806. This early "experiment" did not take root, as only twenty to thirty individuals stayed on into the 1820s.[18] The British revisited this experiment in 1838 and transported some Chinese (but more Indian) coolies to Trinidad and Guyana, while British colonial control over India was consolidating. (The British East India Company arrived in India in 1784; in 1858 Britain asserted official political dominion over India.) Significantly, while mobilizing to abolish the trans-Atlantic slave trade, the British were establishing themselves as the dominant traffickers of Indian and Chinese coolies in the Pacific and Indian Ocean basin. Favored destinations in the British Indian Ocean trading network were Malaya and East Africa. In the Western Hemisphere, the favored destinations were Cuba, Guyana, Trinidad, and Jamaica.

During the same period that the initial 1806 "experiment" began in Trinidad, the British Empire through its navy began imposing in 1809 a unilateral embargo on the trans-Atlantic transport of African slaves. This embargo became more formal when England and Spain signed a treaty in 1817 aimed at abolishing the slave trade.[19] This antislave trading treaty between Spain and England had little impact on the actual trans-Atlantic commerce of African slaves to the Spanish Americas. Although the British suppression of the trans-Atlantic African slave trade did not fully deny Cuban access to African slaves, it did continue to force traders toward more clandestine methods, which drove up prices for the purchase of slaves. The increased purchase costs for African slaves pushed Cuban sugar planters to search for alternate sources of labor and forced Cuban planters to confront a fundamental production problem of cost. Despite increases in the production of sugar and their increased prosperity, Cuban planters were continually beset by the challenge of lowering their labor costs to remain competitive in world commodities markets. Slave imports decreased from 10,000 Africans in 1844 to 1,300 in 1845 and then to 1,000 in 1847—an overall drop of 90 percent. Simultaneously, during this nadir the intensive trafficking of Chinese coolies to Cuba began in 1847.[20]

The ease of introducing Chinese coolie trafficking into the world system was due to colonial access, domestic conditions, and control of labor migration. Beginning in the 1840s, the British effectively "opened" a valuable labor market of displaced or impoverished peasantry in southern China while actively suppressing the African slave trade. After losing the first Opium War (1840–42), China was forced to open five of its major ports to British occupation.[21] After the second Opium War (Arrow War) in which China was defeated again, the British (as well as the French and the Americans) occupied twelve major ports and colonized Hong Kong. One result of the Opium Wars was the deregulation of Chinese immigration, a key demand attained by the British. With unrest, rebellion, and war in China, during a thirty-five-year period alone approximately one million southern Chinese, mostly males of Guangdong Province, were procured as part of Western organized labor traffic from 1840 to 1875, with an estimated 100,000 individuals taken aboard ships to Peru and 142,000 to Cuba.[22]

Lessons of Haiti and the Conditions before Coolie Traffic to Cuba

On the Spanish side, coolie labor was desirable not only due to economic and production demands but also because of other considerations. The higher cost of African slavery was the bane of planters' daily concerns, but the anxiety of the planter class also grew as the numbers of Africans grew. As the African presence increased in Cuba, alarmist sentiments arose among resident whites concerning rebellion. Even with the addition of coolies, Africans still constituted an overwhelmingly larger population. The racialized revolution in French colonial Haiti that led to the overthrow of the white elite provided lessons to the Cuban landowning class. The specter of another Haiti-like revolution, one of a black majority population, never seemed far away. Planters thought that using Chinese coolie labor might

Table 1   Sugar production figures for Jamaica, Brazil, Cuba, and Puerto Rico (tons)

	CUBA	PUERTO RICO	JAMAICA	BRAZIL
1830	105,000	20,000	69,000	83,000
1840	161,000	36,500	26,500	82,000
1850	295,000	50,000	29,000	110,000
1860	429,000	58,000	26,000	57,000
1870	703,000	105,000	24,500	101,500

Sources: Noel Deerr, *The History of Sugar*, vol. 1 (London: Chapman and Hall, 1949), 112, 126, 131, 199; Alan Dye, *Cuban Sugar in the Age of Mass Production* (Stanford: Stanford University Press, 1998), 27; Manuel Moreno Fraginals, *El ingenio: Complejo económico social cubano del azúcar*, 3 vols. (Havana: Ciencias Sociales, 1978), 3:36, 37; and Andrés Ramos Mattei, *La Hacienda Azucarera: Su crecimiento y crisis en Puerto Rico* (San Juan: CEREP, 1981), 33.

help alleviate multiple problems. The control of labor costs and the control of labor as body politic became dual concerns.

Haiti was the primary producer of sugar for the world market until 1791, when the Haitian revolution caused both Haitian and Santo Domingan sugar production to plummet. In 1791, sugar production reached 78,696 tons but then fell to only 1 ton by 1825.[23] After the Haitian slave revolt and revolution the European states imposed a punitive embargo on Haitian sugar, thus driving Haiti out of the sugar market. Cuba seized the lead in sugar production after Haiti and other competing sugar producers emancipated slaves (or the slaves freed themselves) and competitors' sugar production dropped. With Haiti displaced, the colonized territories of Jamaica, Brazil, Cuba, and Puerto Rico rose in prominence.[24] Cuban sugar production began modestly: in the 1780s, Cuba produced only 18,000 tons of sugar per year. Sugar production in Cuba began in earnest in 1798,[25] and the 1830s revealed the flourishing of the sugar economy. During the mid-1830s, Cuba first obtained parity with Jamaica as a sugar producer and then surpassed it when Jamaica emancipated its African slaves during the late 1830s.[26] The emancipation of Jamaican slaves drove up labor costs for Jamaican planters, placing them at a comparative disadvantage with Cuba's sugar planters, who still maintained access to African slave labor at this time. Because of the labor cost advantages available in Cuba, it quickly outpaced Jamaica in sugar production. By the 1840s, Cuba had become the preeminent producer of sugar in the world (161,000 tons), accounting for 21 percent of world production and outdistancing Jamaica, Brazil, and Puerto Rico. Cuba leapt forward with even more phenomenal growth precisely during the period of the 1840s to 1870s, the period when Chinese were introduced as coolies on Cuban sugar plantations. In 1830, Cuba produced 105,000 tons of sugar. Forty years later, Cuba produced almost seven times more (703,000 tons) while its closest competitors produced approximately 100,000 tons. By this time, Cuban sugar accounted for 41 percent of world output.[27] During this period, Cuba used a substantial coolie system grafted onto a continuing slavery system that involved clandestine slave importation.

Tea with Sugar: Empire and the Coolie Trade to Cuba, 1847–1874

During this period the British consumed approximately one third of the world's sugar, and at the same time they were the dominant Western consumers of tea. It is a likely assumption that these two facts are linked as the British consumption of tea was always with sugar. With some irony, one might say the British habit for tea and sugar led to a worldwide movement in capital and labor. The British Opium Wars with China were instigated because of Britain's trade deficit with China concerning Britain's tea imports (which prompted Britain's export of opium to a resistant China to balance the deficit). As a result of the wars, Britain established itself as a major procurer of coolie labor.

It was, of course, Britain's intervention in the African slave trade that led Spanish Cubans to seek alternatives at lower cost—namely, Chinese coolie labor. This source of labor contributed to Cuba's economic success based on sugar production, which benefited Britain's archrival Spain. Spanish Cuba benefited from British colonial hegemony and access to Chinese labor, yet chafed under British anti-slavery measures vis-à-vis African labor. While the British controlled access to a worldwide Asian coolie market, they undertook abolitionist measures against the African slave trade in international waters. This dual approach enabled the British to manipulate access to labor, ultimately affecting the price of labor. Needless to say, this logic affected the labor and capital flows of the era. "Tea with sugar" became a wide circle of political economy. While Britain occupied a major role in the coolie trade (then withdrew from coolie trafficking to Cuba beginning in 1858), they were not the only colonial interests involved. Gary Okihiro draws linkages among the expansion of European imperialism and colonialism in Asia, Africa, and the Americas, the global labor economy, and the trafficking of Indian coolies, Chinese coolies, and African slaves.[28]

Early in their considerations, Cuban planters had discussed the immigration of free whites from Europe. When free white laborers from Europe proved unwilling to work in the sugar cane fields, however, Cuban landowners opted to import labor from the very people who caused the rising prices of African slaves. The Cuban sugar elite began seriously discussing the need to import Chinese laborers from British controlled ports in 1844.[29] Initially, the Spanish bought Chinese coolies from British "agents." Eventually, a multinational network emerged composed of shipping companies and agents, businesses, prominent families, and governing agencies, which turned to the trafficking of coolies and collaborated to realize enormous profits, while continuing to purchase—with increased difficulty and costs—African slaves from the complicated, "clandestine" African slave trade. The network of coolie brokers, shippers, buyers, and investors crossed lines of colonial empires, including monied interests of the British, Americans, Portuguese, French, as well as the Spanish Cubans. To launch the coolie trade in Cuba, Cuban planters used a company called the Real Junta de Fomento y Colonización. This company then engaged Julieta y Cia of London (headed by the cousins Julián Zulueta and Pedro Zulueta), which devised the scheme to transport coolies from China to Cuba. Pedro was the son of the London-based banker/slavetrader/planter Pedro Juan Zulueta de Ceballos who amassed such a fortune that he died the wealthiest man in Spain and the Spanish empire. Pedro Zulueta also was known as a notorious slavetrader, as he was accused, tried, but acquitted of slave trading in London in October 1843.[30] The two main labor agents based in Asia were Fernando Aguirre based in Manila and a Mr. Tait based in Amoy (Xiamen).[31] The Zuluetas engaged Syme Muir and Company and Tait and Company (both based in Amoy and Guangdong) to obtain the first set of Chinese coolies to be shipped to Cuba.[32] While the original financing for this labor-acquisition venture originated in Cuba, supplemental financing came from a multinational network of banks and firms obtained in New York, Boston, London, Paris, Amsterdam, and Liverpool.[33] Participating commercial interests were the same that financed the African slave trade.[34] After first working with Aguirre and Tate, the Cubans replaced them in 1855 with their own labor agents and opened their own offices for this trade in Havana, London, Manila, Macao, and Amoy.

Other labor agents for Cuba operating in China included Francisco Abellá Raldiris and Nicolás Tanco Armero, who generated tremendous capital from coolie trafficking. Armero exemplified a paradox of coolie traffickers. Although he came from a prominent Colombian family and received an elite education in the United States and Paris, he was the descendant of a revolutionary uncle and father who became prominent in the struggle for independence. His own uncle was imprisoned by the Spanish and then killed, with his head put in an iron cage.[35] Armero followed a different path, however: from 1855 to 1873, he and his partner oversaw the buying, selling, and exportation of over one hundred thousand Chinese coolies to the new world.[36] The Cuban finance and insurance firm La Alianza entered the coolie trade in 1859, providing much of the essential financing for Chinese coolie importation. La Alianza then formed a powerful alliance with the Empresa de Colonización (owned by Rafael Rodriguez Torices, Marcial Dupierris, Antonio Ferrán, and Juan A. Colomé). Together these two firms (La Alianza and the Empresa de Colonización) dominated the trade until the re-emergence of the Zulueta firm during the 1870s. Others in the Cuban sugar planting elite were heavily involved in Chinese coolie trafficking. Among those who were prominent in this "trade" were the firms and families of Villoldo, Wardrop y Cía, Pereda Machado y Cía, Don Santiago Drake y Cía, José Maria Morales y Cía, and duPierris y Cía.[37] In addition, most of the prominent slaveholding families on the island (including families by the names of Zulueta, Torices, Drake, Aldama, O'Donnell, Diago, Pedroso, Sotomayor, Baró, Ferrán, Colomé, Ibáñez, Pulido, Moré, Alfonso, Almendares, Francisco, and Morales) were involved in the trade.[38] Many of them operated plantations in the center of the island in Matanzas, where the largest number of coolies were sent.

A ship of five hundred coolies required an average investment of 30,000–50,000 pesos but yielded an average of 100,000–120,000 pesos—a fantastic profit at the time.[39] Juan Peréz de La Riva calculated the costs and overhead of coolie procurement, mortality, and shipping, and approximated the overall profit from coolie sales of this period to be 25–30 million pesos (which in 1975, at the time of his writing, was equivalent to 80 million pesos).[40] He points out, further, that this influx of liquid capital was a factor in helping to industrialize the Cuban economy. The coolie market took on wild characteristics with investors taking advantage of this newest commodity. The travel writer Henry Murray observed speculation by mercantile houses and individuals on the coolie trade driven by incredible profits.[41] In the topic of the coolie trade, in 1872 a correspondent of the *New York Herald* observed: "The 900 human beings brought to the market in the ship I visited were worth some $450,000 to the importers; and, as they had cost originally less than $50,000, the anonymous society (corporation) had some $400,000 as a result of the voyage to meet expenses. Never in the palmiest days of the African trade were such tremendous profits realized."[42] The financing of the slave and coolie trades was made possible by profits that were possible from the sale of sugar. Although sugar prices fluctuated wildly from 1855 to 1857, prices steadily climbed in the 1860s and 1870s during the height of coolie trafficking.

Coolies on Ships: Human Costs

Other than the difficulties of clandestine African slave trading, what were the main reasons for using coolies in particular? Using comparative cost analysis, Chinese coolies were simply much less costly than African slaves. In crude terms, the coolies were more easily obtained and more cheaply purchased, thus making them enormously profitable. Furthermore, they could be brought in as indentured laborers while in actuality used as slaves. The first point regarding purchase price is easily apparent (the second point regarding a "new coolie slavery" is addressed in the next section). Table 2 tracks the differential in prices between African slaves and Chinese coolies from 1847 to 1875, indicating coolies as cheaper to purchase. As production at the sugar plantations and *ingenios* increased during this period, the demand for labor intensified and the importation of African slaves resumed after initially having fallen. With the coerced labor of both coolies and slaves, the Cuban sugar economy boomed.

The critical component to the coolie trade was the actual procuring and transport of this human "cargo" and its eventual profit. On June 3, 1847, the Spanish ship *Oquendo* arrived in Havana after journeying 131 days at sea. Its cargo hold contained 212 Chinese men. Upon disembarking, they were sold for 170 pesos per head to their new masters, Cuban landowners.[43] This cargo of Chinese, brokered by British traffickers and Spanish Cuban buyers,

Table 2 Average prices for coolies and slaves, 1847–1875

YEARS	AFRICAN SLAVES (PESOS)	CHINESE COOLIES (PESOS)
1845–1850	335	125
1851–1855	410	150
1855–1860	580	370
1861–1865	585	310
1866–1870	450	410
1871–1875	715	420

Sources: Laird W. Bergad, Fe Iglesias Garcia, and Maria del Carmen Barcia, *The Cuban Slave Market, 1790-1880* (Cambridge: Cambridge University Press, 1995), 162–73; Du Harthy, "Une Campaigne dans l'extreme Orient" in *Revue des Deux Mondes* 66 (1866): 417; J. Pérez de la Riva, "Aspectos económicos del tráfico de culíes chinos a Cuba, 1853-1874," 269, and E. Phillip Leveen, "A Quantitative Analysis of the Impact of British Suppression Policies on the Volume of the Nineteenth Century Atlantic Slave Trade," in *Race and Slavery in the Western Hemisphere; Quantitative Studies*, edited by Stanley I. Engerman and Eugene D. Genovese (Princeton, N.J: Princeton University Press, 1975), 56 (51–81).

constituted the first significant trafficking of coolies to Cuba. According to several sources, 124,873 to 150,000 Chinese coolies arrived in Havana on 342 ships from 1847 to 1873.[44] Not all coolies survived the journey, which stretched from four to eight months. The British ship *Panama* provided a sobering example of the Chinese coolie middle passage to the harsh "new world": of the 803 coolies taken aboard, only 480 survived. The American ship *Challenger* took 915 coolies on board, but only 620 survived. Cuban ethnographers note that the overall mortality rate of the Chinese coolie passage to Cuba was markedly higher than that of the African passage to Cuba.[45] These few facts scratch the surface of the Chinese coolie period in Cuba, a penetrating history of human loss for some and profit for others.

From 1847 to 1857, coolie trafficking was dominated by the British, Portuguese, and Spanish. Eventually, a vast number of European and American shippers also partook in the lucrative process by investing and providing transport. Ships hailed from twelve European states (England, Spain, France, Denmark, Holland, Portugal, Germany, Austria, Italy, Norway, Russia, Belgium) and the United States. The primary traffickers of Chinese coolies were the British, Portuguese, Spanish, French, Americans, and Dutch. Not surprisingly, these traffickers were the same top six leaders in the trafficking of African slaves.[46] The French and Spanish led in total numbers of

Table 3 Chinese imported into Cuba by nationality of carrier, 1847–1873

	NO. SHIPS	TONNAGE	CHINESE EMBARKED	CHINESE LANDED	CHINESE DIED	% DEATHS
British	35	27,815	13,697	1,457	2,240	16.3
U.S.	34	40,576	18,206	16,419	1,787	9.8
Austrian	3	1,377	936	864	72	7.7
Belgian	3	2,482	1,199	1,182	17	1.4
Chilean	4	1,702	926	743	183	19.8
Danish	1	1,022	470	291	179	38.0
Dutch	19	14,906	8,113	7,132	981	12.1
French	104	64,664	38,540	33,795	4,745	12.3
German	8	4,207	2,176	1,932	244	11.2
Italian	5	5,586	2,832	2,505	327	11.2
Norway	5	2,296	1,366	1,104	262	19.2
Peru	6	4,979	2,609	1,999	610	23.4
Portugal	21	15,847	8,228	7,266	962	11.7
Russia	12	9,857	5,471	5,093	378	6.9
Spain	78	47,604	31,356	28,085	3,271	10.4
Salvadoran	4	4,145	2,031	1,943	88	4.3
Total	**342**	**249,065**	**138,156**	**121,810**	**16,346**	**11.8**

Source: *Report of British Consulate General*, Havana, September 1, 1873.

coolies transported to Cuba and in numbers of coolie ships. Meanwhile, the British were policing the African slave trade but sent the third-highest number of coolie ships to Cuba. The fourth-highest number of coolie ships were brought under the American flag.

The names of coolie ships reflected the legacy of the African trade, such as *Africano* and *Mauritius*. Still others bore incongruous, ironic names such as *Dreams* and *Hope* (British ships) and *Live Yankees* and *Wandering Jew* (North American ships).[47] Approximately 16,400 Chinese coolies died on European and American coolie ships to Cuba during a twenty-six-year period,[48] with some ships formerly used as African slave ships.[49] Mortality rates hovered around 12–30 percent while sometimes reaching as high as 50 percent, such as the case of the Portuguese ship *Cors* in 1857. Violence was the main cause of death. Rebellions, crew assassinations, suicides, thirst, suffocation, and sickness occurred upon the "devil ships" as the Chinese called them.[50] The writer Alexander Laing wrote that the coolie ship

Table 4 Chinese brought to Cuba, 1847–1873

	NO. SHIPS	TONNAGE	CHINESE EMBARKED	CHINESE DIED	CHINESE LANDED	% DEATHS
1847	2	979	612	41	571	6.7
1853	15	8,349	5,150	843	4,307	16.4
1854	4	2,375	1,750	39	1,711	2.2
1855	6	6,544	3,130	145	2,985	4.6
1856	15	10,677	6,152	1,182	4,970	19.2
1857	28	18,940	10,101	1,554	8,547	15.4
1858	33	32,842	16,411	3,027	13,384	18.4
1859	16	13,828	8,539	1,332	7,207	15.6
1860	17	15,104	7,227	1,008	6,219	13.9
1861	16	15,919	7,212	290	6,922	4.0
1862	1	759	400	56	344	14.0
1863	3	2,077	1,045	94	951	9.0
1864	7	5,513	2,664	532	2,132	20.0
1865	20	12,769	6,810	407	6,403	6.0
1866	43	24,187	14,169	1,126	13,043	7.9
1867	42	26,449	15,661	1,247	14,414	8.0
1868	21	15,265	8,400	732	7,668	8.7
1869	19	13,692	7,340	1,475	5,865	20.1
1870	3	2,305	1,312	63	1,249	4.8
1871	5	2,820	1,827	178	1,649	9.7
1872	20	12,886	8,914	766	8,148	8.6
1873	6	4,786	3,330	209	3,121	6.3
Total	342	249,065	138,156	16,346	121,810	11.8

Source: *Report of British Consulate General*, Havana, September 1, 1873.

Sea Witch, with its coolies imprisoned below deck in 1856, was "a Dantean dream: it had become the lid of Hades, and the damned were below."[51] Table 4 gives the mortality rates for coolies from 1847–1873.

Methods of procuring coolies primarily involved kidnapping or decoying peasant men. Resistance and rebellion occurred on ships because the Chinese were mostly taken by duress or deceit. Often, fellow countrymen who were in the employ of colonial coolie traffickers tricked them. Chinese coolies overwhelmingly testified to this case, including one Chao Kun who declared that "Spanish vessels come to China, and suborning the vicious of our countrymen, by their aid carry away full cargoes of men."[52] Other sources for coolie procurement included exprisoners and laborers lured into rigged gambling houses, and gullible young men who went to "recruitment agents" only later to discover that they "were not to be engaged as labourers but to be sold as slaves."[53] Numerous Chinese were so desperate to escape their fate that they committed suicide or jumped overboard. These events and the later coercion of Chinese in Cuba are extensively recorded in *The Cuba Commission Report* (1874). Beginning in 1858, the British began capitalizing on the popular outcry of southern Chinese against the coolie traffic to Cuba. Rumors abounded that the white "barbarians" of Cuba not only abused but also ate the Chinese laborers (a story similar to African rumors of their fate during the slave trade). In response, the Chinese officials began executing Chinese "runners" who were collaborating with the trade to Cuba. The British then withdrew from coolie trafficking to Cuba—a traffic that significantly aided their rivals, the Spanish, in the world sugar economy. The British turned away Spanish coolie ships in Chinese ports and stopped sending British coolie ships to Cuba. While the demand for coolies to Cuba was rising, obtaining coolies was made more burdensome and costly by the new British opposition to selling coolies to Cuba. Coolies were thus smuggled out through the Portuguese and Spanish colonies of Macao and the Philippines, rather than from Hong Kong, Amoy (Xiamen), or Swataw (Shantou). In 1859, records reveal this noticeable shift, with almost all ships departing from Macao. With this added complication, coolie trafficking continued without apparent British participation—with ships hoisting different national flags. In 1865, the British publicly denounced the Spanish coolie traffickers for engaging in a coerced labor system.[54] Meanwhile, however, the British did not cease transporting coolies to their own colonial territories in the West Indies.

Coolies on Land: Coolie Slavery

In 1870, the captain general in Cuba called on Madrid to end coolie imports because coolies were aiding rebels in eastern Cuba.[55] Coolies, who were thought to be passive, displayed a defiant nature and resorted to plantation rebellions, cane field burnings, assassination of overseers, escape, or suicide. Their situation was desperate—in crude terms, the Chinese coolie was a contract slave, with Cuban contracts lasting for "eight years."[56] Yet, studies indicate that "the Chinese and Yucatecan workers were bought, sold, and transferred like slaves, and treated as slaves,"[57] and that "Chinese labor in Cuba in the nineteenth century was slavery in every social aspect except the name."[58] The coolie suffered slave conditions, due to the inability to enforce a contract that provided for certain conditions of "employment" subject to the interpretation of the master. The coolie therefore could be exploited while being provided with minimum or no maintenance. Because of malnourishment and abusive conditions, over 50 percent of coolies died before their eight-year contract ended.[59] The average lifespan of an African slave on a sugar plantation was twenty years. The percentage of coolie attrition due to voluntary exit (coolies who were able to exit Cuba) was negligible:[60] losses were due to death or suicide. In 1860, the American women's rights activist and abolitionist Julia Ward Howe commented insightfully on the coolies in Cuba: "Men will treat a hired horse worse than a horse of their own."[61] "Indenture" in this case was undermined due to the unenforceable nature (or acceptable violation) of the "contract": the coolie contract was routinely ignored and thus generally not enforced in Cuba. The gap between theory versus lived experience disturbs North American paradigms of "contract," "coolie," "slave," and "indentured labor." How does the experience of Chinese coolies in Cuba bring into question and politicize notions of language —that is, what is the meaning of the terms contract, slave, and coolie?

The 1854 regulations concerning the Chinese permitted them to purchase the remainder of their contract at any time—but only after they had compensated their master for their purchase price, the value added since the time of purchase, and any clothing costs, the loss of labor time due to sickness, and the inconvenience of finding a replacement for the Chinese laborer. These conditions were subject to interpretation by the master. Through legal sophistry and the machinations of the labor contract, the planters created a hybrid slave system with Chinese coolies that worked in tandem with African slavery. The contracts with Chinese coolies were patently deceptive. Coolies ostensibly were paid four pesos monthly. From this four peso "salary," deductions were made by the master for the cost of travel from China, the provision of clothing and food, sickness or lost labor time, and a host of other "costs" to the master. Thus, by the time a coolie's eight-year term expired, if he survived (as over half did not), the coolie wound up owing his master. It is no wonder that few Chinese coolies could discharge this cost for the purchase of freedom. The master could invoke a clause in the contract to "renew" the contract, thus renewing at will and keeping the coolie unfree until his death. The notion of the Chinese coolie in Cuba being described under the generic term of "indentured labor" (meaning labor stipulated by legal contract and terms, with the possibility of freedom upon the end of term) becomes problematic if terms for "indenture" were illusory or patently engineered against the possibility of freedom. The description of the coolie experience in Cuba becomes difficult as language and existing definitions are not universal—the varied conditions of "slave" and "coolie," and the notion of "contract" and "indenture" need greater examination.

"Recontracting" at the mercy of the master was not exceptional but rather was common. In rare instances, some indentured coolies managed to escape the island: "There was even one unusual case of a Chinese man who found his way to Trinidad in 1866 all the way from Cardenas in Cuba, after having escaped an attempt to reindenture him."[62] While Cuban laws stipulated "rules" or guidelines for the treatment of African slaves and Chinese coolies, and while methods of resistance (and even attempted legal recourse) were undertaken by slaves and coolies, clearly they were disempowered under the Cuban slave and coolie system. Those coolies who attempted escape were arrested and punished. The condition of the African slave in Cuba and the unfree servitude of the Chinese coolie in Cuba were similar, both resulting in deprivation of liberty and life. The standard labor contract also provided for the sale of a labor contract. Coolies could then be sold as property or recontracted further without cause. The coolie contract also involved rampant misrepresentation of the coolie, with the coolie being put under contracts and renewed contracts under different names. Contracts could also be diverted by planters by claims that the coolie under contract had died when he had not, with the "now-dead" coolie then being resold to another Cuban employer under another name. Chinese coolie runaways, called *cimarrones* like their African counterparts, could be captured and sold by the Cuban police. Also similar to their African counterparts, Chinese were sold at marts and auctions.

Repeatedly, Chinese coolies testified to being kept and treated as slaves. The coolie Wen A-fa declared: "After eight years are completed they refuse us the cedulas and we are forced to remain slaves in perpetuity." The coolie Ku Ch'ias-hsiu declared: "I know of more than one hundred who were with me, who on the completion of their contracts were forced either to accept fresh engagements or to enter prison."[63] Given the condition of being "contracted" at the mercy of the master, the Chinese coolie thus became maximally exploited, and the meaning of "contract" became illusory. The Chinese coolie was disposable or unfree at any time, depending on the vagaries of the system and the master.[64] Contemporary Cuban scholars conclude that the treatment of Chinese coolies was worse than that of an African slave.[65] The innocuous description of coolies as supposed "contract employees" or "Asiatic colonists" neatly allowed coolie traffickers to sidestep accusations of slave trading. As one historian noted: "To avoid the charge of slavery[,] the coolies before sailing signed a contract of eight years indenture, and on arrival at Havana or Lima they were sold in a way differing in a manner but little from a public auction and were at once reduced to the status of slavery."[66]

The Beginning of the End of Coolie and Slave Labor in Cuba

Throughout the 1860s and 1870s, Chinese coolies were prevalent in the *ingenios* or sugar mills. On the smaller plantations, Chinese sometimes accounted for 50 percent of the labor force. They constituted a smaller percentage, however, on the larger plantations.[67] In Cuba, Chinese coolies were a minority in a larger population of African slaves and were concentrated in the sugar plantations of Matanzas, the central province of Cuba, and secondly in Las Villas (Santa Clara).

One might assume that coolie history occupies a lesser role in the history of labor and production in Cuba, given the total number of Chinese coolies versus the overwhelming numbers of African slaves. However, this assumption has been complicated by the recognition that coolie labor was the critical force in reorganizing the Cuban sugar economy and its systems of production, and furthermore, that it constituted an implicit challenge to entrenched paradigms of race and nation. Some scholars have examined the coolies in terms of their relation to racial constructions in Cuba, others emphasize coolie labor as crucial to the economic transition from slavery to wage labor.[68] One scholar has argued that, in fact, the use of coolies as slavelike property in Cuba actually aided in prolonging the institution of slavery.[69] It is generally agreed, however, that coolie labor was significant in a political economy that was moving toward different modes of production and capital acquisition. In effect, the use of coolie labor aided the industrialization and mechanization of the *ingenios* and prompted a paradigm shift in the economy.

Table 5   Chinese population in Cuba (by region), 1861–1877

PROVINCE	1861	1872	1877
Pinar del Rio	2,221	3,396	3,137
Havana	9,456	11,365	10,108
Matanzas	15,782	27,002	20,054
Santa Clara	6,274	15,878	13,301
Puerto Principe	341	297	94
Santiago de Cuba	754	462	422
Total	**34,828**	**54,400**	**47,116**

Sources. For 1861: Cuba Centro de Estadística, *Noticias estadísticas,* "Censo de población segun el cuadro general de la Comisión Ejecutiva de 1861"; for 1872: Expediente General Colonización Asiática, AHN, Ultramar, leg. 87; for 1877: Iglesias, "El censo cubano."

Beginning in 1873, importations of Chinese coolies began to decline significantly because of legal strictures exerted by the Chinese. Later, in 1882, the United States barred Chinese immigration to their shores under the Chinese Exclusion Act. Both resulted in a marked decline in Chinese migration to the Americas. In Cuba, the elimination of Chinese coolie traffic in addition to the costs of Cuba's 1868–1878 Ten Years War of Independence had an impact on the Cuban economy. With these developments regarding the war, labor restrictions, and the economy, Cuban sugar planters needed to make the transition from coerced labor to free labor. Because of ingrained attitudes toward slavery, however, planters still found it difficult to change. Also, the free white laborers who were available were unwilling to participate in the hard work on the sugar cane plantations. Besides the unavailability of free wage laborers, the planters lacked sufficient capitalization to finance a transition to free labor. The engagement of free labor on the sugar plantation would have driven up labor costs at a rate higher than the planters could have withstood. The transition to free labor thus was a risky venture for planters who were accustomed to the old way of engaging labor.

The factors of production in the sugar economy began a slow transformation beginning in the 1880s. Large sugar plantations were slowly broken up. The slaves and the coolies were dispersed upon the abolition of slavery. The large landowning families either sold their properties to newcomers or began entering the business of processing sugar only, which they did in *centrales*. The cultivation of sugar cane was then turned over to sharecroppers who replaced the slaves and coolie system. By the beginning of the twentieth century newer and more efficient refining machinery was introduced in the Cuban sugar industry, leading to economies derived from technological innovation. More efficient technology lowered the cost of production, which led to renewed profitability in the sugar industry and the recovery of the efficiencies lost when coerced labor was eliminated on the island of Cuba.

Today, there are multiple histories of the Chinese Cubans along hybridized lines of class, culture, and race (mixed and "pure" Chinese). However, in respect to the coolie, it is the image of more contemporary Chinese migrations that is generally known in Chinese diaspora and Latin American/Caribbean historiography, with the coolie being a dimmed figure of early "labor." Chinese Cuban clan associations—as the primary keepers of Chinese Cuban history and archives—were mostly founded by the generations of Chinese merchants.[70] They logically interpreted Chinese Cuban history by focusing on the accomplishments of their communities and on their more contemporary history of Chinese Cuban participation in the revolutionary war of 1956–1958. Most recently, attention has been brought to the substantial and fascinating role of Chinese Cuban generals in that revolution, notably in the volume *Our History Is Still Being Written: The Story of Three Chinese-Cuban Generals in the Cuban Revolution* recounted by the generals Armando Choy, Gustavo Chui, and Moises Sio Wong. In comparison, the history of the coolies, their social contexts and their unique story of struggle for emancipation, is distant. The coolie story has been called "la historia de la gente sin historia" (a history of a people without a history).[71] Yet the early coolies not only labored in Cuba, they also participated with Africans and *criollos* in the wars for independence from Spain.[72] The *chinos mambises* asserted themselves and became a permanent part of the history of liberation and independence in Cuba and the Americas.

Notes

Portions of this chapter were originally published as Lisa Yun and Ricardo Rene Laremont, "Chinese Coolies and African Slaves in Cuba, 1847–1874," *Journal of Asian American Studies* 4, no. 2 (2001): 99–122, and are reprinted with permission of Johns Hopkins University Press.

1   Juan Jiménez Pastrana, *Los chinos en la historia de Cuba* (Havana: Editorial de

Ciencias Sociales, 1983), 37, 57. José Baltar Rodríguez, *Los chinos de Cuba* (Habana: Fundación Fernando Ortiz, 1997), 34–37. More on Quesada's writing regarding the Chinese fighters can be found in Guillermo Tejeiro, *Historia ilustrada de la colonia China en Cuba* (Havana: Editorial Hercules, 1947), under the section "Gonzalo de Quesada."

2 Pastrana, *Los chinos en la historia de Cuba*, 84.

3 Mauro García Triano, *Los chinos de Cuba y los nexus entre las dos naciones* (Havana: Sociedad Cubana de Investigaciones Filosóficas, 2003), 175; Pastrana, *Los chinos en la historia de Cuba*, 120, 123.

4 Antonio Chuffat Latour, *Apunte histórico de los chinos en Cuba* (Havana: Molina, 1927), 26.

5 Enrique Cirules, "Algunas reflexiones sobre la presencia de los chinos en Cuba," *Catauro: Revista Cubana de Antropología* 1, no. 2 (2000): 29.

6 Chuffat Latour, *Apunte histórico de los chinos en Cuba*, 27.

7 Ibid., 28.

8 Ibid., 29.

9 Ibid., 22.

10 Chuffat Latour, *Apunte histórico de los chinos en Cuba*; Pastrana, *Los chinos en la historia de Cuba*; Corlia Alonso Valdés, "La immigración china: Su presencia en el Ejército Libertador de Cuba," *Catauro: Revista Cubana de Antropología* 1, no. 2 (2000): 128.

11 Chuffat Latour, *Apunte histórico de los chinos en Cuba*, 36.

12 "Chinese of Cuba" is used in this article to describe a people in loose terms of global diasporic history, as in, for example, "Chinese of Malaysia," "Chinese of Australia," or "Chinese of South Africa." However, the specificities of national identification may be termed differently, carrying particular political histories of identity politics. The Chinese in contemporary U.S. history are often referred to as "Chinese Americans," the term being the result of political and racial struggle linked to the concurrent struggle of other racialized groups in the 1960s and 1970s. The Chinese of Jamaica call themselves "Jamaican" and not "Chinese Jamaican," reflecting the nationalism and political culture of this country. Most of the contemporary Chinese in Cuba interviewed by the author call themselves "cubano/a" in terms of national identity but also call themselves "chino/a" in terms of cultural identity.

13 James O'Kelly, *The Mambi-land, or Adventures of a Herald Correspondent in Cuba* (Philadelphia: Lippincott, 1874), 60.

14 Nancy Morejón, "Race and Nation," in *AfroCuba*, edited by Pedro Peréz Sarduy and Jean Stubbs (Australia: Ocean Press, 1993), 231.

15 Robert Porter, *Industrial Cuba* (New York: Knickerbocker Press, 1899), 101.

16 See Walton Look Lai's *The Chinese in the West Indies 1806–1995* (Kingston, Jamaica: u.w.i. Press, 1998), and *Indentured Labor, Caribbean Sugar: Chinese and Indian Migrants to the British West Indies, 1838–1918* (Baltimore: Johns Hopkins University Press, 1993).

17 Noel Deerr, *The History of Sugar*, vol. 2 (London: Chapman and Hall, 1950), 402.

18 Lai, *Indentured Labor, Caribbean Sugar*, 43.

19 José Luciano Franco, *Comercio clandestino de esclavos* (Havana: Ciencias Sociales, 1980), 139, 159, 257.

20 David R. Murray, *Odious Commerce: Britain, Spain, and the Abolition of the Cuban Slave Trade* (Cambridge: Cambridge University Press, 1980), 244.

21 The Treaty of Nanking (Nanjing) in 1842 opened the ports of Canton (Guangzhou), Fucheu (Fuzhou), Amoy (Xiamen), Ningpo (Ningbo), and Shanghai to the British.

22 Denise Helly, "Introduction," *The Cuba Commission Report*, 1876 (Baltimore: Johns Hopkins University Press, 1993), 20.

23 Deerr, *The History of Sugar*, vol. 1, 240.

24 Herbert S. Klein, *African Slavery in Latin America and the Caribbean* (Oxford: Oxford University Press, 1986), 92.

25 Manuel Moreno Fraginals, *El Ingenio*, vol. 1 (Havana: Ciencias Sociales, 1964).

26 Jamaica gradually emancipated its slaves over the period 1833–1838.

27 See Klein, *African Slavery*, 93; and Fraginals, *El Ingenio*, vol. 3, 35–37.

28 Gary Y. Okihiro, *Margins and Mainstreams* (Seattle: University of Washington Press, 1994), 37–43.

29 *El Diario de la Marina*, Havana, January 1, 1847.

30 Hugh Thomas, *The Slave Trade* (New York: Simon and Schuster, 1997), 802.

31 Juan Pérez de la Riva, *El barracón y otros ensayos* (Havana: Editorial de Ciencias Sociales, 1975), 264.

32 Deerr, *History of Sugar*, vol. 2, 403.

33 Pérez de la Riva, *El barracón y otros ensayos*, 258–59.

34 Juan Pérez de la Riva, *El barracón: Esclavitud y capitalismo en Cuba* (Barcelona: Editorial Critica, 1978), 92.

35 Ibid., 279.

36 Ibid., 267.

37 Félix Erenchun, *Anales de la isla de Cuba* (Havana: Imp. de la Antilla, 1958), Año de 1856, B-E, 1329–1334, *Memoria de la Alianza: Compania de Créditos y Seguros* (Havana: n.p., 1866); Perez de la Riva, *El barracón y otros ensayos*, 257.

38 Erenchum, *Anales de la isla de Cuba*, Año de 1856, B-E, 1329–1334, *Memoria de la Alianza*; Pérez de la Riva, *El barracón y otros ensayos*, 257; Pastrana, *Los Chinos en la Historia de Cuba*, 50–51, 25–26.

39 Pérez de la Riva, *El barracón y otros ensayos*, 92

40 Pérez de la Riva, *El barracón y otros ensayos*, 270. Denise Helly offers a different statistic of US$80 million ("Introduction," *Cuba Commission Report*, 15). The difference between her figure and that of Pérez de la Riva needs to be reconciled.

41 Henry Murray, *Lands of the Slave and the Free* (London: John Parker and Sons, 1855), 310.

42 O'Kelly, *Mambi-land*, 71.

43 *Cuban Commission Report*, 53.

44 See Laird W. Bergad, *Cuban Rural Society in the Nineteenth Century* (Princeton, N.J.: Princeton University Press, 1990), 248; Pérez de la Riva, *El barracón*, 57; Pastrana, *Los chinos en la historia de Cuba*; among others. While 124,873 were documented as sold, larger estimates (150,000) include undocumented "contraband" and Chinese from California and Mexico.

45 Jesus Guanche, *Componentes Etnicos de Cuba* (Havana: Fundación Fernando Ortiz, 1996), 76.

46 Thomas, *The Slave Trade*.

47 It was also common for ships to be bought, sold, and renamed. In addition, Spanish firms began to verticalize their coolie "business" by acquiring the ships from other countries. See Pérez de la Riva, *El barracón*.

48 This only accounts for those who were recorded (see table 5); *Report of the British Consulate General*, Havana, September 1, 1873.

49 Evelyn Hu-DeHart, "Chinese Coolie Labor in Cuba in Nineteenth Century," *Slavery and Abolition* 14, no. 1 (1993): 75.

50 See also Okihiro, *Margins and Mainstreams*, 42, and Helly, "Introduction," 21.

51 Alexander Laing, *The Sea Witch: A Narrative of the Experiences of Capt. Roger Murray and Others in an American Clipper Ship During the Years 1846–1856* (New York: Farrar and Rinehart, 1933).

52 *Cuba Commission Report*, 53.

53 Ibid., 37.

54 Helly, "Introduction," 12.

55 Ibid., 23.

56 Evelyn Hu-DeHart and Walton Look Lai provide their own analyses on this point. Hu-DeHart ("Chinese Coolie Labor," 83) concludes that coolies were legally not slaves, and she emphasizes that actual physical treatment must be separated from legal status. Lai concludes (*Indentured Labor, Caribbean Sugar*, 266) that the considerable differences in state-regulated coolie labor versus private enterprises speculator-run coolie labor raise questions as to whether coolie labor differed greatly from slavery in Cuba and Peru. Lai also questions the contradictions in the laws themselves (British and Spanish) and the nature of coercion.

57 Philip S. Foner, *A History of Cuba* (New York: International Publishers, 1962), 224.

58 Franklin Knight, *Slave Society in Cuba during the Nineteenth Century* (Madison: University of Wisconsin Press, 1970), 119.

59 Helly, "Introduction"; and Pérez de la Riva, *El barracón*, 63.

60 Hu-DeHart, "Chinese Coolie Labor," 77.

61 Julia Ward Howe, *A Trip to Cuba* (New York: Negro Universities Press, 1969 [1860]), 219–20.

62 Lai, *Indentured Labor, Caribbean Sugar*, 193.

63 *Cuba Commission Report*, 53.

64 For information on the legal status of the Chinese, see Juan Pérez de la Riva, "Demografía de los culíes chinos en Cuba (1853–1874)" and "La situación legal del culí en Cuba," in *El barracón y otros ensayos*, 469–507, 209–45; *Tsung li ko kuo shih wu ya mên, Report of the Commission Sent by China to Ascertain the Condition of the Chinese Coolies in Cuba* (Shanghai: Imperial Maritime Customs Press, 1876; reprint edition, Taipei: C'eng Wen Publishing Company, 1970); Denise Helly, *Idéologie et ethnicité: Les Chinois Macao à Cuba* (Montréal: Les Presses de l'Université de Montréal, 1979); and Juan Jiménez Pastrana, *Los chinos en las luchas por la liberación cubana (1847–1930)* (Havana: Instituto de Historia, 1963), 127–40.

65 Rodriguez, *Los Chinos de Cuba*, 21; Jesus Guanche, *Componentes Etnicos de Cuba* (Havana: Fundación Fernando Ortiz, 1996), 75.

66 Deerr, *History of Sugar*, vol. 2, 403.

67 Bergad, *Cuban Rural Society*, 252.

68 For the former view, see Evelyn Hu-DuHart, "Race Construction and Race Relations," in *The Chinese Diaspora*, edited by Ling-Chi Wang and Gungwu Wang (Singapore: Times Academic Press, 1998); for the latter, see Moreno Fraginals, *"El Ingenio"* and "Extent and Significance of Chinese Immigration to Cuba (19th C)," in *Asiatic Migrations to Latin America* (Mexico: Colegio de Mejico 1981), 53–58.

69 Rebecca Scott, *Slave Emancipation in Cuba* (Princeton, N.J.: Princeton University Press, 1985).

70 See Rodriguez's *Los Chinos de Cuba* for an examination of the post-coolie era.

71 Juan Pérez de la Riva, *Contribución a la historia de la gente sin historia* (Havana: Editorial de Ciencias Sociales, 1971).

72 See Pastrana, *Los chinos en las luchas por la liberacion cubana*.

Daniel Widener

Seoul City Sue and the Bugout Blues:
Black American Narratives of the Forgotten War

This essay explores black reactions to and experiences of America's "forgotten war" on the Korean peninsula.[1] Although the Korean conflict raised many of the same issues present in other American conflicts, the timing and parameters of the war guaranteed that particular narratives would arise among African Americans in and out of uniform. This essay traces three aspects of the African American reaction to the war, the most visible of which concerned the role of black troops within an army whose commitment to desegregation was uneven at best. Beyond this issue, black Americans sought to articulate a coherent position on the war as a whole, debating whether the war was a legitimate struggle against aggression or a colonial strike against the self-determination of another "colored" people. Finally, the war generated important domestic changes. Although these changes were in some ways less striking than the mass migration, industrial employment, and new political mobilizations unleashed throughout the "home front" during World War II, the unease, anxiety, and opposition generated between 1950 and 1953 produced lasting impressions among a critical swath of black Americans, including several who would play critical roles in the radical era that accompanied the Vietnam War. Remembering Korea, then, helps to illustrate a moment of African American history caught between peril and progress, between internationalism and patriotism, and between hope and despair.[2]

Black Joes

On January 11, 1951, the NAACP special counsel Thurgood Marshall flew to Japan and Korea in order to investigate the situation of thirty-nine black soldiers convicted by courts-martial as a result of their conduct during the first three months of the Korean conflict. The dispatch of the organization's top troubleshooter highlighted both the serious nature of the charges—one convicted lieutenant had been sentenced to death for refusing an order to lead an attack—and the firestorm of adverse publicity concerning the performance of black soldiers. The convicted soldiers were members of the all-black 24th Infantry Regiment, a former "buffalo soldier" unit that had seen action across the Great Plains, in Cuba, the Philippines, and Mexico, and in both World Wars. The 24th had earlier won the first American victory in the Korean conflict by recapturing a small town (Yech'on) about fifty miles north of Taegu.[3] Subsequent defeats during August and September, however, had led to charges of cowardice and insubordination by white officers openly disdainful of black GIS. The resulting trials of sixty infantrymen, thirty-two of whom were convicted, brought into sharp relief the ongoing debates about the place of race within the armed forces.

Military affairs formed an inherently global arena of postwar black political politicking. In 1948, the trade union leader A. Philip Randolph and the black clergyman Grant Reynolds formed the Committee Against Jim Crow in Military Service and Training. Threatening a campaign of draft resistance and civil disobedience "along the lines of the magnificent struggles of the people of India against British Imperialism," Randolph told members of Congress that "Negroes are in no mood to shoulder a gun for democracy abroad so long as they are denied democracy here at home."[4] The threat of widespread draft evasion by blacks came as relations worsened between the

United States and the Soviet Union and as fears grew within the Truman administration that critical black votes would be lost to the Progressive Party candidate Henry Wallace and the Republican Thomas Dewey. Citing the need to maintain "the highest standards of democracy," Truman authored an executive order (9981) mandating desegregation and announcing the formation of a seven-member committee, chaired by former U.S. Solicitor General Charles Fahy, to review plans submitted by the various military branches.[5]

Testimony before the Fahy committee revealed an uneven commitment to the new order. The U.S. Navy, Coast Guard, and Marine Corps could only come up with three black officers between them out of a total officer corps of nearly seventy thousand. Nearly 80 percent of the African American "sailors" in the navy were cooks, stewards, or steward's mates, job categories that were approximately 98 percent black.[6] Among the service branches with large numbers of ground forces, opposition was open and widespread. Army Chief of Staff General Omar Bradley warned against making the military "an instrument of social policy," while Marine Corps officials added that making the force an "agency for experimentation in civil liberty" threatened the military readiness of the entire nation.[7]

Beyond restricting the ranks of the officer corps, military officials sought to maintain quotas that limited blacks to 10 percent of the enlisted population. The army, in particular, feared inundation at the hands of blacks seeking work in the inflationary economic climate that followed the end of World War II. Fears that African Americans would sign up in large numbers for primarily financial reasons were not without reason. Black unemployment rates had risen considerably between 1946 and 1948. Throughout California, trucks stretched "bumper to bumper" taking former soldiers and defense workers to the expanding cotton fields of California's central valley, where growers offered them $2.50 per one hundred pounds of cotton picked.[8] Against the options of unemployment or picking cotton, many regarded a private's base pay of $95 a month as a workable choice.[9] As a result, black recruits rose from 8.2 percent to 25 percent of all army enlistments in the four months that followed the elimination of recruiting quotas in March 1950.[10]

In claiming segregation as a national defense imperative, army officials recycled old arguments concerning the poor combat reputation of blacks. The purportedly inglorious performance of the 24th Regimental Combat

Team became the primary example of this argument, and allegations regarding the unit's poor performance received widespread publicity. Harold Martin's *Saturday Evening Post* article proved particularly damaging. Martin's essay described "keeping the Negro soldier awake" as "the most harassing" of a list of problems that included laziness, stupidity, and fear.[11] Most damaging, the black soldiers were said to have composed a song in honor of their unwillingness to fight. Set to the tune of "I'm Movin' On," by the country musician Hank Snow, the "Bugout Boogie" reportedly began "when those Chinese mortars begans to thud/the old deuce-four began to bug." Although the song was evidently common to both white and black units, who changed the designation of the retreating unit in order to mock either themselves or rivals, the *Post* suggested that the celebration of "strategic withdrawal," as the U.S. military euphemistically refers to its retreats, was a phenomenon unique to the 24th Infantry.

Martin's *Evening Post* essay appeared six months after the courts-martial trials of sixty members of the 24th Infantry, and some three months before the unit was disbanded. The trials attracted considerable attention, particularly among African Americans. Black newspapers, several of which had sent teams to Korea to cover the process of integration, angrily questioned the military's motives. *Courier* editorials noted that segregation precluded the posting of white reinforcements to black units engaged in combat, a factor that left understrength battalions exposed to destruction through attrition. The *Baltimore Afro-American* openly asserted that the 24th Regimental Combat Team had been set up to fail, noting that it had been assigned too much ground to cover, been left in combat for far too long, and been attacked by what was arguably the toughest North Korean unit, the 6th Division. Another column, entitled "What Gives in Korea?" argued that such exposure was deliberate, as it offered fearful whites a means by which to resist integration.[12]

Legal proceedings against members of the regiment took place throughout September and October 1950. The most serious allegations concerned the refusal to go into combat, and at least one historian notes that the high rate of officer casualties may have generated an unspoken assumption that black enlisted men were "fragging" officers. In the end, the trials were speedy and the sentences were harsh. Lieutenant Leon Gilbert was sentenced to death for refusing to lead an attack against great odds, while fifteen others received sentences of life in prison. Sixteen others received prison sentences of between five and twenty years of hard labor. The most lenient sentence given a black soldier—five years—was the longest term given either of the two whites convicted for dereliction of duty.

In preparing his report on the trials, Marshall concluded that the trials had taken place in an atmosphere that precluded a legitimate outcome. Black soldiers had been denied the counsel of their choice. Witnesses for the prosecution had given conflicting testimony in separate cases, and judging panels had ignored evidence that should have proved exonerating. Marshall noted that four cases ending in life sentences had run between forty-two and fifty minutes, leading him to observe that "even in Mississippi a Negro will get a trial longer than 42 minutes." Several men were convicted of deserting while in the hospital with doctor's orders, while others were tried and punished more than once for the same offense. The ultimate responsibility, Marshall held, lay with Douglas MacArthur, who Marshall noted maintained a segregated command.

As the population of black enlisted men swelled to upward of 30 percent of combat replacements during 1951, assessing the performance of black soldiers came to be seen as a military imperative. Contrasting opinions concerning the strength of black soldiers in integrated combat units prompted the army to convene a study, known as "Project Clear," that ultimately found that integrated units performed as well as white units, provided that blacks comprised no more than 20 percent of the total population. By the time of the report's issue in 1951, military necessities increasingly forced the army to assign replacement soldiers without regard to race. The study thus provided cover to military officials eager to find a face-saving way to concede the necessity of system-wide integration.

Little effort, however, was made toward reducing racist attitudes among white soldiers. The white chaplain of the segregated 24th Infantry frankly admitted his bias, conceding, "I am prejudiced against Negroes even though I am a minister."[13] One soldier asked about the feasibility of integrating domestic bases responded that, "if they'd (blacks) be sent in one at a time, they might as well send in the coffin with them," while another held that "you integrate units and pretty soon it will lead to intermarriage."[14] Another infantryman, betraying a familiarity if not an affinity with black culture, claimed that he would "flatten one on his back if he came up to me and played that game they call 'the dozens' "; hit you on your back and say 'Hello motherfucker!' "[15] Such reactions indicated real and even deadly tension, not simply a transitory prejudice. Wounded soldiers awaiting repatriation told First Lieutenant Adolf Voight in San Francisco that serving with "them nigger bastards" would get him killed.[16] Verbal sparring between black and white soldiers was endemic, and while open conflict on the level of the disturbances during the subsequent conflict in Vietnam was absent, accounts by black soldiers painted a decidedly mixed portrait of race relations among enlisted men.

There is little doubt that the pressures of war spurred rapid desegregation. By the end of 1953, the army reported that more than 90 percent of black enlisted men were serving in integrated units. With the exception of the army and the Air National Guards, which remained nearly 99 percent white throughout the Vietnam War, the armed forces were by 1954 unquestionably more mixed than any other single institution in civil society (excepting, of course, prisons). As a result, the military became the forum for precisely the sort of debate that Omar Bradley and others had sought to avoid. Some argued that the U.S. military stood as the ultimate symbol of national possibility, while others lamented that dying seemed to be the primary thing that whites were willing to share with blacks.[17]

At the time, it seems, small numbers of black soldiers evidently preferred serving in all-black units. The percentage of black soldiers who told army interviewers that they would rather serve in black units or live in all-black housing ran between 6 percent and 22 percent.[18] One black infantryman stated that he "would rather be in a colored unit for the simple reason that I don't like them [white people].[19] Such attitudes, however rare, pointed to a problem that faced an American military confronting both the terms and the forces of national liberation. As American officials sought to portray the war as a struggle against communism that had nothing to do with the color line, publicity regarding American racism toward black GIs threatened— in ways much more direct than during World War II—to open fissures throughout the cold war edifice. The communist press concluded as much, editorializing that, "although the Negro press . . . does not question the unjust character of the war, its clamor for the abolition of jimcrow indirectly raises the question of the war's character."[20] Here, the domestic and the international fused once again, leading many to suggest that the question of continued black support for the war might turn, not simply on the experience of black soldiers but on the larger question of how the war would be defined or spun.

Mister Charlie's War?

Six months after the publication of Marshall's report, a group of fifty-four black soldiers wrote the *Courier* columnist P. L. Prattis in the hopes of publicizing their unhappiness with the aims and the conduct of the Korean War. Citing discrimination against black soldiers at home and abroad, the authors argued that ultimately the war was about denying self-determination to another "colored" population. Terming the conflict "Mister Charlie's War," they ended by mocking Supreme Commander Douglas MacArthur's famous edict by noting that, while "old soldiers never die, plenty of young ones do."[21]

Today, the notion of an essentially defensive struggle against communist aggression constitutes a common American understanding of the Korean War. As a result, contemporary denunciations of the conflict as an imperialist and colonial war, more similar to U.S. efforts in the Philippines or Iraq than to World War II, are largely forgotten. Forgotten too is the extent to which significant swaths of African America saw the conflict as heavily racialized. For the most part, the erasure of the Korean conflict as an imperialist intervention is understandable, given both the general lack of interest in the war on the part of Americans and their conviction that American expeditionary forces sought only to check communist expansion.[22] At the time, however, a diverse group of black communists, independent progressives, left nationalists, and pacifists saw the war less as a desperate struggle against Moscow's surrogates than as another untimely and self-serving effort to influence the political processes of a nonwhite people.

African Americans had long seen American excursions into the Pacific, especially the Pacific War of 1931–1945, through an internationalist and anti-imperialist lens.[23] As a number of key studies have shown, the struggle between Japan and the United States was waged across a racialized landscape that influenced everything from cultural perceptions and media representations to military campaigns and strategic planning.[24] The aftermath of the war scattered soldiers and sailors across the ocean, transforming the "black Pacific" from an imagined community of transnational anti-racism into an actually existing arc of complex social interactions. In the South Pacific, the site of armed, uniformed "Black Joes" working alongside white soldiers stoked an anticolonial consciousness among Solomon Islanders.[25] Black soldiers assigned occupation duties in Japan reported favorable attitudes on the part of Japanese citizens, and they vehemently blamed white officers and military policies for what they regarded as growing racism among Japanese as the occupation continued. The social status, conduct, and influence of African American soldiers—overrepresented among the American garrisons in Japan—formed a nagging question within an occupation incapable of fully masking its racial overtones.[26]

Whereas the conflict with Japan had often been debated as a "race" war, the conflict in Korea increasingly revealed a subtle shift toward a terminology that replaced "race" with "color." This, it should be stressed, was a tendency and not an absolute, and the terms "race" and "color" were occasionally used interchangeably, primarily among supporters of the U.S. intervention. Nevertheless, to the extent that the language of "race war" seemed to suggest competing racial concepts or orders, as in the case of the U.S. and Japan, the notion of a "war of color" opened a space for viewing the Korean conflict, the Chinese Revolution, and the insurgencies in Indonesia, Indochina, and the Philippines as part of a worldwide struggle against what the African American radical Malcolm X termed "world white supremacy."

As John Dower has noted, prewar fears of an anticolonial "race" war pitting India, China, Japan, and other Asian nations against the West reemerged well before the conclusion of hostilities in 1945. An article in *Catholic World* in July of that year, entitled "Which War Comes Next?" noted Russia's "Asiatic" character in order to argue that the struggle against communism and the threatened race war might well fuse together.[27] Although such sentiments became less histrionic during the 1950s, the thinking behind them expanded with Chinese revolution and the rise of the ostensibly "socialist" regimes of Nasser and Nehru. By the time of the 1955 gathering of nonaligned nations in Bandung, Indonesia, the notion of an independent foreign policy among developing countries was seen as little more than a communist trick.

In the immediate postwar period, events in Korea proved difficult to separate from larger discussions of decolonization. Communists, progressives, and Left nationalists saw a worldwide war of color between reputable nationalists like Mao and Kim Il Sung and "quislings" and "uncle toms" like the Chinese nationalist leader Chiang Kai-Shek and the South Korean president Syngman Rhee, whom the columnist J. A. Rogers called "senile" and "incompetent."[28] The perception that the United States was preventing unification caused many to view events in Korea as part of a global struggle for self-determination. Thus the black paper with the most extensive coverage of the war, the *Baltimore Afro-American,* compared the struggle in Korea to the Boxer rebellion, noting that the 1950s did not mark the first time that Asians had fought against combined armies drawn from Europe and Japan.[29] Another journalist wrote that "the Korean people, north and south, have no 'welcome' on their doormats for Americans."[30] Closer to home, nationalist expatriates living in Los Angeles published a bilingual weekly paper, *Korean Independence,* relentlessly critical of both the Rhee government and the American intervention. The *California Eagle,* published a few miles away from the Jefferson Boulevard offices of the Korean Independence Co., often echoed *Korean Independence,* as when the publisher Charlotta Bass denounced the U.N.'s decision to intervene as a "purchased parliamentary victory" that meant little, given the absence of North Korean or Chinese participation in the U.N. debate.[31]

The composition of U.N. expeditionary forces did little to reassure those who saw the U.S.-led intervention as a colonial crusade. Ostensibly "First World" nations provided the bulk of the U.N. coalition, with Australia, Belgium, Canada, Greece, New Zealand, and tiny Luxembourg sending combat units. Some of the largest contingents came from England, the Netherlands, and France, each of which was busily confronting Southeast Asian guerrilla insurgencies. One observer tried to connect the dots by arguing that "the smoke of battle in Korea has not yet cleared, and the French capitalists are already crying for our boys to be used to protect their interests."[32]

Among those skeptical of American motivations in Korea, one ally provoked particular ire. As Thomas Borstelmann notes, the Korean conflict confirmed the Republic of South Africa as the United States' closest African ally. The Korean conflict erupted just as the legal framework of apartheid was being established, with the Group Areas Act, the Prohibition of Mixed Marriages Act, and the Suppression of Communism Act offering clear parallels with the United States.[33] South Africa contributed an air force squadron to the U.N. effort, and at least one official offered to raise a levy of 100,000 colored soldiers. Beyond soldiers or airmen, however, an alliance with South Africa promised a steady supply of uranium, a key resource for an American military openly considering the use of nuclear weapons against Chinese and Korean targets.

Anti-imperialist black activists criticized the expanding strategic alliance between the segregated United States, apartheid South Africa, and Europe's colonial powers. Claiming that "South Africa in her treatment of colored people represents a greater challenge to world peace than Korea," the Council on African Affairs added that "neither might of wealth nor military power can settle struggles in Asia and Africa."[34] The council's call, authored by W. E. B. Du Bois, was endorsed by more than one hundred black activists, journalists, artists, labor leaders, professionals, and clergy, including the council leaders Robeson and Du Bois, the Baltimore *Afro-American* editor Wes Matthews, the producer Carlton Moss, the naval officer Capt. Hugh Mulzac, the artists Aaron Douglas and Charles White, and several regional NAACP secretaries. Charlotta Bass asked how Americans could debate "losing China and Korea, as if they were ours in the first place," while another woman wrote caustically that she was "personally tired of having Ralph Bunche dangled from flag poles" before adding, "if this is a living example of democracy that we are spreading in Korea, then heaven help the dark Korean people."[35]

Even more moderate observers seemed inclined to regard events in Korea as part of a broad transformation underway throughout the world. A news release from the Associated Negro Press wire service termed the conflict "a clash of white versus colored, of imperialism versus nationalism." Claiming that "America is the last bulwark of the colonial powers," the wire service release concluded, "if she is beaten in Korea, the whole structure of colonialism will be shaken and toppled." A *Pittsburgh Courier* columnist wrote: "[In] Korea, in Indo-China, in Tunisia, in South Africa, in India, the West Indies, South America and the United States, the magic that made chattel slaves of some, peons of many and sharecroppers of others is furiously losing its charm."[36] Despite his own feelings against communism, the NAACP head Walter White warned that the animosity of China and North Korea showed an "implacable hatred" toward white people worldwide. Having earlier spoken of a growing connection between black Americans and the colonial world, White predicted that a worldwide racial conflict was "inevitable" unless "white nations" completed "an about-face on the issue of race."

Others disputed claims of a racialized war. The *Los Angeles Sentinel* called claims of a race war "ill founded," instead informing readers that the war constituted a clash between political ideologies with "adherents among all racial groups."[37] An *Ebony* photo-editorial entitled "Is It a War of Color?" compared communist efforts to mobilize antiwar sentiment through anti-racist appeals to Japanese wartime propaganda. A letter to the editor published in the *Afro-American* concurred, noting that the presence of "tan yanks" and troops from the Philippines, Siam, and the Chinese Kuomin-tang proved the war "against aggression" rather than "one of white's against a colored race." The *Chicago Defender,* writing only days before China's intervention changed the parameters of the war, argued that the UN victory offered a lesson to the Russians, who, the newspaper maintained, were behind the initial attack. The NAACP offered a more conditional endorse-ment, arguing that, "if the United States is to win the support of noncom-munist Asia and Africa, it will have to demonstrate that democracy is a living reality which knows no limitation of race."[38]

Despite these claims, the war's obvious racial overtones proved difficult to ignore. Battlefield reports often made explicit reference to racial issues. The *Afro-American* reported on a unit of North Korean soldiers in "black face" attempting to infiltrate American positions.[39] On another occasion, the paper led with a headline discussing North Korean broadcasts aimed at black soldiers, placing the article over another article describing the bomb-ing of the 24th Infantry Regiment by American aircraft. The latter issue particularly vexed black soldiers, who complained repeatedly of launching costly attacks on enemy positions that had to be abandoned following poorly aimed air and artillery barrages. More than one soldier, in fact, prefaced his comments in support of military integration by noting that he thought he was less likely to be bombed by American planes if he were in a mixed unit.

Newspaper accounts provided some sense of a growing disenchantment with the war on the part of black enlisted men. The *Courier* printed a let-ter from fifty-four black soldiers asking, "Why is this country fighting in Korea?" The *Daily People's World* reprinted a song penned by an injured private that included a stanza proclaiming, "Till our discharge we must take it/many good things we must miss/don't let the draft board get you/and for God's sake don't enlist." Critical opinions by other black soldiers prompted Curtis Morrow, who had volunteered for the army, to declare the war "bull-shit."[40] Unhappiness extended to white and Latino soldiers as well. Quoting a GI who described the war as "damned useless," the *New York Times* argued that an "unawareness" of the mission was hampering American efforts.[41] A correspondent from the *Atlanta Constitution* overhead a soldier who, upon being informed that he was part of an "international police force," asked sarcastically "when do I git my horse?"[42]

As in the war with Japan, racist depictions of a savage and inhuman enemy became commonplace. Chinese soldiers, attacking en masse without artillery or air support, were referred to as "ants" or other insects. The second-highest-ranking American military officer in Korea, Major General Edward "Ned" Almond, sought to rally a group of marines destined for annihilation at the Chosin Reservoir with instructions not "to let a bunch of Chinese laundrymen stop you."[43] The ostensible aims of the war, however, as well as the presence of Asian armies among allied troops, limited the official tolerance for openly derogatory references to the enemy. MacArthur's segregated headquarters issued an advisory instructing soldiers to avoid using the word "gook," while an article published in the military paper *Tips* informed readers that "insulting and alienating" language provided "ammunition for the propaganda war waged against democratic nations."[44] Although the epithet continued to grow in popularity among American soldiers, newspaper accounts reported black unease with the epithet, perhaps as a result of the perception, articulated clearly by the *New York Age*, that "gook was a new way of saying n——r."[45]

Endemic racism constituted the primary challenge for observers seeking to recast the war narrative away from discussions of race. Institutional racism extended beyond the presence of ill-equipped and poorly led segregated battalions. Black soldiers repeatedly claimed that their requests for air and artillery support were ignored. Donated blood was labeled by race until protests by U.N. staff forced a change. And although military cemeteries had been formally desegregated in 1948, the Congressional Medal of Honor winner Sergeant Cornelius Charlton was denied burial in Arlington National Cemetery, suggesting that while there may not have been any racists in the foxholes, there were still a few directing the burial procedures of the armed forces.

Nowhere was the war's sharply racial relief brought into greater focus than in the prisoner of war camps spread along North Korea's mountainous northern frontier. The seesaw battles of the war's first year saw large numbers of American servicemen fall prisoner to advancing North Korean and Chinese forces. The latter took charge of administrative duties relating to U.N. prisoners of war, conducting sustained political work among their charges. More than seven thousand captured American troops were separated according to their political leanings, with "progressives" and "reactionaries" standing on opposite sides of the political spectrum. The extent and apparent effect of these efforts—postwar estimates put the number of troops said to have collaborated with their captors as high as one-third—led to a decade of debate concerning the mental and physical stamina of American soldiers.[46]

Much of this debate turned on the question of the purported "brainwashing" of American servicemen. Amid more coercive methods, interrogation and indoctrination efforts contained political education and "struggle sessions" focused on generating a critique of both the war and American society among soldiers and airmen. As with every other U.S. war in Asia, black soldiers were seen as logically open to precisely such a critique. Discussions of racial conditions in the United States formed part of the core of Chinese propaganda efforts, and black soldiers were among those most pressed to write letters, sign peace petitions, or participate in radio broadcasts denouncing the war.[47] Roger Fletcher, a captured member of the segregated 24th Infantry, noted that racial themes surfaced more commonly during education sessions than during interrogations. Told "to go back to your country and help start a revolution," Fletcher decided that "the Chinese did not like white people very much."[48]

Postwar surveys of POW behavior, otherwise bitterly opposed, are unified in proclaiming "the Negro GI" as no more susceptible to red propaganda than his white cohorts. Indeed, as one recent study notes, postwar research concerning POW conduct deliberately avoids using race as an analytical tool, ignoring, for example, the segregation of returning prisoners by American officials after the armistice for purposes of interrogation.[49] One notable exception, Edward Hunter's book *Brainwashing*, contains an entire chapter devoted to what he terms the "Korean miracle" of black resistance to communist entreaties. Hunter, a former propagandist for the Office of Strategic Services whose political work had centered on coordinating anticommunist opposition among American journalists, actually seems to have coined the term "brainwashing." Both the term itself and Hunter's insistence that black Americans proved no more susceptible than whites are worthy of note. In the context of cold war struggle, both changing race relations and the purported superiority of American life were shot through with questions of national security. As a result, the conscious desire to minimize incidents of race difference during wartime and the insistence than anyone who preferred life under socialism was clinically insane can be seen as the ideological imperatives of a society locked in a struggle as all-encompassing as it was fierce.[50]

Given these gaps, it is entirely possible that black soldiers agreed tacitly with Chinese commentary linking capitalism with racism and imperialism. Perhaps black soldiers, eager to press their claims toward full citizenship, saw little of value in the mandatory political education classes that prisoners attended. On the other hand, Chinese efforts may simply have come one war too early. Unlike Vietnam where hundreds if not thousands of black G Is would eventually create autonomous black zones like Saigon's "Soul Alley," refuse to fight, or publicly agree with Muhammad Ali's observation concerning his refusal to quarrel "with them Viet Cong," the pattern of separating black soldiers into their own areas during the Korean conflict generated considerable resentment among soldiers reminded of domestic conditions.

Chinese efforts made an impression on white prisoners as well. Approximately 22 percent of returning prisoners listed members of minority groups as the primary group to whom Chinese propaganda efforts were directed. Prison life exacerbated preexisting tensions, and at least some white prisoners angrily rejected what they saw as "preferences of treatment given to minority group Americans." Small groupings of "reactionary" prisoners organized into groups like the "Free Hearts of America," the "Non-Benedict Arnold Club," the "War Camp," and the "Un-American Activities Committee." As one of the studies most sympathetic to American prisoners notes, however, the most prevalent resistance organization among servicemen was called the Ku Klux Klan. Cells of between two and four Klan members sought to intimidate prisoners away from collaboration with their captors through threats and occasional acts of violence.[51]

"Collaboration" was generally in the eye of the beholder. The daughter of one serviceman who refused repatriation pointedly asked, "when someone points out something you already know, such as racism, is that brainwashing?"[52] In addition to political education classes, soldiers were encouraged to sign peace petitions and to write letters questioning the aims and value of the war. Most notable, however, were the daily radio broadcasts recorded in Korea and broadcast over shortwave radio from Beijing.[53] Both white and black servicemen participated in the broadcasts, which also featured Chinese announcers. Details of the broadcasts were carried in the mainstream media, the communist press, and in African American periodicals, as when the *Courier* described a "Seoul City Sue" broadcast excoriating black soldiers as "slaves to the American white man" and claiming "we are all of the colored race."[54]

Although the overall effect of such missives is difficult to gauge, postwar authors took pains to portray black soldiers as equal partners in resisting communist entreaties. Nevertheless, at least three African American prisoners of war refused repatriation. Unlike several of the eighteen white soldiers who chose to remain in North Korea, none of the three African American detainees possessed a background of familiarity with Marxism. None was even said by the army to have known the location of Korea before the outbreak of war. Thus the effort to survive America, rather than any affinity with either scientific socialism or East Asian life, explained the decisions of the three. Corporal LaRance Sullivan, an impoverished soldier from Santa Barbara who had not known "the habit of breakfast" as a child and had seen his sisters placed in foster homes following the incarceration of his mother, while his own life had been sufficiently bad that the authors of a book on GI deserters conceded, "you cannot find anyone in Santa Barbara who is willing to condemn LaRance Sullivan for turning his back on America." Captured in the chaotic days following the initial Chinese intervention, Sullivan's treatment in a People's Liberation Army (PLA) military hospital prompted him to oppose a war, as he declared in a letter to his grandmother, that "is not being fought for the common people."[55]

Like Sullivan, Private William White and Private Clarence Adams refused to return to the United States. Both were southerners. Few familiar with White, of Plumerville, Arkansas (pop. 550), could understand why he elected to stay in China, although his description by a former employer as "a good worker, not one of those rowdy niggers," suggests something of what he chose to leave behind. A Memphis native, Adams had been assigned to an all-black artillery unit ordered to advance even as white soldiers retreated past them. Convinced that his unit had been sacrificed in order to save white lives, Adams was incensed by what he saw as pervasive racism among white prisoners. Openly critical of American society, Adams was seen as a "progressive" prisoner by the Chinese and placed in charge of a prison library.[56] Choosing to remain, Adams earned a university degree, married a Chinese academic, and started a family. During the early years of open American involvement in Vietnam (1963–1966), Adams was involved in making radio broadcasts aimed at American troops. Adams and his wife left for the United States in 1966, pushed by political criticisms launched at them as the Cultural Revolution began.[57] Despite death threats and a federal investigation, Adams remained in the United States, where in Memphis he and his family operated a restaurant until his death in 1999.

G.I. Fever or Korea Blues?

Midway through 1949, the San Francisco–based Spire records released a sparse 78 rpm single by the California blues pianist (and migrant agricultural worker) Mercy Dee Walton. In lyrics familiar to many a young man, "G.I. Fever" describes unsuccessful efforts to compete for the attention of women against soldiers. As Walton sang:

> I can dress up in my finest
> she don't even look my way
> I can dress up in my finest
> she don't even look my way
> just starts talkin' bout some Sergeant she saw downtown that day
> Now I'm going down to the draft board
> I'm going to fall down on my knees
> I'm going to babu du du lay
> Going down to the draft board
> I'm going to fall down on my knees
> I'm asking them to give me some position
> in this man's army please[58]

Walton had written and performed "G.I. Fever" during the heady years of World War II, as defense employment ignited a boom in nightclub business from Oakland to San Diego. Against the backdrop of a new mobilization, Spire records founder Chester Lu doubtlessly imagined that the record would capture audiences gearing up for a new war. With the outbreak of war several months away, however, Walton's single sold poorly among audiences dealing less with wartime fever than with reconversion blues.

The explosion of new hostilities led to expectations of a new economic boom. Charlotta Bass described the streets of South Los Angeles as looking as they had during World War II.[59] Unemployment among nonwhites declined by nearly half nationwide, from 8.5 percent to 4.8 percent, and music industry executives and club owners claimed that sheet music sales and orchestra prospects were better than any time since 1940–41. Commentators predicted that orchestras, in decline since the early days of World War II, would stage a comeback to displace singers and beboppers.[60]

Ultimately, however, few saw a dramatic improvement in their economic fortunes. Wage and price controls slowed but did not eliminate inflationary pressures on household items and foodstuffs. Much of the war was initially fought with surplus equipment, and the Truman Administration's initial unwillingness to commit to a full national mobilization—owing in part to the generally suspect level of support for the war—created an uneven employment picture. In Southern California, for example, defense production increasingly shifted from multiracial Los Angeles to predominantly white Orange County. The percentage of African Americans employed in heavy industry in Los Angeles continued to decline in any event, dropping to less than 5 percent. Writing more than a year after the outbreak of war, the communist leader Pettis Perry stated, "Negro women, who were driven from industry right after the Second World War, have never regained any mass base in industry anywhere in the country."[61] Efforts to create a new Fair Employment Practices Commission went nowhere, with African American leaders committed to a cold war civil rights strategy unwilling to threaten widespread protest against the backdrop of rising state repression. A Korean War-era version of the "Double Victory" campaign, it seems, was to be limited to struggling over the terms of military integration.[62]

Mostly, the war found black folks at home anxious and uneasy. B. B. King's mournful lament "Sweet Sixteen" included the lyrics "well my brother's in Korea baby, my sister's down in New Orleans . . . you know I'm having so much troubles people, baby I wonder what in the world is gonna happen to me."[63] During 1951 and 1952, J. B. Lenoir recorded several songs critical of the war and its effects, including the "Eisenhower Blues," "I'm in Korea," and "Korea Blues." In the latter, the guitarist asked "who you gonna let lay down in my bed" when "the Chinese shoot me down . . . in Korea somewhere."[64] Confusion over the war was aptly summarized in an editorial cartoon published in the Pittsburgh *Courier*. In it, a woman looking in on a neighbor listens as her friend complains about: "That no-good Bootsie . . . he keeps that television AND radio goin' all day long and all you can hear 'round here is "Jackie's at the bat, count's two and one . . . the North Koreans done run MacArthur back another ten miles . . . there's a sharp hit to the shortstop and MacArthur say pay it no mind . . . Sister, I'm so mixed up I find myself tryin' to sweep the hallway with a fire-extinguisher."[65]

African Americans were not alone in experiencing difficulty coming to grips with the meaning of the war. With the exception of the recent invasion of Iraq, the American intervention in Korea was arguably the least popular American military effort in the twentieth century. After an initial surge in patriotic sentiment, Americans wearied quickly of a war seemingly without progress or end. As in Vietnam, organized opposition came from pacifists as well as the Left. Few of any political persuasion wanted to shoulder the increased tax burden the war was sure to bring, while others viewed the participation of only sixteen of the United Nations' sixty member states as evidence of a civil conflict that the United States should seek to avoid. Many business leaders resented the imposition of price controls, while rightist opposition came from hawkish politicians concerned that the United States was fighting without using the full contents of its arsenal (i.e., nuclear weapons). Reservations extended to the very top of the military chain of command. Having initially refused to divert units based in Europe for duty in Asia, the Joint Chiefs of Staff chairman Omar Bradley termed the conflict "the wrong war, in the wrong place, at the wrong time, against the wrong enemy." For some, the war was not simply wrong but deeply uninteresting. One Vancouver paper reportedly ran the same combat dispatches—complete with identical headlines and punctuation—for three days without eliciting complaint from readers.[66]

Most black opposition to the war came from the Left. Harlem communists led one of the conflict's first antiwar rallies, meeting only ten days after the first commitment of U.S. troops. Paul Robeson joined the recently ousted communist city councilman Ben Davis, who told a crowd of fifteen hundred that "if Truman, Dulles and MacArthur have ants in their pants, let them send troops into Mississippi and Georgia."[67] Calling the struggles for peace and equality "indivisible," Davis noted a "growing acuteness of the contradiction between the war program of the American billionaires and the struggle for Negro liberation."[68] William Patterson wrote that "the wanton murder of Negroes has been a dress rehearsal for the murders of Koreans and Chinese," while Pettis Perry, secretary of the party's Negro commission, called the use of napalm "genocidal."[69] Writing in *Masses and Mainstream,* John Pittman detailed widespread opposition to the war on the part of urban blacks. Quoting a white unionist who had claimed to have gathered more than one thousand signatures in favor of the antinuclear Stockholm peace petition, Pittman wrote: "In the ghetto, you get a different kind of response. The people aren't afraid. They may say they don't see how a petition campaign can avert war, but they aren't scared to sign it."[70]

Party activists and affiliates sought to build a base of support among African Americans by linking the conduct of a racist war to the continuing oppression of African Americans at home. Civil Rights Congress activists led the initial struggle to publicize the case of Lieutenant Gilbert, earning his thanks even as the NAACP seized control of his legal fight.[71] In California, the Civil Rights Congress national secretary Aubrey Grossman joined the Korean American publisher Dr. Diamond Kim at an antiwar rally held in Watts.[72] Local congress members played a key role in mobilizing support, organizing legal defense, and finding bail money for the architect David Hyun, who was threatened with deportation to South Korea despite his arrest as an alleged "North Korean" agent.[73]

While these efforts may have facilitated an early degree of black antiwar opinion, internal contradictions hampered efforts conceived or led by the Communist Party. Pettis Perry warned sharply that white chauvinism threatened the struggle for peace, while the party's attempt to rearticulate "the national question" of black self-determination ran counter to the increasingly promising possibilities of integration. More seriously, the Korean War was the first in which members of the political Left found themselves obligated not simply to advocate peace but often to champion the cause of the enemy. Even when the latter contradiction could be finessed, ideological and practical challenges remained. Upholding domestic anti-racism and international anti-imperialism found the Communist Party advocating somewhat schizophrenic demands for more rapid military integration and an immediate end to hostilities. Perhaps units were to have been integrated on the way back to the United States.

Beyond these problems, the increasingly draconian environment faced by party cadre prevented the Communist Party in the United States from leading the struggle against the war. The preceding years had seen the decline of popular front institutions such as the National Negro Congress, the purge of communist locals from the ranks of the CIO, new legislation aimed at preventing "subversion," and an increasingly effective campaign to convince Americans that secretive groups threatened national security. Attempts to move the party to the center foundered, as former allies like

Henry Wallace became ardent supporters of war. New security laws made normal operations impossible, and entire sections of the party were ordered to begin preparations for existence underground. Against this backdrop, aboveground activities focused on defensive efforts to free jailed party members, such as those promoted by the Committee to Defend Negro Leadership and the Committee for the Defense of the Foreign Born. With the targeting of immigrants a key element of cold war repression, the latter committee often found itself working in conjunction with civil rights and anti-racist activists. Although many Smith Act and McCarran Act (1952) defendants were white, many were not. The Trinidadians C. L. R. James and Claudia Jones confronted deportation, as did the Guatemalan Luisa Moreno, the Filipino Ernesto Mangaoang, and the Koreans Sang Ryup Park and David Hyun.[74]

State repression against identifiable communists and the decline of the interracial Left meant that the most visible black opposition to war came from Left-leaning black radicals formally independent of any group affiliation. This included Robeson, Du Bois, and Bass, as well as artists like Aaron Douglas and Charles White, clergymen like Edward D. McGowan and J. Raymond Henderson, and the journalist Wes Mathews. During the war's first year, the Council on African Affairs constituted the primary political home of this tendency, at least for the dissemination of information. In her guise as Progressive Party vice-presidential candidate, Bass toured the United States denouncing the war. Du Bois addressed rallies on both coasts, gathering signatures for the Stockholm appeal against the use of atomic weapons as students began practicing "duck and cover" drills nationwide. Robeson joined a group of schoolchildren in New York who staged a sit-in at the United Nations to protest ambiguous American comments that seemed to suggest a possible nuclear strike against China.[75]

Neither the poor electoral fortunes of the Progressive Party nor the subsequent marginalization of Robeson and Du Bois should be taken as evidence that proponents of peace lacked a mass base. More than one million Americans signed the Stockholm appeal, with up to thirty-five thousand signing in Los Angeles during one long Fourth of July weekend. Accounts published in the *Daily People's World* reported strong support for the petition among African Americans, a factor that perhaps explains why the petition drive became the basis of the federal government's legal complaint against the octogenarian Du Bois.[76] An antiwar rally held at Madison Square Garden drew eighteen thousand.[77] Polls taken in March 1952 revealed that only 13 percent of black women supported the U.S. effort in Korea, making black women the group of Americans most opposed to continuing the war.[78] According to the journalist John Pittman, opposition was the "dominant" black view of the war, extending from "Negroes in uniforms" through "farmers, industrial workers, white collar workers, domestic workers, housewives, small businessmen, and many professionals."[79] Although Pittman was biased, he wasn't wrong. Two years into the war, a majority of African Americans (55 percent) supported continued negotiation or an immediate withdrawal, options that a slight minority (44 percent) of whites found more appealing than continuing to seek a decisive victory.[80]

Although most opposition to the war in Korea was verbal in nature, draft resistance was more pronounced than in either World War. Nearly 1.5 percent of draftees sought conscientious objector status, a rate ten times that of World War II, and the federal government investigated thousands of cases of draft resistance. Estimates of draft evasion ran as high as 30 percent in Harlem alone, and African Americans ultimately represented some 20 percent of those arrested for violating the Selective Service Act of 1948. The low overall number of blacks prosecuted for refusing induction (131) likely attests less to the level of resistance than to the limited means the government brought to bear upon those refusing to fight.[81]

The war caused deep divisions among pacifist organizations seeking a common position on what many regarded as communist aggression. James Farmer, for example, argued that he saw "no practical alternative to war" during the conflict. His stance brought him into direct conflict with the Fellowship of Reconciliation member Bayard Rustin and the Peacemakers activist Bill Sutherland, both of whom spent the war organizing rallies and practicing nonviolent civil disobedience. Citing religious beliefs, the Tennessean activist James Lawson chose prison over Korea, serving three years, while Bob Moses, a key figure in the Student Nonviolent Coordinating Committee during the 1960s, spent the war in European and Japanese camps run by the Quakers. Although the federal government had made efforts to tighten the requirements for those claiming conscientious objector status, members of the growing Nation of Islam and black Jehovah's Witnesses refused to serve.[82]

It is difficult to ascertain precisely the extent to which domestic opposition changed the political calculus in Washington regarding the war. Certainly, the eventual critiques of the *Wall Street Journal* and the Joint Chiefs of Staff carried more weight than the missives of Paul Robeson or Charlotta Bass. Ultimately, the answer matters little. American antiwar sentiment has historically functioned less to produce a cessation of hostilities than to narrow the range of motion for policymakers eager to maintain a full quiver of options. Unintended consequences often form the most important legacy of war, from the outpouring of political and cultural radicalism following World War I to the birth of the modern civil rights movement after 1941.

Korea proved no different. Beyond the ostensibly successful integration of the armed forces, one lasting effect of the conflict was the radicalization of a cadre of former black military personnel who would go on to play important roles in the subsequent civil rights and Black Power movements. In addition to those like Lawson and Moses who sought to avoid the military, many black radicals active during the 1960s served in the military during the war. A decorated serviceman with a Purple Heart, a Korean Service Medal, the Republic of Korea Presidential Unit Citation, a Combat Infantry Badge, and United Nations and Japanese Occupation duty ribbons, Ivory Perry served prison time after a questionable arrest and court-martial. Perry later stated, "I shouldn't have been in Korea in the first place."[83] Dishonorably discharged from the Marine Corps, the Black Power pioneer Robert Williams termed the conflict in Korea a "stupid waste."[84] The Black Panther Party cofounder Bobby Seale listed racial incidents during the war as one reason for his subsequent radicalization, as did James Forman, the eventual director of the Student Nonviolent Coordinating Committee's international affairs bureau who served an unhappy stint in the Air Force during the war.[85]

The war played a similar role in facilitating the development of black cultural radicalism during the 1960s. As the airman Amiri Baraka observed, "The fifties took on their own peculiar foreboding shape because of the grim catalyst of the Korean War and the emotional chaos that went with it. The Negro could not help but be affected; neither could his music."[86] Whether as volunteers or draftees, an important cross-section of the 1960s jazz avant-garde served between 1950 and 1954. The Chicago-based Association for the Advancement of Creative Musicians' collective members Roscoe Mitchell and Joseph Jarman and the saxophonist Albert Ayler served in Europe during the war years. The Saint Louis Black Arts Group members Julius Hemphill and Hamiet Bluiett were in uniform during this time as well, as were the

Los Angeles free jazz pioneers Horace Tapscott, Bobby Bradford, and Eric Dolphy. For these men, some of whom had never before left the cities of their birth, military service facilitated contact with like-minded musicians under conditions conducive to artistic experimentation. In at least one case, the effect was even more direct. While in Korea, the multi-instrumentalist Bilal Abdurrahman was given a woodwind instrument called a *p'iri* by a Korean farmer, which Abdurrahman then used in developing his signature jazz/Middle Eastern compositions.[87]

As the latter case suggests, the Korean War formed only one part of a broad-based internationalist counternarrative to the domesticating impulses of the cold war liberalism during the early-to-mid 1950s. Black interest in India and China, in African liberation and Puerto Rican nationalism, and in the West Indies and the Middle East all expanded during the 1950s.[88] War in Korea, however, facilitated the mobilization of people and resources, bringing individuals into new contexts. Debates over the pace of military and civilian desegregation, over the place of African Americans in a world seemingly fracturing along the global color line, and over the opportunities and challenges provided, again, by war all contributed to making the Korean conflict a critical one for African Americans. Responses vacillated between support for military integration and fury at the representations of black soldiers, between the desire for fuller participation in American life and the growing appeal of a proto Third Worldism, and between the desire to force change at a moment of national crisis and the growing implausibility of public dissent. Highlighting the insolubility of "African" and "American," the war illustrated what one recent account calls the "great divide in the modern black freedom movement" between those who saw "an identification with the U.S. State . . . as the answer to black mass discontent" and those for whom the national frame—and therefore the American state—was part of a problem that could only be solved across continents and seas.[89]

Coda: Fighting the Last War

In a recent article, the former army specialist Jorge Mariscal noted the cold ironies at play on a day when National Security Advisor Condoleeza Rice defended the Bush administration before the 9/11 commission while, eight time zones away, Lieutenant-General Ricardo Sanchez explained Iraq's deteriorating security situation at a military press briefing. Both Rice, an African

American of working-class origins from one of the most racist areas of the United States, and Sanchez, a Tejano of similarly humble economic origins for whom the military proved a path to education, success, and respect, found themselves publicly defending decisions made by "a group of privileged white men whose commitment to telling the truth has proven to be negligible."[90] Rice and Sanchez, like Secretary of State Colin Powell or the four-star General John Abizaid, constitute some of the most visible faces of American power on the world stage. The political effect—intentional or otherwise—is clear. Echoing Stokely Carmichael ("you can't eat Ralph Bunche for lunch"), the Palestinian MK (Member of Knesset) Azmi Bishara noted caustically: "People are sick and tired of the sound bites of John Abi Zeid and Ricardo Sanchez. If one were to land in Iraq from another planet, one would suspect that there are more non-whites in America than whites. America is using identity politics of the cheapest sort."[91]

This "military multiculturalism" fulfills a clear role. Media representations of a colorblind army facilitate many of the moral imperatives placed at the heart of America's contemporary "war on terror." Promoting a colorblind army arrayed against an implacable foe contrasts a modern and Western universalism with a provincial, premodern region, deflects accusations of imperialism by proposing instead a struggle between competing ideologies, and suggests that the entire world—as represented by our Arab and Latino commanders and black statesmen—shares an interest in the outcomes that American policymakers desire.[92]

The story was similar fifty years ago. The Korean War provided the impetus for a specific reordering of American racial relations, paving the way for the emergence of the belief that the U.S. military—the primary purveyors of organized violence on the planet today—somehow represents the most meritocratic, socially equal, and ultimately progressive institution in American society. The American-led world war against Islam—like the American-directed world war against communism—confronts an enemy whose long record of racial mixing necessitates a very public presentation of American universalism.

This universalism, of course, went unobserved at home. Racial progress consistently stalled in the interests of national security, from the collapse of interracial unionization efforts in the 1940s Jim Crow South amidst red-baiting through the fiscal evisceration of the war on poverty as a result of

Vietnam. The postwar red scare, moreover, explicitly targeted noncitizens and cast communism as a foreign-borne illness treatable with summary arrests, jailing, and deportation.

Neither racial reaction nor military multiculturalism forms the only link between the cold war and the War on Terror. Events in Iraq, Afghanistan, and the Philippines have raised anew the idea that some small, weak, confused, and dangerous segment of our own populace may hold strange ideas, planted from afar, that are germinating slowly in our putatively open society. A poor Chicagoan converts in prison. An affluent white kid turns his back on America. From the outside, they seem normal enough. Inside, however, they seethe with rage inculcated in foreign schools. Brainwashing, it would seem, is back. Or so the recent decisions of Hollywood suggest. Although World War II and Vietnam constitute the primary analogies utilized by the Right and Left, respectively, in framing the War on Terror, it is perhaps less than accidental that rather than remaking either *The Big Red One* or *Apocalypse Now*, Paramount Pictures spent eighty million dollars making—and thirty-five million dollars advertising—their remake of the 1962 classic of cold war paranoia, *The Manchurian Candidate.*

Paramount's 2004 effort perhaps reflects little more than the desperation of a film industry engaged in the sorts of recycling decried by Theodor Adorno. The replacement of "Manchuria" with a deterritorialized corporate concern certainly suggests little in the way of continuity with an early historical epoch. Still the figure of Sergeant Marco (Denzel Washington) as a confused former serviceman whose loyalty to the United States provides his sole path to clarity following his captivity, suggests powerfully the idea that America can in the end be seen as the only possible affiliation for African Americans in or out of uniform. And so, for those whom integration has failed, perhaps there are lessons to be learned from a war—and a world—where an infantryman could enter enthused with patriotism, or just needing a job, and ultimately elect to remain a permanent resident of the People's Republic of China. Like other political projects, memory and history involve the active organization and mobilization of consciousness and resources. Thus in considering a counternarrative of opposition and unease during the Korean War, we might, at the very least, begin to make space for alternative histories, alternative imaginations, and therefore alternative politics imagined outside—and perhaps arrayed against—the national frame.

Notes

1. For an overview on the political and military dimensions of the conflict, see Clay Blair, *The Forgotten War: America in Korea* (New York: Times Books, 1987); Bruce Cumings, *The Origins of the Korean War*, 2 vols. (Princeton, N.J.: Princeton University Press, 1981, 1990); Max Hastings, *The Korean War* (New York: Simon and Schuster, 1987); and William Stueck, *The Korean War: An International History* (Princeton, N.J.: Princeton University Press, 1995), and *Rethinking the Korean War* (Princeton, N.J.: Princeton University Press, 2002). On the postwar relationship between black liberation and international relations, see Robin D. G. Kelley, "Stormy Weather: Reconstructing Black (Inter) Nationalism in the Cold War Era," in *Is It Nation Time? Contemporary Essays on Black Power and Black Nationalism*, edited by Eddie S. Glaude, Jr. (Chicago: University of Chicago Press, 2002); Thomas Bortelsman, *The Cold War and the Color Line* (Cambridge, Mass.: Harvard University Press, 2003); Mary Dudziak, *Cold War Civil Rights: Race and the Image of American Democracy* (Princeton, N.J.: Princeton University Press, 2002); Brenda Plummer, *Rising Wind: Black Americans and U.S. Foreign Affairs, 1935–1960* (Chapel Hill: University of North Carolina Press, 1997); and Nikhil Pal Singh, *Black Is a Country: Race and the Unfinished Struggle for Democracy* (Cambridge, Mass.: Harvard University Press, 2004). For background on the question of black internationalism prior to 1945, see Robin D. G. Kelley, "But a Local Phase of a World Problem"; Black History's Global Vision, 1883–1950," *Journal of American History* 86, no. 3 (December 1999): 1045–77.

2. A number of historians have taken up the issues raised in this essay. Plummer's *Rising Wind* contains a short section on the war, while George Lipsitz's *George, a Life in the Struggle: Ivory Perry and the Culture of Opposition* (Philadelphia: Temple University Press, 1988), contains a section detailing the Missourian's experience as an infantryman during the war.

3. T. H. Pettigrew, *The Kunu-ri (Kumori) Incident* (New York: Vantage Press, 1963). This victory, coming against a backdrop of serious setbacks suffered by an unprepared U.S. military, was widely reported in both the black and the white press. In addition, accounts of the valor of black soldiers were read into the *Congressional Record* (vol. 96, part 8, p. 10866).

4. Here, Randolph returned to a strategy he had employed during World War II, when his threat to organize a mass march on the nation's capital resulted in the passing of an executive order desegregating defense-related industries. See Randolph's testimony before the U.S. Congress Committee on Armed Services, Universal Military Training (80th Cong., 1st sess., 1948), reprinted in Bernard Nalty and Morris MacGregor, *Blacks in the Military: Essential Documents* (Wilmington, Del.: Scholarly Resources Inc., 1981), 237.

5. Executive Order 9981, July 26, 1948, Harry S. Truman Library, Independence,

Missouri. On the Fahy committee, see Morris MacGregor, *Integration of the Armed Forces* (Washington D.C.: Center of Military History, United States Army, 1981), 291–378.

6 Nalty and MacGregor, *Blacks in the Military,* 300.

7 MacGregor, *Integration of the Armed Forces,* 317, 336. Richard Dalfiume, *Desegregation of the U.S. Armed Forces: Fighting on Two Fronts, 1939–1953* (Columbia: University of Missouri Press, 1969), 173.

8 "Dixie Comes to California," *Baltimore Afro-American,* October 16, 1950.

9 Michael Varhola, *Fire and Ice: The Korean War, 1950–1953* (Da Capo Press, 2000), 284.

10 Operations Research Office, Johns Hopkins University, *Utilization of Negro Manpower in the Army: A 1951 Study* (Bethesda, Md.: Research Analysis Corporation, 1963), 5; Lee Nichols, *Breakthrough on the Color Front* (New York: Random House, 1954), 109–11.

11 Harold H. Martin, "How Do Our Negro Troops Measure Up?" *Saturday Evening Post* 23 (June 16, 1951): 30–33, 139.

12 "What Gives in Korea?" *Baltimore Afro-American,* September 9, 1950.

13 *Pittsburgh Courier,* September 9, 1950.

14 Leo Bogart, *Social Research and the Desegregation of the U.S. Army;* Two Original 1951 Field Reports (Chicago: Markham Pub. Co., 1969), 209.

15 Ibid., 81.

16 William T. Bowers, William M. Hammond, George L. MacGarrigle, *Black Soldier, White Army: The 24th Infantry Regiment in Korea* (Washington, D.C.: Center of Military History, 1996), 185.

17 MacGregor, *Integration of the Armed Forces,* 609–24.

18 Bogart, *Social Research,* 344–52.

19 Ibid., 93.

20 Editorial, *Daily People's World,* October 2, 1950.

21 "Negro GI's Ask: Why Are We fighting?" *Daily People's World,* July 24, 1951.

22 Bruce Cumings has argued at length that the Korean War should be seen first and foremost as a revolutionary civil war between Koreans whose origins are to be found in the unreconstructed political situation on the peninsula following the collapse of Japanese rule. From this vantage point, the events of June 1950 represent less a premeditated general assault by northern forces than a sharp escalation of the "border" hostilities that had taken place throughout the previous year. See Cumings, *The Origins of the Korean War,* vol. 2, 568–85.

23 African Americans have consistently viewed America's "politics by other means" in Asia through a distinct lens. Asian wars have repeatedly challenged African Americans torn between the desire to use wartime opportunities to advance claims toward full citizenship and equality with their sympathy for and affiliation with others on the dark side of the color line. On the nineteenth-century effort to colonize the Philippines, see George Marks, *The Black Press Views American Imperialism (1898–1900)* (New York: Arno, 1971); Willard

Gatewood, *Smoked Yankees and the Struggle for Empire: Letters from Negro Soldiers* (Urbana: University of Illinois Press, 1971). According to Scot Brown ("The Dilemma of the African American Soldier in the Philippine-American War, 1899–1902," M.A. thesis, Cornell University, 1993), between 700 and 1,000 of the nearly 6,000 black soldiers assigned to the occupation chose to remain in the islands rather than return to the United States. See also Frank Schubert, "David Fagen: An Afro-American Rebel in the Philippines, 1899–1901," *Pacific Historical Review* 44 no. 1 (February 1975): 68–83. For information on pro-Japanese sentiment among African Americans, see Ernest Allen, "When Japan Was 'Champion of the Darker Races': Satokata Takahashi and the Flowering of Black Messianic Nationalism," *Black Scholar* 24 (winter 1994): 23–46; George Lipsitz, "Frantic to Join . . . the Japanese Army," in *Perilous Memories: The Asia-Pacific War(s)*, edited by T. Fujitani, Geoffrey M. White, and Lisa Yoneyama (Durham, N.C.: Duke University Press, 2000); Reginald Kearney, *African American Views of the Japanese: Solidarity or Sedition?* (Albany: State University of New York Press, 1998); Marc Gallicchio, *The African American Encounter with Japan and China* (Chapel Hill: University of North Carolina Press, 2000). For information on the influence of the Chinese Revolution on African Americans, see Robin D. G. Kelley and Betsy Esch, "Black Like Mao: Notes on Red China and the Black Revolution," this volume. Finally, on Southeast Asia, see William Duiker, *Ho Chi Minh: A Life* (New York: Criterion Books, 2000), 50–51, 56; Brent Hayes Edwards, "The Shadow of Shadows," *positions: east asia cultures critique* 11, no. 1 (spring 2003): 11–49. Analysts continue to debate whether Ho Chi Minh's interest in African American politics was fostered primarily in France or in the United States. Whichever the case, his 1924 essay "On Lynching and the Ku Klux Klan" remains an insightful exposé concerning black resistance and American political economy.

24 On the racial dimensions of World War II and its aftermath, see John Dower, *War without Mercy: Race and Power in the Pacific War* (New York: Pantheon Books, 1986); John Dower, *Embracing Defeat: Japan in the Wake of World War II* (New York: Norton, 1999); Yukiko Koshiro, *Transpacific Racisms and the Occupation of Japan* (New York: Columbia University Press, 1999); Gerald Horne, *Race War: White Supremacy and the Japanese Attack on the British Empire* (New York: New York University Press, 2004).

25 Geoffrey White, *The Big Death: Solomon Islanders Remember World War II* (Suva, Fiji: University of the South Pacific Press, 1988), 218–19, 223–25.

26 On black soldiers in occupation-era Japan, see Dower, *Embracing Defeat*; and Koshiro, *Transpacific Racisms*.

27 H. C. McGinnis, "Which War Comes Next?" *Catholic World*, July 1945; Dower, *War without Mercy*, 170–73.

28 Gerald Gill, "Afro-American Opposition to the United States' Wars of the 20th Century" (Ph.D. dissertation, Howard University, 1985), 84.

29 *Baltimore Afro-American*, 16 September 1950.

30   Milton Smith, "No Welcome Mat Out for U.S. in Korea," *Baltimore Afro-American*, December 16, 1950.

31   Milton Smith, "No Welcome Mat Out for U.S. in Korea," *California Eagle*, 11 August 1950.

32   Letter to the editor, *Daily People's World*, October 19, 1950. By September of 1950, four years before the French surrender at Dien Bien Phu, the American military had formed a military assistance group to coordinate American support for France.

33   Thomas Bortelsmann, *Apartheid's Reluctant Uncle* (New York: Oxford University Press, 1993), 137–68.

34   "100 Negro Leaders Demand That U.S. Quit Foreign Intervention," *California Eagle*, July 28, 1950.

35   Charlotta Bass, "Who Lost What?" *California Eagle*, November 16, 1950; Marie Bowden, "Open Letter to President Truman," *California Eagle*, July 28, 1950.

36   Joseph Bibb, "Who's Inferior?" *Pittsburgh Courier*, 26 July 1950.

37   "This Is No Race War," *Los Angeles Sentinel*, August 31, 1950.

38   "Is It a War of Color?" *Ebony*, October 1950; *Baltimore Afro-American* [n.d., 1950].

39   Lacking heavy artillery or air cover, Chinese and North Korean forces typically attacked at night in order to create greater confusion among U.N. forces. As the editors of the *Afro-American* were more than likely aware that camouflage face paint was often employed in war, their specific discussion of "blackface" makeup suggests the possibility of a desire to heighten a racialized angle on the conflict. Such an effort might be read either as an effort to rearticulate a racial narrative in defiance of moderate claims to the contrary or as an attempt to cast the enemy as utilizing means offensive to African American sensibilities (see "Red Soldiers Use Black Face in War," *Baltimore Afro-American*, August 26, 1950).

40   Curtis Morrow, *What's a Commie Ever Done to Black People? A Korean War Memoir of Fighting in the U.S. Army's Last All Negro Unit* (Jefferson, N.C.: McFarland, 1997), 34.

41   "GI's in Korea Handicapped by Unawareness of Mission," *New York Times*, August 13, 1950.

42   "GI's resent 'useless' war on alien soil," *Daily People's World*, August 18, 1950.

43   Blair, *The Forgotten War*, 462.

44   "GIS Warned Not to Use Word 'Gook,'" *Baltimore Afro-American*, October 16, 1950.

45   Editorial, *New York Age*, 12 August 1950.

46   The conduct of American servicemen captured in Korea remained a topic of public interest and debate for more than a decade after the war: the number of academic studies, policy documents, captivity narratives, prisoner-of-war novels, government research and archival holdings, and feature films range into the low hundreds. For a summary bibliographic overview, see Lewis Carlson,

Remembered Prisoners of a Forgotten War: An Oral History of Korean War POWS (New York: St. Martin's Press, 2002).

47   Eugene Kinkead, *Why They Collaborated* (London: Longmans, 1959), 104. After the war, black servicemen made efforts to reject claims that they had collaborated with their captors. For a representative account by a black marine, see Freeman Pollard's *Seeds of Turmoil: A Novel of American* POW*'s Brainwashed in Korea* (New York: Exposition Press, 1959).

48   Carlson, *Remembered Prisoners of a Forgotten War,* 193.

49   On at least one occasion, captured Puerto Rican soldiers clashed with racist white prison gangs. Despite this, and although the Chinese made concerted efforts to politicize captured African Americans, subsequent American researchers made little effort to study racial attitudes or interactions among repatriates. According to Ron Rubin, in *The Making of the Cold War Enemy: Culture and Politics in the Military-Intellectual Complex* (Princeton, N.J.: Princeton University Press, 2001, chapter 8), material collected from interviews that detailed serious racial tension among prisoners was purged from published studies, perhaps in an effort to avoid suggestions that integration had been less than a complete success.

50   Hunter, Edward. *Brainwashing: The Story of Men Who Defied It* (New York: Farrar, Straus and Cudahy, 1956), 89–116.

51   Albert Biderman, *March to Calumny: The Story of American* POW*'s in the Korean War* (New York: Macmillan, 1963), 60–61.

52   Carlson, *Remembered Prisoners of a Forgotten War,* 209.

53   "U.S. POWS Appeal for Peace in Radio Program from Peking," *Daily People's World,* May 4, 1951.

54   "Go Back Home: Seoul City Sue tells Negro GIS," *Pittsburgh Courier,* September 9, 1950.

55   Virginia Pasley, *21 Stayed: The Story of the American* GI*'s Who Chose Communist China—Who They Were and Why They Stayed* (New York: Farrar, Straus and Cudahy, 1955), 73.

56   Ibid., 132. Camp libraries typically contained both nonfiction and fiction works.

57   Adams's wife, a professor of Russian at Wuhan University, was suspended after being criticized for having a suspect background (large landowner) and for marrying a foreigner, while Adams was criticized for spending too much time at the Ghanaian and Cuban embassies. See Carlson, *Remembered Prisoners of a Forgotten War,* 208–10.

58   Mercy Dee Walton, "G.I. Fever," Crown Prince Records IG 406.

59   Charlotta Bass, "On the Sidewalk," *California Eagle,* November 16, 1950.

60   "Upswing in Music Biz Ascribed to Korean War," *Baltimore Afro-American,* September 16, 1950.

61   Pettis Perry, *White Chauvinism and the Struggle for Peace* (New York: New Century Publishers, 1952), 3.

62 The brainchild of a cafeteria worker from Wichita, James G. Thompson, the call for a simultaneous struggle against fascism abroad and racism at home offered a contrast with the unconditional support many African American leaders had offered during World War I. Popularized by the *Pittsburgh Courier* and supported by the NAACP and A. Philip Randolph, the "Double V" campaign might properly be considered a fundamental part of the birth of the postwar civil rights movements.

63 B. B. King, "Sweet Sixteen," Kent Records 330.

64 J. B. Lenoir, "Korea Blues," Chess Records 1449; "Eisenhower Blues/I'm in Korea," Parrot Records 802.

65 Ollie Harrington, "Dark Laughter," *Pittsburgh Courier,* August 19, 1950.

66 The story of opposition to the war in Vietnam is well known. What is often forgotten, however, is that antiwar sentiment in the United States peaked only as the U.S. government began actively seeking disengagement. Polls showed higher support for the war in Vietnam after the 1968 Tet offensive than after three years of inconclusive warfare in Korea. The relevant point is less the effort to quantify one war or the other as having had broader, longer, or deeper support at home, but rather to acknowledge the eventual breadth of opposition to both. For comparative surveys regarding public sentiment during Korea and Vietnam, see Philip Caine, "The United States in Korea and Vietnam: A Study in Public Opinion," *Air University Quarterly Review* 20, no. 1 (spring 1968), 49–58; Alonzo Hamby, "Public Opinion: Korea and Vietnam," *Wilson Quarterly* 2, n. 3 (fall 1978), 137–41; Matthew Mantell, "Opposition to the Korean War: A Study in American Dissent" (Ph.D. dissertation, New York University, 1973); Hugh Wood, "American Reaction to Limited War in Asia: Korea and Vietnam, 1950–1968" (Ph.D. dissertation, University of Colorado, 1974).

67 Gerald Horne, *Black Liberation/Red Scare: Ben Davis and the Communist Party* (Newark: University of Delaware Press, 1994), 247.

68 Editorial, *Daily People's World,* January 4, 1951.

69 Developed by researchers at Harvard University and later trademarked by Dow Chemical Co., Napalm (and other incendiary materials) were used with great destructive force in Europe and the Pacific theater during World War II. The repeated use of chemical, biological, nuclear, and other special munitions against Japanese, Korean, Vietnamese, and Iraqi targets raises issues regarding the use of particular types of killing technologies against particular ethnonational groups.

70 John Pittman, "Korea and the Negro People," *Masses and Mainstream,* September 1950.

71 Much as had been the case with the Scottsboro trials a generation earlier, efforts to defend African American soldiers accused in Korea opened sharp rifts between mainstream civil rights organizations and more radical left groups.

72 Editorial, *California Eagle,* September 21, 1950.

73 Series III: Case Files: David Hyun. Box 8, Folder 4–7. Los Angeles Committee for the Defense of the Foreign Born. Civil Rights Congress Collection. Southern California Library for Social Research.

74 "Foreign Born first McCarran Victims." *Daily People's World*, October 23, 1950.

75 Martin Duberman, *Paul Robeson* (London: Pan Books, 1989), 387–92; W. E. B. Du Bois, *In Battle for Peace: The Story of My 83rd Birthday* (New York: Masses and Mainstream, 1952); Charlotta Bass. *Forty Years: Memoirs from the Pages of a Newspaper* (Los Angeles: Charlotta Bass, 1960).

76 "35,000 sign Stockholm Pledge for Peace in LA over Holiday," *Daily People's World*, July 6, 1950.

77 Gerald Horne, *Communist Front? The Civil Rights Congress, 1946–1956* (Rutherford, N.J.: Farleigh Dickinson University Press, 1988), 176.

78 Gill, "Afro-American Opposition to the United States' Wars of the 20th Century," 308.

79 Pittman, "Korea and the Negro People," 27.

80 Gill, "Afro-American Opposition to the United States' Wars of the 20th Century," 308.

81 Ibid., 210.

82 Ibid., 168–69; Clayborne Carson, *In Struggle: SNCC and the Black Awakening of the 1960s* (Cambridge, Mass.: Harvard University Press, 1981), 22, 46; Malcolm X, with the assistance of Alex Haley, *The Autobiography of Malcolm X* (New York: Grove Press, 1965), 202–3.

83 As the biographer George Lipsitz notes in *George, a Life in the Struggle: Ivory Perry and the Culture of Opposition*, 57–62, Perry was convicted of a drug possession charge despite the fact that he had been arrested wearing another man's coat, which in any event contained too little heroin residue to be tested by army technicians. Perry saw his arrest and conviction as punishment for his repeated clashes with white officers.

84 Timothy Tyson, *Radio Free Dixie: Robert F. Williams and the Roots of Black Power* (Chapel Hill: University of North Carolina Press, 1999), 72.

85 James Foreman, *The Making of Black Revolutionaries* (Seattle: Open Hand Publishing, 1985), 60–66.

86 LeRoi Jones [Imamu Amiri Baraka], *Blues People* (New York: William Morrow, 1963), 215.

87 On the development of a radical internationalist intelligentsia of black artists and musicians during this time, see Robin D. G. Kelley, "Dig They Freedom: Meditations on History and the Black Avant-Garde," *Lenox Avenue* 1, no. 3 (1997): 13–27; George Lipsitz, "Like a Weed in a Vacant Lot: The Black Artists Group in St. Louis" (unpublished manuscript, 1999); Scot Saul, *Freedom Is, Freedom Ain't: Jazz and the Making of the Sixties* (Cambridge, Mass.: Harvard University Press, 2003); Daniel Widener, "Something Else: Creative Community and Black Liberation in Los Angeles" (Ph.D. dissertation. New York University, 2003).

88 See Kelley, "Stormy Weather."

89 Singh, *Black Is a Country,* 109.

90 Jorge Mariscal, "The Condi and Ricardo Show: The Perils of Bootstraps," *Counterpunch* 11 (April 2004): http://www.counterpunch.org/mariscalo4102004 .html.

91 Azmi Bishara, "The Logic of Occupation," *Al-Ahram Weekly,* no. 687, April 22– 28, 2004.

92 The term military multiculturalism is taken from Melani McAlister, *Epic Encounters: Culture, Media, and U.S. Interests in the Middle East, 1945–1990* (Berkeley: University of California Press, 2001).

PART II

FROM BANDUNG TO THE BLACK PANTHERS: NATIONAL LIBERATION, THE THIRD WORLD, MAO, AND MALCOLM

Part 2 explores the fertile period of Afro Asian liberation and exchange during the period of national liberation and the rise of the Third World. It begins with Mao Zedong's two statements—delivered in 1963 and 1968, respectively—in support of black liberation. The statements came as responses to appeals by black radicals like Robert F. Williams, and they were received by black radicals in the United States as true signs of international solidarity. Robin D. G. Kelley and Betsy Esch's essay "Black Like Mao" is a comprehensive overview of the influence of Maoism on African American leftists, nationalists, and internationalism from the time of the Chinese revolution of 1949 to the 1960s. Fred Ho's "The Inspiration of Mao and the Chinese Revolution on the Black Liberation Movement and the Asian

Movement on the East Coast" offers a framework for assessing the impact of Mao and Maoism on African American and Asian Pacific American liberation struggles. Diane Fujino in her essay "The Black Liberation Movement and Japanese American Activism" assesses two of the groundbreaking Asian American activists of the 1960s, Richard Aoki and Yuri Kochiyama, and their relationship to Malcolm X and the Black Panthers, respectively. Finally, Kalamu Ya Salaam's essay, "Why Do We Lie about Telling the Truth?" is a tour de force, trenchant polemic and commentary on African American internalized oppression and the need for internationalist militant unity.

Mao Zedong

Statement Supporting the Afro-American in Their Just Struggle Against Racial Discrimination by U.S. Imperialism, August 8, 1963

An Afro-American leader now taking refuge in Cuba, Mr. Robert Williams, the former president of the Monroe, North Carolina, chapter of the National Association for the Advancement of Colored People, has twice this year asked me for a statement in support of the Afro-Americans' struggle against racial discrimination. On behalf of the Chinese people, I wish to take this opportunity to express our resolute support for the Afro-Americans in their struggle against racial discrimination and for freedom and equal rights. Chinese com. supports black lib.

There are more than nineteen million Afro-Americans in the United States, or about 11 percent of the total population. They are enslaved, oppressed, and discriminated against—such is their position in society. The overwhelming majority are deprived of their right to vote. In general, only the most backbreaking and despised jobs are open to them. Their average wages are barely a third or a half of the white people. The proportion of unemployment among the Afro-Americans is the highest. In many states they are forbidden to go to the same school, eat at the same table, or travel in the same section of a bus or train as the white people. Afro-Americans are often arrested, beaten up, or murdered at will by the U.S. authorities at various levels and by members of the Ku Klux Klan and other racists. About half the Afro-Americans are concentrated in eleven southern states, where the discrimination and persecution they suffer are especially shocking.

The Afro-Americans are awakening and their resistance is growing stronger and stronger. Recent years have witnessed a continuous expansion of their mass struggle against racial discrimination and for freedom and equal rights. In 1957 the black people in Little Rock, Arkansas, waged a fierce struggle against the barring of their children from public schools. The authorities used armed force against them, creating the Little Rock incident that shocked the world.

In 1960 Negroes in more than twenty states held "sit-in" demonstrations protesting against racial segregation in local restaurants, shops, and other public places.

In 1961 the Negroes launched the "freedom riders" campaign to oppose racial segregation in public transportation, a campaign that rapidly spread to many states.

In 1962 the Negroes in Mississippi fought for the equal right to enroll in colleges and met with bloody suppression by the authorities.

This year, the American Negroes started their struggle early in Birmingham, Alabama. Unarmed and bare-handed Negro people were arrested en masse and most barbarously suppressed merely for holding meetings and parades against racial discrimination. On June 12 Mr. Medgar Evers, a leader of the Negro people in Mississippi, was murdered in cold blood. Defying brutality and violence, the indignant black masses waged their struggle even more heroically and quickly won the support of Negroes and other people of various strata throughout the United States. A gigantic and vigorous nationwide struggle is going on in nearly every city and state, and the struggle is mounting. American Negro organizations have decided to start a "freedom march" on Washington on August 28, in which 250,000 people will take part.

The speedy development of the struggle of the Afro-Americans is a manifestation of sharpening class struggle and sharpening national struggle within the United States; it has been causing increasing anxiety among U.S. ruling circles. The Kennedy administration is insidiously using dual tactics. On the one hand, it continues to connive and take part in discrimination against Negroes and their persecution, and it even sends troops to suppress them. On the other hand; in the attempt to numb the fighting will of the black people and deceive the masses of the country the Kennedy administration is parading as an advocate of "the defense of human rights" and "the protection of the civil rights of Negroes," calling upon the black people to exercise "restraint" and proposing the "civil rights legislation" to Congress. But more and more Afro-Americans are seeing through these tactics of the Kennedy administration. The fascist atrocities of the U.S. imperialists against the black people have exposed the true nature of so-called American democracy and freedom and revealed the inner link between the reactionary policies pursued by the U.S. government at home and its policies of aggression abroad.

I call on the workers, peasants, revolutionary intellectuals, enlightened elements of the bourgeoisie and other enlightened persons of all colors in the world, whether white, black, yellow, or brown, to unite to oppose the racial discrimination practiced by U.S. imperialism and support the black people in their struggle against racial discrimination. In the final analysis, national struggle is a matter of class struggle. Among the whites in the United States it is only the reactionary ruling circles who oppress the black people. They can in no way represent the workers, farmers, revolutionary intellectuals, and other enlightened persons who comprise the overwhelming majority of the white people. At present, it is the handful of imperialists headed by the United States, and their supporters, the reactionaries in different countries, who are oppressing, committing aggression against, and menacing the overwhelming majority of the nations and peoples of the world. We are in the majority and they are in the minority. At most, they make up less than 10 percent of the three thousand million population of the world. I am firmly convinced that, with the support of more than 90 percent of the people of the world, the Afro-Americans will be victorious in their just struggle. The evil system of colonialism and imperialism arose and throve with the enslavement of Negroes and the trade in Negroes, and it will surely come to its end with the complete emancipation of the black people.

↑ rebuttal: KKK

Statement by Mao Tse-Tung, Chairman of the Central Committee of the Communist Party of China, in Support of the Afro-American Struggle Against Violent Repression, April 16, 1968

Some days ago, Martin Luther King, the Afro-American clergyman, was suddenly assassinated by the U.S. imperialists. Martin Luther King was an exponent of nonviolence. Nevertheless, the U.S. imperialists did not on that account show any tolerance toward him, but used counter-revolutionary violence and killed him in cold blood. This has taught the broad masses of the black people in the United States a profound lesson. It has touched off a new storm in their struggle against violent repression sweeping well over a hundred cities in the United States, a storm such as has never taken place before in the history of that country. It shows that an extremely powerful revolutionary force is latent in the more than twenty million black Americans.

The storm of Afro-American struggle taking place within the United States is a striking manifestation of the comprehensive political and economic crisis now gripping U.S.

imperialism. It is dealing a telling blow to U.S. imperialism, which is beset with difficulties at home and abroad.

The Afro-American struggle is not only a struggle waged by the exploited and oppressed black people for freedom and emancipation, it is also a new clarion call to all the exploited and oppressed people of the United States to fight against the barbarous rule of the monopoly capitalist class. It is a tremendous support and inspiration to the struggle of the people throughout the world against U.S. imperialism and to the struggle of the Vietnamese people against U.S. imperialism. On behalf of the Chinese people, I hereby express resolute support of the just struggle of the black people in the United States. *shouldn't be about just race*

Racial discrimination in the United States is a product of the colonialist and imperialist system. The contradiction between the black masses in the United States and U.S. ruling circles is a class contradiction. Only by overthrowing the reactionary rule of the U.S. monopoly class and destroying the colonialist and imperialist system can the black people in the United States win complete emancipation. The black masses and the masses of white working people in the United States share common interests and have common objectives to struggle for. Therefore, the Afro-American struggle is winning sympathy and support from increasing numbers of white working people and progressives in the United States. The struggle of the black people in the United States is to merge with the American workers' movement, and this will eventually end the criminal rule of the U.S. monopoly capitalist class. *race struggle will only happen via class revol.*

In 1963, in my "Statement Supporting the Afro-American in Their Just Struggle Against Racial Discrimination by U.S. Imperialism" I said that "the evil system of colonialism and imperialism arose and throve with the enslavement of Negroes and the trade in Negroes, and it will surely come to its end with the complete emancipation of the black people." I still maintain this view.

At present, the world revolution has entered a great new era. The struggle of the black people in the United States for emancipation is a component part of the general struggle of all the people of the world against U.S. imperialism, a component part of the contemporary world revolution. I call on the workers, peasants, and revolutionary intellectuals of every country and all who are willing to fight against U.S. imperialism to take action and extend strong support to the struggle of the black people in the United

States! People of the whole world, unite still more closely and launch and sustain a vigorous offensive against our common enemy, U.S. imperialism, and against its accomplices! It can be said with certainty that the complete collapse of colonialism, imperialism, and all systems of exploitation and the complete emancipation of all the oppressed peoples and nations of the world are not far off.

Robin D. G. Kelley and Betsy Esch

Black Like Mao: Red China and Black Revolution

This is the era of Mao Tse-Tung, the era of world revolution and the Afro-American's struggle for liberation is a part of an invincible world-wide movement. Chairman Mao was the first world leader to elevate our people's struggle to the fold of the world revolution.—ROBERT WILLIAMS, 1967

It seems as if the Chairman, at least as a symbol, has been enjoying a resurgence in popularity among youth. Mao Zedong's image and ideas consistently turn up in a myriad of cultural and political contexts. For example, The Coup, a popular Bay Area hip hop group, restored Mao to the pantheon of black radical heroes and, in so doing, placed the black freedom struggle in an international context. In a song simply called "Dig It" (1993), The Coup refers to its members as "The Wretched of the Earth"; tells listeners to read *The Communist Manifesto*; and conjures up revolutionary icons such as Mao Zedong, Ho Chi Minh, Kwame Nkrumah, H. Rap Brown, Kenya's Mau Mau movement, and Geronimo Ji Jaga Pratt. In classical Maoist fashion, The Coup seizes upon Mao's most famous quote and makes it their own: "We realize that power [is] nickel plated."[1] Even though members of The Coup were not born until after the heyday of black Maoism, "Dig It" captures the spirit of Mao in relation to the larger colonial world—a world that included African Americans. In Harlem in the late 1960s and early 1970s, it seemed as though everyone had a copy of *Quotations from Chairman Mao Tse-Tung*, better known as the "Little Red Book."[2] From time to time supporters of the Black Panther Party would be seen selling the Little Red Book on street corners as a fund-raiser for the party. And it wasn't unheard of to see a young black radical strolling down the street dressed like a Chinese peasant—except for the Afro and sunglasses, of course.

Like Africa, China was on the move and there was a general feeling that the Chinese supported the black freedom struggle; indeed, real-life blacks were calling for revolution in the name of Mao as well as Marx and Lenin. Countless black radicals of the era regarded China, not unlike Cuba or Ghana or even Paris, as the land where true freedom might be had. It wasn't perfect, but it was much better than living in the belly of the beast. When the Black Panther leader Elaine Brown visited Beijing in fall 1970, she was pleasantly surprised by what the Chinese revolution had achieved in terms of improving people's lives: "Old and young would spontaneously give emotional testimonies, like Baptist converts, to the glories of socialism."[3] A year later she returned with the Panther founder Huey Newton, whose experience in China he described as a "sensation of freedom—as if a great weight had been lifted from my soul and I was able to be myself, without defense or pretense or the need for explanation. I felt absolutely free for the first time in my life—completely free among my fellow men."[4]

More than a decade before Brown and Newton set foot on Chinese soil, W. E. B. Du Bois regarded China as the other sleeping giant poised to lead the colored races in the worldwide struggle against imperialism. He had first traveled to China in 1936—before the war and the revolution—during an extended visit to the Soviet Union. Returning in 1959, when it was illegal to travel to China, Du Bois discovered a new country. He was struck by the transformation of the Chinese, in particular what he perceived as the emancipation of women, and he left convinced that China would lead the underdeveloped nations on the road toward socialism. "China after long centuries," he told an audience of Chinese communists attending his ninety-first birthday celebration, "has arisen to her feet and leapt forward. Africa arise, and stand straight, speak and think! Act! Turn from the West and your slavery and humiliation for the last 500 years and face the rising sun."[5]

W. E. B. Du Bois with Mao Zedong at Mao's villa in south-central China, April 1959. (Reprinted by permission of the Special Collections Department, W. E. B. Du Bois Library, University of Massachusetts at Amherst)

How black radicals came to see China as a beacon of Third World revolution and Mao Zedong thought as a guidepost is a complicated and fascinating story involving literally dozens of organizations and covering much of the world—from the ghettos of North America to the African countryside. The text following thus does not pretend to be comprehensive;[6] instead, we have set out in this essay to explore the impact that Maoist thought and, more generally, the People's Republic of China have had on black radical movements from the 1950s through at least the mid-1970s. In addition, our aim is to explore how radical black nationalism has shaped debates within Maoist or "anti-revisionist" organizations in the United States. It is our contention that China offered black radicals a "colored" or Third World Marxist model that enabled them to challenge a white and Western vision of class struggle—a model that they shaped and reshaped to suit their own cultural and political realities. Although China's role was contradictory and problematic in many respects, the fact that Chinese peasants, as opposed to the European proletariat, made a socialist revolution and carved out a position in world politics distinct from the Soviet and U.S. camps endowed black radicals with a deeper sense of revolutionary importance and power. Finally, not only did Mao prove to blacks the world over that they need not wait for "objective conditions" to make revolution, but also his elevation of cultural struggle profoundly shaped debates surrounding black arts and politics.

The Long March

Anyone familiar with Maoism knows that it was never a full-blown ideology meant to replace Marxism-Leninism. On the contrary, if anything it marked a turn against the "revisionism" of the post-Stalin Soviet model. What Mao did contribute to Marxist thought grew directly out of the Chinese revolution of 1949. Mao's insistence that the revolutionary capacity of the peasantry wasn't dependent on the urban proletariat was particularly attractive to black radicals skeptical of the idea that they must wait for the objective conditions to launch their revolution. Central to Maoism is the idea that Marxism can be (must be) reshaped to the requirements of time and place, and that practical work, ideas, and leadership stem from the masses in movement and not from a theory created in the abstract or produced out of other struggles.[7] In practice, this meant that true revolutionaries must possess a revolutionary will to win. The notion of revolutionary will cannot be underestimated, especially for those in movements that were isolated and attacked on all sides. Armed with the proper theory, the proper ethical behavior, and the will, revolutionaries in Mao's words can "move mountains."[8] Perhaps this is why the Chinese communist leader Lin Biao could write in the foreword to *Quotations* that "once Mao Tse-Tung's thought is grasped by the broad masses, it becomes an inexhaustible source of strength and a spiritual atom bomb of infinite power."[9]

Both Mao and Lin Biao recognized that the source of this "atom bomb" could be found in the struggles of Third World nationalists. In an age when the cold war helped usher in the nonaligned movement, when leaders of the "colored" world were converging in Bandung, Indonesia, in 1955 to try to chart an independent path toward development, the Chinese hoped to lead the former colonies on the road to socialism. The Chinese (backed by Lin Biao's theory of the "new democratic revolution") not only endowed nationalist struggles with revolutionary value but also reached out specifically to Africa and people of African descent. Two years after the historic Bandung meeting of nonaligned nations—China formed the Afro-Asian People's Solidarity Organization. Mao not only invited W. E. B. Du Bois to spend his ninetieth birthday in China after he had been declared a public enemy by the U.S. state, but three weeks prior to the great March on Washington in 1963, Mao issued a statement criticizing American racism and casting the African American freedom movement as part of the worldwide struggle against imperialism. "The evil system of colonialism and imperialism," Mao stated, "arose and throve with the enslavement of Negroes and the trade in Negroes, and it will surely come to its end with the complete emancipation of the black people."[10] A decade later, the novelist John Oliver Killens was impressed by the fact that several of his books, as well as works by other black writers, had been translated into Chinese and were widely read by students. Everywhere he went, it seemed, he met young intellectuals and workers who were "tremendously interested in the Black movement and in how the art and literature of Black folks reflected that movement."[11]

The status of people of color served as a powerful political tool in mobilizing support from Africans and African-descended people. In 1963, for example, Chinese delegates in Moshi, Tanzania, proclaimed that the Russians had no business in Africa because of their status as white. The Chinese, on the other hand, were not only part of the colored world but also unlike Europeans they never took part in the slave trade. Of course, most of these claims served essentially to facilitate alliance building. The fact is that African slaves could be found in Guangzhou during the twelfth century, and African students in communist China occasionally complained of racism. (Indeed, after Mao's death racial clashes on college campuses occurred more frequently, notably in Shanghai in 1979, in Nanjing in 1980, and in Tianjin in 1986.)[12] Furthermore, Chinese foreign policy toward the black world was often driven more by strategic considerations than by a commitment to Third World revolutionary movements, especially after the Sino-Soviet split. China's anti-Soviet position resulted in foreign policy decisions that ultimately undermined their standing with certain African liberation movements. In southern Africa, for example, the Chinese backed movements that also received support from the apartheid regime of South Africa.[13]

Yet, Mao's ideas still gained an audience among black radicals. While Maoist projects in the United States never achieved the kind of following enjoyed by Soviet-identified communist parties in the 1930s, they did take root in this country. And like a hundred flowers, Mao's ideas bloomed into a confusing mosaic of radical voices all seemingly at war with each other. Not surprisingly, at the center of the debate over the character of class struggle in the United States was the "Negro Question": that is, what role would blacks play in world revolution.

The World Black Revolution

Maoism in the United States was not exported from China. If anything, for those Maoists schooled in the Old Left the source of Maoism can be found in Khrushchev's revelations at the twentieth Congress of the Communist Party Soviet Union in 1956 that prompted an anti-revisionist movement throughout the pro-Stalinist Left. Out of the debates within the Communist Party USA emerged several organizations pledging to push the communists back into the Stalinist camp, including the Provisional Organizing Committee (POC) in 1958, Hammer and Steel in 1960, and the Progressive Labor Party (PLP) in 1965.[14]

The Progressive Labor Party, an outgrowth of the Progressive Labor movement founded three years earlier, was initially led by excommunists who believed that the Chinese had the correct position. Insisting that black workers were the "key revolutionary force" in the proletarian revolution, the PLP attracted a few outstanding black activists such as John Harris in Los Angeles and Bill Epton in Harlem. Epton had become somewhat of a cause célèbre after he was arrested for "criminal anarchy" during the 1964 rebellion in Harlem.[15] Two years later, the PLP helped organize a student strike to establish a black studies program at San Francisco State University, and its Black Liberation Commission published a pamphlet titled *Black Liberation Now!* that attempted to place all of these urban rebellions within a global context. But by 1968, the PLP abandoned its support for "revolutionary" nationalism and concluded that all forms of nationalism are reactionary. As a result of its staunch anti-nationalism, the PLP opposed affirmative action and black and Latino trade union caucuses—positions that undermined the PLP's relationship with black community activists. In fact, the PLP's connections to the New Left in general were damaged in part because of its attack on the Black Panther Party and on the black student movement. Members of the PLP were thrown out of Students for a Democratic Society (SDS) in 1969 with the help of several radical nationalist groups, including the Panthers, the Young Lords, and the Brown Berets.[16]

Nevertheless, the predominantly white Marxist-Leninist-Maoist parties were not the primary vehicle for the Maoist-inspired black Left. Most black radicals of the late 1950s and early 1960s discovered China by way of anti-colonial struggles in Africa and the Cuban revolution. Ghana's independence in 1957 was cause to celebrate, and the CIA-sponsored assassination of Patrice Lumumba in the Congo inspired protest from all black activist circles. The Cuban revolution and Fidel Castro's infamous residency at Harlem's Hotel Theresa during his visit to the United Nations brought black people face to face with an avowed socialist who extended a hand of solidarity to people of color the world over. Indeed, dozens of black radicals not only publicly defended the Cuban revolution but also visited Cuba through groups like the Fair Play for Cuba Committee.[17] One of these visitors was Harold Cruse, himself an excommunist still committed to Marxism. He believed the Cuban, Chinese, and African revolutions could revitalize radical thought because they demonstrated the revolutionary potential of nationalism. In a provocative essay published in the *New Leader* in 1962, Cruse wrote that the new generation was looking to the former colonial world for its leaders and insights, and among its heroes was Mao: "Already they have a pantheon of modern heroes—Lumumba, Kwame Nkrumah, Sekou Toure in Africa; Fidel Castro in Latin America; Malcolm X, the Muslim leader, in New York; Robert Williams in the South; and Mao Tse-Tung in China. These men seem heroic to the Afro-Americans not because of their political philosophy, but because they were either former colonials who achieved complete independence, or because, like Malcolm X, they dared to look the white community in the face and say: 'We don't think your civilization is worth the effort of any black man to try to integrate into.' This to many Afro-Americans is an act of defiance that is truly revolutionary."[18]

In another essay, which appeared in *Studies on the Left* in 1962, Cruse was even more explicit about the global character of revolutionary nationalism. He argued that black people in the United States were living under domestic colonialism and that their struggles must be seen as part of the worldwide anticolonial movement. "The failure of American Marxists," he wrote, "to understand the bond between the Negro and the colonial peoples of the world has led to their failure to develop theories that would be of value to Negroes in the United States." In his view, the former colonies were the vanguard of the revolution, and at the forefront of this new socialist revolution were Cuba and China.[19]

Revolutions in Cuba, Africa, and China had a similar effect on Baraka, who a decade and a half later would found the Maoist-inspired Revolutionary Communist League. Touched by his visit to Cuba and the assassination of Lumumba, Baraka began contributing essays to a new magazine called *African Revolution* edited by the Algerian nationalist leader Ahmed Ben Bella. As Baraka explained it: "India and China had gotten their formal independence before the coming of the 50s, and by the time the 50s had ended, there were many independent African nations (though with varying degrees of neocolonialism). Ghana's Kwame Nkrumah had hoisted the black star over the statehouse in Accra, and Nkrumah's pronouncements and word of his deeds were glowing encouragement to colored people all over the world. When the Chinese exploded their first A-bomb I wrote a poem saying, in effect, that *time* for the colored peoples had rebegun."[20]

The Ghana-China matrix is perhaps best embodied in the career of Vickie Garvin, a stalwart radical who traveled in Harlem's black Left circles during the postwar period. Raised in a black working-class family in New York, Garvin spent her summers working in the garment industry to supplement her family's income. As early as high school she became active in black protest politics, supporting efforts by Adam Clayton Powell Jr. to obtain better-paying jobs for African Americans in Harlem and creating black history clubs dedicated to building library resources. After earning her B.A. in political science from Hunter College and her M.A. in economics from Smith College in Northhampton, she spent the war years working for the National War Labor Board and continued on as an organizer for the United Office and Professional Workers of America (UOPWA-CIO) and as national research director and co-chair of the Fair Employment Practices Committee. During the postwar purges of the Left in the CIO, Garvin was a strong voice of protest and a sharp critic of the CIO's failure to organize in the South. As executive secretary of the New York chapter of the National Negro Labor Council and vice president of the national organization, Garvin established close ties to Malcolm X and helped him arrange part of his tour of Africa.[21]

Garvin joined the black intellectual exodus to Nkrumah's Ghana where she initially roomed with the poet Maya Angelou and eventually moved into a house next to Du Bois. She spent two years in Accra surrounded by several key black intellectuals and artists, including Julian Mayfield, the artist Tom Feelings, and the cartoonist Ollie Harrington. As a radical who taught conversational English to the Cuban, Algerian, and Chinese diplomatic core in Ghana, it was hard *not* to develop a deep internationalist outlook. Garvin's conversations with Du Bois during his last days in Ghana only reinforced her internationalism and kindled her interest in the Chinese revolution. Indeed, through Du Bois Garvin got a job as a "polisher" for the English translations of the *Peking Review* as well as a teaching position at the Shanghai Foreign Language Institute. She remained in China from 1964 to 1970, building bridges between the black freedom struggle, the African independence movements, and the Chinese revolution.[22]

For Huey Newton, the future founder of the Black Panther Party, the African revolution seemed even less crucial than events in Cuba and China. As a student at Merritt College in the early 1960s he read a little existentialism, began attending meetings sponsored by the Progressive Labor Party, and supported the Cuban revolution. Not surprisingly, Newton began to read Marxist literature voraciously. Mao, in particular, left a lasting impression: "My conversion was complete when I read the four volumes of Mao Tse-Tung to learn more about the Chinese Revolution."[23] Thus well before the founding of the Black Panther Party, Newton was steeped in Mao Zedong thought as well as in the writings of Che Guevara and Frantz Fanon. "Mao and Fanon and Guevara all saw clearly that the people had been stripped of their birthright and their dignity, not by a philosophy or mere words, but at gunpoint. They had suffered a holdup by gangsters, and rape; for them, the only way to win freedom was to meet force with force."[24]

The Chinese and Cubans' willingness "to meet force with force" also made their revolutions attractive to black radicals in the age of nonviolent passive resistance. Of course, the era had its share of armed struggle in the South, with groups like the Deacons for Defense and Justice and Gloria Richardson's Cambridge movement defending nonviolent protesters when necessary. But the figure who best embodied black traditions of armed self-defense was Robert Williams, a hero to the new wave of black internationalists whose importance almost rivaled that of Malcolm X. As a former U.S. Marine with extensive military training, Williams earned notoriety in 1957 for forming armed self-defense groups in Monroe, North Carolina, to fight the Ku Klux Klan. Two years later, Williams's statement that black people must "meet violence with violence" as the only way to end injustice in an uncivilized South led to his suspension as president of the Monroe chapter of the NAACP.[25]

Williams's break with the NAACP and his open advocacy of armed self-defense pushed him further Left and into the orbit of the Socialist Workers Party, the Workers World Party, and among some members of the old CPUSA. However, Williams had had contact with communists since his days as a Detroit auto worker in the 1940s. He not only read the *Daily Worker* but also published a story in its pages called "Some Day I Am Going Back South." Williams was also somewhat of an intellectual dabbler and auto-didact, having studied at West Virginia State College, North Carolina College, and Johnson C. Smith College. Nevertheless, his more recent Left associations led him to Cuba and the Fair Play for Cuba Committee. Upon returning from his first trip in 1960, he hoisted the Cuban flag in his backyard and ran a series of articles in his mimeographed publication, the *Crusader,* about the transformation of working peoples' lives in Cuba as a result of the revolution. In one of his editorials published in August 1960, Williams insisted that African Americans' fight for freedom "is related to the Africans,' the Cubans,' all of Latin Americans' and the Asians' struggles for self-determination." His support of the Chinese revolution was evident in the pages of the *Crusader* as well, emphasizing the importance of China as a beacon of strength for social justice movements the world over. Like Baraka, Williams took note of China's detonation of an atomic bomb in 1960 as a historic occasion for the oppressed. "With the bomb," he wrote, "China will be respected and will add a powerful voice to those who already plead for justice for black as well as white."[26]

By 1961, as a result of trumped-up kidnapping charges and a federal warrant for his arrest, Williams and his family were forced to flee the country and seek political asylum in Cuba. During the next four years, Cuba became Williams's base for promoting black world revolution and elaborating an internationalist ideology that embraced black nationalism and Third World solidarity. With support from Fidel Castro, Williams hosted a radio show called *Radio Free Dixie* that was directed at African Americans, continued to edit the *Crusader* (which by now had progressed from a mimeograph to a full-blown magazine), and completed his book *Negroes with Guns* (1962). He did not, however, identify himself as a Marxist. At the same time, he rejected the "nationalist" label, calling himself an "internationalist" instead: "That is, I'm interested in the problems of Africa, of Asia, and of Latin America. I believe that we all have the same struggle; a struggle for liberation."[27]

Although Williams recalls having had good relations with Castro, political differences over race did lead to a rift between him and the Cuban communists. "The Party," Williams remembered, "maintained that it was strictly a class issue and that once the class problem had been solved through a socialist administration, racism would be abolished."[28] Williams not only disagreed but had moved much closer to Che Guevara, who embodied much of what Williams had been advocating all along: Third World solidarity, the use of armed struggle, and a deep and unwavering interest in the African revolution. Indeed, Che's leanings toward China undoubtedly made an impact on Williams's decision to leave Cuba for Beijing. Given Che's break with Fidel and the solidification of Cuba's links to the Soviet Union, Williams saw no need to stay. He and his family packed up and moved to China in 1966.

As an exiled revolutionary in China during its most tumultuous era, Williams nevertheless predicted that urban rebellions in America's ghettoes would transform the country. Although one might argue that by publishing the *Crusader* from Cuba and then China Williams had very limited contact with the black freedom movement in the United States, his magazine reached a new generation of young black militants and promoted the vision of black world revolution articulated by critics such as Harold Cruse. The fact is, the *Crusader* and Williams's own example compelled a small group of black radical intellectuals and activists to form what might loosely be called the first black Maoist-influenced organization in history: the Revolutionary Action Movement (RAM).

The Revolutionary Action Movement and the Coming Black Revolution

Williams's flight to Cuba partly inspired the creation of RAM. In Ohio around 1961, black members of Students for a Democratic Society as well as activists in the Student Nonviolent Coordinating Committee (SNCC) and the Congress of Racial Equality (CORE) met in a small group to discuss the significance of Williams's work in Monroe and his subsequent exile. Led by Donald Freeman, a black student at Case Western Reserve in Cleveland, the group's main core consisted of a newly formed organization, named "Challenge," made up of Central State College students at Wilberforce. Members of Challenge were especially taken with Harold Cruse's essay "Revolutionary Nationalism and the Afro-American," which was circulated widely among young black militants. Inspired by Cruse's interpretation of the global importance of the black freedom struggle, Freeman hoped to turn Challenge into a revolutionary nationalist movement akin to the Nation of Islam but that would adopt the direct action tactics of sncc. After a lengthy debate, Challenge members decided to dissolve the organization in spring 1962 and form the Revolutionary Action Committee (originally called the "Reform" Action Movement so as not to scare the administration), with its primary leaders being Freeman, Max Stanford, and Wanda Marshall. A few months later they moved their base to Philadelphia, began publishing a bi-monthly paper called *Black America* and a one-page newsletter called raм *Speaks,* and made plans to build a national movement oriented toward revolutionary nationalism, youth organizing, and armed self-defense.[29]

Freeman and raм members in Cleveland continued to work publicly through the Afro-American Institute, an activist policy-oriented think tank formed in fall 1962. Under Freeman's directorship, its board—dubbed the Soul Circle—consisted of a small group of black men with ties to community organizations, labor, civil rights, and student groups. Board members such as Henry Glover, Arthur Evans, Nate Bryant, and Hanif Wahab gave lectures on African history and politics, organized forums to discuss the future of the civil rights movement, black participation in Cleveland politics, and the economic conditions of urban blacks. The institute even recruited the great drummer Max Roach to help organize a panel titled "The Role of the Black Artist in the Struggle for Freedom." Institute members also used random leaflets and pamphlets to influence black community thinking on a number of local and international issues. Addressed "To Whom It May Concern," these short broadsides were intended to stimulate discussion and offer the black community a position on pressing topics such as "elections, urban renewal, black economic subservience, the 'arms race,' and the struggle in the South." Within a year, the institute graduated from printing leaflets to publishing to a full-blown newsletter titled *Afropinion.* Through the Afro-American Institute, raм members in Cleveland worked with core activists and other community organizers to demand improvements in hospital care for black patients and to protest the exclusion of African and Afro-American history from the public school curriculum. The institute's most important campaign of 1963 was the defense of Mae Mallory, a black woman who was being held in the county jail in Cleveland for her association with Robert Williams in Monroe, North Carolina. Soon after Williams's flight to Cuba, Mallory was arrested in Ohio and awaited extradition charges. The institute and its allies, including the Nation of Islam in Cleveland, petitioned the governor of Ohio to revoke the warrant of extradition, and they also organized a mass demonstration in front of the county jail demanding Mallory's immediate release.[30]

In Northern California, RAM grew primarily out of the Afro-American Association. Founded by Donald Warden in 1962, the Afro-American Association consisted of students from the University of California at Berkeley and from Merritt College—many of whom, such as Leslie and Jim Lacy, Cedric Robinson, Ernest Allen, and Huey Newton, would go on to play important roles as radical activists and intellectuals. In Los Angeles, the president of the Afro-American Association was a young man named Ron Everett, who later changed his name to Maulana Karenga and went on to found the U.S. organization. The Afro-American Association quickly developed a reputation as a group of militant intellectuals willing to debate anyone. By challenging professors, debating groups such as the Young Socialist Alliance, and giving public lectures on black history and culture, these young activists left a deep impression on fellow students as well as on the black community. In the East Bay, where the tradition of soapbox speakers died in the 1930s (with the exception of the individual campaigns by the communist-led Civil Rights Congress during the early 1950s), the Afro-American Association was walking and talking proof that a vibrant, highly visible militant intellectual culture could exist.[31]

Meanwhile, the Progressive Labor movement (PL) had begun sponsoring trips to Cuba and recruited several radical black students in the East Bay to go along. Among them was Ernest Allen, a UC Berkeley transfer from Merritt College who had been forced out of the Afro-American Association. A working-class kid from Oakland, Allen was part of a generation of black radicals whose dissatisfaction with the civil rights movement's strategy of nonviolent, passive resistance drew them closer to Malcolm X and Third World liberation movements. Not surprisingly, through his trip to Cuba in 1964 he discovered the Revolutionary Action Movement. Allen's travel companions included a contingent of black militants from Detroit: Luke Tripp, Charles ("Mao") Johnson, Charles Simmons, and General Baker. All were members of the student group Uhuru, and all went on to play key roles in the formation of the Dodge Revolutionary Union Movement and the League of Revolutionary Black Workers. Incredibly, the RAM leader Max Stanford was already on the island visiting Robert Williams. When it was time to go back to the states, Allen and the Detroit group were committed to building

RAM. Allen stopped in Cleveland to meet with RAM members on his cross-country bus trip back to Oakland. Armed with copies of Robert Williams's *Crusader* magazine and related RAM material, Allen returned to Oakland intent on establishing RAM's presence in the East Bay. As a result, activists such as Isaac Moore, Kenn Freeman (Mamadou Lumumba), Bobby Seale (future founder of the Black Panther Party), and Doug Allen (Ernie's brother) established a base at Merritt College through the Soul Students Advisory Council. Although the group never grew larger than a handful of people, its intellectual and cultural presence was broadly felt. Allen, Freeman, and others founded a journal called *Soulbook: The Revolutionary Journal of the Black World*, which published prose and poetry that is best described as Left black nationalist in orientation. Freeman, in particular, was highly respected among RAM activists and widely read. He constantly pushed his members to think about black struggle in a global context. The editors of *Soulbook* also developed ties with Old Left black radicals, most notably the former communist Harry Haywood whose work they published in an early issue.[32]

Although RAM had established itself in Northern California and in Cleveland, by 1964 Philadelphia appeared to be RAM's "home base." It was in Philadelphia, after all, that RAM maintained an open existence, operating under its own name rather than a variety of "front" organizations. The strength of the Philadelphia chapter has much to do with the fact that it was also the home of Max Stanford, RAM's national field chairman. It was out of Philadelphia that RAM published a bimonthly paper called *Black America* and a one-page newsletter called RAM *Speaks*; made plans to build a national movement oriented toward revolutionary nationalism, youth organizing, and armed self-defense; and recruited several Philadelphia activists to the group, including Ethel Johnson (who had also worked with Robert Williams in Monroe), Stan Daniels, and Playthell Benjamin.[33] Subsequently, RAM recruited a group of young Philadelphia militants who would go on to play key roles in radical organizations, including Michael Simmons, one of the authors of SNCC's famous "Black Consciousness Paper," whose resistance to the draft resulted in his serving a two-and-a-half-year prison sentence, and Tony Monteiro, who went on to become a leading national figure in the CPUSA during the 1970s and 1980s.[34]

The RAM organization represented the first serious and sustained attempt in the postwar period to wed Marxism, black nationalism, and Third World internationalism into a coherent revolutionary program. In Max Stanford's view, RAM "attempted to apply Marxism-Leninism Mao Tse-Tung thought" to the conditions of black people and "advanced the theory that the black liberation movement in the United States was part of the vanguard of the world socialist revolution." Young RAM militants sought political guidance from a number of former black communists who had either been expelled for "ultra-leftism" or "bourgeois nationalism," or had left the party because of its "revisionism." Among this group of elders were Harold Cruse, Harry Haywood, Abner Berry, and "Queen Mother" Audley Moore. Indeed, Moore would go on to become one of RAM's most important mentors on the East Coast, offering members training in black nationalist thought and in Marxism. The Queen Mother's home, which she affectionately called Mount Addis Ababa, practically served as a school for a new generation of young black radicals. Moore had founded the African-American Party of National Liberation in 1963, which formed a provisional government and elected Robert Williams as premier in exile. These young black radicals also turned to Detroit's legendary ex-Trotskyists James Boggs and Grace Lee Boggs, the former comrades of C. L. R. James whose Marxist and pan-Africanist writings greatly influenced RAM members as well as other New Left activists.[35]

Although RAM as a movement never received the glory publicity bestowed on groups like the Black Panther Party, its influence far exceeded its numbers—not unlike the African Blood Brotherhood (ABB) four decades earlier. Indeed, like the African Blood Brotherhood RAM remained largely an underground organization that devoted more time to agitprop work than actual organizing. Leaders such as Max Stanford identified with the Chinese peasant rebels who led the Communist Party to victory. They seized upon Mao's famous line—"The enemy advances, we retreat; the enemy camps, we harass; the enemy tires, we attack; the enemy retreats, we pursue"—and they took it quite literally by advocating armed insurrection and drawing inspiration and ideas directly from Robert Williams's theory of guerrilla warfare in the urban United States. The leaders of RAM actually believed that such a war was not only possible but could be won in ninety days. The combination of mass chaos and revolutionary discipline was the key to victory. The Fall 1964 issue of *Black America* predicted Armageddon:

Black men and women in the Armed Forces will defect and come over to join the Black Liberation forces. Whites who claim they want to help the revolution will be sent into the white communities to divide them, fight the fascists and frustrate the efforts of the counter-revolutionary forces. Chaos will be everywhere and with the breakdown of mass communications, mutiny will occur in great numbers in all facets of the oppressors' government. The stock market will fall; Wall Street will stop functioning; Washington, D. C. will be torn apart by riots. Officials everywhere will run—run for their lives. The George Lincoln Rockwellers, Kennedys, Vanderbilts, Hunts, Johnsons, Wallaces, Barnetts, etc., will be the first to go. The revolution will "strike by night and spare none." . . . The Black Revolution will use sabotage in the cities, knocking out the electrical power first, then transportation and guerrilla warfare in the countryside in the South. With the cities powerless, the oppressor will be helpless.[36]

The revolution was clearly seen as a man's job since women barely figured in the equation. Indeed, one of the striking facts about the history of the anti-revisionist left is how male dominated it remained. Although Wanda Marshall had been one of the founding members of RAM, she did not hold a national leadership post in 1964. Besides promoting the creation of "women's leagues" whose purpose would be "to organize black women who work in white homes," RAM remained relatively silent on women's liberation until the later 1960s, when the organization had begun to collapse. In 1969, RAM issued a statement on the role of "Soul Sisters" in the movement. An auxiliary of RAM, the Soul Sisters were to be trained in self-defense and work to organize the female youth, but they were also supposed to educate, care for, and positively influence potential black male revolutionaries. Their immediate tasks included "influencing non-militant Negro men to involve themselves into organized self-defense," promote efforts to keep "white women away from all areas of Negro political and sexual life," report any incidents of "harassment by police or any other *white* men in the ghetto or the schools," and "promote the image of Robert Williams as the international symbol of Negro freedom struggle." The two most telling tasks that revealed the subordinate status of women involved training "girls for taking a census of the black population" and having them "design and buy sweaters for an identity symbol."[37]

The masculinist orientation of RAM should not be surprising given the masculinist orientation of black nationalist (not to mention white New Left) organizations in the 1960s, whether they were advocating civil rights or some incipient version of Black Power. The masculinism of RAM, however, was heightened by the fact that its leaders saw themselves as urban guerrillas—as members of an all-black version of Mao's Red Army. Not all RAM members saw themselves in this way, but those who did were deeply committed to a set of revolutionary ethics that Mao laid down for his own party cadre and for members of the People's Army. We see this very clearly in RAM's "Code of Cadres," a set of highly didactic rules of conduct that members were expected to live by. Some examples of this code are as follows:

A Revolutionary nationalist maintains the highest respect for all authority within the party. . . .

A Revolutionary nationalist cannot be corrupted by money, honors or any other personal gains. . . .

A Revolutionary nationalist will unhesitatingly subordinate his personal interest to those of the vanguard [without] hesitation. . . .

A Revolutionary nationalist will maintain the highest level of morality and will never take as much as a needle or single piece of thread from the masses—Brother and Sisters will maintain the utmost respect for one another and will never misuse or take advantage of one another for personal gain—and will never misinterpret, the doctrine of revolutionary nationalism for any reason. . . .[38]

The code's similarities to the *Quotations from Chairman Mao Tse-Tung* are striking. Indeed, the last example comes straight out of Mao's "Three Main Rules of Discipline," which urges cadre to "not take a single needle or piece of thread from the masses." Selflessness and total commitment to the masses is another theme that dominates *Quotations*. Again, the comparisons are noteworthy: "At no time and in no circumstances," says Mao, "should a Communist place his personal interests first; he should subordinate them to the interests of the nation and of the masses. Hence, selfishness, slacking, corruption, seeking the limelight, and so on are most contemptible, while selflessness, working with all one's energy, whole-hearted devotion to public duty, and quiet hard work will command respect."[39]

Maoism's emphasis on revolutionary ethics and moral transformation, in theory at least, resonated with black religious traditions (as well as with American Protestantism more generally), and like the Nation of Islam it preached self-restraint, order, and discipline. It's quite possible that in the midst of a counterculture that embodied elements of hedonism and drug use, a new wave of student and working-class radicals found Maoist ethics attractive. (Indeed, many in the New Left and in the women's liberation movement also found Mao's idea of revolutionary ethics attractive.) Upon his return from China, Robert Williams—in many respects RAM's founding father—insisted that all young black activists "undergo personal and moral transformation. There is a need for a stringent revolutionary code of moral ethics. Revolutionaries are instruments of righteousness."[40] For black revolutionaries, the moral and ethical dimension of Mao's thought centered on the notion of personal transformation. It was a familiar lesson embodied in the lives of Malcolm X and (later) George Jackson—namely, the idea that one possesses the revolutionary will to transform *himself*. (These narratives are almost exclusively male despite the growing number of memoirs by radical black women.) Whether or not RAM members lived by the "Code of Cadres," Maoist ethics ultimately served to reinforce Malcolm's status as a revolutionary role model.

The twelve-point program created by RAM called for the development of freedom schools, national black student organizations, rifle clubs, black farmer cooperatives (not just for economic development but to keep "community and guerrilla forces going for a while"), and a liberation guerrilla army made up of youth and the unemployed. They also placed special emphasis on internationalism—on pledging support for national liberation movements in Africa, Asia, and Latin America as well as the adoption of "pan-African socialism." In line with Cruse's seminal essay, RAM members saw themselves as colonial subjects fighting a "colonial war at home." As Stanford wrote in an internal document titled "Projects and Problems of the Revolutionary Movement" (1964), "RAM's position is that the Afro-American is not a citizen of the U.S.A., denied his rights, but rather he is a colonial subject enslaved. This position says that the black people in the U.S.A. are a captive nation suppressed and that their fight is not for integration into the white community but one of national liberation."[41]

As colonial subjects with a right to self-determination, RAM saw Afro-America as a de facto member of the nonaligned nations. They even identified themselves as part of the "Bandung world," going so far as to hold a conference in November 1964 in Nashville titled "The Black Revolution's Relationship to the Bandung World." In a 1965 article published in RAM's journal *Black America,* the group started to develop a theory called Bandung Humanism, or Revolutionary Black Internationalism, which argued that the battle between Western imperialism and the Third World—more than the battle between labor and capital—represented the most fundamental contradiction in our time. The organization linked the African American freedom struggle with what was happening in China, Zanzibar, Cuba, Vietnam, Indonesia, and Algeria, and it characterized its work as part of Mao's international strategy of encircling Western capitalist countries and challenging imperialism. After 1966, however, the term Bandung Humanism was dropped entirely and replaced with Black Internationalism.[42]

Precisely what was meant by Black Internationalism was laid out in an incredibly bold thirty-six-page pamphlet, *The World Black Revolution,* which was published by RAM in 1966. Loosely patterned on the Communist Manifesto, the pamphlet identifies strongly with China against both the capitalist West and the Soviet Empire. The "emergence of Revolutionary China began to polarize caste and class contradictions within the world, in both the bourgeoisie imperialist camp and also in the European bourgeois communist-socialist camp."[43] In other words, China was the wedge that sharpened the contradictions between colonial peoples and the West. Rejecting the idea that socialist revolution would arise in the developed countries of the West, RAM insisted that the only true revolutionary solution was the "dictatorship of the world by the Black Underclass through World Black Revolution." In this, of course, they were working from today's definitions: RAM used "underclass" to encompass all peoples of color in Asia, Latin America, Africa, and elsewhere; the "Black Underclass" was merely a synonym for the colonial world. China was in a bitter fight to defend its own freedom. Now the rest of the "black" world must follow suit: "The Black Underclass has only one alternative to free itself of colonialism, imperialism, capitalism and neo-colonialism; that is to completely destroy Western (bourgeois) civilization (the cities of the world) through a World Black Revolution[,] and establishing a Revolutionary World Black Dictatorship can bring about the end of exploitation of man by mankind and the new revolutionary world [can] be created."[44] To coordinate this revolution, RAM called for the creation of a Black International and the creation of a "People's Liberation Army on a world scale."[45]

For all of its strident nationalism, *The World Black Revolution* concludes that black nationalism "is really internationalism." Only by demolishing white nationalism and white power can liberation be achieved for everyone. Not only will national boundaries be eliminated with the "dictatorship of the Black Underclass," but "the need for nationalism in its aggressive form will be eliminated." This is a pretty remarkable statement given RAM's social and ideological roots. But rather than represent a unified position, the statement reflects the various tensions that persisted throughout RAM's history. On one side were nationalists who felt that revolutionaries should fight for the black nation first and build socialism separate from the rest of the United States. On the other side were socialists like James Boggs and Grace Lee Boggs who wanted to know who would rule the "white" nation and what such a presence would mean for black freedom. They also rejected efforts to resurrect the "Black Nation" thesis—the old communist line that people in the black-majority counties of the South (the "black belt") have a right to secede from the union. The Boggses contended that the real source of power was in the cities and not the rural black belt.[46]

After years as an underground organization, a series of "exposés" in *Life* magazine and *Esquire* that ran in 1966 identified RAM as one of the leading extremist groups "plotting a war on 'whitey.'" The "Peking-backed" group was not only considered armed and dangerous, but "impressively well read in revolutionary literature—from Marat and Lenin to Mao, Che Guevara and Frantz Fanon."[47] The Harlem Branch of the Progressive Labor Party responded to the articles with a pamphlet titled *The Plot Against Black America,* which argued that China is not financing revolution, just setting a revolutionary example by its staunch anti-imperialism. The real causes of black rebellion, they insisted, can be found in the conditions of ghetto life.[48] Not surprisingly, these highly publicized articles were followed by a series of police raids on the homes of RAM members in Philadelphia and New York City. In June 1967, RAM members were rounded up and charged with conspiracy to instigate a riot, poison police officers with potassium cyanide, and assassinate Roy Wilkins and Whitney Young. A year later, under the repressive atmosphere of the FBI's Counter Intelligence Program (COINTELPRO), RAM transformed itself into the Black Liberation Party, or the African American Party of National Liberation. By 1969, RAM had pretty much dissolved itself, though its members opted to "melt back into the community and infiltrate existing Black organizations," continue to push the twelve-point program, and develop study groups that focused on the

"Science of Black Internationalism, and the thought of Chairman Rob [Robert Williams]."[49]

The COINTELPRO operations only partly explain the dissolution of RAM. Some of its members moved on to other organizations, such as the Republic of New Africa and the Black Panther Party. But RAM's declining membership and ultimate demise can be partly attributed to strategic errors on its part. Indeed, its members' understanding of the current situation in the ghettoes and their specific strategies of mobilization suggest that they were not very good Maoists after all. Mao's insistence on the protracted nature of revolution was not taken to heart; at one point they suggested that the war for liberation would probably take ninety days. And because RAM's leaders focused their work on confronting the state head on and attacking black leaders whom they deemed reformists, they failed to build a strong base in black urban communities. Furthermore, despite their staunch internationalism, they did not reach out to other oppressed "nationalities" in the United States. Nevertheless, what RAM and Robert Williams did do was to elevate revolutionary black nationalism to a position of critical theoretical importance for the anti-revisionist Left in general. They provided an organizational and practical example of what Harold Cruse, Frantz Fanon, and Malcolm X were trying to advance in their writings and speeches. More importantly, they found theoretical justification for revolutionary black nationalism in Mao Zedong thought, especially after the launching of the Cultural Revolution in China.

"Finally Got the News": The League of Revolutionary Black Workers

Although RAM might have been on the decline, its leaders continued to shape some of the most radical movements of the decade. Several leading figures in the League of Revolutionary Black Workers in Detroit had been leaders in RAM, most notably Luke Tripp, General Baker, Charles (Mao) Johnson and, later, Ernie Allen. Tripp, Baker, Johnson, and John Watson were Wayne State University students active in the nationalist collective Uhuru, which in some respects served as the public face of RAM much like Challenge had done in Ohio and the Soul Students Advisory Council had done in California. Watson, who apparently was not in RAM, had worked with a number of organizations, including the Freedom Now Party (an all-black political party that endorsed the socialist Clifton DeBerry for president in 1964), SNCC, and the Negro Action Committee. Upon General Baker's return from Cuba, he moved even deeper into Detroit's labor and Left circles, taking a job as a production worker at the Chrysler-Dodge main plant and taking classes on Marx's *Capital* with Marty Glaberman, a veteran radical of the Johnson-Forest tendency (a breakaway goup from the Socialist Workers Party led by C. L. R. James and Raya Dunayevskaya that included James Boggs and Grace Lee Boggs).[50]

The *Inner City Voice* (*ICV*), which Watson began editing after the Detroit riots in 1967, was conceived as a revolutionary publication that could build links between black radicals, particularly students and labor activists, with the broader black community. Having studied the works of Lenin, and to a lesser degree Stalin and Mao, the militants who started *ICV* regarded the newspaper as "the focus of a permanent organization [that] could provide a bridge between the peaks of activity."[51] And they tried to live up to this injunction: in 1968 Baker organized a discussion group consisting largely of Dodge main plant workers at the *ICV*'s office. Not long afterward—the Vday after May Day, 1968, to be exact—four thousand workers at the Dodge main plant walked out in a wildcat strike, the first in that factory in fourteen years and the first organized and led entirely by black workers. The strike was over the speedup of the assembly line, which in the previous week had increased from forty-nine to fifty-eight cars per hour. Black radical trade unionists characterized the speedups as part of a broader process of "nigger-mation," or as one worker explained it, the practice of hiring one black worker to do the work formerly done by three white workers. In spite of the fact that many pickets were white, the greatest company reprisals were against black workers. General Baker, accused of leading the strike, was among those summarily fired. In an "Open Letter to Chrysler Corporation," Baker wrote: "In this day and age . . . the leadership of a wildcat strike is a badge of honor and courage. . . . You have made the decision to do battle with me and therefore to do battle with the entire Black community in this city, this state, this country and in this world which I am part of. Black people of the world are united in a common struggle."[52]

No matter what role Baker played in the walkout, it is clear that the individuals involved in the *ICV* study group were at the forefront of the strike. This core of radical workers around Baker and the *ICV* group gave birth to DRUM—the Dodge Revolutionary Union Movement. The spirit and militancy that DRUM represented spread to other plants: ELRUM rose out of the Eldon Avenue Gear and Axle Plant, JARUM was started at Chrysler Jefferson Avenue, MERUM at Mound Road Engine, CADRUM at Cadillac Fleetwood, FRUM at the Ford Rouge, and GRUM at General Motors. Though most of these committees actively involved relatively small numbers of workers, the spread of the movement revealed the level of frustration and anger that black workers felt toward both the auto industry and the leadership of the United Auto Workers (UAW).

From the outset, black student radicals at Wayne State University were committed to building DRUM and the other revolutionary union movements because they saw working-class struggles as the fundamental wedge against capitalism. Besides, at a public institution like Wayne State in which 10 percent of its student body was black, it wasn't unusual to find part-time students in the plants or workers whose kids leapt into the revolutionary movement feet first. During the wildcat strikes at the Dodge main and Eldon Avenue plants, students walked the picket line after court injunctions prevented the striking workers from coming near the plant gates. Thus the distinctions between "intellectuals" and "workers" were always somewhat blurred. As Geoffrey Jacques, a black Detroit native active in radical politics during the 1970s recalled, "I would ride the bus full of auto workers on their way to the plant and there was always somebody reading Stalin, Lenin, or Mao. It seemed like everyone was part of a study group."[53]

It is not an exaggeration to state that most DRUM leaders were self-identified Marxist-Leninist-Maoists or Trotskyists of some variety. However, at the outset their main concern was unity within the revolutionary union movement. In large measure through the work of the original core group from the ICV, but with the important additions of workers who had become active on the shop floor, the League of Revolutionary Black Workers came into being in 1969. Its constitution called on workers to "act swiftly to organize DRUM-type organizations wherever there are black workers, be it in Lynn Townsend's kitchen, the White House, White Castle, Ford Rouge, the Mississippi Delta, the plains of Wyoming, the mines of Bolivia, the rubber plantations of Indonesia, the oil fields of Biafra, or the Chrysler plant in South Africa."[54] The organization's belief that world revolution was imminent and that people of color throughout the world were in the vanguard reflects the Maoist-inspired vision characteristic of RAM. Indeed, when Ernie

Allen became the League's director of political education, he recalled that practically everyone was reading Mao and Giap (the Vietnamese theoretician on guerrilla warfare). It wasn't uncommon for members to use the Chinese revolution as a framework for understanding the history of the black workers' struggles. Besides, League activists were reading more than Mao: they were interested in some of the Italian and French New Left movements, particularly Potere Operaio, Lotta Continua, and several French "workerist" organizations. Allen brought some of these heated discussions of world events back home by introducing books and articles on African American labor history.[55]

Despite their deep sense of internationalism and their radical vision of trade unionism, League members were divided over strategy and tactics. One group, led by General Baker, believed that the movement should focus on shop-floor struggles, while Watson, Mike Hamlin, and Cockrel felt that the League needed to organize black communities beyond the point of production. One outgrowth of their community-based approach was the Black Economic Development Conference (BEDC) held in spring 1969. At the urging of the former SNCC leader James Forman, who had recently arrived in Detroit, the League became heavily involved in the planning and running of the conference. Originally called by the Inter-religious Foundation for Community Organizations, the conference was taken over by the revolutionary left in Detroit and essentially produced a call for black socialism. Out of BEDC came Forman's proposal for a Black manifesto, which demanded, among other things, five hundred million dollars in reparations from white churches.[56]

The work in BEDC led the League leadership, of which Forman was now a part, away from its local emphasis. Their efforts led to the founding of the Black Workers Congress (BWC) in 1970. The BWC was conceived more or less as a coalition of black revolutionary labor activists, and it attracted a number of Maoist and Left nationalist movements, including the Puerto Rican Revolutionary Workers Organization (which went on to help found the Revolutionary Workers League) and the Communist Party (Marxist-Leninist). Forman was deeply influenced by Kathy Amatniek, a major theorist in the women's liberation movement, with whom he had a relationship. She had studied Chinese at Harvard and introduced consciousness-raising based on the "speak bitterness" campaigns in China. And according to Rosalyn Baxandall, one of the founding members of the radical feminist group Redstockings, Amatniek was a serious anti-revisionist who appreciated Stalin and sympathized with Albania.[57] Eventually the Forman-led BWC became a Marxist-Leninist-Maoist organization in its own right, calling for workers' control over the economy and the state to be brought about through cooperatives, united front groups, neighborhood centers, student organizations, and ultimately a revolutionary party. With Forman at the helm, the BWC called for an end to all forms of racism, imperialism, speedups, and wage freezes, and it expressed its support for the South Vietnamese Provisional Revolutionary Government.

Meanwhile, the League's local base began to disintegrate. Several League activists, including Chuck Wooten and General Baker, had been fired and all of the revolutionary union movements were barely functional by 1972. The "General Policy Statement" of the League, which based everything on the need for vibrant "DRUM-type" organizations, seemed to have fallen by the wayside. Divisions between the leadership groupings were so entrenched that no one could hear criticism from "the other side" without assuming hostile motivations. These contradictions came to a head when Cockrel, Hamlin, and Watson left the League in June 1971 to build the Black Workers Congress. In their document "The Split in the League of Revolutionary Black Workers: Three Lines and Three Headquarters" they described themselves as "the proletarian revolutionaries" and the two other tendencies as "the petty bourgeois opportunists" and "the backward reactionary nationalist lumpen proletarians." Not long after their departure from the League the remaining core, led by General Baker, joined the Communist League under the leadership of the veteran black Marxist Nelson Peery. Several members of the Dodge Revolutionary Union Movement and the League of Revolutionary Black Workers rose to leadership positions within the Communist Labor Party (CLP) and significantly shaped its industrial orientation. They studied Mao and Stalin with even greater rigor and built a highly disciplined party in Detroit that concentrated on the plants and factories. Although the League (which was to become the Communist Labor Party in 1972) opened the China-Albania Bookstore in Detroit, it never tried to operate as a mass organization or recruit on college campuses. Baker, especially, remained committed to the Communist League through all of its manifestations—as the CLP and, most recently, as the League of Revolutionaries.

In many respects, the League's leaders turned out to be very good Maoists—whether or not they identified with Mao. Through the newspapers and the revolutionary union movements, they always looked for ways to relate their overall political analysis to the conditions around them. They established strategic guidelines rather than a rigid blueprint for organizing. And they constantly struggled over the relationship of Marxist intellectuals, which they were in large part, to the workers they wanted to reach. In so doing they succeeded in creating a revolutionary language and making it available to black workers. Yet the promise of the League was also its peril: when the phenomenon of the revolutionary union movements began to dissipate, and as struggles led by the revolutionary union movements were defeated, the League itself was called into question. As Ken Cockrel puts it, "We had to develop a concept of what to do when workers are fired for doing organizational activity, and you are not in a position to feed them, and you are not in a position to force management to take them back, and you are not in a position to relate concretely to any of their needs. . . . If you make no response you are in a position of having led workers out of the plant on the basis of an anti-racist, anti-imperialist, anti-capitalist line and having the man respond and you can't do anything."[58]

But this is not the whole story. Perhaps the greatest tragedy for the League was the failure of white workers to support the revolutionary union movements. Had the UAW used its resources to support League demands rather than lining up with the auto companies to isolate and destroy the movements, the outcome probably would have been different. Race, once again, contributed to the downfall of a potentially transformative American labor movement. It was yet another installment of a very old (and continuing) saga.

Return of the Black Belt

By most accounts, an explicit Maoist ideology and movement did not emerge on the U.S. political landscape until Mao initiated the Great Proletarian Cultural Revolution in 1966. A precursor to the revolution had erupted in China nine years earlier, when Mao appealed to his countrymen to "let a hundred flowers blossom" and "let a hundred schools of thought contend." That campaign was just a flash in the pan, however, and it was quickly silenced after too many flowers openly criticized the Chinese Communist Party.

But the Cultural Revolution was different. Hierarchies in the party and in the Red Army were ostensibly eliminated. Criticism and self-criticism was encouraged—as long as it coincided with Mao Zedong thought. Communists suspected of supporting a capitalist road were brought to trial. Bourgeois intellectuals in the academy and government were expected to perform manual labor, to work among the people as a way of breaking down social hierarchies. And all vestiges of the old order were to be eliminated. The youth, now the vanguard, attacked tradition with a vengeance and sought to create new cultural forms to promote the revolution. The people of China were now called on to educate themselves. The Cultural Revolution intensified the constituent elements of Maoism: the idea of constant rebellion and conflict; the concept of the centrality of people over economic laws or productive forces; the notion of revolutionary morality.

No matter what one's view of the Cultural Revolution might be, it projected to the world—particularly to those sympathetic to China and to revolutionary movements generally—a vision of society where divisions between the powerful and powerless are blurred, and where status and privilege do not necessarily distinguish leaders from the led. The socialists Paul Sweezey and Leo Huberman, editors of the independent socialist journal *Monthly Review,* recognized the huge implications of such a revolution for the urban poor in the United States: "Just imagine what would happen in the United States if a President were to invite the poor in this country, with special emphasis on the blacks in the urban ghettos, to win the war on poverty for themselves, promising them the protection of the army against reprisals!"[59] Of course, the United States is not a socialist country and has never pretended to be one, and despite a somewhat sympathetic President Lyndon Johnson, black people in the United States were not regarded by the state as "the people." Their problems were a drain on society and their ungrateful riots and the proliferation of revolutionary organizations did not elicit much sympathy for the black poor.

For many in the New Left, African Americans were not only "*the* people" but also the most revolutionary sector of the working class. The Cultural Revolution's emphasis on eliminating hierarchies and empowering the oppressed reinforced the idea that black liberation lay at the heart of the new American revolution. Mao Zedong himself gave credence to this view in his widely circulated April 1968 statement "In Support of the Afro-American Struggle Against Violent Repression." The statement was delivered during a massive demonstration in China protesting the assassination of Dr. Martin

Luther King Jr., at which Robert Williams and Vicki Garvin were among the featured speakers. According to Garvin, "millions of Chinese demonstrators" marched in the pouring rain to denounce American racism.[60] Responding to the rebellions touched off by King's assassination, Mao characterized these urban uprisings as "a new clarion call to all the exploited and oppressed people of the United States to fight against the barbarous rule of the monopoly capitalist class."[61] Even more than the 1963 statement, Mao's words endowed the urban riots with historic importance in the world of revolutionary upheaval. His statement, as well as the general logic of Lin Biao's "theory of the new democratic revolution" justified support for black nationalist movements and their right of self-determination.

It was in the context of the urban rebellions that several streams of black radicalism, including RAM, converged and gave birth in Oakland, California, to the Black Panther Party for Self-Defense. Perhaps the most visible black organization promoting Mao Zedong thought, by some accounts they also were probably the least serious about reading Marxist, Leninist, or Maoist writings and developing a revolutionary ideology. Founded by Huey Newton and Bobby Seale, a former RAM member, the Black Panther Party went well beyond the boundaries of Merritt College and recruited the "lumpenproletariat." Much of the rank-and-file engaged in sloganeering more than anything else, and their bible was the Little Red Book.

That the Panthers were Marxist, at least in rhetoric and program, was one of the sources of their dispute with Ron Karenga's U.S. organization and other groups they derisively dismissed as cultural nationalists. Of course, the Panthers not only had their own cultural nationalist agenda, but the so-called cultural nationalists were neither a monolith nor were they uniformly pro-capitalist. And the divisions between these groups were exacerbated by COINTELPRO. Still, there was a fundamental difference between the Panthers' evolving ideology of socialism and class struggle and that of black nationalist groups, even on the left. As Bobby Seale explained in a March 1969 interview, "We're talking about socialism. The cultural nationalists say that socialism won't do anything for us. There's the contradiction between the old and the new. Black people have no time to practice black racism and the masses of black people do not hate white people just because of the color of their skin. . . . We're not going to go out foolishly and say there is no possibility of aligning with some righteous white revolutionaries, or other poor and oppressed peoples in this country who might come to see the light about the fact that it's the capitalist system they must get rid of."[62]

How the Panthers arrived at this position and the divisions within the party over their stance is a long and complicated story that we cannot address here. For our purposes, we want to make a few brief points about the party's embrace of Mao Zedong thought and its position vis-à-vis black self-determination. For Huey Newton, whose contribution to the party's ideology rivals that of Eldridge Cleaver and George Jackson, the source of the Panther's Marxism was the Chinese and Cuban revolutions precisely because their analysis grew out of their respective histories rather than from the pages of *Capital*. The Chinese and Cuban examples, according to Newton, empowered the Panthers to develop their own unique program and to discard theoretical insights from Marx and Lenin that had little or no application to black reality.[63] Indeed, a quick perusal of the Panthers' "Ten Point Program" reveals quite clearly that Malcolm X continued to be one of their biggest ideological influences.

Eldridge Cleaver was a little more explicit about the role of Maoism and the thought of the Korean communist leader Kim Il Sung in reshaping Marxism-Leninism for the benefit of the national liberation struggles of Third World peoples. In a 1968 pamphlet titled "On the Ideology of the Black Panther Party (Part 1)," Cleaver makes clear that the Panthers were a Marxist-Leninist party, but he adds that Marx, Engels, Lenin, and their contemporary followers did not offer much insight on understanding and fighting racism. The lesson here is to adopt and alter what is useful and reject what is not. "With the founding of the Democratic People's Republic of Korea in 1948 and the People's Republic of China in 1949," Cleaver wrote, "something new was interjected into Marxism-Leninism, and it ceased to be just a narrow, exclusively European phenomenon. Comrade Kim Il Sung and Comrade Mao Tse-Tung applied the classical principles of Marxism-Leninism to the conditions of their own countries and thereby made the ideology into something useful for their people. But they rejected that part of the analysis that was not beneficial to them and had only to do with the welfare of Europe."[64] In Cleaver's view, the sharpest critique of Western Marxism's blindness with regard to race came from Frantz Fanon.

By seeing themselves as part of a global national liberation movement, the Panthers also spoke of the black community as a colony with an inherent right to self-determination. Yet, unlike many other black or interracial Mao-ist groups, they never advocated secession or the creation of a separate state. Rather, describing black people as colonial subjects was a way of characteriz-ing the materialist nature of racism; that is, it was more of a metaphor than an analytical concept. Self-determination was understood to mean commu-nity control within the urban environment, not necessarily the establish-ment of a black nation.[65] In a paper delivered at the Peace and Freedom Party's founding convention in March 1968, Cleaver tried to clarify the relationship between interracial unity in the U.S. revolution and, in his words, "national liberation in the black colony." He essentially called for an approach in which black and white radicals would work together to create coalitions of revolutionary organizations and to develop the political and military machinery that could overthrow capitalism and imperialism. Going further, he also called for a United Nations–sponsored plebiscite that would allow black people to determine whether they wished to integrate or sepa-rate. Such a plebiscite, he argued, would bring clarity to black people on the question of self-determination, just as the first-wave independence move-ments in Africa had to decide whether they wanted to maintain some altered dominion status or achieve complete independence.[66]

Cleaver represented a wing of the Black Panther Party more interested in guerrilla warfare than in rebuilding society or doing the hard work of grassroots organizing. The Panthers' attraction to Mao, Kim Il Sung, Giap, Che, and for that matter Fanon, was based on their writings on revolution-ary violence and people's wars. Many self-styled Panther theoreticians fo-cused so much on developing tactics to sustain the immanent revolution that they skipped over a good deal of Mao's writings. Recognizing the prob-lem, Newton sought to move the party away from an emphasis on guer-rilla warfare and violence to a deeper, richer discussion of what the party's vision for the future might entail. Shortly after his release from prison in August 1970, Newton proposed the creation of an "Ideological Institute" where participants actually read and taught what he regarded as the "clas-sics"—Marx, Mao, and Lenin as well as Aristotle, Plato, Rousseau, Kant, Kierkegaard, and Nietszche. Unfortunately, the Ideological Institute did not amount to much; few Party members saw the use of abstract theorizing or the relevance of some of these writings to revolution. Besides, the fact that *Quotations from Chairman Mao* read more or less like a handbook for guer-rillas didn't help matters much. Even Fanon was read pretty selectively, with his chapter "Concerning Violence" being the perpetual favorite among militants. George Jackson contributed to the Panther's theoretical emphasis on war since much of his own writings, from *Soledad Brother* to *Blood in My Eye,* drew on Mao primarily to discuss armed resistance under fascism. Efforts to read the works of Marx, Lenin, or Mao beyond issues related to armed rebellion did not always find a willing audience among the Panthers.[67] Sid Lemelle, then a radical activist at California State University in Los Angeles, recalls being in contact with a few Panthers who had joined a study group sponsored by the California Communist League. The reading, which included Mao's *Four Essays on Philosophy* and lengthy passages from Lenin's selected works, turned out to be too much and the Panthers eventually left the group amid a stormy debate.[68]

Perhaps the least-read section of *Quotations from Chairman Mao,* at least by men, was the five-page chapter on women. In an age when the metaphors for black liberation were increasingly masculinized and black movement leaders not only ignored but also perpetuated gender oppression, even the most Marxist of the black nationalist movements belittled the "woman question." The Black Panther Party was certainly no exception. Indeed, it was during the same historic meeting of the Students for a Democratic Society in 1969, where the Panthers invoked Marx, Lenin, and Mao to expel the Progressive Labor Party for their position on the national question, that the Panther minister of information Rufus Walls gave his infamous speech about the need to have women in the movement because they possessed "pussy power." Although Walls's statement clearly was a vernacular take-off from Mao's line that "China's women are a vast reserve of labour power [that] . . . should be tapped in the struggle to build a great socialist country,"[69] it turned out to be a profoundly antifeminist defense of women's participation.

While China's own history on the "woman question" is pretty dismal, Mao's dictum that "women hold up half the sky" as well as his brief writings on women's equality and participation in the revolutionary process endowed women's liberation with some revolutionary legitimacy on the Left. Of course, Maoism didn't make the movement: the fact is, women's struggles within the New Left played the most important role in reshaping Left movements toward a feminist agenda, or at least putting feminism on the table. But for black women in the Panthers who were suspicious of "white feminism," Mao's language on women's equality provided space within the party to develop an incipient black feminist agenda. As the newly appointed minister of information, the Panther Elaine Brown announced to a press conference soon after returning from China in 1971 that "the Black Panther Party acknowledges the progressive leadership of our Chinese comrades in all areas of revolution. Specifically, we embrace China's correct recognition of the proper status of women as equal to that of men."[70]

Even beyond the rhetoric, black women Panthers such as Lynn French, Kathleen Cleaver, Erica Huggins, Akua Njere, and Assata Shakur (formerly Joanne Chesimard) sustained the tradition of carving out free spaces within existing male-dominated organizations in order to challenge the multiple forms of exploitation that black working-class women faced daily. Through the Panther's free breakfast and educational programs, for example, black women devised strategies that, in varying degrees, challenged capitalism, racism, and patriarchy. And in some instances, African American women radicals rose to positions of prominence and, sometimes by sheer example, contributed toward developing a militant, class-conscious black feminist perspective. The most important figures in this respect include Kathleen Cleaver, Erica Huggins, Elaine Brown, and Assata Shakur.[71] In some instances, the growing strength of a black Left feminist perspective, buttressed by certain Maoist slogans on the woman question, shaped future black Maoist formations. One obvious example is the Black Vanguard Party, another Bay Area Maoist group active in the mid to late 1970s whose publication *Juche!* maintained a consistent socialist-feminist perspective. Michelle Gibbs (also known as Michelle Russell, her married name at the time) promoted a black feminist ideology as a Detroit supporter of the League of Revolutionary Black Workers and as a member of the Black Workers Congress. As a red-diaper baby whose father, Ted Gibbs, fought in the Spanish Civil War, and who grew up in a household where Paul Robeson and the artist Elizabeth Catlett were occasional guests, Gibbs's black socialist-feminist perspective flowed from her political experience; from the writings of black feminist writers; and from a panoply of radical thinkers ranging from Malcolm, Fanon, and Cabral to Marx, Lenin, and Mao.[72] Conversely, the predominantly white radical feminist organization Redstockings not only was influenced by Mao's writings but also modeled itself somewhat off of the Black Power movement, particularly the movement's separatist strategies and identification with the Third World.[73]

Ironically, the Black Panther Party's greatest identification with China occurred at the very moment when China's status among the Left began to decline worldwide. Mao's willingness to host President Nixon and China's support of the repressive governments of Pakistan and Sri Lanka left many Maoists in the United States and elsewhere disillusioned. Nevertheless, Huey Newton and Elaine Brown not only visited China on the eve of Nixon's trip but also they announced that their entry into electoral politics was inspired by China's entry into the United Nations. Newton argued that the Black Panther's shift toward reformist electoral politics did not contradict "China's goal of toppling U.S. imperialism nor [was it] an abnegation of revolutionary principles. It was a tactic of socialist revolution."[74] Even more incredible was Newton's complete abandonment of black self-determination, which he explained in terms of developments in the world economy. In 1971, he concluded quite presciently that the globalization of capital rendered the idea of national sovereignty obsolete, even among the socialist countries. Thus black demands for self-determination were no longer relevant; the only viable strategy was global revolution. "Blacks in the U.S. have a special duty to give up any claim to nationhood now more than ever. The U.S. has never been our country; and realistically there's no territory for us to claim. Of all the oppressed people in the world, we are in the best position to inspire global revolution."[75]

In many respects, Newton's position on the national question was closer to Mao's than that of most of the self-proclaimed Maoist organizations that popped up in the early to late 1970s. Despite his own statements in support of national liberation movements and of Lin Biao's "theory of democratic revolutions," Mao did not support independent organizations along nationalist lines. To him, black nationalism looked like ethnic/racial particularism. He was, after all, a Chinese nationalist attempting to unify peasants and proletarians and eliminate ethnic divisions *within his own country*. We might recall his 1957 statement in which he demanded that progressives in China "help unite the people of our various nationalities . . . not divide them."[76] Thus while recognizing that racism is a product of colonialism and imperialism, his 1968 statement insists that the "contradiction between the black masses in the United States and U.S. ruling circles is a class contradiction. . . . The black masses and the masses of white working people in the United States share common interests and have common objectives to struggle for."[77] In other words, the black struggle is bound to merge with the working-class movement and overthrow capitalism.

On the issue of black liberation, however, most American Maoist organizations founded in the early to mid 1970s took their lead from Stalin, not Mao. Black people in the United States were not simply proletarians in black skin but rather a nation—or as Stalin put it, "a historically evolved, stable community of language, territory, economic life, and psychological make-up manifested in a community of culture."[78] The anti-revisionist groups that embraced Stalin's definition of a nation, such as the Communist Labor Party (CLP) and the October League, also resurrected the old Communist Party's position that African Americans in the black belt counties of the South constitute a nation and have a right to secede if they wished. On the other hand, groups like the Progressive Labor Party—once an advocate of "revolutionary nationalism"—moved to a position repudiating all forms of nationalism by the start of the Cultural Revolution.

The CLP was perhaps the most consistent advocate of black self-determination among the anti-revisionist movements. Founded in 1968 largely by African Americans and Latinos, the CLP's roots can be traced to the old Provisional Organizing Committee (POC)—itself an outgrowth of the 1956 split in the CPUSA that led to the creation of Hammer and Steel and the Progressive Labor movement. Ravaged by a decade of internal splits, the POC had become a predominantly black and Puerto Rican organization divided between New York and Los Angeles. In 1968, the New York leadership expelled their L.A. comrades for, among other things, refusing to denounce Stalin and Mao. In turn, the L.A. group, largely under the guidance of the veteran black Marxist Nelson Peery, founded the California Communist League that same year and began recruiting young black and Chicano radical workers and intellectuals. Peery's home in South-Central Los Angeles had already become somewhat of a hangout for young black radicals after the Watts uprising; there, he organized informal groups to study history, political economy, and classic works in Marxism-Leninism-Mao Zedong thought and he entertained all sorts of activists, including Black Panthers and student activists ranging from Cal State Los Angeles to L.A. Community College. The California Communist League subsequently merged with a group of SDS militants called the Marxist-Leninist Workers Association and formed the Communist League in 1970. Two years later they changed their name again to the Communist Labor Party.[79]

Except for, perhaps, Harry Haywood's long essay "Toward a Revolutionary Position on the Negro Question," Nelson Peery's short book *The Negro National Colonial Question* (1972) was probably the most widely read defense of black self-determination in Marxist-Leninist-Maoist circles at the time.[80] Peery was sharply criticized for his defense of the term "Negro," a difficult position to maintain in the midst of the Black Power movement. But Peery had a point: national identity was not about color. The Negro nation was a historically evolved, stable community with its own unique culture, language (or, rather, dialect), and territory—the black belt counties and their surrounding areas, or essentially the thirteen states of the Old Confederacy. Because southern whites shared with African Americans a common territory, and by Peery's account a common language and culture, they were also considered part of the "Negro nation." More precisely, southern whites comprised the "Anglo-American minority" within the Negro nation. As evidenced in soul music, spirituals, and rock and roll, Peery insisted that what emerged in the South was a hybrid culture with strong African roots manifest in the form of slave folktales and female headwraps. Jimi Hendrix and Sly and the Family Stone, as well as white imitators like Al Jolson, Elvis Presley, and Tom Jones, are all cited as examples of a shared culture. Peery saw "soul" culture embedded in forms of daily life; for example, "the custom of eating pigs' feet, neck bones, black-eyed peas, greens, yams, and chitterlings are all associated with the region of the South, particularly the Negro Nation."[81]

Peery's positioning of southern whites as part of the Negro Nation was a stroke of genius, particularly since one of his intentions was to destabilize racial categories. However, at times his commitment to Stalin's definition of a nation weakened his argument. At the very moment when mass migration and urbanization depleted the rural South of its black population, Peery insisted that the black belt was the natural homeland of Negroes. He even attempted to prove that a black peasantry and stable rural proletariat still existed in the black belt. Because the land question is the foundation upon which his understanding of self-determination was built, he ends up saying very little about the nationalization of industry or socialized production. Thus he could write in 1972 that "the Negro national colonial question can only be solved by a return of the land to the people who have toiled over it for centuries. In the Negro Nation this land redistribution will demand a combination of state farms and cooperative enterprises in order to best meet the needs of the people under the conditions of modern mechanized agriculture."[82]

The Communist Party (Marxist-Leninist) also promoted a version of the black belt thesis, which it inherited from its earlier incarnation as the October League. The CP(ML) was formed out of a merger between the October League, based mainly in Los Angeles, and the Georgia Communist League in 1972.[83] Many of its founding members came out of the Revolutionary Youth Movement II (a faction within SDS), and a handful were Old Left renegades like Harry Haywood and Otis Hyde. Haywood's presence in the CP(ML) is significant since he is considered one of the architects of the original black belt thesis formulated at the Seventh Congress of the Communist International in 1928. According to the updated CP(ML) formulation, Afro-Americans had the right to secede "to their historic homeland in the Black Belt South."[84] But they added the caveat that the recognition of the right of self-determination does not mean they believe separation is the most appropriate solution. They also introduced the idea of regional autonomy (i.e., that urban concentrations of African Americans can also exercise self-determination in their own communities) and they extended the slogan of self-determination to Chicanos, Puerto Ricans, Asian Americans, Native Americans, and indigenous people in U.S. colonies (in the Pacific Islands, Hawaii, Alaska, etc.). They were selective as to what sort of nationalist movements they would support, promising to back only revolutionary nationalism as opposed to reactionary nationalism.

The Revolutionary Union, an outgrowth of the Bay Area Revolutionary Union (BARU) founded in 1969 with support from ex-CPUSA members who had visited China, took the position that black people constituted "an oppressed nation of a new type." Because black people were primarily workers concentrated in urban, industrial areas (what they called a "deformed class structure"), they argued that self-determination should not take the form of secession but rather be realized through the fight against discrimination, exploitation, and police repression in the urban centers. In 1975, when the Revolutionary Union transformed itself into the Revolutionary Communist Party (RCP), it continued to embrace the idea that black people constituted a nation of a new type, but it also began to uphold "the right of Black people to return to claim their homeland."[85] Not surprisingly, these two contradictory lines created confusion, thereby compelling RCP leaders to adopt an untenable position of defending the right of self-determination without advocating it. Two years later, they dropped the right of self-determination altogether and, like the PLP, waged war on all forms of "narrow" nationalism.

Unlike any of the Maoist-oriented organizations mentioned above, the

Revolutionary Communist League (RCL)—founded and led by none other than Amiri Baraka—grew directly out of the cultural nationalist movements of the late 1960s. To understand the RCL's (and its precursors') shifting positions with regard to the black liberation, we need to go back to 1966 when Baraka founded Spirit House in Newark, New Jersey, with the help of local activists as well as folks he had worked with in Harlem's Black Arts Repertory Theater. While Spirit House artists were from the beginning involved in local political organizing, the police beating of Baraka and several other activists during the Newark uprising in 1967 politicized them even further. After the uprising they helped organize a Black Power conference in Newark that attracted several national black leaders, including Stokely Carmichael, H. Rap Brown, Huey P. Newton of the Black Panther Party, and Imari Obadele of the newly formed Republic of New Africa (partly an outgrowth of RAM). Shortly thereafter, Spirit House became the base for the Committee for a Unified Newark (CFUN), a new organization made up of United Brothers, Black Community Defense and Development, and Sisters of Black Culture. In addition to attracting black nationalists, Muslims, and even a few Marxist-Leninist-Maoists, CFUN bore the mark of Ron Karenga's U.S. organization. Indeed, CFUN adopted Karenga's version of cultural nationalism and worked closely with him. Although tensions arose between Karenga and some of the Newark activists over his treatment of women and the overly centralized leadership structure that CFUN had imported from the US organization, the movement continued to grow. In 1970, Baraka renamed CFUN the Congress of African Peoples (CAP), transformed it into a national organization, and at its founding convention broke with Karenga. Leaders of CAP sharply criticized Karenga's cultural nationalism and passed resolutions that reflected a turn to the left—including a proposal to raise funds to help build the Tanzania-Zambia railroad.[86]

Several factors contributed to Baraka's turn to the Left during this period. One has to do with the painful lesson he learned about the limitations of black "petty bourgeois" politicians. After playing a pivotal role in the 1970 election of Kenneth Gibson, Newark's first black mayor, Baraka witnessed an increase in police repression (including attacks on CAP demonstrators) and a failure on the part of Gibson to deliver what he had promised the African American community. Feeling betrayed and disillusioned, Baraka broke with Gibson in 1974, though he did not give up entirely on the electoral process. His role in organizing the first National Black Political

Assembly in 1972 reinforced in his mind the power of black independent politics and the potential strength of a black united front.[87]

One source of Baraka's turn to the Left was the CLP East Coast regional coordinator William Watkins. Harlem born and raised, Watkins was among a group of radical black students at Cal State Los Angeles who helped found the Communist League. In 1974 Watkins got to know Baraka, who was trying to find someone to advance his understanding of Marxism-Leninism. "We'd spend hours in his office," Watkins recalled, "discussing the basics— like surplus value." For about three months, Baraka met regularly with Watkins, who taught him the fundamentals of political economy and tried to expose the limitations of cultural nationalism. These meetings certainly influenced Baraka's leftward turn, but when Watkins and Nelson Peery asked Baraka to join the CLP, he refused. Although he had come to appreciate Marxism-Leninism-Mao Tse-Tung thought, he wasn't ready to join a multiracial organization. The black struggle was first and foremost.[88]

It is fitting that the most important source of Baraka's radicalization came out of Africa. Just as Baraka's first turn to the Left after 1960 was inspired by the Cuban revolution, the struggle in southern Africa prompted his post-1970 turn to the left. The key event was the creation of the African Liberation Support Committee in 1971, which originated with a group of black nationalists led by Owusu Sadaukai, the director of Malcolm X Liberation University in Greensboro, North Carolina, who traveled to Mozambique under the aegis of FRELIMO (Front for the Liberation of Mozambique). The president of FRELIMO, Samora Machel (who, coincidentally, was in China at the same time as Huey Newton), and other militants persuaded Sadaukai and his colleagues that the most useful role that African Americans could play in support of anticolonialism was to challenge American capitalism from within and let the world know the truth about their just war against Portuguese domination. A year later Amilcar Cabral, the leader of the anticolonial movement in Guinea-Bissau and the Cape Verde Islands, said essentially the same thing during his last visit to the United States. Moreover, Cabral and Machel represented explicitly Marxist movements; they rejected the idea that precolonial African societies were inherently democratic and that they practiced a form of "primitive communism" that could lay the groundwork for modern socialism. Rather, they asserted that African societies were not immune from class struggle, nor was capitalism the only road to development.

The African Liberation Support Committee reflected the radical orientation of the liberation movements in Portuguese Africa. On May 27, 1972 (the anniversary of the founding of the Organization of African Unity), the ALSC held the first African Liberation Day demonstration, drawing approximately thirty thousand protesters in Washington alone, and an estimated thirty thousand more across the country. The African Liberation Day Coordinating Committee consisted of representatives from several nationalist and black Left organizations, including the Youth Organization for Black Unity (YOBU); the All-African People's Revolutionary Party (AAPRP), headed by Stokely Carmichael (Kwame Toure); the Pan-African People's Organization; and the Maoist-influenced Black Workers Congress.[89] Because the ALSC brought together such a broad range of black activists, it became an arena for debate over the creation of a black radical agenda. While most ALSC organizers were actively anti-imperialist, the number of black Marxists in leadership positions turned out to be a point of contention. Aside from Sadaukai, who would go on to play a major role in the Maoist-oriented Revolutionary Workers League (RWL), the ALSC's main leaders included Nelson Johnson (future leader in the Communist Workers Party) and the brilliant writer/organizer Abdul Alkalimat. As early as 1973, splits occurred within the ALSC over the role of Marxists, though when the dust settled a year later, Marxists from the RWL, the Black Workers Congress (BWC), the Revolutionary Workers Congress (an offshoot of the BWC), CAP, and the Workers Viewpoint Organization (the precursor to the Communist Workers Party) were victorious. Unfortunately, internal squabbling and sectarianism proved to be too much for the ALSC to handle. Chinese foreign policy struck the final blow; its support for UNITA during the 1975 Angola civil war and Vice-Premier Li Xiannian's suggestion that dialogue with white South Africa was better than armed insurrection, placed black Maoists in the ALSC in a difficult position.[90] Within three years the ALSC had utterly collapsed, bringing to an inauspicious close perhaps the most dynamic anti-imperialist organization of the decade.

Nevertheless, Baraka's experience in the ALSC profoundly altered his thinking. As he recalls in his autobiography, by the time of the first African Liberation Day demonstration in 1972, he was "going left, I was reading Nkrumah and Cabral and Mao." Within two years he was calling on CAP members to examine "the international revolutionary experience—namely the Russian and Chinese Revolutions—and integrate it with the practice of the Afrikan revolution."[91] Their study lists expanded to include works such as Mao Zedong's *Four Essays on Philosophy,* Stalin's *Foundations of Leninism,* and *History of the Communist Party Soviet Union (Short Course).* By 1976, CAP had dispensed with all vestiges of nationalism, changed its name to the Revolutionary Communist League, and sought to remake itself into a multiracial Marxist-Leninist-Maoist movement. Perhaps as a way to establish its ideological moorings as an anti-revisionist movement, the RCL followed in the noble tradition of resurrecting the black belt thesis. In 1977, the organization published a paper titled "The Black Nation" that analyzed black liberation movements from a Marxist-Leninist-Maoist perspective and concluded that black people in the South and in large cities constitute a nation with an inherent right to self-determination. While rejecting "bourgeois integration," the essay argued that the struggle for black political power was central to the fight for self-determination.[92]

The RCL attempted to put its vision of self-determination in practice through efforts to build a Black United Front. They organized coalitions against police brutality, mobilized support for striking cafeteria workers and maintenance workers, created a People's Committee on Education to challenge budget cuts and shape educational policy, and protested the Bakke decision. The RCL's grassroots organizing and coalition building brought them in contact with the League of Revolutionary Struggle (LRS), a California-based movement formed out of a merger between I Wor Kuen, the Chinese-American Maoist organization, and the predominantly Chicano August 29th Movement (Marxist-Leninist). In 1979, the RCL and the LRS decided to unite, and one of the foundations of their joint program was their support of the black nation thesis. As a result of the merger and the debates that preceded it, the RCL's position changed slightly: southern black people and Chicanos in the Southwest constituted oppressed nations with the right to self-determination. By contrast, for black people locked in northern ghettoes the struggle for equal rights obviously took precedent over the land question.

Invariably the merger was short-lived, in part because of disagreements over the issue of self-determination and the continuing presence of what LRS members regarded as "narrow nationalism" in the RCL. The LRS chair Carmen Chang was never comfortable with the black nation thesis but accepted the position for the sake of unity. Baraka's group, on the other hand, never abandoned black unity for multiracial class struggle. And as an artist with deep roots in the Black Arts movement, Baraka persistently set his cultural and political sights on the contradictions of black life under capitalism, imperialism, and racism. For Baraka, as with many of the characters discussed in this essay, this was not a simple matter of narrow nationalism. On the contrary, understanding the place of racist oppression and black revolution within the context of capitalism and imperialism was fundamental to the future of humanity. In the tradition of Du Bois, Fanon, and Harold Cruse, Baraka insisted that the black (hence colonial) proletariat was the vanguard of world revolution, "not because of some mystic chauvinism but because of our place in objective history. . . . We are the vanguard because we are at the bottom, and when we raise to stand up straight everything stacked upon us topples."[93]

Moreover, despite Baraka's immersion in Marxist-Leninist-Maoist literature, his own cultural work suggests that he knew, as did most black radicals, that the question of whether black people constituted a nation was not going to be settled through reading Lenin or Stalin or resurrecting M. N. Roy. If the battle ever could be settled it would take place, for better or for worse, on the terrain of culture. While the Black Arts movement was the primary vehicle for black cultural revolution in the United States, it is hard to imagine what that revolution would have looked like without China. Black radicals seized the Great Proletarian Revolution by the horns and reshaped it in their own image.

The Great (Black) Proletarian Cultural Revolution

Less than a year into the Cultural Revolution, Robert Williams published an article in the *Crusader* titled "Reconstitute Afro-American Art to Remold Black Souls." While Mao's call for a cultural revolution meant getting rid of the vestiges (cultural and otherwise) of the old order, Williams—not unlike members of the Black Arts movement in the United States—was talking about purging black culture of a "slave mentality." Although adopting some of the language of CCP's manifesto (the "Decision of the Central Committee of the Chinese Communist Party Concerning the Great Proletarian Cultural Revolution, published August 12, 1966 in the *Peking Review*), Williams's essay sought to build on the *idea* rather than on the ideology of the Cultural Revolution. Like Mao, he called on black artists to cast off the shackles of the old traditions and only make art in the service of revolution. "The Afro-American artist must make a resolute and conscious effort to reconstitute our art forms to remold new proud black and revolutionary soul. . . . It must create a new theory and direction and prepare our people for a more bitter, bloody and protracted struggle against racist tyranny and exploitation. Black art must serve the best interest of black people. It must become a powerful weapon in the arsenal of the Black Revolution."[94] The leaders of RAM concurred. An internal RAM document circulated in 1967, titled *Some Questions Concerning the Present Period,* called for a full-scale black cultural revolution in the United States whose purpose would be "to destroy the conditioned white oppressive mores, attitudes, ways, customs, philosophies, habits, etc., which the oppressor has taught and trained us to have. This means on a mass scale a new revolutionary culture." It also meant an end to processed hair, skin lighteners, and other symbols of parroting the dominant culture. Indeed, the revolution targeted not only assimilated bourgeois Negroes but also barbers and beauticians.

The conscious promotion of art as a weapon in black liberation is nothing new—it can be traced back at least to the Left wing of the Harlem Renaissance, if not earlier. And the Black Arts movement in the United States, not to mention virtually every other contemporary national liberation movement, took this idea very seriously. Fanon says as much in *The Wretched of the Earth,* English translation of which was making the rounds like wildfire during this period.[95] Still, the Cultural Revolution in China loomed large. After all, many if not most black nationalists were familiar with China and had read Mao, and even if they did not acknowledge or make explicit the influence of Maoist ideas on the need for revolutionary art or the protracted nature of cultural revolution, the parallels are striking nonetheless. Consider Maulana (Ron) Karenga's 1968 manifesto "Black Cultural Nationalism." First published in *Negro Digest,* the essay derived many of its ideas from Mao's "Talks at the Yenan Forum on Literature and Art." Like Mao, Karenga insisted that all art must be judged by two criteria—"artistic" and "social" ("political"); that revolutionary art must be for the masses; and that, in Karenga's own words, art "must be functional, that is useful, as we cannot accept the false doctrine of 'art for art's sake.' " One can definitely see the influence of Maoism on Karenga's efforts to create an alternative revolutionary culture. Indeed, the seven principles of Kwanzaa (the African American holiday that Karenga invented and first celebrated in 1967)—unity, self-determination, collective work and responsibility, collective economics (socialism), creativity, purpose, and even faith—are nearly as consonant with Mao's ideas as they are with "traditional" African culture.[96] And it is not a coincidence, perhaps, that at least one of the principles, Ujamaa, or "cooperative economics," was the basis of Tanzania's famous Arusha Declaration in 1964 under president Julius Nyerere—with Tanzania being China's earliest and most important ally in Africa.

Although Karenga's debt to Mao went unacknowledged, the Progressive Labor Party took note. The PLP's paper, the *Challenge,* ran a scathing article that attacked the entire Black Arts movement and its theoreticians. Titled "[LeRoi] Jones-Karenga Hustle: Cultural 'Rebels' Foul Us Up," the article characterized Karenga as a "pseudo-intellectual" who "has thoroughly read Mao's Talks on Literature and Art. In fact he can quote from this work as if he wrote it himself. What he did with this Marxist classic is to take out its heart—the class struggle—and substitute no-struggle. In addition he has put 'art' above politics and has MADE ART THE REVOLUTION." " 'Cultural nationalism,' " the article continued, "is not only worshipping the most reactionary aspects of African history. It even goes so far as measuring one's revolutionary commitment by the clothes that are being worn! This is part of the 'Black awareness.' "[97]

Of course, revolution did become a kind of art, or more precisely, a distinct style. Whether it was Afros and dashikis or leather jackets and berets, most black revolutionaries in the United States developed their own aesthetic criteria. In the publishing world, Mao's Little Red Book made a tremendous impact on literary styles in black radical circles. The idea that a pocket-sized book of pithy quotes and aphorisms could address a range of subjects, from ethical behavior, revolutionary thought and practice, economic development, philosophy, etc., appealed to many black activists, irrespective of political allegiance. The Little Red Book prompted a cottage industry of miniature books of quotations compiled expressly for black militants. *The Black Book,* edited by Earl Ofari Hutchison (with assistance from Judy Davis), is a case in point. Published by the Radical Education Project (circa 1970), *The Black Book* is a compilation of brief quotes from W. E. B. Du Bois, Malcolm X, and Frantz Fanon that address a range of issues related to domestic and world revolution. The resemblance to *Quotations from Chairman Mao* is striking: chapter titles include "Black Culture and Art," "Politics," "Imperialism," "Socialism," "Capitalism," "Youth," "The Third World," "Africa," "On America," and " Black Unity." Earl Ofari Hutchison's introduction places black struggle in a global context and calls for revolutionary ethics and "spiritual as well as physical unification of the Third World." "True blackness," he adds, "is a collective life-style, a collective set of values and a common world perspective" that grows out of distinct experiences in the West. *The Black Book* was not written as defense of black nationalism against the encroachments of Maoism. On the contrary, Earl Ofari Hutchison closes by telling "freedom fighters everywhere, continue to read your red book, but place alongside of it the revolutionary BLACK BOOK. To win the coming battle, both are necessary."[98]

Another popular text in this tradition was the *Axioms of Kwame Nkrumah: Freedom Fighters Edition*.[99] Bound in black leather with gold type, it opens with a line in the frontispiece underscoring the importance of revolutionary will: "The secret of life is to have no fear." And with the exception of its African focus, the chapters are virtually indistinguishable from the Little Red Book. Topics include "African Revolution," "Army," "Black Power," "Capitalism," "Imperialism," "People's Militia," "The People," "Propaganda," "Socialism," and "Women." Most of the quotes are either vague or fail to transcend obvious sloganeering (e.g., "The foulest intellectual rubbish ever invented by man is that of racial superiority and inferiority," or "A revolutionary fails only if he surrenders").[100] More importantly, many of Nkrumah's insights could have come straight from Mao's pen, particularly those quotations dealing with the need for popular mobilization, the dialectical relationship between thought and action, and issues related to war and peace and imperialism.

On the question of culture, most Maoist and anti-revisionist groups in the United States were less concerned with creating a new, revolutionary culture than with destroying the vestiges of the old or attacking what they regarded as a retrograde, bourgeois commercial culture. In this respect, they were in step with the Great Proletarian Cultural Revolution. In a fascinating review of the film *Superfly* published in the CP(ML) paper *The Call*, the writer seizes the opportunity to criticize the counterculture as well as the capitalists' role in promoting drug use in the black community. "Looking around at all the people overdosing on drugs, getting killed in gun fights among themselves, and getting shredded up in industrial accidents while stoned on the job, it's clear that dope is as big a killer as any armed cop." Why would a film marketed to black people glorify the drug culture? Because "the imperialists know the plain truth—if you're hooked on dope, you won't have time to think about revolution—you're too busy worrying about where the next shot is coming from!" The review also included a bit of Chinese history: "The British did everything they could to get the Chinese people strung out [on opium]. It was common for workers to get part of their wages in opium, turning them into addicts even quicker. It was only revolution that got rid of the cause of this misery. By taking their countries back, and turning their society in to one that really served the people, there was no more need to escape into drugs."[101]

Maoist attacks were not limited to the most reactionary aspects of mass commercial culture. The Black Arts movement—a movement that, ironically, included figures very much inspired by developments in China and Cuba—came under intense scrutiny by the anti-revisionist Left. Groups like the PLP and the CP(ML), despite their many disagreements over the national question, did agree that the Black Arts movement and its attraction to African culture was misguided, if not downright counterrevolutionary. The PLP dismissed black cultural nationalists as petty bourgeois businessmen who sold the most retrograde aspects of African culture to the masses and "exploit[ed] Black women—all in the name of 'African culture' and in the name of 'revolution.'" The same PLP editorial castigates the Black Arts movement for "teaching about African Kings and Queens, African 'empires.' There is no class approach—no notice that these Kings, etc., were oppressing the mass of African people."[102] Likewise, an editorial in *The Call* in 1973 sharply criticized the Black Arts movement for "delegitimizing the genuine national aspirations of Black people in the U.S. and to substituting African counter-culture for anti-imperialist struggle."[103]

While these attacks were generally unfair, particularly in the way they lumped together a wide array of artists, a handful of black artists had come to similar conclusions about the direction of the Black Arts movement. For the novelist John Oliver Killens, the Chinese Cultural Revolution offered a model for transforming black cultural nationalism into a revolutionary force. As a result of his travels to China during the early 1970s, Killens published an important essay in *The Black World* (later reprinted by the U.S.-China People's Friendship Association as a pamphlet titled *Black Man in the New China*) praising the Cultural Revolution for being, in his view, a stunning success. In fact, he ostensibly went to China to find out why their revolution succeeded "while our own Black cultural revolution, that bloomed so brightly during the Sixties, seems to be dying on the vine."[104] By the time Killens was ready to return to the United States, he had reached several conclusions regarding the limitations of the black cultural revolution and the strength of the Maoist model. First, he recognized that all successful revolutions must be continuous—permanent and protracted. Second, cultural activism and political activism are not two different strategies for liberation but rather two sides of the same coin. The cultural revolution and the political revolution go hand in hand. Third, a revolutionary movement must be self-reliant; it must create self-sustaining cultural institutions. Of course, most radical nationalists in the Black Arts movement figured out most of this independently and Killens's article merely reinforced these lessons. However, China taught Killens one other lesson that few other males in the movement paid attention to at the time: " 'Women hold up one-half of the world.' " "In some very vital and militant factions of the Black cultural revolution, women were required to metaphorically 'sit in the back of the bus.' . . . This is backward thinking and divisive. Many women voted with their feet and went into Women's Lib. And some of the brothers seemed upset and surprised. We drove them to it."[105]

The other major black critic of the Black Arts movement's cultural nationalism who ended up embracing Maoism was Amiri Baraka, himself a central figure in the black cultural revolution and an early target for Maoist abuse. As the founder and leader of CAP and later the RCL, Baraka offered more than a critique; instead, he built a movement that attempted to synthesize the stylistic and aesthetic innovations of the Black Arts movement with Marxism-Leninism-Mao Zedong thought and practice. Just as his odyssey from the world of the Beats to the Bandung World provide insight into Mao's impact on black radicalism in the United States, so does his transition from a cultural nationalist to committed communist. More than any other Maoist or anti-revisionist, Baraka and the RCL epitomized the most conscious and sustained effort to bring the Great Proletarian Cultural Revolution to America's inner cities and to transform it in a manner that spoke to the black working class.

Having come out of the Black Arts movement in Harlem and Spirit House in Newark, Baraka was above all else a cultural worker. As he and the Congress of African Peoples moved from cultural nationalism to Marxism, this profound ideological shift manifested itself through changes in cultural practice. Dismissing the "Black petty bourgeois primitive cultural nationalist" as unscientific and metaphysical, he warned his comrades against "the cultural bias that might make us think that we can return to pre-slave trade Afrika, and the romance of feudalism."[106] Further, CAP changed the name of its publication from *Black Newark* to *Unity and Struggle* to reflect its transition from a cultural nationalist perspective to a deeper understanding of "the dialectical requirements of revolution."[107] The Spirit House Movers (CAP's theater troupe) was now called the Afrikan Revolutionary Movers (ARM), and a group of cultural workers associated with Spirit House formed a singing group called the Anti-Imperialist Singers. They abandoned African dress as well as "male chauvinist practices that had been carried out as part of its 'African traditionalism' such as holding separate political education classes for men and women."[108] And CAP's official holiday, known as "Leo Baraka" for Baraka's birthday, became a day devoted entirely to studying Marxism-Leninism-Mao Zedong thought, the "woman question," and the problems of cadre development.[109]

By 1976, the year CAP reemerged as the Revolutionary Communist League, Baraka had come a long way since his alliance with Ron Karenga. In a poem titled "Today," published in a small book of poetry titled *Hard Facts* (1976), Baraka's position on cultural nationalism vis-à-vis class struggle is unequivocal:

Frauds in leopard skin, turbaned hustlers w/skin
type rackets, colored capitalists, negro
exploiters, Afro-American Embassy gamers
who lurk about Afrikan embassies fightin for
airline tickets, reception guerrillas, whose
only connection w/a party is the Frankie
Crocker kind.
Where is the revolution brothers and sisters?
Where is the mobilization of the masses led
by the advanced section of the working class?
Where is the unity criticism unity. The self criticism
& criticism? Where is the work & study. The
ideological clarity? Why only poses &
postures & subjective one sided non-theories
describing only yr petty bourgeois upbringing
Black saying might get you a lecture gig, 'wise man.' but will not alone bring
    revolution.[110]

In fact, one might argue that Baraka's *Hard Facts* was written as a kind of Marxist-Leninist-Maoist manifesto on revolutionary art. Like his former mentor Ron Karenga, Baraka builds on Mao's oft-cited "Talks at the Yenan Forum on Art and Literature," though to very different ends. In his introduction to *Hard Facts*, Baraka insists that revolutionary artists must study Marxism-Leninism; produce work that serves the people, not the exploiters; jettison petty bourgeois attitudes and learn from the people, taking ideas and experiences and reformulating them through Marxism-Leninism. No artist, he asserts, is above study or should produce his or her opinions unconnected to the struggle for socialism. As Mao put it, "through the creative labour of revolutionary artists and writers the raw material of art and literature in the life of the people becomes art and literature in an ideological form in the service of the people."[111]

Baraka tried to put this manifesto in practice through intense community-based cultural work. One of the RCL's most successful projects was the Anti-Imperialist Cultural Union (AICU), a New York-based multinational cultural workers' organization founded in the late 1970s. In November 1978, the AICU sponsored the Festival of People's Culture, which drew some five hundred people to listen to poetry read by Askia Toure, Miguel Algarin, and Sylvia Jones along with musical performances by an RCL-created group called the Proletarian Ensemble. Through groups like the Proletarian Ensemble and the Advanced Workers (another musical ensemble formed by the RCL), the RCL spread its message of proletarian revolution and black self-determination and its critique of capitalism to community groups and schoolchildren throughout black Newark, New York, and other cities on the Eastern seaboard.

Theater seemed to be Baraka's main avenue for the Black Proletarian Cultural Revolution. Among the AICU's many projects, the Yenan Theater Workshop clearly projected Mao's vision of revolutionary art. The Yenan Theater produced a number of his plays, including a memorable performance of *What Was the Lone Ranger's Relationship to the Means of Production?* In 1975–76, Baraka wrote two new plays, *The Motion of History* and *S-1*, that perhaps represent the clearest expression of his shift, as he stated, "from petty bourgeois radicalism (and its low point of bourgeois cultural nationalism) on through to finally grasping the science of revolution, Marxism-Leninism-Mao Tse-Tung Thought."[112] *The Motion of History* is a long epic play that touches upon just about everything under the sun—including slavery and slave revolts, industrial capitalism, civil rights and Black Power, and Irish immigration and white racism. And practically every revolutionary or reformist having something to do with the struggle for black freedom makes an appearance in the play, including John Brown, H. Rap Brown, Lenin, Karenga, Harriet Tubman, Denmark Vesey, and Nat Turner. Through scenes of workers discussing politics on the shop floor or in Marxist study groups, the audience learns about the history of slavery, the rise of industrial capitalism, imperialism, surplus value, relative overproduction, and the day-to-day racist brutality to which African Americans and Latinos are subjected. In the spirit of proletarian literature, *The Motion of History* closes on an upbeat note with a rousing meeting at which those present pledge their commitment to building a revolutionary multiracial, multiethnic working-class party based on Marxist-Leninist-Mao Zedong thought.

S-1 shares many similarities with *The Motion of History*, although it focuses primarily on what Baraka and the RCL saw as the rise of fascism in the United States. As a play about a Marxist-Leninist-Maoist group fighting antisedition legislation, Baraka wrote it as a response to the Senate Bill "Criminal Justice Codification, Revision & Reform Act," known as *S-1*, which would enable the state to adopt extremely repressive measures to combat radical movements. *S-1* gave police and the FBI greater freedom to search and seize materials from radical groups, as well as permission to wiretap suspects for forty-eight hours without court approval. The bill also proposed mandatory executions for certain crimes, and it revived the Smith Act by subjecting any group or person advocating the "destruction of the government" to a possible fifteen-year prison sentence and fines up to $100,000. The most notorious aspect of the bill was the "Leading a Riot" provision, which allowed courts to sentence to three years in prison and a $100,000 fine anyone promoting the assembly of five people with the intention of creating "a grave danger to Property."[113]

We don't know how activists and working people responded to Baraka's plays during the ultraradical period of the AICU and the RCL, and most cultural critics act as if these works are not worthy of comment. No matter what one might think about these works, as art, as propaganda, or as both, it is remarkable to think that in the late 1970s a handful of inner-city kids in Newark could watch performances that advocated revolution in America and tried to expose the rapaciousness of capitalism. And all this was going on in the midst of the so-called "me" generation, when allegedly there was no radical Left to speak of. (Indeed, Reagan's election in 1980 is cited as evidence of the lack of a Left political challenge as well as the reason for the brief resurrection of Marxist parties in the United States between 1980 and 1985.)

Farewell for Mao, the Party's Over?

Depending on where one stands politically, and with whom, one could easily conclude that American Maoism died when Mao passed away in 1976. In China that rings true; the crushing of Mao's widow Jian Quing and the rest of the Gang of Four and the rapid ascendancy of Deng Xiaoping suggests that Maoism doesn't stand a ghost of a chance of returning. And while some protesters in Tiananmen Square in the mid 1980s saw themselves in the tradition of the student radicals of the Cultural Revolution, the vast majority did not—nor did they invoke Mao's name in the service of their own democratic (some might say "bourgeois") movement.

But to say that Maoism somehow died on the vine is to overstate the case. Maoist organizations still exist in the United States, and some are very active on the political scene. The Maoist Internationalist Movement maintains a Web site, as does the Progressive Labor Party (though they can hardly be called "Maoist" today), and the RCP is as ubiquitous as ever. Indeed, there is some evidence to suggest that the RCP played a role in helping to draft the Bloods and Crips' post-L.A. rebellion manifesto, "Give Us the Hammer and the Nails and We Will Rebuild the City." The former CLP, now called the League of Revolutionaries, has a strong following in Chicago as well as some incredibly talented radicals, including General Baker and Abdul Alkalimat. More importantly, even if we acknowledge that the number of activists has dwindled substantially since the mid-1970s, the individuals who stayed in those movements remained committed to black liberation, even if their strategies and tactics proved insensitive or wrong-headed. Anyone who knows anything about politics knows that Jesse Jackson's 1984 presidential campaign was overrun by a rainbow coalition of Maoists, or that a variety of Maoist organizations were represented in the National Black Independent Political Party. In other words, now that so many American liberals are joining the backlash against poor black people and affirmative action, either by their active participation or their silence, some of these self-proclaimed revolutionaries are still willing to "move mountains" in the service of black folk. The most tragic and heroic example comes from Greensboro, North

Carolina, where five members of the Communist Workers Party (formerly the Workers Viewpoint Organization) were murdered by Klansmen and Nazis during an anti-Klan demonstration on November 3, 1979.

The fact remains, however, that the heyday of black Maoism has passed. The reasons are varied, having to do with the overall decline of black radicalism, the self-destructive nature of sectarian politics, and China's disastrous foreign policy decisions vis-à-vis Africa and the Third World. Besides, most of the self-described black Maoists in our story—at least the most honest ones—probably owe their greatest intellectual debt to Du Bois, Fanon, Malcolm X, Che Guevara, and Harold Cruse, not to mention Stalin and Lenin. But Mao Zedong and the Chinese revolution left an indelible imprint on black radical politics—an imprint whose impact we've only begun to explore in this essay. At a moment when a group of nonaligned countries sought to challenge the political binaries created by cold war politics, when African nationalists tried to plan for a postcolonial future, when Fidel Castro and a handful of fatigue-clad militants did the impossible, when southern lunch counters and northern ghettoes became theaters for a new revolution, there stood China—the most powerful "colored" nation on earth.

Mao's China, along with the Cuban revolution and African nationalism, internationalized the black revolution in profound ways. Mao gave black radicals a non-Western model of Marxism that placed greater emphasis on local conditions and historical circumstances than on canonical texts. China's Great Leap Forward challenged the idea that the march to socialism must take place in stages, or that one must wait patiently for the proper objective conditions to move ahead. For many young radicals schooled in student-based social democracy and/or antiracist politics, "consciousness-raising" in the Maoist style of criticism and self-criticism was a powerful alternative to bourgeois democracy. But consciousness-raising was more than propaganda work; it was intellectual labor in the context of revolutionary practice. "All genuine knowledge originates in direct experience," Mao said in his widely read essay "On Practice" (1937). This idea of knowledge deriving dialectically from practice to theory to practice empowered radicals to question the expertise of sociologists, psychologists, economists, etc., whose grand pronouncements on the causes of poverty and racism often went unchallenged. Thus in an age of liberal technocrats, Maoists—from black radical circles to the women's liberation movement—sought to overturn bourgeois notions of expertise. They developed analyses, engaged in debates, and published journals, newspapers, position papers, pamphlets, and even books. And while they rarely agreed with one another, they saw themselves as producers of new knowledge. They believed, as Mao put it, that "these ideas turn into a material force which changes society and changes the world."[114]

Ideas alone don't change the world, however; people do. And having the willingness and energy to change the world requires more than the correct analysis and direct engagement with the masses: instead, it takes faith and will. Here Maoists have much in common with some very old black biblical traditions. After all, if little David can take Goliath with just a slingshot, certainly a "single spark can start a prairie fire."[115]

Notes

We would like to thank Ernest Allen, Harold Cruse, the late Vicki Garvin, Michael Goldfield, Fred Wei-Han Ho, Geoffrey Jacques, Sid Lemelle, Josh Lyons, Eric Mann and Liann Hurst Mann, Manning Marable, David Roediger, Tim Schermerhorn, Akinyele Umoja, Alan Wald, Billy Watkins, Komozi Woodard, and Marilyn Young for their insights, recollections, and advice. Finally we wish to express our deepest gratitude to the staff at the Tamiment Collection at NYU, especially Andrew Lee and Jane Latour. A slightly different version of this essay first appeared in *Souls* 1, no. 4 (fall 1999): 6–41; we are grateful to the editors of *Souls* for granting permission to publish this revised version.

1 The Coup, "Dig It," *Kill My Landlord* (Wild Pitch Records, 1993).

2 Mao Tse-Tung [Mao Zedong], *Quotations from Chairman Mao Tse-Tung* (Beijing: Foreign Language Press, 1966).

3 Elaine Brown, *A Taste of Freedom* (New York: Doubleday Books, 1992), 231–32.

4 Huey Newton, *Revolutionary Suicide* (New York: Ballantine Books, 1973), 110.

5 W. E. B. Du Bois, *The Autobiography of W. E. B. Du Bois,* ed. Herbert Aptheker (New York: International Publishers, 1968), 404.

6 In fact, several organizations (namely, Ray O. Light, the Communist Workers Party, the Black Vanguard Party, the Maoist Internationalist Movement, and others) are only mentioned in passing or are omitted altogether for lack of information. We recognize that only a book-length study can do justice to this story. Fortunately, since the first version of this essay appeared in 1999, Max Elbaum published an excellent and comprehensive study of anti-revisionist movements in the United States. See Elbaum, *Revolution in the Air: Sixties Radicals Turn to Lenin, Mao and Che* (London: Verso, 2002).

7 A. Belden Fields, *Trotskyism and Maoism: Theory and Practice in France and the United States* (New York: Praeger, 1988), 16–19.

8   The allegory in *Quotations from Mao Tse-Tung* titled "The Foolish Old Man Who Removed the Mountains" instilled a missionary zeal in many radicals that enabled them to jump quickly to the question of guerrilla war, as if revolution were immanent. Of course, chapters of the Little Red Book such as "People's War," "The People's Army," "Education and the Training of Troops," and "Revolutionary Heroism" certainly helped promote the idea that "political power grows out of the barrel of a gun," despite the fact that efforts to apply China's experience to the United States contradicts Mao's own argument that each revolution must grow out of its own specific circumstances.

9   Mao Tse-Tung, *Quotations*, iv.

10 Mao Tse-Tung, *Statement Supporting the American Negroes in Their Just Struggle Against Racial Discrimination in the United States* (Beijing: Foreign Languages Press, 1963), 2.

11 John Oliver Killens, *Black Man in the New China* (Los Angeles: U.S.-China People's Friendship Association, 1976), 10.

12 Philip Snow, "China and Africa: Consensus and Camouflage," in *Chinese Foreign Policy: Theory and Practice*, edited by Thomas W. Robinson and David Shambaugh (New York: Clarendon Press, 1994), 285–99.

13 Fields, *Trotskyism and Maoism*, 213. Silber criticized Chinese policy in Angola where the Chinese were on the same side as the South African apartheid regime and the United States. Chinese foreign policy was a hindrance to the American Maoists in a variety of contexts, not just southern Africa: China's reception of Nixon while U.S. bombs continued to drop on Vietnam and its support for Pinochet in Chile are two particularly striking examples.

14 Vertical Files on the Provisional Organizing Committee, Hammer and Steel, and the Progressive Labor Party, Tamiment Collection, Bobst Library, New York University.

15 Amiri Baraka, *The Autobiography of LeRoi Jones/Amiri Baraka* (New York: Freundlich Books, 1984), 220; Fields, *Trotskyism and Maoism*, 185; Bill Epton, conversation with Robin D. G. Kelley, January 2000.

16 Fields, *Trotskyism and Maoism*, 185–97. See also Jim O'Brien, *American Leninism in the 1970s* (Somerville, Mass.: New England Free Press, n.d.).

17 Van Gosse, *Where the Boys Are: Cuba, Cold War America and the Making of a New Left* (London: Verso, 1993), 147–48; Brenda Gayle Plummer, *Rising Wind: Black Americans and U.S. Foreign Affairs, 1935–1960* (Chapel Hill: University of North Carolina Press, 1996), 285–97.

18 Harold Cruse, "Negro Nationalism's New Wave," *New Leader* (1962), in *Rebellion or Revolution?* (New York: Morrow, 1968), 73.

19 Harold Cruse, "Revolutionary Nationalism and the Afro-American" (1962), in *Rebellion or Revolution?* 74–75.

20 Baraka, *Autobiography*, 184; LeRoi Jones [Baraka], "Cuba Libre" (1966), in *Home: Social Essays* (Hopewell, N.J.: Ecco Press, 1998), 11–62; Komozi Wood-

ard, A *Nation within a Nation: Amiri Baraka (LeRoi Jones) and Black Power Politics* (Chapel Hill: University of North Carolina Press, 1998), 52–63.

21 Vicki Garvin, interview by the authors, January 16, 1996. Unpublished speech by Garvin in the authors' collection.

22 Vertical file on Vicki Garvin, Tamiment Collection, Bobst Library, New York University.

23 Newton, *Revolutionary Suicide*, 70.

24 Ibid., 111.

25 On Robert Williams, see Timothy B. Tyson, *Radio Free Dixie: Robert Williams and the Roots of Black Power* (Chapel Hill: University of North Carolina Press, 1999); Marcellus C. Barksdale, "Robert Williams and the Indigenous Civil Rights Movement in Monroe, North Carolina, 1961," *Journal of Negro History* 69 (spring 1984): 73–89; and Williams's own writings and interviews, particularly Robert F. Williams, *Negroes with Guns* (New York: Marzani and Munsell, 1962); Robert Williams, *Listen, Brother* (New York: World View Publishers, 1968); "Interview: Robert Williams," *Black Scholar* 1, no. 7 (May 1970): 5–18; and Kalamu ya Salaam, "Robert Williams: Crusader for International Solidarity," *Black Collegian* 8, no. 3 (January-February, 1978): 53–60. See also the excellent article by Timothy B. Tyson, "Robert Williams, 'Black Power,' and the Roots of the African American Freedom Struggle," *Journal of American History* 85, no. 2 (September 1998): 540–70. For discussions of armed self-defense movements during the civil rights era, see Akinyele O. Umoja, "The Ballot and the Bullet: A Comparative Analysis of Armed Resistance in the Civil Rights Movement," *Journal of Black Studies*, 29, no. 4. (March 1999): 558–78; Anita K. Foeman, "Gloria Richardson: Breaking the Mold," *Journal of Black Studies* 26 (1996): 604–15; and Lance Hill, *The Deacons for Defense: Armed Resistance and the Civil Rights Movement* (Chapel Hill: University of North Carolina Press, 2004), which appeared after the first version of this essay.

26 *Crusader* 2, no. 6 (August 20, 1960); *Crusader* 2, no. 21 (December 31, 1960).

27 Williams, *Negroes with Guns*, 120.

28 "Interview: Robert Williams," 5.

29 Maxwell C. Stanford, "Revolutionary Action Movement (RAM): A Case Study of an Urban Revolutionary Movement in Western Capitalist Society," (M.A. thesis, Atlanta University, 1986), 75–80.

30 Donald Freeman, "The Cleveland Story," *Liberator* 3, no. 6 (June 1963): 7, 18.

31 See Gerald Horne, *Communist Front? The Civil Rights Congress, 1946–1956* (London: Fairleigh Dickinson University Press, 1988).

32 Ernest Allen Jr., interview by the authors, June 8, 1997; Huey P. Newton, *Revolutionary Suicide*, 71–72.

33 *Crusader* 8, no. 4 (May 1967); Maxwell C. Stanford, "Revolutionary Action Movement," 75–80.

34 Michael Simmons and Tony Monteiro, conversation with Robin D. G. Kelley, October 24, 1998, Philadelphia.

35 Stanford, "Revolutionary Action Movement," 197; "Queen Mother" Audley Moore, interview with Mark Naison and Ruth Prago, Oral History of the American Left, Tamiment Library, New York University; Grace Lee Boggs, *Living for Change* (Minneapolis: University of Minnesota Press, 1997), 134; Stanford, "Revolutionary Action Movement," 40; Tim Schermerhorm, interview by Betsy Esch, May 11, 1998.

36 Max Stanford, "We Can Win!" *Black America* (fall 1964), 22.

37 Stanford, "The Revolutionary Action Movement," 110.

38 Max Stanford, "Soul Sisters," ca. 1969, RAM Papers.

39 Mao Tse-Tung, *Quotations*, 256, 269.

40 "Interview: Robert Williams," 14.

41 "The 12 Point Program of RAM (Revolutionary Action Movement) 1964," May-June 1964. RAM Papers; Max Stanford, "Projects and Problems of the Revolutionary Movement" (1964), "Revolutionary Action Movement," General File, Tamiment Library, NYU.

42 Rolland Snellings (Askia Muhammad Touré), "Afro American Youth and the Bandung World," *Liberator* 5, no. 2 (February 1965): 4; RAM, *The World Black Revolution*, RAM Papers. See also Don Freeman, "Black Youth and Afro-American Liberation," *Black America* (fall 1964): 15–16.

43 RAM, *The World Black Revolution*, 5. Echoing the *Communist Manifesto*, the pamphlet begins, "All over Africa, Asia, South, Afro and Central America a revolution is haunting and sweeping."

44 RAM, *The World Black Revolution*, 29.

45 RAM, *The World Black Revolution*, 31. See also Max Stanford, "The African American War of National Liberation," ca. fall 1965, RAM Papers.

46 See Boggs, *Living for Change*, 134–37.

47 R. Sackett, "Plotting a War on Whitey: Extremists Set for Violence," *Life* 60 (June 10, 1966): 100–100B; D. MacDonald, "Politics: Black Power," *Esquire* 65 (October 1967): 38; Gary Wills, "Second Civil War," *Esquire* 69 (March 1968): 71–78.

48 Harlem Branch of the Progressive Labor Party, "The Plot Against Black America" (pamphlet, 1965), Vertical File, Tamiment Collection, Bobst Library, NYU. See also A. B. Spellman, "The Legacy of Malcolm X," *Liberator* 5, no. 6 (June 1965): 13, which also challenges the press's attacks on RAM.

49 *Afro-American*, July 1, 1967; Stanford, "Revolutionary Action Movement," 210–15; "Interview: Robert Williams," 5–7, 14.

50 Dan Georgakas and Marvin Surkin, *I Do Mind Dying: A Study in Urban Revolution* (New York: St. Martin's Press, 1975), 17; Stanford, "Revolutionary Action Movement," 82. See also John C. Leggett, *Class, Race, and Labor: Working-Class Consciousness in Detroit* (New York: Oxford University Press, 1968); James A. Geschwender, *Class, Race, and Worker Insurgency: The League of Revolutionary Black Workers* (Cambridge: Cambridge University Press, 1977), for studies of DRUM and the League of Revolutionary Black Workers.

51 John Watson, interview by George Rawick, *Radical America* (July-August 1968): 31. Watson was referring to a pamphlet written by Lenin in 1903 entitled "Where to Begin," which preceded the more well-known "What Is to Be Done?"

52 Georgakas and Surkin, *I Do Mind Dying*, 27.

53 Geoffrey Jacques, interview by Robin D. G. Kelley, December 4, 1995.

54 From the film *Finally Got the News* by Stewart Bird, Rene Lichtman, and Peter Gessner (First Run Icarus Films, 1970).

55 Ernest Allen Jr., interview with the authors, June 8, 1997.

56 James Forman, *The Black Manifesto*; James Forman, *The Making of Black Revolutionaries* (Washington, D.C.: Open Hand Publishers, 1985).

57 Rosalyn Baxandall, correspondence to Robin D. G. Kelley, March 10, 1999.

58 From the film *Finally Got the News*.

59 Paul Sweezy and Leo Huberman, "The Cultural Revolution in China," *Monthly Review* (January 1967): 17.

60 Vicki Garvin, interview by the authors, January 16, 1996.

61 Mao Tse-Tung, *Statement by Comrade Mao Tse-Tung, Chairman of the Central Committee of the Communist Party of China, in Support of the Afro-American Struggle Against Violent Repression, April 6, 1968* (Beijing: Foreign Languages Press, 1968).

62 "Interview with Bobby Seale from Radical Education Project," in *An Introduction to the Black Panther Party* (Ann Arbor, Mich.: Radical Education Project, 1969), 26.

63 Newton, *Revolutionary Suicide*, 70.

64 Eldridge Cleaver, *On the Ideology of the Black Panther Party* (pamphlet, 1968), Black Panther Party, Organizational File, Tamiment Collection, Bobst Library, NYU.

65 Radical Education Project, *An Introduction to the Black Panther Party*, 19, 26.

66 Eldridge Cleaver, "National Liberation in the Black Colony," Black Panther Organizational File, Tamiment Collection, Bobst Library, NYU.

67 George Jackson, *Soledad Brother: The Prison Letters of George Jackson* (New York: Coward-McCann, 1970); George Jackson, *Blood in My Eye* (New York: Random House, 1972).

68 Sid Lemelle, interview by Robin D. G. Kelley, November 11, 1995.

69 Mao Tse-Tung, *Quotations*, 298; Fields, *Trotskyism and Maoism*, 197.

70 Brown, *A Taste of Freedom*, 304.

71 There is a lot of excellent work documenting the role of black women in the Black Panther Party. See, for example, Tracye Matthews, " 'No One Ever Asks What a Man's Role in the Revolution Is': Gender and Sexual Politics in the Black Panther Party, 1966–1971" (Ph.D. diss., University of Michigan, 1998); Angela Le Blanc-Ernest, "Surviving Revolution: A History of the Community Programs of the Black Panther Party for Self-Defense, 1966–1982" (Ph.D. diss., Stanford University, 2000); Charles Jones, ed., *The Black Panther Party Reconsidered* (Baltimore: Black Classic Press, 1998); and Kathleen Cleaver and

George N. Katsiaficas, eds., *Liberation, Imagination, and The Black Panther Party: A New Look at the Panthers and Their Legacy* (New York: Routledge, 2001).

72 Michelle Gibbs, interview by Robin D. G. Kelley, April 26, 1996.

73 For this insight we are grateful to Rosalyn Baxandall, a historian and participant in radical feminist and Left struggles.

74 Quoted in Brown, *A Taste of Freedom*, 313.

75 Ibid., 281

76 Mao Tse-Tung, *Mao Tse-Tung on Art and Literature* (Beijing: Foreign Languages Press, 1960), 144.

77 Mao Tse-Tung, *Statement by Comrade Mao Tse-Tung, Chairman of the Central Committee of the Communist Party of China, in Support of the Afro-American Struggle Against Violent Repression*, 2.

78 Joseph Stalin, *Marxism and the National Question* (Calcutta: New Book Centre, 1975), 11.

79 Communist League, *Dialectics of the Development of the Communist League* (Los Angeles: Communist League, 1972) [mimeograph in author's collection]; Sid Lemelle, interview by Robin Kelley, November 11, 1995; William Watkins, interview by Robin D. G. Kelley, October 11, 1995; Fields, *Trotskyism and Maoism*, 200.

80 Harry Haywood, "Toward a Revolutionary Position on the Negro Question" (Provisional Organizing Committee for the Reconstruction of a Marxist-Leninist Party, 1959, mimeograph); Nelson Peery, *The Negro National Question* (Chicago: Workers Press, 1975 [1972]).

81 Peery, *The Negro National Question*, 82–83.

82 Ibid., 80.

83 "The Communist Party (Marxist-Leninist) and the October League," Vertical Files, Tamiment Collection, Bobst Library, NYU.

84 "The Negro National Question," founding document from the Communist Party (Marxist-Leninist), Vertical Files, Tamiment Collection, Bobst Library, NYU.

85 The Revolutionary Union, Vertical Files, Tamiment Collection, Bobst Library, NYU.

86 "The Revolutionary Communist League (MLM) and the League of Revolutionary Struggle (M-L) Unite!" *Forward: Journal of Marxism-Leninism-Mao Zedong Thought* 3 (January 1980): 29–38; Woodard, *A Nation within a Nation*, 63–254.

87 "The Revolutionary Communist League (MLM) and the League of Revolutionary Struggle (M-L) Unite!" 89–90; Woodard, *A Nation within a Nation*, 219–54.

88 William Watkins, interview with Robin D. G. Kelley, October 11, 1995.

89 "The Revolutionary Communist League (MLM) and the League of Revolutionary Struggle (M-L) Unite!" 80–81; Rod Bush, *"We Are Not What We Seem": Black Nationalism and Class Struggle in the American Century* (New York: New York University Press, 1999), 211–13; Woodard, *A Nation within a Nation*, 173–80.

90 See Philip Snow, *The Star Raft: China's Encounter with Africa* (Ithaca, N.Y.: Cornell University Press, 1989).

91 Baraka, *Autobiography,* 298; Imamu Amiri Baraka, "Revolutionary Party: Revolutionary Ideology" (speech delivered at the Congress of Afrikan People, Midwestern Conference, March 31, 1974), Vertical Files, Tamiment Collection, Bobst Library, NYU.

92 Komozi Woodard, interview by Robin D. G. Kelley, December 12, 1995; "The Revolutionary Communist League (MLM) and the League of Revolutionary Struggle (M-L) Unite!" 100, 121.

93 Baraka, "Revolutionary Party," 5.

94 Robert Williams, "Reconstitute Afro-American Art to Remold Black Souls," *Crusader* 9, no. 1 (July 1967): 1.

95 Frantz Fanon, *The Wretched of the Earth* (New York: Grove Press, 1963).

96 Ron Karenga, "Black Cultural Nationalism," in *The Black Aesthetic,* edited by Addison Gayle (Garden City, N.J.: Anchor Books, 1971), 32.

97 "Jones-Karenga Hustle: Cultural 'Rebels' Foul Us Up," in *Black Liberation,* 1969, n.p. (pamphlet containing articles by the Progressive Labor Party, originally published in their paper *Challenge*).

98 Radical Education Project, *The Black Book* (Ann Arbor, Mich.: Radical Education Project, ca. 1970).

99 Kwame Nkrumah, *Axioms of Kwame Nkrumah: Freedom Fighters Edition* (New York: International Publishers, 1969).

100 Ibid., 114.

101 *The Call,* September 1972, 6.

102 "Jones-Karenga Hustle," n.p.

103 *The Call,* September 1973, 3.

104 Killens, *Black Man in the New China,* 18.

105 Ibid., 19.

106 Baraka, "Revolutionary Party," 2.

107 "The Revolutionary Communist League (MLM) and the League of Revolutionary Struggle (M-L) Unite!" 94.

108 Ibid., 94–95; Baraka, *Autobiography,* 301.

109 Baraka, *Autobiography,* 89–94.

110 Amiri Baraka, *Hard Facts* (New York: William Morrow, 1976), 15.

111 Mao Tse-Tung, "Talks at the Yenan Forum on Art and Literature," in *Mao Tse-Tung on Art and Literature,* 100.

112 Amiri Baraka, *The Motion of History and Other Plays* (New York: William Morrow, 1978), 13–14.

113 Ibid.

114 Mao Tse-tung, "Where Do Correct Ideas Come From?" *Four Essays on Philosophy* (Peking: Foreign Languages Press, 1968).

115 Mao Tse-tung, *A Single Spark Can Start a Prairie Fire* (Peking: Foreign Languages Press, 1953).

Fred Ho

The Inspiration of Mao and the Chinese Revolution on the Black Liberation Movement and the Asian Movement on the East Coast

Presentation written for the panel "Mao, the Black Panthers and the Third World Strike," as part of the thirtieth anniversary conference on the Third World Strike, University of California, Berkeley, April 8, 1999.

The Chinese revolution led by the Chinese Communist Party and Mao Zedong has been a great source of inspiration and example to Third World peoples both internationally and within the United States. The Chinese Revolution of 1949 established the Peoples Republic of China as a socialist government among one quarter of the world's population, a population that is "nonwhite."

Relative to the Bolshevik revolution that established the Soviet Union, the Chinese Revolution had major differences. As a Third World country, China had a history of colonial penetration and domination at the hands of the U.S., Western European, and Japanese imperialism. Compared to India, virtually all of Africa, and much of Latin America and the Caribbean, China was never fully colonized. China was a semicolony—its major port cities had come under control of competing foreign powers. These foreign concessions obeyed no Chinese laws and were islands of privilege that humiliated Chinese sovereignty.

Unlike Russia and other Western countries, China's industrial proletariat was tiny—less than 1 percent of the population. Like the rest of the Third World, most of China's enormous laboring population was comprised of peasantry. This is why Chinese communist historiography has characterized China as a "semicolonial, semifeudal" society.

As members of an oppressed Third World country the Chinese people were subjected to racist stereotyping—notably, deemed inferior and inscrutable—and thus were seen as in need of Western Christian missionary salvation, despite its long history as a highly advanced civilization. China confounded Karl Marx who, incapable of explaining China's socioeconomic history in the formulation of Western European social history, devised the transhistorical category of the Asiatic Mode of Production in a circular explanation for China's and India's "Asiatic despotism"—that is, to explain why such societies, even with their with long histories as highly developed civilizations and state bureaucracies, nonetheless were not capable of advancing to capitalism on their own. In this view, Marx was guilty of the prevailing orientalist and Eurocentric scholarship.

The Chinese revolution could not be explained in Eurocentric Marxist formulation. It was a massive peasantry led by a communist party, with a leader, Mao Zedong, who advanced the concept of a united front against imperialism for a national democratic revolution that would lead to socialism. Eurocentric white chauvinist Marxists and Trotskyists would criticize and condemn the Chinese revolution as petit-bourgeois nationalism, and its leader Mao as a "nationalist." To this day, virtually all Trotskyists, the sell-out Communist Party USA and its ideological adherents (such as members of the nonrevolutionary Committees of Correspondence) who, despite breaking with the tyrannical and senile CPUSA old guard, still cannot accept Mao or the Chinese revolution as the true extension of Marxism-Leninism (Angela Davis is one example).

But for most of us, what the white chauvinist socialist Left thinks isn't important. The Chinese revolution and Mao inspired most of the world to seek revolutionary socialism and Marxist ideology, because most of the world was the victim of Western imperialist superexploitation and brutal national oppression. Most Third World workers have time and time again been sold out by the white socialist and workers movement, whether it be the classic case of the French workers and peasants in the 1950s, or the 1960s with the CPUSA calling Malcolm X a police agent and denouncing the Black Panthers, or the Trotskyist parties opposing the Vietnamese national liberation struggle and supporting only the demand to "bring the boys home," thus valuing the lives of white boys over Asian peoples. Even today, the term national liberation is equated and dismissed as "nationalism" (deemed a dirty word) by these racist socialists and fake leftists.

Most of the New Left in the United States emerged and demarcated itself from the Old Left (primarily the CPUSA and the Trotskyist Socialist Workers Party) in 1969. Several momentous historical factors propelled this emergence: the questions of supporting the Vietnamese national liberation struggle against U.S. imperialism; the rise of the Black Panther Party and the re-raising of the gun into U.S. Left politics or continuing Malcolm X's prophetic question of the bullet vs. the ballot; and the Cultural Revolution in China in which a tremendous wave of militant radicalism was being spearheaded by students and youth.

Malcolm X had perceptively remarked (and I'll paraphrase) that the once-common racist slur "a Chinaman's chance"—meaning no chance at all—had gone the way of oblivion as the Chinese now had more chance than most of the dark peoples of the world, having made a revolution, kicked out the white imperialist, and created its own nuclear device, joining the up-to-then all-white-boys nuclear club, pushing the question of removing the pipsqueak runt of a country called Taiwan out of the United Nations and putting the PRC into its rightful seat as representing the Chinese people. China could be free

All of the great twentieth-century radical and revolutionary African American activists and artists have extolled and looked to China. In the late 1920s the great radical poet Langston Hughes, inspired by and supporting the upsurge of Chinese workers' struggles, wrote the magnificent poem "ROAR CHINA ROAR!" Paul Robeson learned to speak Chinese and often sang the revolutionary Chinese anthem "CHI LAI!" ("Rise Up!"). W. E. B. Du Bois and his family moved to China, where Du Bois eventually died. The fugitive Robert F. Williams, who took up armed self-defense against the KKK in North Carolina and was forced to flee the United States, ended up in China for a very long stay. There he raised his two sons, both of whom speak Chinese fluently. The Williams family members were treated as honored political refugees in the PRC. Upon Williams's request, Chairman Mao issued two profound statements in support of the black American liberation struggle.

The first statement was made in 1963 to condemn the rise of racist violence against the U.S. civil rights movement. The final sentence of this historic statement sent profound reverberations through the quickly radicalizing sectors of the black struggle. As Mao stated: "The evil system of colonialism and imperialism arose and throve with the enslavement of Negroes and the trade in Negroes, and it will surely come to its end with the complete emancipation of the black people." Along with many others, I have interpreted Mao's statement as indicating that the struggle for black liberation, and the liberation of oppressed nations and nationalities in general, is objectively a revolutionary struggle with or without the support or unity of white oppressor nation workers.

The second statement was made on April 6, 1968, after the heinous assassination of Dr. Martin Luther King Jr. As black ghettos across the United States began to erupt in violent rebellion, Mao made his famous statement in support of the Afro-American Struggle Against Violent Repression, in which he called for total support for black liberation "to end the rule of the U.S. monopoly capitalist class." By the end of summer 1968, over one hundred U.S. cities had gone up in smoke. Robert Williams, exiled in China, was conferred the status of president in exile by the Republic of New Afrika, a pro-nationhood radical black activist movement in the U.S. Many years later, he would finally return to the United States to take a job teaching Chinese studies at a small college in Michigan. He died in 1997.

By the late 1960s in the United States a New Left had begun to emerge. It rejected several key positions of the Old (white) Left: namely, it supported China as a socialist state and Mao as a genuine Marxist-Leninist and rejected the Soviet Union as having turned into being a social-imperialist power (meaning socialism in words, imperialism in deeds) after its invasion of Hungary, Poland, and Czechoslovakia and its maneuvers to turn Third World liberation organization and newly independent countries into Soviet puppets. The New Left was fervently revolutionary and rejected the electoral politics and mainstreaming as the CPUSA succumbed from the terror of McCarthyism and its own internal rising reformism and liquidationism. Further, the New Left looked seriously toward the Third World, including Third

World peoples inside its own borders (whom I prefer to call oppressed nationalities instead of the depoliticized mainstream term "people of color"). By the early 1970s, many in the New Left focused on building a new revolutionary communist party. *New Left*

I won't discuss the critical importance of China, Mao, and the Black Panthers as others are in a better position to do so. Instead I wish to address some important examples on the East Coast that reflect this connection and catalyst.

In the early 1970s in New York City, a new revolutionary Asian American organization emerged, comprised mostly of college students. They took the name I Wor Kuen, the Cantonese name for the Boxers who were part of an anti-Manchu and anti-imperialist uprising in China at the turn of the century. At first I Wor Kuen described itself as an anti-imperialist revolutionary nationalist organization, though its program, closely modeled after the Black Panther Party's 10-Point Program, did call for socialism. The Serve the People programs started by Wor Kuen were modeled on the Panthers' Survival Programs. I Wor Kuen soon merged with a Bay Area revolutionary Asian American group, the Red Guard Party, and became national IWK.

At several college campuses, IWK led the demand for Asian studies as part of the call for Ethnic or Third World studies overall. The first Asian studies curriculum on the East Coast was at the City College of New York in Harlem, where IWK played a major role. A quick look at the manifestos of all these early ethnic studies programs reveals how revolutionary they were, and how much of that revolutionary mission has been totally gutted today. Here are some of the main features in the revolutionary vision for Asian and Third World studies: *Asian studies*

1   The curriculum serves the people and promotes revolution. These programs were supposed to be liberated zones to wage the protracted struggle against the mainstream racist, sexist, and elitist academy. Instead of producing bureaucrats and yuppies to serve the system, Third World studies would produce revolutionaries with skills and expertise for the movement. The Asian Student Unions, Movimiento Estudiantil Chicano de Atzlán (MECHA), Black Student Unions, etc., were to be the student wing of the revolutionary liberation movements. They were to be the incubators for future organizers and warriors. In discrediting and eliminating Marxist and revolutionary theory, postmodernism was promoted in the 1980s and

early 1990s as a pretentious justification for hyperindividualism and political inactivity by the current crop of anti-activist intellectuals who want to pose as radical. Here I am specifically naming, among others, bell hooks, Tricia Rose, Andrew Ross, and the whole bankrupt gamut of what has fashionably become "cultural studies"—that is, studying culture by people who can't create culture.

2   The main way a revolutionary education was to happen was through student-community control over these institutions. The first to be eliminated by the administration and their professorial career-climbing lackeys was the community. So-called "outsiders" were accused of lowering academic standards and wanting political control. It is true that many horror stories from both sides can be cited—of students being allowed to pass courses simply by political membership, or of progressive faculty being denied tenure and fired due to red-baiting. Whatever the case, the key questions of what standards and who creates them were clearly decided by the administration in favor of what we see today. People like myself, who have proven our revolutionary commitment and intellectual/artistic excellence in the real world, without a Ph.D., won't get hired. On the other hand, I now have no desire for a faculty job because I'm having more fun and doing more of what I want outside of academia. Not only am I self-taught in my professional career, I paid off my mortgage three years ago at the age of thirty-eight. Now, how many professors can match that? And I'm still a revolutionary!

education is a business 3   These institutions, perhaps too naively we thought, could direct resources and talents back to the oppressed communities. Now they've become self-perpetuating and career-aggrandizing vehicles.

The New Left was engaged in many fierce battles, both with the external enemy and with its own members. One of the key questions it fought over was what is called the National Question, or the question of how liberation for the oppressed nations and nationalities in the United States would be won. This issue continues to be debated. Most of the U.S. oppressed nationality Left started out as anti-imperialist, revolutionary nationalists. But many quickly moved to Marxism, and certainly the prestige and weight of socialist China and Mao had much influence. I can remember this period in the early 1970s, the great debates between nationalism and Marxism, because I started as a yellow revolutionary nationalist. I strongly identified with the revolutionary thrust of the black liberation movement, Malcolm X, Robert Williams, the Black Panther Party, and the African Liberation Support Committee (ALSC).

Let me now discuss the ALSC, which although it was one of the most significant projects in the history of the U.S. Left in the twentieth century it is now virtually forgotten and given almost no attention or recognition by today's social movement scholars or Left historians.

While the ALSC was short-lived, spanning the years 1972 to 1978, it was possibly the center of anti-imperialist, pan-Africanist motion in the black liberation struggle in the United States. It gathered together a broad ideological range including Karenga, Haki Madhubuti, Amiri Baraka, Abdul Akalimat, Mark Smith, and many others. In May 1972, as a part of Malcolm X's birthday, the ALSC sponsored a mass demonstration that became African Liberation Day in Washington, D.C. Over forty thousand workers, students, youths, and activists came to support the African liberation struggles in Guinea-Bissau/Cape Verde Islands, Angola, Mozambique, Zimbabwe (then Rhodesia), Azania (South Africa), and Namibia (formerly South-West Africa). As the black liberation struggle moved to the Left, so too did the African American working class assume anti-imperialist positions. African American dockworkers in North Carolina and South Carolina boycotted Rhodesian chrome, refusing to unload it from South African ships. The campaign "Ban the Krugerrand" came out of this movement. stop funding apartheid

In June 1974, the Sixth Pan-African Congress was hosted by Julius Nyerere in Tanzania, a country that had been friendly to and hosted many an exiled-African liberation movement. Black activists from the United States attended the event and were sternly lectured by their African revolutionary brothers and sisters, who were engaged in life-and-death armed struggle, to check their narrow nationalism and to check out scientific socialism. In a few months, former nationalists like Baraka would discard nationalism and turn to Marxism-Leninism-Mao Zedong thought. One of the most dynamic organizers and theoreticians in this transition from nationalism to Marxism was Owusu Sadauki, a college activist turned Marxist and factory worker in North Carolina and leader of Revolutionary Workers League—a black-originated now-Marxist organization. Others were making the move to Marxism, including the Dodge Revolutionary Movement (DRUM) in Detroit and other black auto worker–based radical groups, which came together to form the Black Workers Congress. By 1975, the largest cultural nationalist organization (with chapters in over thirteen cities)—the Congress of Afri-kan Peoples under Baraka's leadership—would adopt MLMTT (Marxism-Leninism-Mao Tse-tung Thought) and become the Revolutionary Commu-nist League (RCL). At this time I was only a young teenager, but I attended every meeting in this great debate, vigorously trying to defend nationalism against Marxism as a "white boys" ideology.

During this time, Stokely Carmichael would become Kwame Toure and take up Pan-African scientific socialism with its strange political orientation of primarily focusing on the mother continent and the struggle of U.S. blacks as secondary and only to be supportive of struggles on the mother continent.

But even the most die-hard cultural nationalists still gave props to China. Karenga learned to speak Chinese and has visited China on a number of oc-casions. The poet Sonia Sanchez, who, when I first studied under her, was into the Nation of Islam, had gone on an American delegation to the PRC in 1972 as one of the trips sponsored by the U.S.-China Peoples Friendship Association, a mass movement that favored recognition of the PRC and pro-moted pro-China opinion in the United States. Joining Sonia was another prominent Black American writer, Earl Ofari, who wrote *The Myth of Black Capitalism.*

In 1977, with support from the USCPFA, the all-black cultural nationalist Council in Independent Black Institutions brought the first all-black delega-tion to the PRC after the Black Panthers' historic visit in 1971. These were hard-core cultural nationalists who were building totally independent insti-tutions such as schools, community centers, and communal businesses and presses. The delegation of twenty included Jitu Weusi, the founder and leader of The East, an independent community-controlled school and cul-tural center in black Brooklyn; Kalamu Ya Salaam, the writer/activist/editor of *The Black Collegian* magazine and member of Adhiamma, a cultural nationalist communal-activist group in New Orleans; and members from Haki Madhubuti's Institute for Positive Education in Chicago with its pub-lishing wing, Third World Press, the most successful black-owned indepen-dent publishing house.

These were cultural nationalists who disagreed adamantly with Marxism but who recognized that socialist China had eliminated illiteracy, wiped out drug addiction (when before 1949 one out of four Chinese men were opium addicts), and created miraculous social changes in a Third World country without any white Western help. Indeed, the Chinese had extended much aid to other Third World countries, including sending its own engineers and workers who ate, worked, and slept alongside Africans in the building of the TanZam railway that connected the island of Zanzibar with the African mainland in Tanzania. African guerrillas also secretly trained for armed struggle inside the PRC.

Unlike today, where divisions and mutual stereotypes are held between African Americans and Asian Americans, back in the days of greater "Third World Unity," much of the black nationalist leadership looked at Asians as Third World brothers and sisters. The force of China's example played a major factor in this attitude. *not competitive minority-ism*

It was Muhammad Ali, refusing the draft, who proclaimed: "No Vietnamese ever called me Nigger." A proud and glorious tradition of Afro Asian anti-imperialist solidarity has existed, from Ho Chi Minh spending time in Harlem as a student to a rap group today calling itself the Wu-Tang Clan after a Taoist anti-Manchu and anti-imperialist sect (though one would hope these rappers would be more politically conscious).

Before closing, I want to state that I maintain that the two questions that distinguish revolution from reformism in the United States are:

1   The national question and recognizing the independent revolutionary character of Third World peoples' struggle; the need to reject forced assimilation and the falseness of integration—that is, the white chauvinist position that our struggles need to be validated by the inclusion of and proximity to white people and traditions.

2   The question of upholding Mao Zedong Thought as Marxism-Leninism *legitimacy at mercy of whiteness* applied to the struggle for national liberation against imperialism. By the late 1970s the U.S. anti-revisionist communist movement (which all started upholding China over the sell-out Soviet Union and its American shadow, the CPUSA), was unraveling in bitter disagreement over post-Mao China, and in my opinion, not so coincidentally rehabilitating the Soviet Union on international lines and adopting a thoroughly white chauvinist line domestically by totally liquidating the black nation and the Chicano nation and calling for a repellant socialist integrationism and assimilation. Condemning all nationalism as reactionary, narrow, and totally rejecting national consciousness, national identity, national pride in the context that our struggles are for liberation and not integration.

Last year I started my own cultural production company, Big Red Media, which produces the Sheroes Calendars and my recordings. The name Big Red comes from two of my most important political icons: Malcolm X, who was known as Big Red for being tall with reddish hair; and for Mao Zedong, who truly was a big Red.

Diane C. Fujino

The Black Liberation Movement and Japanese American Activism: The Radical Activism of Richard Aoki and Yuri Kochiyama

T his essay explores the impact of the black liberation movement on the radicalization of Japanese American activism in the 1960s. The case examples of Yuri Kochiyama, arguably the most influential Asian American activist to emerge in the 1960s, and Richard Aoki, a former leader of the Black Panther Party, are presented to examine the ways in which the revolutionary black movement affected the development of Japanese American radicalism. Two areas of this issue need further explanation. First, it was the radical black liberation or Black Power movement, rather than the civil rights movement, that exerted a radicalizing force. The black liberation movement developed in response to frustrations with the moderate goals and gains of the civil rights movement. By the early 1960s there were visible shifts toward revolutionary goals and increasingly militant tactics, and by the mid-1960s the radical black movement was flourishing.[1] It was in this historical context that Kochiyama's and Aoki's politics developed. Had they come to political consciousness in a different period, and had they not lived in working-class black communities, their ideological development and political participation most likely would have taken a different form.[2] Second, while I discuss the radicalization of these 1960s activists, it is more appropriate to frame this event as the *reemergence* of Japanese American radicalism. But the earlier radical organizing, particularly strong in the 1920s and 1930s, did not directly impact the 1960s activists.[3] In fact, most of these activists were not even aware of a preexisting Japanese American Left until after they became politically active and began to seek their roots. Nonetheless, that this history existed and that some of the Issei or older Nisei[4] radicals worked with the 1960s activists are facts that helped shape the latter's political development.[5] Moreover, experiences as Japanese Americans, notably in the World War II concentration camps, shaped their political consciousness, racial awareness, and ethnic identities. But, it was the black liberation movement that triggered the development of a radical consciousness.

black lib →
radical that

Impact of the Concentration Camps

The events of World War II had a dual effect on Japanese American radicalism. First and foremost, the state repression that culminated in the forced incarceration of 120,000 West Coast Japanese Americans along with internal contradictions within the U.S. Left combined to spell the demise of visible radical organizing. Moreover, the arrests and imprisonment of Issei community leaders immediately following Japan's bombing of Pearl Harbor created a vacuum of leadership in a period of crisis.[6] Into this void stepped the Japanese American Citizens League (JACL), the largest Nisei organization, with its ultra-patriotic, assimilationist, and political accommodationist beliefs. The JACL national leadership not only promoted a policy of cooperation with the U.S. government's evacuation orders, the organization also actively opposed any type of protest within the Japanese American community and pushed for the military enlistment of Japanese Americans. Some JACL leaders went so far as to gather intelligence on the Japanese American community—information that enabled the arrests of the Issei leaders.[7]

Prior to the 1940s, Japanese American leftists were particularly active in the Communist Party USA (CPUSA) and in the militant labor movements.

But by late 1941, internal contradictions within the CPUSA contributed to the disintegration of visible radical organizing. In 1940, in response to the Smith Act, the CPUSA decided to purge its immigrant membership and, following the December 1941 bombing of Pearl Harbor, to suspend all Japanese American members and their non-Japanese spouses. The rationale for suspending Japanese American members, Karl Yoneda contends, is that CPUSA General Secretary Earl Browder believed that "the best place for any Japanese fifth columnist to hide is within the Communist Party ranks and consequently no Japanese American should be kept in the Party while the war against Japan is going on."[8]

But the mistakes of the CPUSA went beyond membership purges. In following the dictates of the Soviet Communist Party and allying itself with President Roosevelt's policies, the CPUSA prioritized its fight against fascism, to the exclusion of any critical analysis of the war or of U.S. or European militarism. When World War II first began in 1939, the National Committee of the Communist Party declared: "The war that has broken out in Europe is a Second Imperialist War. . . . It is a war between rival imperialists for world domination." And the Communist Party sought to keep the United States out of the "Imperialist War."[9] But following Japan's attack on Pearl Harbor, the CPUSA immediately pledged complete support for the U.S. war effort. Consequently, the CPUSA failed to oppose the unconstitutional incarceration of West Coast Japanese Americans. The CPUSA further urged its members, including the newly suspended Japanese Americans like Karl Yoneda and the Communist sympathizers like James Oda, to fight in the U.S. military, which did help defeat Axis fascism but also strengthened U.S. global dominance. While the CPUSA's goal of fighting fascism was reasonable and just, that they did so after 1941 in the absence of any critical analysis of the inter-imperialist nature of the war was treacherous. In retrospect, the CPUSA leader Dorothy Healey has acknowledged as much: "With the Soviet Union and the United States as allies, we felt no conflict at all between our patriotic sentiments and our political beliefs. So unquestioning was our support for the war that a few months later we raised no objections when Japanese-American citizens . . . were sent to relocation camps. . . . It was yet another example of our inability to find or even conceive of a way to be simultaneously supportive and critical in our judgments, the flaw that was the basis of the 'pendulum' appearance of our policies." The CPUSA's World War II policies and practices resulted in capitulating to U.S. and European imperialist goals and abandoning domestic struggles against racism and capitalism.[10]

The CPUSA and JACL's activities during World War II were, for the most part, indistinguishable. Both organizations supported the U.S. war efforts, though the CPUSA certainly placed a greater emphasis on fighting fascism. Both groups urged Japanese Americans to cooperate with the U.S. government, including the forced removal from the West Coast; pushed for Japanese American enlistment in the U.S. military; volunteered to go to Manzanar early to help prepare the concentration camp for new arrivals; helped the U.S. war efforts from inside the concentration camps; and in general, worked inside the concentration camps to promote pro-American sentiment and to suppress any resistance, including that of the Nisei draft resisters. The political consequence of this dual effort—from the moderate and the so-called radical segments of the Japanese American community—was to strengthen a moderate politic, promote assimilationist aspirations, and further suppress Left organizing.[11] By the mid-1960s, the absence of militant labor struggles and radical activism helped set the conditions for the rise of the model minority image of Japanese America.

But even as resistance was being suppressed, the harsh and unjust conditions inside the concentration camps spurred political protest.[12] Many internees voiced strong objections to their incarceration and what many saw as the capitulation of the JACL and CPUSA to the U.S. government. "It is believed that at least 90 percent of the people in the centers are opposed to the JACL," editorialized the *Rocky Shimpo* journalist James Omura in 1944. And some, particularly within the pro-Japanese Kibei[13] community, went so far as to physically assault several JACL and CPUSA leaders and sympathizers inside the concentration camps. Many who engaged in protest activities did so for the first time inside the camps. By and large, the leaders of the Fair Play Committee inside the Heart Mountain, Wyoming, concentration camp, for example, were not politically active prior to their decision to oppose military conscription of internees. Neither were the 315 Nisei men who risked prison time for refusing induction into the U.S. military. Their rationale centered on the violation of civil liberties—reasoning that they should not have to fight for a government that unconstitutionally incarcerated their families—in the absence of any radical critique of U.S. militarism or imperialism. For these draft resisters—as well as for some who later developed radical politics—it was the conditions of confinement that triggered their racial and political awakening.[14] radical from life

The Black Liberation Movement

It was not until the social movements of the 1960s that Japanese American radicalism reignited. At the time, Japanese American politics were dominated by JACL's focus on legalistic, integrationist challenges within the established system to obtain fair housing and nondiscriminatory employment practices and to promote nonracist images of Japanese Americans. This politic matched that of the NAACP and other moderate civil rights organizations, in contrast to high-risk direct action confrontations, including CORE's freedom rides and SNCC's sit-ins, or more radical efforts to transform oppressive structures.[15] In the absence of any Japanese American militancy, the black liberation movement inspired the radicalization of many Japanese and Asian American activists in the 1960s. So did the predominantly white New Left. But the residential proximity of Japanese and blacks—shaped to a large degree by racially discriminatory housing policies and practices— helps explain why the black movement had such a large influence on Japanese American activism. In fact, it was the Japanese, to a greater extent than the other major Asian American group at the time, who lived in or near black communities. The Chinese, by contrast, tended to be segregated into their own ethnic enclaves, especially before World War II.[16] adjacent

Two leading examples of Japanese American radicalism, Yuri Kochiyama and Richard Aoki, emerged in this period. Living in Harlem in the 1960s enabled Kochiyama to meet and work with Malcolm X, her principal political mentor, as well as other influential black revolutionary nationalists. Having grown up in Oakland in the postwar years, Aoki's social networks facilitated his development into an early leader of the Black Panther Party and the most prominent Asian American leader in the struggle for ethnic studies at the University of California at Berkeley. These two activists differ from the majority of Japanese American 1960s activists in that they were significantly older in age and developed their radical consciousness in the early to mid-1960s. By contrast, most 1960s activists gained their political consciousness as youth participating in the Asian American movement that emerged in the late 1960s and early 1970s. Still, the black movement exerted a powerful influence on the development of Asian American activism throughout the 1960s and 1970s and arguably to this day. Kochiyama and Aoki are important to study because they were significant political mentors to the younger cohort of 1960s activists and they influenced the developments of the Asian American movement. Moreover, both are credited with being among the chief architects in building African-Asian unity and solidarity grounded in anti-imperialist, revolutionary politics. These case examples are based on my extensive oral history interviews and participant observations as well as on primary source materials.[17]

Richard Aoki: Drawing from Black Cultural Roots

Though Aoki was only three years old when his family entered the Tanforan assembly center in spring 1942, the experience of incarceration had a major impact on his life. Not only did the three-and-a-half year incarceration result in economic decline, as it did for many Japanese Americans, it also lead to the break up of Aoki's nuclear family. Aoki's parents separated in the all-Japanese environment of the Topaz, Utah, concentration camp, in a community where divorce was both rare and taboo. Even more unusual, Aoki and his brother, fifteen months his junior, lived with their father's family both inside the concentration camp and after their return to Oakland.[18]

Aoki recalls the concentration camp experience shaping his racial attitudes, even at a young age: "In kindergarten I was chosen to play George Washington in the school pageant. . . . I got real excited about it and ran home and told my father what the big deal was. Disasterville struck. . . . My father was incensed that I didn't have the good sense to realize that I was not the father of 'our country,' no way, shape or form. . . . There was no way I could forget the message: I should not think in terms of George Washington, this was not my country by a long shot. In fact 'my country' put me in this camp."[19] His father's views were influenced by his own segregated confinement. As Aoki recounted, "My father [then a junior high school teacher] resigned after he got to the section on American democracy because he looked at the kids while speaking about democracy, freedom, and justice; and all the kids had to do was look out the window and see the barbed wire fences, the watch towers with search lights, the half track with 50 caliber machine gun. It didn't compute."[20]

Returning to the black ghetto of West Oakland in 1945, Aoki faced not only being the new kid on the block but also the anti-Japanese sentiment engendered by the war. When his black peers picked fights with him, as they regularly did, his father demanded that he fight back. As Aoki recalled: "My father was starting to become an accomplished barroom brawler. . . . Also my uncle Ruizo had a black belt in jujitsu, so he was very patient and taught me the basics or fundamentals involving jujitsu. . . . In jujitsu, it's not the size of your opponent that is that important." And soon, Aoki became an accomplished street fighter. In time, he was drawn into the petty criminal activities of street life—"five-finger shopping," "second-story work," "midnight auto supply," and gangs. He also adopted black music, dance, food, and culture, as well as a love for reading that was influenced by the substantial libraries of his paternal grandfather, his father, and his uncle Ruizo. After many years of being home schooled by his father, he entered public junior high school and graduated co-valedictorian.[21]

Following his high school graduation in 1957 Aoki joined the army, where he served on active duty for the first six months and reserve duty for the next seven-and-a-half years. In the military he saw contradictions that helped to fuel his very early opposition to the Vietnam War. He also gained weapons training—skills he would further develop in his activist work. After completing his active duty, Aoki began a series of working-class jobs where he gained a proletarian consciousness. At one of these jobs, in a paint factory, Aoki made a grave error in calculating the ingredients to make a huge batch of paint, thereby ruining, in Aoki's estimate, "ten thousand dollars" worth of paint. "The color was off, the viscosity was off, the pH was off," he explained. Because the paint would be "chipping and cracking and peeling in a week," he expected it to be thrown out and anticipated his own reprimand or firing. Instead, he was shocked that the bosses would sell the defective paint: "They made a decision to can the product. . . . put them into one gallon containers, put [on] another label, not the company label." That day, he learned a lesson in the greed of capitalism. His understanding of capitalism was further enhanced when his fellow workers, many of whom were labor organizers, socialists, and communists, introduced him to reading materials, including books by Carey McWilliams and John Steinbeck, the speeches of Eugene Debs, Art Preis's *Labor's Giant Steps,* and Michael Harrington's *The Other America.* Members of the Socialist Workers Party (swp) urged him to read the classics, and he delved into Hegel, Marx, Engels, and Lenin. After an intensive self-study in Marxist-Leninist literature, Aoki joined the swp and its youth group, the Young Socialist Alliance, around 1963. By this time, he publicly identified as a "revolutionary socialist" and cofounded the Socialist Discussion Club in 1964 at Oakland City College (later Merritt College), where he had just begun his full-time studies.[22]

Aoki's study of black nationalism began through regular exchanges between his group and the Soul Students Advisory Council and one of its leaders, Bobby Seale. He was also "reading everything anybody in a Marxist or Leninist, Maoist tradition had written about nationalism." By the time he participated as the only nonblack at a Black Power conference held in San Francisco in September 1966, he was an advocate of revolutionary nationalism. In a report on the conference for the swp, Aoki asserted that "the origin and development of black nationalism is the direct result of the American capitalist system, which has placed black people into a position analogous to the colonial peoples." He also noted that "the Black nationalist movement is in an embryonic stage of development, and is constantly undergoing transformations." He called upon the swp to recognize the need for "Blacks . . . to organize themselves independently," even as "the Black liberation struggle does not exist in isolation from other forces and conflicts at home and abroad." He also admonished that "the swp must begin to lay down the foundations that will lead to a principled alliance between Black people and the White workers so that they can together destroy American capitalism." Though he did not yet have a term for the various forms of nationalism, Aoki had come to the conclusion that there was a distinction between what he soon called cultural nationalism (promoting African culture and racial pride, but lacking a class analysis) and revolutionary nationalism (promoting race and class liberation in its anti-capitalist, anti-imperialist, and pro-socialist analysis). Aoki's advocacy of revolutionary nationalism contradicted the swp Trotskyist line that all nationalism is reactionary, and by early 1967 he left the swp "without breaking stride."[23]

Contrary to what many would assume, while growing up in Oakland Aoki did not know the Black Panther Party co-founders Huey Newton and Bobby Seale. Aoki, after all, had been home schooled until junior high. But by living in Oakland, he met Huey's older brother, Melvin, and through Melvin, he met Huey. In contrast to Bobby Seale's unwavering descriptions of Huey Newton as the intellectually and politically savvy one of their duo,[24] Aoki remembers Seale as the more intellectually engaging and the better orator, and Newton as the street-smart one with the quick street-fighting skills. In fact, even with his revolutionary socialist politics and political understanding of exploitation, Aoki, along with Huey, entertained the idea of becoming pimps. They were impressed with the fancy clothes and imposing guns of a big-time pimp they knew. But, after further exploration of the idea, they changed their minds. As Aoki explained: "[We] got to talk to a lot of prostitutes. And he and I could just not become pimps. We talked to the women and they were in bad shape. I mean they were out there because they were mothers and trying to make ends met . . . Huey and I couldn't see profiting over somebody's misery."[25] That Aoki could seriously consider becoming a pimp in the mid-1960s illustrates the inconsistencies of his street upbringing and his developing political ideas.

As Seale remembers it, he met Aoki through Newton: "It was at one of the restaurants across the street from Merritt College . . . in the Spring of 1963. Richard happened to pop in, or [he] was at the table and I came in, one of the two. And Huey says, 'Bobby this is Richard Aoki, he's a friend of mine.' . . . We got to talking about basic politics. Huey was always getting into . . . discussions with Richard about politics, international politics, socialist politics, that kind of stuff." Seale and Aoki were soon having regular interactions through their respective organizations at Merritt College. But, as Seale recounted: "Our friendship with Richard was more than just around the college campus. We would drop over to Richard's house, me and Huey, my god we must've dropped into Richard's apartment several times just to sit and sip on some wine, drink some beer, eat some cheese. We were intellectuals. We had these long broad intellectual discussions with each other . . . ten or twelve times over a two to three year period. [This was] all before the Party started." Seale credits Aoki with teaching him about the distinctions among the different forms of socialism and, in the first couple of years of the BPP, being the party member most well versed in Marxist-Leninist thought. Seale respected Aoki's affiliation with the SWP, particularly its publication of Malcolm X's speeches, and he appreciated the SWP newspaper subscription that Aoki gave him.[26]

When Seale and Newton organized the now renowned Black Panther Party for Self-Defense (BPP) in Oakland in October 1966, they sought Aoki's advice on their newly written Ten-Point Platform. Aoki was also among the first to help to duplicate and distribute copies of the document. He further embodied the Panthers' belief in self-defense by supplying them with their first two guns—a .45 for Seale and a M-1 carbine for Newton. In fact, because of Aoki's consistent presence in Newton's and Seale's political lives and his active support in the early days of the party's formation, it was hard for Aoki to pinpoint the exact moment of his Panther membership. But after joining the party some time within the first month, Aoki became one of the few nonblacks (perhaps the only one) to hold leadership positions within the BPP, in which he served briefly as the first branch captain of the Berkeley chapter, worked as a field marshal who reported directly to Huey, and, informally, acted as the minister of education in the BPP's earliest months.[27]

In 1968, Aoki began working in the Asian American movement at UC Berkeley, to which he had transferred two years earlier to complete his bachelor's degree. As a founding member of the Asian American Political Alliance (AAPA), initiated by Yuji Ichioka and Emma Gee, Aoki was among the earliest participants of the nascent Asian American movement in the Bay Area and throughout the nation. He was respected for his dynamic oratory skills, developed in the black culture of West Oakland; his political study of revolutionary nationalism and classic Marxism-Leninism; and his activist experience in the revolutionary nationalist black movement, in the antiwar movement with the radical Vietnam Day Committee, and in Third World solidarity struggles. After becoming AAPA's official spokesperson, he soon found himself embroiled in a historic struggle to establish ethnic studies at UC Berkeley, a movement that followed closely on the heels of the 1968–69 five-month strike at San Francisco State College, which resulted in the nation's first School of Ethnic Studies. As Aoki became intensely involved in Asian American organizing in 1968–69, he began drifting away from the activities of the BPP, which, unlike its active role in the San Francisco State College strike, provided little direction to the strike at UC Berkeley.[28]

In 1968 at UC Berkeley, the black, Chicana and Chican/o, and Asian American students began approaching the administration for ethnic studies curriculum. When the AAPA-initiated pioneering Asian American studies class was offered at UC Berkeley in winter 1969, Aoki, then a graduate student in social welfare at UC Berkeley, served as one of the class's four teaching assistants. And when various student groups decided to begin a strike for ethnic studies and formed the Third World Liberation Front

(TWLF), Aoki became the chair of AAPA for the duration of the strike and the Asian American spokesperson within the TWLF. He was the most visible Asian American leader of the strike and a member of the TWLF decision-making body, the central committee. Consistent with Aoki's ultra-Left approach, he was more interested in the military aspects of the strike than in sitting in lengthy meetings. In this capacity, he tirelessly and meticulously attended to the details of planning various tactics for confronting the police and administration. Though he considered himself more radical than most in AAPA, there is consensus that in his role as spokesperson, he fairly and accurately represented the organization's views.[29]

After establishing the School of Ethnic Studies at UC Berkeley, Aoki became one of the first coordinators of the nascent Asian American Studies Program and taught many of its first classes. For Aoki, it was important to teach academically rigorous classes and maintain a community-based focus in that program. But by 1972, with internal struggles in the department, Aoki was ready to move on.[30] He would spend the next twenty-six years working as a counselor, instructor, and administrator with the Peralta Community College district in the East Bay. During this period, a combination of political burnout and personal crises led to his being politically inactive, though he continued to follow political events in the mainstream news and was aware of grassroots struggles. Significantly, it was through the reemergence of Black Panther activities following Huey Newton's death in 1989 that Aoki reconnected with the grassroots social movements. Following his retirement in 1998 his activist life reignited, and currently he is active in the movement to oppose the U.S. war and occupation of Iraq.[31]

In reflecting on his life, Aoki contends that the Black Panther Party remains the single most important political influence on his life. As he adamantly states: "I never left the Party and I was never expelled." Even when politically inactive, he found jobs for party members at the various community colleges where he worked and provided other concrete support to the BPP, particularly through the mid-1970s.[32] To the present day, his loyalties to the party are so strong that it is hard for him to offer criticisms of the organization's controversial history. The legacy of the Panthers in Aoki's life is evident in his revolutionary nationalist ideology; his current activism, often centering on BPP commemorations or antiwar organizing with former Panthers; the personal sacrifices he has made in his life; his oratory skills; and his black cultural style. Indeed, his reputation among Asian American activists in the 1960s and today stems in large part from his Panther affiliation.

Yuri Kochiyama: Living in Harlem in the "Sizzling Sixties"

Yuri Kochiyama is one of the most prominent Asian American activists to emerge in the 1960s.[33] Yet her early years hold few clues that explain her radical transformation during that period. Born in 1921, Kochiyama grew up in a predominantly white, middle-class neighborhood in South Los Angeles. There were acts that could be interpreted as rebellious in her youth. In particular, she managed to evade doing much housework. This was unusual, when social norms in 1930s America dictated that daughters, especially only daughters as was the case with Yuri, would help lighten their mother's domestic load and, perhaps more importantly, gain training for becoming a "good wife" and "good mother." Still, Yuri's rebelliousness did not stem from any conscious feminist impulse, but rather from a desire to participate actively in extracurricular activities. Her whirlwind of community service activities, including being a fanatical sports journalist, a member of her high school tennis team, the first female student body officer at her high school, a counselor to multiple girls' clubs, and a dedicated Sunday school teacher, was a second area that signaled a potential activist future. But she was drawn to helping others from a humanitarian base, in the absence of any pursuit of social justice. In her youth, her racial outlook could best be described as colorblind and assimilationist. She fit into the predominantly white world surrounding her in San Pedro. She was not only well integrated into school activities—"one of the most popular students," remarked several of her friends—she even dated white boys at a time when Asian-white romantic relationships were legally and culturally prohibited. Kochiyama acknowledges that even as she attended Japanese language school and was raised in a Japanese home culture, she barely identified as being Japanese American.[34]

World War II inaugurated her racial awakening. For the first time, she perceived race discrimination in, for example, organizations asking her to leave and the local police accusing her of spying for Japan. Under conditions of segregated confinement, Kochiyama began listening to the lengthy discussions of older internees, many with grievances about their unjust racist treatment. These experiences challenged her colorblind worldview. But even as she began recognizing instances of race discrimination, she still clung to her faith in America as a land of equality and democracy. She was able to reconcile these seemingly contradictory views by adopting a moderate, legalistic, and assimilationist politic—one that matched the politics of the JACL. Race discrimination was an aberrant event that could be eradicated through reforms to the system. This is far different from the worldview Kochiyama would adopt by the mid-1960s—that racism was a deeply embedded and widespread feature of the United States, intricately linked to the historical development of the country itself. Still, her concentration camp experiences triggered a racial awakening and her community service activities began, for the first time, taking on an explicitly racial focus. From inside the Santa Anita assembly center and the Jerome, Arkansas, concentration camp, Kochiyama organized her Sunday school class to began an extensive letter-writing campaign to Nisei soldiers, in large part because they were facing race discrimination at home and abroad on the battlefield. In the postwar years, after moving to New York City to marry a war veteran, Bill Kochiyama, she and her husband started an organization to support Japanese American and later Chinese American soldiers on their way to the Korean warfront.[35]

In the 1950s, as Kochiyama followed newspaper accounts of the civil rights movement and invited political speakers to her family's open houses —where scores of people, strangers and friends alike, gathered every weekend—she began to gain a political consciousness. But her 1960 move from midtown Manhattan to Harlem, with its pulsating black social movements, was key in her radical transformation. In 1963, she began struggling for quality education for inner-city children and for nondiscriminatory hiring *education* practices for construction workers—work that matched the goals (integration) and methods (nonviolent, direct action) of the civil rights movement. But within two short years she had developed an incipient radical consciousness. That she developed a moderate political consciousness was not surprising. In the context of the civil rights movement surrounding her in Harlem, her community service activities took on a political cast. But given her experiences, it would have been hard to predict the development of a radical politic. What triggered this radicalization?

The historic moment—the "sizzling sixties," as Kochiyama has called it—

Big Q: why me
Big R for ppl

and her location in Harlem were key. She became radicalized at precisely the moment when the moderate civil rights movement was shifting into the radical Black Power movement. Moreover, she was located in a black community that was rife with radical and nationalist tendencies and that had a rich history of political and cultural resistance. In this milieu, Kochiyama met Malcolm X, who would become her foremost political mentor. In October 1963, when Kochiyama met Malcolm at a courtroom hearing for her arrest along with others for using their bodies to block construction trucks, her politics reflected that of the predominant civil rights movement. She told Malcolm that she disagreed with his "harsh stance on integration," and she asked, in her first letter to him, "If each of us, white, yellow, and what-have-you, can earn our way into your confidence by actual performance, will you . . . could you . . . believe in 'togetherness' of all people?"[36] In these statements, Kochiyama clearly promotes integrationism as a goal, yet she also acknowledges the need for nonblack people to prove through "actual performance" their genuine commitment to racial equality.

The day after meeting Malcolm, Kochiyama heard him speak for the first time. She soon began to attend his talks at the Audubon Ballroom. In June 1964, Malcolm spoke at a program, held at the Kochiyama home, in honor of Japanese *hibakusha* (atomic-bomb survivors) on a world tour against nuclear proliferation. At that program, Malcolm acknowledged receiving the numerous letters from Kochiyama and promised to write during his lengthy travels abroad in Africa, the Middle East, and England. Yuri and Bill were surprised to receive eleven postcards from Malcolm, in the midst of his meeting with foreign national leaders. But something about Kochiyama touched Malcolm. As Mae Mallory, a respected Harlem activist, recalled: "Mary [as Kochiyama was then known] was the only person in the area that Malcolm wrote to, except for Mr. Micheaux [the black nationalist bookstore owner]." Although her statement is exaggerated, Mallory is expressing a perception that exists to this day—that Kochiyama was special to Malcolm. As he expressed in one of his postcards: "I read all of your wonderful cards and letters of encouragement and I think you are the most beautiful family in Harlem."[37]

By the end of the year, Kochiyama was attending, at Malcolm's invitation, his Organization of Afro-American Unity's Liberation School. From lessons about Fannie Lou Hamer's jailhouse beating to the European colonialists' division of Africa to a political-economic analysis of slavery, Kochiyama learned lessons about how this country's "congenital deformity" of racism could not be reformed. Contained in these lessons, and in readings by Fanon, Nkrumah, and Aptheker, were anti-capitalist, anti-imperialist, and even implicitly pro-socialist messages. At Kochiyama's first class, on December 5, 1964, she was impressed with the instructor's ability to connect cross-culturally: "To my surprise, Brother [James] Shabazz started talking about linkages between Africans and Asians. I was the only non-Black there. I don't know if he spoke about this because I was there, to help me connect my heritage to what we were learning, or if he would have lectured on this anyway. Brother Shabazz, who speaks some Japanese, Korean, and Chinese, wrote the *kanji* [Japanese and Chinese characters] for Tao and various martial art forms on the board. He explained the spirituality underlying these martial arts—that they were exercises to help one move towards God similar to how Islam did." The Liberation School not only presented a different view ınʰᵉʳˢᵉᶜᵗᵒⁿˢ of nationalism, one that contained elements of Third World solidarity and internationalism, it also challenged the reformist, integrationist, and non-violent beliefs contained within Kochiyama's civil rights ideology. As she questioned the possibility of gaining equality and liberation in a system built on racism, she began to fathom that an entirely different system needed to be established.[38]

That Malcolm too was undergoing a political and racial transformation following his 1964 departure from the Nation of Islam had a profound impact on Kochiyama. In May 1964, upon returning from Africa where he met white revolutionary Muslims, particularly the Algerian ambassador to Ghana, Malcolm revealed: "In the past, I have permitted myself to be used to make sweeping indictments of all white people, and these generalizations have caused injuries to some white people who did not deserve them. . . . My pilgrimage to Mecca . . . served to convince me that perhaps American whites can be cured of the rampant racism which is consuming them and about to destroy this country. In the future, I intend to be careful not to sentence anyone who has not been proven guilty. I am not a racist and do not subscribe to any of the tenets of racism."[39] Had Malcolm maintained his previous antiwhite views, Kochiyama, who believed in the possibility of genuine interracial unity based on her own experiences growing up in San Pedro, probably would not have become such a close supporter.

Nationalist politics were growing in other ways in Harlem as well. Following Malcolm's assassination in 1965, LeRoi Jones (later Amiri Baraka) established the Black Arts Repertory Theater and School, which according to Kochiyama, "became so well known that black literary people and artists from all over the country came to Harlem to check it out." Jones, a prominent poet, dramatist, and writer who initially emerged as a Beat poet, had undergone an ideological transformation from integrationism to black revolutionary nationalism. Jones's first organization in Harlem, the On Guard for Freedom Committee, was interracial—a policy he defended when some of the young nationalists in Harlem objected to the presence of whites at their meetings. But by 1965, Jones argued that the Black Arts School should be, in the words of Harold Cruse, "a black theater about black people, with black people, for black people, and only black people." Kochiyama observed how this policy affected the political community in Harlem: "It was the first kind of institution that upset a lot of people, and certainly it upset whites, because the idea was that it was open only to blacks, or nonwhites. Harlem Freedom School was integrated and most everything else that was political in Harlem was integrated, until this new kind of nationalism emerged. Even a lot of whites who had been in the civil rights movement were upset by it."[40]

The racially exclusionary policy of the Black Arts School and other instances of separatist organizing must have challenged Kochiyama's own evolving views on integrationism and self-determination. Just two years earlier, she had rebuked Malcolm X's separatist ideas. But by listening to Malcolm's speeches and studying at his Liberation School, she was beginning to understand the need for autonomous spaces to solidify unity and realize self-determination. The effects of white supremacy were felt in a variety of ways in the movement, including white people dominating discussions and leadership positions and black people, in subscribing to internalized racism, accepting subordinate roles. As a result, Kochiyama reasoned, autonomous spaces—that is, racially exclusionary ones—served to counter the powerful effects of white supremacy on black activists as well as on well-meaning white activists. So while Kochiyama probably disliked the fact that white activists felt hurt by being excluded on the basis of race, she also believed that the separation of races was necessary for black self-determination, but only as a stepping stone to the eventual "togetherness of all people" in a transformed society. Her own racial identity placed her in an ambiguous position vis-à-vis black nationalism. But in a period of growing Third World solidarity, and given Kochiyama's humble and respectful manner, she was one of the few nonblacks to be included in the Black Arts School and other black nationalist formations in Harlem.

Not only was Kochiyama becoming increasingly nationalist, she also was moving from believing in philosophical nonviolence to accepting the right to self-defense. Certainly the teachings of Malcolm X and his associates at the Liberation School influenced her thinking. In contrast to many civil rights leaders, particularly Martin Luther King Jr. and Bob Moses, both of whom raised nonviolence to a principle to be adhered to in all situations, Malcolm X viewed nonviolence as a tactic to be used depending on the circumstances: "We're nonviolent with people who are nonviolent with us. But we're not nonviolent with people who are not nonviolent with us." He elaborated on this concept in his 1963 "Message to the Grass Roots" speech:

> As long as the white man sent you to Korea, you bled. . . . You bleed for white people, but when it comes to seeing your own churches being bombed and little black girls murdered, you haven't got any blood. . . . How are you going to be nonviolent in Mississippi, as violent as you were in Korea? . . . If violence is wrong in America, violence is wrong abroad. If it is wrong to be violent defending black women and black children and black babies and black men, then it is wrong for America to draft us and make us violent abroad in defense of her. And if it is right for America to draft us, and teach us how to be violent in defense of her, then it is right for you and me to do whatever is necessary to defend our own people right here in this country.

Robert F. Williams, president of the NAACP chapter in Monroe, North Carolina, who gained the respect of black nationalists for daring to promote armed defense against Ku Klux Klan attacks in the 1950s, concurred with the tactical use of self-defense: "Nonviolence is a very potent weapon when the opponent is civilized, but nonviolence is no repellent for a sadist." As he further observed: "When Hitler's tyranny threatened the world, we did not hear much about how immoral it is to meet violence with violence." Likewise, nonviolence would not prove an effective weapon against white supremacists, argued Williams.[41]

In the 1960s, Williams became one of the most prominent leaders within black revolutionary nationalist circles, second only to Malcolm X. The black intellectual Harold Cruse, under whom Kochiyama studied at the Black Arts School, views this as a curious fact; as he asserted, "Robert Williams himself was never a nationalist, but an avowed integrationist." There is certainly much evidence to support this position. As president of the Monroe NAACP, integration appeared to be Williams's solution to white supremacy, as he worked diligently for the desegregation of swimming pools and other public facilities. Believing that the federal government would defend civil rights activists against the segregationist practices of southern politicians and Ku Klux Klan, he consistently informed the federal officials, including the FBI, about local racial problems. He supported diverse political tendencies, including the interracial Freedom Riders and the predominantly white Trotskyists—all pro-integrationist. Moreover, Williams considered the black nation position unfeasible and was never a nationalist, in his words, "to the point that I would exclude whites or that I would discriminate against whites or that I would be prejudiced against whites." So why, inquires Cruse, were the bulk of Williams's supporters in Harlem in the early 1960s nationalists? And why, I might add, did revolutionary nationalist organizations in the late 1960s invite Williams to be their leader? Cruse offers a succinct response: "The young nationalists celebrated Williams as their leader, since his self-defense stand coincided with their rising interests in the adoption of force and violence tactics in the North." Williams's advocacy of self-defense certainly inspired many revolutionary nationalists, including the Black Panther Party's armed stance against police brutality. This position contrasted sharply with the nonviolent philosophy of prominent civil rights leaders and made Williams an adversary of the NAACP executive director Roy Wilkins and an ally to revolutionary nationalists.[42]

By the late 1960s, Kochiyama was a firm believer in revolutionary nationalism, with its promotion of self-determination and self-defense and its anti-racist, anti-capitalist, and implicitly or explicitly pro-socialist politics. Even here, the influences of Malcolm X and Robert Williams are apparent. Both adhered to what Williams's biographer called "eclectic radicalism." In the late 1950s and early 1960s, Williams believed in nationalist ideas about self-reliance, he relied on the militant tactic of self-defense, and he strove toward racial equality through integration without fundamentally contesting the economic or political structures of the United States. By the late 1960s, Williams, after living in exile in Cuba and China, stated, "I envision a democratic socialist economy wherein the exploitation of man by man will be abolished." Malcolm X's Organization of Afro-American Unity contained cultural nationalist, revolutionary nationalist, and revolutionary

Marxist elements. And it is unclear whether Malcolm, whose politics were evolving rapidly in the last year of his life, remained a nationalist (some associates claim that given his treatment as an ex-officio head of state during his 1964 travels abroad, he acted out the concept of nationalism) or repudiated narrow nationalism (as Malcolm stated in a January 1965 interview with the Socialist Workers Party). But it can be argued that he was becoming increasingly internationalist, anti-capitalist, and pro-socialist toward the end of his life.[43] Moreover, compared to West Coast black radicals who drew sharp divisions between cultural and revolutionary nationalism, on the East Coast, particularly in Harlem, the boundaries between various forms of nationalism appeared more fluid. While the New York Panthers adopted African names and culture, the Oakland Panthers emphasized class over race, harshly condemned "porkchop nationalists," and forbid New York Black Panthers from working closely with cultural nationalists.[44] It was in this more eclectic East Coast nationalist environment that Kochiyama's politics—strongly influenced by revolutionary nationalism but also drawing from cultural nationalism, civil rights discourse, and socialism—flourished.

In the mid-1960s, Kochiyama was a supporter of the Revolutionary Action Movement, a clandestine revolutionary nationalist organization, which, according to William Sales, "was the first of many organizations in the black liberation movement to attempt to construct a revolutionary nationalism on the basis of a synthesis of the thought of Malcolm X, Marx and Lenin, and Mao Tse Tung . . . [giving] its variant of black nationalism a particularly leftist character." The Revolutionary Action Movement was headed by Muhammad Ahmed (Max Stanford), who relied on Kochiyama's wide political networks to help to recruit members in Harlem. As Ahmed recounted: "Yuri opened up her apartment as a meeting place, where we met for lunch two or three times a week. She'd fix sandwiches and we would listen to Malcolm's unedited speeches, which would go for maybe two hours or so. And we would have discussions. . . . She could introduce people to us. She would circulate any information that we had to a whole network of people. . . . Yuri was a constant communicator, constant facilitator, constant networker." Through RAM and others in Harlem, Kochiyama began writing to Robert Williams while he was in exile, distributing his U.S.-government banned publication *The Crusader.* Upon their return from exile in 1969, Robert and Mabel Williams visited the Kochiyama home.[45]

Based on her consistent and fervent support for revolutionary politics and black self-determination, Kochiyama was among the very few non-blacks invited to join the Republic of New Africa (RNA), which was established in 1968 and known for its ultimate nationalist position advocating a separate black nation in the U.S. South. Kochiyama was so influenced by RNA's "nation-building" classes and the revolutionary nationalist milieu in Harlem that when the RNA had an internal split over the form and location of revolutionary struggle, despite her own location in a northern city she sided with the need to build an independent black nation in the South over the struggle for equality in northern cities, where large numbers of blacks had migrated since World War II. Though Kochiyama took a clear stance by allying with Imari Obadele's faction, given that her pragmatic approach consistently took precedent over a strong ideological position, it is not surprising that she worked simultaneously to promote Obadele's "nation within a nation" position and to work for black liberation in Harlem.[46]

By 1967, the year that the FBI director J. Edgar Hoover officially launched the counterintelligence program, or COINTELPRO, "to expose, disrupt, misdirect, discredit or otherwise neutralize the activities of black nationalist, hate-type organizations and groupings, their leadership, spokesmen, membership, and supporters, and to counter their propensity for violence and civil disorder," Kochiyama began what would became her most intense area of struggle—supporting political prisoners. Initially drawn in because many of her comrades were being harassed, arrested, and imprisoned by the FBI and local police, her own experiences of incarceration during World War II help explain the intensity of her commitment. Drawing parallels between the two situations, Kochiyama proclaimed: "These things could happen when there is no support; when no one even knows what is happening; and when people are afraid to even know you because they might be found guilty by association. . . . If we don't support one another, and stand by one another, it will be easy for those in power to pick off one group at a time, as they have done so successfully in the past." Kochiyama soon became one of the central figures in the political prisoner movement in Harlem and nationally, supporting political prisoners not only for humanitarian reasons, given their excessively harsh treatment and long prison sentences, but also defending their anti-racist, anti-imperialist politics. She was the first person many turned to when arrested or when released from prison, either by calling her home or dropping by her work. "When we were captured by the enemy, our first call went to WA6–7412," recounted the political prisoner Mutulu Shakur, rattling off her telephone number from memory thirty years after his first post-prison phone call to Kochiyama. "Everybody just remembered that number," continued Shakur: "Anybody getting arrested, no matter black, Puerto Rican, or whatever, our first call was to her number. Her network was like no other. She would get a lawyer or get information out to our family and the Movement. You knew she wasn't going to stop until somebody heard from you." Kochiyama, dubbed the "Internet in those days," was also a storehouse of political information and updates on political prisoner cases. As her fellow RNA citizen Bolanile Akinwole recalled, "She had little cardboard boxes [of files] stacked up everywhere. One of her back rooms was just filled with these boxes. And there used to be boxes in the hallway and in the kitchen. The kitchen table always had bunches of stuff on it, and underneath it. But everything was very organized and it was amazing how quickly she could put her hands on information." And Ahmed Oba-femi adds, "So if you wanted information on a political prisoner, say to organize a conference or a tribunal, all we had to do was go to Yuri." And with the same intensity she had while writing letters to Nisei soldiers during World War II, Kochiyama would stay up until the wee hours of the morning writing letters to political prisoners, composing articles for newsletters or letters to the editor, completing a mass mailing, or organizing an event.[47]

Kochiyama's commitment to political prisoners and to working cross-culturally continues to this day. She has become an ardent supporter of Puerto Rican independence and of those imprisoned for their efforts to decolonize their homelands. As the Puerto Rican leader Richie Perez ob-served: "Yuri was an activist in a movement to free political prisoners in almost every community—not only for the Panthers but also for the people up in prison fighting for Puerto Rican independence—and [she] worked very closely with some of the cases that were dear to our community. . . . In each of these, [she worked] amazingly with the same kind of enthusiasm as if they were people from her own community." She has traveled inter-nationally to Peru, the Philippines, and Japan to generate international support for the Peruvian political prisoner and Shining Path leader Abimael Guzman. Significantly, Kochiyama almost single-handedly is responsible for generating Asian American support for political prisoners and, in the 1990s, for establishing support groups for the Asian American political prisoners Yu Kikumura and David Wong. As the former Puerto Rican political prisoner Dylcia Pagan proclaimed, "I have the utmost admiration for Yuri. She is the most incessant activist I've ever met."[48]

The Radicalizing Effect of the
Black Liberation Movement

My discussion of Richard Aoki and Yuri Kochiyama attends to the ways in which the black liberation movement exerted a radicalizing force on their ideological development and political activities. Their proximity to the working-class black community was important. For Aoki, his growing up in the black ghetto in West Oakland shaped his ideas about the nature of black oppression, which he saw grounded in not only racism and capitalism but also internal colonialism.[49] Had he been raised in a middle-class, predominantly white suburb, he may well have adopted a civil rights analysis of the racist nature of black oppression or a Left analysis of the capitalist nature of black oppression. For Kochiyama, it was in listening to her black neighbors' daily experiences with racism that she gained an understanding of the systemic nature of racism.

Still, as Kochiyama observed, it was not simply living in a working-class black community, as she had throughout the 1950s in the predominantly black Amsterdam Housing Projects in midtown Manhattan, but being surrounded by the emerging black power movement in Harlem that triggered her radicalization. That her politics developed in the early to mid-1960s, precisely in the period when the civil rights movement was transforming into the more radical black power movement, profoundly shaped her activism. These influences are particularly salient in Kochiyama's ideological development from her civil rights promotion of integrationism and nonviolence to her revolutionary nationalist advocacy of self-determination, self-defense, and armed struggle. For Aoki, his participation in the budding black nationalist movement transformed his politics from the Trotskyism of the swp to the revolutionary nationalism of the bpp. For both of these Japanese American radicals, living in working-class black communities in the midst of the emerging Black Power movement provided them with opportunities to meet numerous black radicals and nationalists. These were invaluable connections and experiences. To this day, Malcolm X is Kochiyama's greatest political mentor and the Black Panther Party is the single greatest political influence in Aoki's life.

As much as black radicalism impacted Aoki and Kochiyama's politics, these Japanese American radicals also helped to shape the emerging black power movements locally and nationally. The Black Panther Party cofounder Bobby Seale finds Aoki's contributions significant enough to identify him by name in his 1960s classic book *Seize the Time,* and in his current Black Panther Web site, even though Aoki was in neither the primary nor secondary tier of party leadership.[50] To Seale, Aoki's ideological and material support was critical to the formation of the BPP. He and Huey Newton trusted and respected Aoki's political analysis, so much so that they engaged in lengthy discussions with him and sought his advice on, for example, their party's platform. That a person—and nonblack at that—would be willing to supply them with their first guns for their audacious and controversial police patrols must have affirmed their ideas and signaled Aoki's commitment in action, and not just words, to black liberation.

In the New York black liberation movement, Kochiyama can be characterized as a behind-the-scenes worker—making stylistically designed leaflets, archiving materials, writing and visiting political prisoners, arranging meetings, and writing articles for movement publications. She readily acknowledges her ordinariness: "I was never an officer or leader [in RNA]. . . . I never spoke." In emphasizing her respect for black self-determination, she is adamant "that [it] would be sort of ridiculous for a non-Black to speak for the Black nation." But to see her contributions to black liberation as merely that of a rank-and-file activist is misguided. As Mutulu Shakur, Kochiyama's New York comrade in RNA and the National Committee to Defend Political Prisoners (NCDPP), asserts: "She was more than just a leaflet maker. . . . She was essential to that decision-making process. . . . When there were like only five of us active in the NCDPP, Yuri would be there at every meeting. So how can you minimize her decision-making role in that?" The NCDPP comrade Nyisha Shakur concurred: "Yuri, out of all of us, was in touch with people the most. People would call her relentlessly, just all the time—frequently collect. And she would somehow just never refuse them. So she was always the one who people looked to to find out where [prisoners and activists] moved to. . . . She was the one seemingly writing and visiting most of [the] political prisoners and really staying on top of it. . . . When I was still young,

I said to myself, I never want to be as busy as she was. Yuri literally worked until two or three in the morning every night." Because of the dedication, consistency, and selflessness with which Kochiyama has worked through thick and thin, she has emerged as a leading figure in the New York black liberation movement and in the national political prisoners movement. In the early 1990s, for example, Kochiyama was listed on the Malcolm X Commemoration Committee's letterhead as a founding member of the Organization of Afro American Unity (OAAU), though she was merely a budding activist when Malcolm X established the OAAU in 1964. It seems that Kochiyama is so revered in black revolutionary nationalist circles that she is placed among the closest associates of Malcolm X.[51]

It was from their roots in the Black Power movement that both Kochiyama and Aoki emerged as early leaders of the Asian American Movement. Young Asian American activists respected both leaders for their connections with the militant Black Power movement. Kochiyama helped build bridges between the Asian and black radical movements by, for example, writing or speaking about Malcolm X, Robert Williams, and political prisoners in many Asian American movement publications and events, and writing or speaking about the Japanese American incarceration, the bombings of Hiroshima and Nagasaki, the Vietnam War, and the Japanese American redress movement to Asian and black audiences. As she worked for Japanese American redress in the 1980s, she consistently advocated the need for black reparations. Aoki's leadership in the Asian American Political Alliance and the Third World Liberation Front at UC Berkeley stemmed from, in large part, his connections to the Black Power movement on the West Coast. Not only was he a dynamic orator grounded in black street style and an advanced student of revolutionary black nationalism, he also exuded the macho style of the Black Panthers that drew the admiration of young Asian American men and women looking for alternative role models.

The black liberation movement was a radicalizing force in the lives of Aoki and Kochiyama, both of whom in turn helped shape the emerging radical black movement. Both activists were influential leaders in the nascent Asian American movement and inspired the activism of countless Asian American youth. In helping to forge revolutionary African-Asian unity, Japanese American radicals like Kochiyama and Aoki were instrumental in helping to build the Left wing of the Asian American movement.[52]

Notes

1   See, for example, Clayborne Carson, David J. Garrow, Gerald Gill, Vincent Harding, and Darlene Clark Hine, eds., *The Eyes of the Prize Civil Rights Reader* (New York: Penguin Books, 1991), 244–47.

2   It is likely that Kochiyama and Aoki would have maintained their original political ideology, that of civil rights and Old Left activism, respectively, if not for the emergence of the black liberation movement and their location in black working-class communities.

3   Though little known, Japanese Americans have a long history of radical resistance. Beginning in the earliest years of the twentieth century, Japanese immigrants formed socialist study groups and the immigrant Sen Katayama, already known in Japan for his instrumental role in the Japanese labor and communist movements, helped found the Communist Party USA (CPUSA). Japanese Americans, leftists and nonleftists alike, engaged in intensive labor struggles, including numerous militant strikes. On the Japanese American Left, see Yuji Ichioka, "A Buried Past: Early Issei Socialists and the Japanese Community," *Amerasia Journal* 1 (1971): 1–25; Hyman Kublin, *Asian Revolutionary: The Life of Sen Katayama* (Princeton, N.J.: Princeton University Press, 1964); Karl G. Yoneda, "The Heritage of Sen Katayama," *Political Affairs* (1975) (reprinted as pamphlet); Scott Kurashige, *Transforming Los Angeles: Black and Japanese American Struggles for Racial Equality in the 20th Century* (Ph.D. dissertation, University of California, Los Angeles, 2000); Diane Fujino, "Japanese American Radicalism and Radical Formation," paper presented at the National Association for Asian American Studies conference, San Francisco, May 2003; and Karl Yoneda, *Ganbatte: Sixty-Year Struggle of a Kibei Worker* (Los Angeles: UCLA Asian American Studies Center, 1983). On labor organizing, see Tomas Almaguer, *Racial Faultlines: The History of White Supremacy in California* (Berkeley: University of California Press, 1994), 153–204; Edward D. Beechert, *Working in Hawaii: A Labor History* (Honolulu: University of Hawaii Press, 1985); Chris Friday, *Organizing Asian American Labor: The Pacific Coast Canned-Salmon Industry, 1870–1942* (Philadelphia: Temple University Press, 1994); Yuji Ichioka, *The Issei: The World of the First Generation Japanese Immigrants, 1885–1924* (New York: Free Press, 1988); Craig Scharlin and Lilia V. Villanueva, *Philip Vera Cruz: A Personal History of Filipino Immigrants and the Farmworkers Movement* (Seattle: University of Washington Press, 2000 [1992]); Ronald Takaki, *Pau Hana: Plantation Life and Labor in Hawaii, 1835–1920* (Honolulu: University of Hawaii Press, 1983).

4   Issei refers to first-generation or immigrant Japanese Americans, most of whom immigrated to the United States between 1885 and 1924. Nisei refers to second-generation Japanese Americans, the children of immigrants, most of whom were born between 1910 and 1940.

5 Paul Kochi, *Imin no Aiwa (An Immigrant's Sorrowful Tale)* (Los Angeles: self-published, 1978); Ryan Yokota, "Activism for Communism and Community: The Life and Times of Paul Shinsei Kochi," unpublished manuscript, 2003; Mo Nishida, interview by Diane Fujino, April 15, 2003.

6 The U.S. government arrested and imprisoned 1,291 Japanese Americans within the first forty-eight hours after the attack on Pearl Harbor. Those arrested had been placed on the "ABC List" of allegedly "known and potentially dangerous" suspects, when in fact, the U.S. government and military's own investigations, conducted as late as fall 1941, showed that Japanese America posed no threat of espionage, sabotage, or fifth-column activity. See Michi Weglyn, *Years of Infamy: The Untold Story of America's Concentration Camps* (New York: Morrow Quill, 1976); Roger Daniels, *Prisoners without Trial* (New York: Hill and Wang, 1993); and Bob Kumamoto, "The Search for Spies: American Counterintelligence and the Japanese American Community, 1931–1942," *Amerasia Journal* 6 (1979): 45–75.

7 Deborah Lim, "The Lim Report," 1990, unpublished report commissioned by the JACL but suppressed because of its findings critical of JACL's role in incarceration—the report was, however, widely distributed via the Internet, see www.resisters.com or www.javoice.com; Paul Spickard, "The Nisei Assume Power: The Japanese American Citizens League, 1941–1942," *Pacific Historical Review* 52 (1983): 147–74; Jere Takahashi, *Nisei Sansei: Shifting Japanese American Identities and Politics* (Philadelphia: Temple University Press, 1997), 48–112; Bill Hosokawa, *JACL: In Quest of Justice* (New York: William Morrow, 1982).

8 The purging of immigrants resulted in the loss of four thousand members, including more than one hundred Japanese Americans. The clause was overturned in 1944. See Yoneda, *Ganbatte*, 105, 115; William Z. Foster, *History of the Communist Party of the United States* (New York: Greenwood Press, 1968), 392–93.

9 Foster, *History of the CPUSA*, 387–88. Regarding CPUSA interpretations of U.S. motives for entering the war, the CPUSA national chair William Foster wrote: "The main enemy and by far the most powerful fascist power in World War II was Nazi Germany. . . . Actually, however, the United States struck its hardest blows against Japan. . . . due to the fact that American imperialism felt itself much more affected by the far-flung conquests of Japan in the Pacific and Far East, areas which American imperialism had staked out for itself" (402–403).

10 Foster, *History of CPUSA*, 383–407; Dorothy Ray Healey and Maurice Isserman, *California Red: A Life in the American Communist Party* (Urbana: University of Illinois Press, 1993), 86; Yoneda, *Ganbatte*, 111–65; James Oda, *Heroic Struggles of Japanese Americans: Partisan Fighters From America's Concentration Camps* (North Hollywood, Calif.: KNI, 1980).

11 Weglyn, *Years of Infamy*, 121–33; Yoneda, *Ganbatte*, 111–65; Oda, *Heroic Struggles of Japanese Americans*; Hosokawa, *JACL*; Lim, "The Lim Report."

12 Morris and Braine theorize that physical segregation facilitates the develop-

ment of an oppositional political consciousness. This is particularly the case when group members control their segregated spaces, as existed to a fair degree under Japanese American community control of the internal functioning of the concentration camps. See Aldon Morris and Naomi Braine, "Social Movements and Oppositional Consciousness," in *Oppositional Consciousness: The Subjective Roots of Social Protest*, ed. Jane Mansbridge and Aldon Morris (Chicago: University of Chicago Press, 2001), 20–37.

13 Kibei refers to Japanese born in the United States and educated in Japan, who then return to the United States often as young adults. Those educated in Japan in the 1920s and early 1930s tended to have more progressive views, whereas those educated in militaristic Japan in the mid to late 1930s tended to have pro-Japanese militaristic views.

14 Jimmie Omura, "Freedom of the Press," *Rocky Shimpo*, March 29, 1944, in *Frontiers of Asian American Studies*, edited by Gail Nomura, Russell Endo, Steven Sumida, and Russell Leong (Pullman: Washington State University Press, 1989), 79; Weglyn, *Years of Infamy*, 121–33. On draft resistance, see Fair Play Committee, Bulletin no. 3, 1944; Frank Emi, letters to the editor, *Heart Mountain Sentinel*, March 25, 1944; Frank Emi, "Draft Resistance at the Heart Mountain Concentration Camp and the Fair Play Committee," in Nomura et al., *Frontiers of Asian American Studies*, 41–50; William Hohri, ed., *Resistance: Challenging America's Wartime Internment of Japanese-Americans* (Lomita, Calif.: Epistolarian, 2001); and Mike Mackey, *A Matter of Conscience: Essays on the World War II Heart Mountain Draft Resistance Movement* (Power, Wyo.: Western History Publications, 2002).

15 On JACL's postwar activities, see issues of *Pacific Citizen*, the Japanese American Citizens League's organ, Japanese American National Museum, Los Angeles. On differences among civil rights organizations, see Taylor Branch, *Parting the Waters: America in the King Years, 1954–63* (New York: Simon and Schuster, 1988), 467–68; Clayborne Carson, *In Struggle: SNCC and the Black Awakening of the 1960s* (Cambridge, Mass.: Harvard University Press, 1981), 137, 186–89; James Forman, *The Making of Black Revolutionaries* (Seattle, Wash.: Open Hand Publishing, 1985), 147–48; Charles Payne, *I've Got the Light of Freedom: The Organizing Tradition and the Mississippi Freedom Struggle* (Berkeley: University of California Press, 1995), 77–102; and Barbara Ransby, *Ella Baker and the Black Freedom Movement* (Chapel Hill: University of North Carolina Press, 2003), 116–18, 142–47, 281–86.

16 Diane C. Fujino, "Race, Place, and Political Development: Japanese American Radicalism in the 'Pre-Movement' 1960s," *Social Justice*, forthcoming; Davis McEntire, *Residence and Race* (Berkeley: University of California Press, 1960), 46–48, 260; Earl Hanson and Paul Beckett, *Los Angeles: Its People and Its Homes* (Los Angeles: Haynes Foundation, 1944), 36–41. On Marxist influences on the Asian American Movement, see Fred Ho, ed., *Legacy to Liberation: Politics and Culture of Revolutionary Asian Pacific America* (San Francisco: AK

Press, 2000); Miriam Ching Louie, "'Yellow, Brown & Red': Towards an Appraisal of the Marxist Influences on the Asian American Movement," 1991, unpublished manuscript; Roy Nakano, "Marxist-Leninist Organizing in the Asian American Community of Los Angeles, 1969–79," unpublished manuscript, 1984 (available at the UCLA Asian American Studies Reading Room); Laura Pulido, *Black, Brown, Yellow and Left: Radical Activism in Los Angeles, 1968–78* (Berkeley: University of California Press, 2006).

17 My interviews with Kochiyama culminated in the biography *Heartbeat of Struggle: The Revolutionary Practice of Yuri Kochiyama* (Minneapolis: University of Minnesota Press, 2005). My interviews with Aoki will produce a book-length oral history narrative on his life. These interviews, as well as those with other Japanese American radicals, are part of a long-term project on twentieth-century Japanese American radicalism.

18 "[I'm told] I had an unhappy childhood," lamented Richard Aoki, who was born in 1938 in Northern California. "And to a certain extent, that may be correct because [the time before World War II] was probably the happiest period of my childhood and yet I don't remember it" (Richard Aoki, interview by Diane Fujino, May 18–21, 2003).

19 Richard Aoki, interview by Dolly Veale, in Ho, *Legacy to Liberation*, 320; Richard Aoki, interview by Diane Fujino, May 18–21, 2003.

20 Aoki, *Legacy to Liberation*, 320.

21 Richard Aoki, interview by Diane Fujino, June 16–20, 2003.

22 Ibid.; Richard Aoki's military yearbook; Judie Hart, "'Revolutionary Socialist' Leads New Club," *Tower* (Oakland City College), February 26, 1964.

23 [Richard Aoki], "Nationalism, S.F. Black Power Conference, and the SWP," October 8, 1966; Richard Aoki, interviews by Diane Fujino, July 16–18, 2003, and July 30-August 1, 2003.

24 When discussing how the BPP Ten-Point Platform was created, Seale and Newton independently explain that Newton dictated and Seale recorded the points; see *Seize the Time: The Story of the Black Panther Party and Huey P. Newton* (Baltimore: Black Classic Press, 1991 [1968]), 59–69; Huey P. Newton, *Revolutionary Suicide* (New York: Ballantine Books, 1973), 129. Newton also describes his intellectual hunger and passion for study in *Revolutionary Suicide*, 72–78.

25 Aoki, *Legacy to Liberation*, 325.

26 In his autobiography, Huey Newton relays that Seale had collected all of Malcolm's speeches from, among other publications, SWP's newspaper, *The Militant*. According to Seale, his *Militant* subscription came from Aoki. See Newton, *Revolutionary Suicide*, 125; Bobby Seale, interview by Diane Fujino, September 2, 2003; Richard Aoki, interview by Diane Fujino, July 30-August 1, 2003.

27 Two corrections need to be made regarding Richard Aoki's important interview in *Legacy to Liberation*. First, Aoki implies that Newton, Seale, and he wrote the Black Panther Party's Ten-Point Platform (326–27). While Newton

and Seale may well have gained political insights from Aoki, Aoki did not write the platform. A more accurate interpretation is contained in Seale, *Seize the Time*, 59–62, and Newton, *Revolutionary Suicide*, 129, explaining that Newton dictated and Seale recorded the ten points. Aoki remembers helping to reproduce and distribute the platform. I clarified this issue in separate interviews with Richard Aoki, July 30-August 1, 2003, and with Bobby Seale, September 2, 2003. Second, after relaying that he was the "first minister of education" for the Black Panther Party, Aoki allegedly adds, "and there ain't been one since that time" (331). Certainly the latter statement is false, and it was not in the original interview transcript, which Aoki showed to me (Richard Aoki, interviews by Diane Fujino, July 16–18, and July 30-August 1, 2003). Aoki identifies himself as "Minister of Education" in a speech on January 29, 1968.

28   Harvey Dong, *The Origins and Trajectory of Asian American Political Activism in the San Francisco Bay Area, 1968–78* (Ph.D. dissertation, University of California, Berkeley, 2002), 28–79; Floyd Huen, "The Advent and Origins of the Asian American Movement in the San Francisco Bay Area: A Personal Perspective," in Steve Louie and Glenn Omatsu, eds., *Asian Americans: The Movement and the Moment* (Los Angeles: UCLA Asian American Studies Center, 2001), 276–83; Karen Umemoto, "'On Strike!' San Francisco State College Strike, 1968–69: The Role of Asian American Students," *Amerasia Journal* 15 (1989): 3–41; Richard Aoki, interview by Diane Fujino, August 21–26, 2003; Harvey Dong, interviews by Diane Fujino, May 11 and 20, 2003; Bryant Fong, interview by Diane Fujino, January 19, 2004; Alan Fong, interview by Diane Fujino, January 20, 2004. In the context of the brutal FBI and police repression against the BPP during those years, resulting in the killings of twenty-eight Panthers in 1969 alone, Aoki often remarks: "Dolly [Veale] says my going into the Asian American Movement saved my life."

29   "UC Berkeley to Continue Asian Studies Experiment," *Hokubei Mainichi*, April 3, 1969; Ray Okamura, "Asian Studies at U.C. Attract 375 Berkeley Students," *Hokubei Mainichi*, April 23, 1969; syllabus, Asian Studies 100x, winter 1969; "Third World Students Want MS to Tell Their Story First," *Muhammad Speaks*, February 7, 1969; Dong, *Asian American Political Activism*, 28–79; Richard Aoki, "The Asian American Political Alliance: A Study of Organizational Death," graduate student paper, University of California, Berkeley, June 9, 1970; Miriam Ching Louie, "Yellow, Brown & Red"; Richard Aoki, interviews by Diane Fujino, August 21–26, September 8–10, and December 21–23, 2003; Harvey Dong, interviews by Diane Fujino, May 11 and 20, 2003; Bryant Fong, interview by Diane Fujino, January 19, 2003; Alan Fong, interview by Diane Fujino, January 20, 2003.

30   Richard Aoki, "The Asian American Studies Division: A Study in Administrative Behavior," graduate student paper, University of California, Berkeley, June 10, 1970; various Asian American studies curriculum documents, University of California, Berkeley; Richard Aoki, interviews by Diane Fujino, August 21–

26, September 8–10, and December 21–23, 2003; Alan Fong, interview by Diane Fujino, January 20, 2003.

31 Richard Aoki, interviews by Diane Fujino, December 21–23, 2003, January 18–19, 2004, March 14–16, 2004; Richard Aoki, resume.

32 Richard Aoki, interview by Diane Fujino, July 30–August 1, 2003.

33 Unless otherwise noted, the information presented here on Kochiyama is based on the following sources: extensive interviews by Diane Fujino, 1995–1998, along with participant observations, informal interactions, and conversations, 1995-present; Fujino, *Heartbeat of Struggle*; Diane C. Fujino, "To Serve the Movement: The Political Practice of Yuri Kochiyama," in Ho, *Legacy to Liberation*, 257–66; Diane C. Fujino, "Revolution's from the Heart: The Making of an Asian American Women Activist, Yuri Kochiyama," in *Dragon Ladies: Asian American Feminists Breathe Fire*, edited by Sonia Shah (Boston: South End Press, 1997), 169–81; Arthur Tobier, ed., *Fishmerchant's Daughter: Yuri Kochiyama, An Oral History*, vol. 1 (New York: Community Documentation Workshop, 1981); Kochiyama, *Christmas Cheer*, 1951–1968; Kochiyama, *North Star*, 1965–1969.

34 On Kochiyama's popularity, see Yuriko (Endo) Yoshihara, letter to author, February 2000; Norma (Benedetti) Brutti, interview by Diane Fujino, January 16, 2000; and Sumi (Seo) Seki, interview by Diane Fujino, February 13, 2000. Japanese Americans, even those well accepted into white friendship circles, rarely crossed the interracial dating barrier; see Mei Nakano, *Japanese American Women: Three Generations, 1890–1990* (Berkeley: Mina Press, 1990), 111; Takahashi, *Nisei Sansei*, 42–44; Paul Spickard, *Mixed Blood: Intermarriage and Ethnic Identity in Twentieth-Century America* (Madison: University of Wisconsin Press, 1989), 70, 279–80, 374–75; Yuri Kochiyama, interview by Diane Fujino, June 29–July 6, 1997; Peter Nakahara, interview by Diane Fujino, January 12, 2000; Monica Miya (Miwako Oana), interview by Diane Fujino, January 17, 2000; and Sumi (Seo) Seki, interview by Diane Fujino, February 13, 2000.

35 For a more extensive coverage of the influence of the concentration camps on Kochiyama's political development, see Fujino, *Heartbeat of Struggle*; and Fujino, "Race, Place, and Political Development."

36 "Mrs. Mary Kochiyama & family," letter to Malcolm X, October 17, 1963; Yuri Kochiyama, interview by Diane Fujino, December 8–11, 1995.

37 Malcolm X, eleven postcards to "Mr. & Mrs. Wm Kochiyama & Family," 1964, collection of Yuri Kochiyama; Yuri Kochiyama, interview by Diane Fujino, December 8–11, 1995; Mae Mallory, interview by Diane Fujino, February 23, 2000.

38 Yuri Kochiyama, handwritten class notes from the OAAU Liberation School, December 5, 1964, to April 3, 1965, copy in author's collection; James Campbell, interview by Diane Fujino, January 25, 2000; *Backlash*, September 28, 1964; Yuri Kochiyama, interview by Diane Fujino, December 8–11, 1995. For a detailed analysis of the transformation of Kochiyama's ideology, see Diane

Fujino, *Heartbeat of Struggle*. On the OAAU, see William Sales, *From Civil Rights to Black Liberation: Malcolm X and the Organization of Afro-American Unity* (Boston: South End Press, 1994).

39 George Breitman, *The Last Year of Malcolm X* (New York: Schocken Books, 1967), 32, 40–51, 58–59; Sales, *The Organization of Afro-American Unity*, 83–84; Malcolm X, *The Autobiography*, 340. Malcolm's associate Herman Ferguson asserts that although Malcolm no longer made sweeping anti-white indictments, he remained suspicious of the motives of the majority of white Americans raised in a deeply racist society. If American whites could adopt Islam, Malcolm believed they might learn to practice the anti-racist humanity it espoused. But, Ferguson adds, "Malcolm doubted most White Americans would adopt Islam or shed their racism" (Herman Ferguson, letter to author, February 14, 1999).

40 Harold Cruse, *The Crisis of the Negro Intellectual* (New York: Quill, 1984), 355–64, 535–36; Tobier, *Fishmerchant's Daughter*, 7–8.

41 Malcolm X, "Message to the Grass Roots," in *Malcolm X Speaks* (New York: Grove Press, 1965, 7–8); Timothy Tyson, *Radio Free Dixie: Robert F. Williams and the Roots of Black Power* (Chapel Hill: University of North Carolina Press, 1999), 214. Though I contrast the general ideology of the civil rights movement, symbolized by King, and the black liberation movement, symbolized by Malcolm X, it is recognized that many civil rights activists—rank-and-file members as well as some leaders—protected themselves with guns, even as they advocated nonviolence. Other civil rights activists and organizations, notably the SNCC, moved from a position of philosophical nonviolence to self-defense.

42 Cruse, *Crisis of the Black Intellectual*, 359; Tyson, *Radio Free Dixie*, 82–87, 114–15, 206–7, 244–60, 284–85; Williams, *Negroes with Guns*, 117, 120; Newton, *Revolutionary Suicide*, 124.

43 Tyson, *Radio Free Dixie*, 206–7; Robert Sherrill, "We Also Want Four Hundred Billion Dollars Back Pay," *Esquire*, January 1969, 73, 75; Breitman, *The Last Year of Malcolm X*, 26–39; Sales, *The Organization of Afro-American Unity*, 53–94, 99–109; James Campbell, interview by Diane Fujino, January 25, 2000; Muhammad Ahmad, interview by Diane Fujino, January 30, 2000; A. Peter Bailey, conversation with Diane Fujino, July 24, 2000.

44 Ollie A. Johnson, III, "Explaining the Demise of the Black Panther Party: The Role of Internal Factors," in *The Black Panther Party Reconsidered*, edited by Charles E. Jones (Baltimore: Black Classic Press, 1998), 401; Linda Harrison, "On Cultural Nationalism," *The Black Panther*, February 2, 1969, reprinted in *The Black Panthers Speak*, edited by Philip S. Foner (Philadelphia: Lippincott, 1970), 151–54.

45 Sales, *The Organization of Afro-American Unity*, 106, 179; Max Stanford, *Revolutionary Action Movement: A Case Study of an Urban Revolutionary Movement in Western Capitalist Society* (M.A. thesis, Atlanta University, 1986), 2, 74–109, 125–26; Muhammad Ahmad (Max Stanford), interview by Diane Fujino,

January 30, 2000; Kochiyama, interview by Diane Fujino, November 3–10, 1997; Kochiyama, "The Power of Positive Thinking," *North Star*, December, 1966, 1, 8.

46   On RNA's split and the logic of nation building, see Imari Obadele, *Foundations of the Black Nation* (Detroit: House of Songhay, 1975); and Imari Obadele, *War in America: The Malcolm X Doctrine* (Chicago: Ujamaa Distributors, 1977). On the logic of struggling in northern cities, see James Boggs, *Racism and the Class Struggle* (New York: Modern Reader, 1970), 39–50; and Grace Lee Boggs, *Living for Change: An Autobiography* (Minneapolis: University of Minnesota Press, 1998), 36–137.

47   Director, FBI, "Counterintelligence Program, Black Nationalist-Hate Groups, Internal Security," August 25, 1967, reprinted in Ward Churchill and Jim Vander Wall, *The COINTELPRO Papers* (Boston: South End Press, 1990), 92–93; Yuri Kochiyama, "A Generation of Struggle," speech, November 21, 1986, New York City, November 21, 1986; Mutulu Shakur, interview by Diane Fujino, October 19, 1998; Bolanile Akinwole, interview by Diane Fujino, February 21, 2000; Ahmed Obafemi, interview by Diane Fujino, February 7, 2000.

48   Richie Perez, speaking in Rea Tajiri and Patricia Saunders, *Yuri Kochiyama*, video; Yuri Kochiyama, "Eyewitness in Peru: A Learning Experience of People in Struggle," speech, St. Mary's Episcopal Church, New York, April 23, 1993; Yuri Kochiyama, letter to "PP/POWs in the U.S.," May 2, 1993; Yuri Kochiyama, "The IEC's Tour of Philippines and Japan: Why?" speech, New York University Law School, April 13, 1994; International Emergency Committee to Defend the Life of Dr. Abimael Guzman (IEC), "The International Campaign to Defend the Life of Dr. Abimael Guzman," booklet, September, 1993; IEC, "4th IEC Delegation to Peru Completes Successful Mission" and "Findings of the 4th Delegation," *Emergency Bulletin* no. 28, April 9, 1993; Dylcia Pagan, interview by Diane Fujino, October 6, 1998.

49   On theorizing internal colonialism, see Harold Cruse, *Rebellion or Revolution* (New York: William Morrow, 1968), 74–76, 232; Stokely Carmichael and Charles V. Hamilton, *Black Power: The Politics of Liberation in America* (New York: Vintage Books, 1967), 3–32; Robert Blauner, *Racial Oppression in America* (New York: Harper and Row, 1972), 51–110.

50   In *Seize the Time*, Bobby Seale identifies Aoki by name, misspelled as "Richard Iokey," with reference to giving the Party their first guns and with selling Mao's *Red Book*; Seale, *Seize the Time* (Baltimore: Black Classic Press, 1991 [1968]), 72–73, 79, 81; see also www.bobbyseale.com.

51   Mutulu Shakur, interview by Diane Fujino, October 19, 1998; Nyisha Shakur, interview by Diane Fujino, October 15, 1998; Yuri Kochiyama, letter to Herman and Iyaluua Ferguson, November 8, 1993; Minutes, various MXCC meetings.

52   While this essay focuses on the influences of the black liberation movement on Japanese American radicalism, there are examples throughout of how Asian and Asian American influences also shaped black social movements. For more

on Black-Asian political connections, see Vijay Prashad, *Everybody Was Kung Fu Fighting: Afro Asian Connections and the Myth of Cultural Purity* (Boston: Beacon Press, 2001); Gary Okihiro, *Margins and Mainstreams: Asians in American History and Culture* (Seattle: University of Washington Press, 1994), 31–63; Marc Gallicchio, *The African American Encounter with Japan and China: Black Internationalism in Asia, 1895–1945* (Chapel Hill: University of North Carolina Press, 2000); and the essays in this volume.

Kalamu ya Salaam

Why Do We Lie about
Telling the Truth?

"I put his head sort of on my lap. I just hoped and prayed he was still alive. It was hard to tell. He was having difficulty breathing. And other people came and they tore open the shirt. I could see that he was hit so many times."

This is a description of the death of El-Hajj Malik El-Shabazz, aka Malcolm X. Who said these words?

A Betty Shabazz, Malcom's wife who was present with their children when Malcolm was assassinated.

B Gene Roberts, an undercover police agent who had infiltrated Malcolm's organization and was attempting to save Malcolm with mouth-to-mouth resuscitation.

C Yuri Kochiyama, a Japanese American member of Malcom's organization who was present in the Audubon Ballroom on February 21, 1965.

If you have seen Spike Lee's movie *Malcolm X* you will be forgiven in believing the answer is A. Betty Shabazz. If you have seen the death scene photo of a man leaning over

Malcolm desperately trying to revive him, it is understandable that you believe it is B. Gene Roberts. But actually, the correct answer is C. Yuri Kochiyama, a follower and supporter of Malcolm X.

Photos from the grisly death scene clearly show Malcolm's head cradled in Ms. Kochiyama's lap. Spike Lee's colorful and fictionalized pseudo-biography liquidates Ms. Kochiyama and replaces the truth with an untruth. Lee's fictionalization is particularly troubling when we consider the fact that Lee argued that a black director should do the Malcolm X movie because no white director could honestly portray the real story of Malcolm X.

Lee said Malcolm was a black man, and in the process of zoot-suiting and focusing on the Nation of Islam, he completely ignored the internationalist that Malcolm became; as a result, one could see the movie and never know that Yuri Kochiyama was a welcomed and active member of Malcolm's organization, the OAAU. Although Spike Lee is not an elected leader, he is, unquestionably, revered as a major force in the imaging of black people and has often cast himself (or agreed to be cast) as a spokesperson for a "black" point of view.

Malcolm died trying to tell us something important, trying to lead us away from a morbid fascination with color and a limited conception of our struggle. Using the camera, the editing booth, and falsification of facts, Spike Lee re-assassinated Malcolm X the internationalist. Why? Who knows. Lee may not know. But I'm willing to bet that a racial focus devoid of progressive politics had a lot to do with Lee doing the wrong thing.

Why do we lie about truths of our existence? Because even as we oppose racism we often end up believing in racial essentialism.

Black people in America are victims of racism. Many of us—particularly our "appointed" leaders—manifest a terminal case of internalized oppression. Far too many of us are incapable not only of loving ourselves as "mixed-race" human beings (or mulattoes) forcibly born out of the crucible of chattel slavery, but also are incapable of relating to other so-called minorities without exhibiting a warped and essentially racist assessment of people of color.

Misled by leaders (many of whom are media created) who don't pro-actively lead but who instead pander to mass prejudices and misconceptions, many of us U.S. blacks tend toward a twisted and self-destructive color-based antagonism toward other so-called minorities, or in an equally self-destructive manner advocate a mole-like insistence on color blindness that liquidates diversity in the name of an idealized humanism. Both self-centered chauvinism and romantic humanism are, I believe, manifestations of white-supremacy victimization. This skewed perspective of other ethnic groups is particularly troubling in terms of black/Asian relations.

A graphic illustration of where the "I'm human not black" system-induced viewpoint leads us is the movie *One Night Stand* starring Wesley Snipes. In the movie, Wesley's character is a West Coast–based advertising video director who is in New York to see a former best friend who just happens to be white and dying of AIDS. The character has a one-night stand with a blonde rocket scientist and returns home to his Asian wife and two lovely mixed-race children. The movie ends with spouse-swapping; yes, Wesley's character gets the white woman and his Asian wife gets with the cuckolded white husband.

What's wrong with this picture?

Neither the Asian wife nor the African American husband exhibit any cultural self-awareness as people of color. They are portrayed as individuals who are culturally white and who just happen to have been born people of color. Although their race is obvious, they are oblivious to the culture of their people. They go through life neither identifying with other people of color nor advocating black or Asian culture. This acceptance of racial difference but liquidation of cultural differences and distinctions and avoidance of active identification with other people of color is not ethnic diversity. This is white supremacy under the guise of "humanism" and "racial tolerance."

We can approach ethnicity as a racial matter or as a cultural matter. If we focus on race and create a fetish out of color, regardless of what we may think, we are essentially adopting a white supremacist point of view that out-and-out propagandizes the notion that skin color is the essential determinant of human existence. Of course, when it comes to black manifestations of white supremacy's racial essentialism, there are two approaches. One is that black is intrinsically good, moral, and beautiful because of color, and the other is that white is intrinsically good, moral, and beautiful because of power.

Those who argue the "scientific" melanin thesis—i.e., that essentially people born with melanin are better (more moral and beautiful) than people born without melanin—have simply flipped the racist script, including the pseudo-scientific justifications. Indeed, some even argue that whites are a separate species from people of color, hence the Yacub-derived theories from the Nation of Islam that whites are grafted or manufactured people and not human beings like people of color. Those who are entranced by political (actually, economic and military) power basically believe that since whites are at the top, being white is the best one can be. In either case, there is a basic assumption that things are the way they are because of some sort of racial essentialism, some immutable result of racial origins and existence.

I think the basic problem is that we blacks have become Americanized in our social thought via our formal integration into American society, an integration that earnestly began in the mid-1970s and has accelerated ever since. We have become nearly as jingoistic and racist as the dominant society that shapes and influences our psyches—which may be why "skin creams" (i.e., lye-based cosmetics that purportedly lighten the skin) and "hair relaxers" are reported to sell more today than ever before. In terms of our relationship to other people of color—whether continental African, Asian, Hispanic, or Native American, many of us are as racist or as color blind (and, as I argue above, the willful ignoring of real differences is also a form of racism) as the average American, if not more so. Indeed, as far as our attitudes toward others go, many of us might best be defined as brown-skinned rednecks!

While it is common to hear blacks argue that we are the most oppressed people in American history—as if that were some sort of badge of honor—nevertheless, what we don't often do is acknowledge the depth of our wretchedness as the most oppressed. If we are the leading victims of racism, it follows that we along with those who create and maintain this barbaric system are the most affected by the system. No one else is as mesmerized by the splendor of the big house as are the master and his most loyal slave; the master out of material self-interest and the slave out of vicarious self-interest—i.e., psychic identification with the master.

This brings us to the recent rise of black American jingoism—recall the excessive flag waving of the black athletes at the 1996 Olympics in Atlanta, particularly in view of the sharp contrast to the Black Power salutes of the 1968 Olympics in Los Angeles. Admittedly, 1968 then is not 1998 now; there are major differences in the conditions that our people live and struggle under. However, what is remarkable is the embracing of America as though black churches were not being burned to the ground, multinational corporations were not superexploiting Third World labor, African American males were not being systematically victimized by the criminal justice system, etc., etc. Judging from the mindless rah-rahing of how great America is, one would not know that our communities and neighborhoods have been devastated by drugs, riddled by bullets, sickened by disease, and dumbed-down by educational neglect, and, oh yes, that the best and the brightest have left the least and the darkest to fend for themselves in the concrete jungles of urban America. Can anyone really argue that America is the greatest country in the world if one looks at the living conditions of the majority of people of color in the United States?

We have boarded the bus of mindless patriotism and we ride in the front. Regardless of where the stop is, whenever we step off the bus we step off, and proudly so, as full-fledged American patriots with all the racism that such blind patriotism implies. I'm waiting for the melanin experts to explain the ultra patriotism of American blacks in embracing the twin evils of racism and capitalism—is it because in being black we do it better than the whites who introduced it?

No, our skin color is neither the most important part of our oppression nor are color-based proposals the solution to our problems. Moreover, the more important truth is that if we are the most oppressed, we are also the most affected by oppression and, psychologically speaking, that effect has been overwhelmingly negative. Indeed, black racial chauvinism is simply a manifestation of the pathology of oppression, and it is, in the final analysis, nothing more than a variation on the classic white lie of racial superiority.

My first encounters with Asians happened in 1966 when I was in the U.S. Army stationed on a Nike-Hercules nuclear missile base, atop a mountain near the DMZ in Korea. The base was remote and the nearest city was a day's truck ride away. On one peak there were missiles and on another peak nearby there was the radar site. In the valley was the garrison area and a small Korean village separated by a dirt road, barbed wire, and armed guards. The village's main function was to supply cheap labor and cheap thrills to the U.S. soldiers stationed there. I wrote a short story that heavily drew on my experiences and the experiences of my fellow soldiers during my army years. At that time the only locations for the Hercules missiles were the United States, Germany, and Korea. By general consensus, the "brothers" loved Korea and the whites loved Germany. The following excerpt from the story illustrates the social education I received in Korea.

I AIN'T NEVER GOING BACK NO MORE

It was raining by the bucketful. The door to Soulville, which is what we called our collectively rented hooch, was open and it was early afternoon. Rain softened daylight streaming in. And warm, a typical summer monsoon day.

Em, which was the only name I knew her by, was near me. She was reading the paper. I had a Korean bootleg Motown record spinning on the cheap portable player plugged into the extension cord that snaked out the window to some generator source that supplied this small village with a modicum of juice. Did I say village? The place was erected for one reason, and one reason only, to service the service men stationed on the other side of the road, to supply the base with cheap labor and even cheaper pussy. I know it sounds crude, but that's the way occupying armies work.

I had never fucked Em, and, as it turned out, never would. I remember one wrinkled old sergeant, a holdover from World War II, talking on the base one day about Em sucking his dick, but that was not the Em I knew. Somehow, the Em I knew, the woman reading the paper I couldn't read because I couldn't read as many languages as she could, somehow, the lady who put down the paper and, as the rain fell, calmly carried on a conversation with me, clearly that Em was not the same Em that the sergeant knew.

It would be many, many years later before I realized that Sarge never knew Em. How can one ever really know a person if one buys that person? If you buy someone, the very act of the sale cuts you off from thinking of that someone as a human equal. Sarge simply consumed the pleasure given by a female body to whom he paid money, a body which kneaded his flesh and opened her flesh to him, made him shudder as her thighs pulled him in or as she sucked him. A business transaction. Nobody buys pleasure in order to get to know the prostitute. In fact, the whole purpose of the deal is to remove the need for a human connection while satisfying a desire.

I didn't think like that at that time, laying in the hooch with my boots off, day dreaming as I gazed out into the rain, my chin on my arm. In Soulville, just like in all the other hooches, which were usually little more than a large room that doubled as both a living room and a bedroom, we took our boots off upon entering. Even now I like to take my shoes off inside. At the time it was a new thing to me, a difficult thing to get used to, especially with combat boots rather than the slip-ons which most of the Koreans wore. But that's the good thing about going to a foreign country: learning something that you don't already know, something that you can use for the rest of your life.

It's funny how stuff can catch up with you years later, and only after rounding a bunch of corners does the full impact of an experience become clear. I mean more than a delayed reaction, more like a delayed enlightenment . . .

My reminiscence was broken by Em's hand on my arm. I looked over at her. This wasn't no sexual thing. We both knew and observed the one rule of Soulville: no fucking in Soulville. Soulville was a place to hang out and cool out. We put our money together and rented Soulville so as anytime day or night when you didn't feel like being around the white boys, if you was off you could come over to Soulville and just lay. And you didn't have to worry about interrupting nothing. It didn't take long for all the girls in the village to know Soulville was like that. So a lot of time was spent in here with Black GIs and Korean women just talking or listening to music. It was the place where we could relate to each other outside of the flesh connection.

From time to time we had parties at Soulville. And of course, some one of us was always hitting on whoever we wanted for the night. But when it came to getting down to business, you had to vacate the premises. We had had some deep conversations in Soulville. One or two of the girls might cook up some rice or something, and we'd bring some beer or Jim Beam—although I personally liked Jack Daniels Black, Jim Beam was the big thing cause it was cheap, cheap, cheap—and, of course, we brought our most prized possessions, our personal collections of favorite music. We'd eat, drink, dance and argue about whether the Impressions or the Temptations were the baddest group. As I remember it, there wasn't much to argue about among the girl groups, cause none of the others was anywhere near Martha and The Vandellas. Soulville, man, we had some good times there.

Em was getting old. She had been talking about her childhood and stuff. And when she touched my arm and I looked over at her, I could see a bunch of lines showing up in her face. Most of the time, when you saw the girls it was at night or they had all kinds of makeup on their face. But it was not unusual for some of us to sleep over at Soulville and if we were off duty we'd just loll around there all day. Early in the morning we would hear the village waking up and watch the day unfold. Invariably, one of the girls would stop by to chat for ten or fifteen minutes. Or sometimes, two or three of them would hang out for awhile.

On days like this one, you'd get to see them as people. Talking and doing whatever they do, which is different from seeing them sitting around a table, dolled up with powder and lipstick, acting—or should I say, "trying to act"— coy or sexy, sipping watered-down drinks through a straw and almost reeking of the cheap perfume they doused on themselves in an almost futile attempt to cover the pungent fragrance associated with the women of the night.

Just like when we was in Soulville we was off duty, well it was the same way for them. And I guess without the stain and strain of a cash transaction clouding the picture, we all got a chance to see a different side of each other.

I started wondering what it must have felt like to be a prostitute, a middle-aged prostitute getting old and knowing you ain't had much of a future. A prostitute watching soldiers come and go, year after year. What it must have been like to have sex with all them different men, day in and day out and shit. Especially for somebody like Em who spoke Korean, English, Japanese, and Chinese, and could read in Korean, English, and Chinese. I mean, from the standpoint of knowing her part of the world, she was more intelligent than damn near all of us put together.

Her touch was soft on my arm. I looked down at her small hand, the unpainted fingernails, the sort of dark cream color of her skin. I looked up into her face. Her eyes were somber but she was half smiling.

"Same-o, same-o." She said, rubbing first my bare arm and then her bare arm. "Same-o, same-o."

Like most of my peers, my first encounter with Asians was a politically unconscious encounter. Although I may like to think otherwise and under-standably was reluctant to publicly admit it, I was an armed agent of im-perialism—no matter that I told myself, for example, that I was in Korea to avoid going to Vietnam; no matter that I tried to have more respect for the Korean people than did the white soldiers on the base; no matter that I understood that there was a connection of color between myself and the Koreans. Just like a Japanese American friend whom it turns out was born in an internment camp during World War II and who served in the U.S. Army at the same time I did, regardless of all the historical and individual contra-dictions I had with America's domestic and foreign policies, regardless of my personal beliefs or how I dressed up my involvement, the reality was that I was a soldier in the army, a collaborator with the dictators of democracy. Although I had my rationalizations, and though my "reasoning" did have some merit, there is a big difference between admitting one's contradictions and lying to oneself about the existence of those contradictions. That's what Em was telling me—prostitute to soldier, we're same-o, same-o.

My second major encounter with Asians was a horse of a different mule. In 1974 I was a delegate to the fifth Pan-African Congress in Dar es Salaam, Tanzania. I was an active organizer in my home community of New Orleans and considered myself a Pan-Africanist. Upon arriving in Tanzania one of my first quests was to stand on the TanZam railroad, a vital rail linkage between Zambia and Tanzania that gave landlocked Zambia seaport access for copper shipments. The railroad was built through the lead partnership of the People's Republic of China. During that time I also had the opportunity to visit Zanzibar where I took a tour of a cigarette factory that was built and transitionally managed by the Chinese. I spoke to none of the Chinese managers or workers, but I watched and wondered.

Our relationship to "foreigners" is inevitably a major barometer of our political consciousness. By 1974, the internal clash among black radicals between the philosophies of black nationalism and Marxism was at an all-time high. By then Amiri Baraka, the former chief propagandist of Kawaida-style black nationalism had declared himself a Marxist. Also, within the Black Power movement, the teachings of Chairman Mao were widely studied by nationalists and Marxists alike. Moreover, struggles around the Vietnam War had also come to a head. Within this social context, political considerations were primary and alliances between ethnic groups were forged for purposes of collective struggle against racism and capitalism. This was a high point in interethnic alliances, not because of liberal "we are all humans" sentiments but because of militant political calls for Third World liberation abroad and Third World self-determination at home. Hence, even though he has never been a Marxist, Haki Madhubuti (formerly Don L. Lee) named the press he cofounded "Third World Press."

Less than two decades ago, we were identifying with people of color rather than antagonistic toward people whom many of us now contemptuously regard as competitors for "our jobs" and replacements for white neighborhood merchants who price gouge us in corner stores where we are charged a nickel to change a dime. What the Third World had in common was not really color but rather anticolonial struggle, and we within the

United States were equally, if not more so, colonial subjects. Within that context, identification with the Third World was led by a political understanding that in many ways was much more mature than the good-old-boy "buy American" rhetoric we mindlessly spout today.

This same political concern with the Third World led our nationwide grouping of black nationalists, all of whom operated independent black educational institutions for young black children, to organize the first all-black tour to China in 1977. We worked in cooperation with the Marxist-led U.S.-China Friendship Association. During the course of the year-long effort to arrange the trip and raise money for it, we encountered, confronted, and attempted to change anti-Asian sentiments in our community without liquidating our basic black nationalist stance. In fact, at one point there was a concerted effort by some members of the Friendship Association to force us to exclude Maulana Ron Karenga from our twenty-member delegation. We took the stance that the makeup of our delegation was an internal matter not subject to the dictates of outsiders, and if it meant that we had to forgo the trip then so be it. After some weeks of high-level wrangling, our delegation proceeded as originally planned. We spent eighteen days traveling throughout China, and we happened to be in Beijing (then Peking) when the rehabilitation of Deng Xiaoping was announced.

Although there was a massive demonstration in the city center by the literally millions of people supporting Deng, I remained skeptical of Deng's line. He had argued that it doesn't make a difference what color the cat is as long as the cat catches the mice. Some of us argued that "color" (Deng was referring to ideology) did make a difference because if black cats never learned to catch mice, black cats would continue to be dependent on white cats for food. At the same time, I was not inclined to simply dismiss the Chinese view out of hand because by then I realized that there was a lot more to Chinese ideological developments than initially met the eye.

While we were in Beijing some of us met Robert Williams, the former NAACP organizer who had fled to Cuba then China after an attempted frame-up by the FBI. Williams was recuperating from an operation for which he had returned to China. When Nixon visited China and officially reopened diplomatic relations with the Chinese government, Robert Williams parlayed his knowledge and acceptance within the Chinese government into an opportunity to return to the United States. Williams made the trade-off after over a decade of being in exile; after being on the FBI's most-wanted list and on the CIA's hit list for his international activities, which included publishing the militant newspaper *The Crusader;* and after, while in Cuba, broadcasting an incendiary radio program known as Radio Free Dixie. Indeed, our delegation had a photocopy of the issue of Dan Watts's *Liberator* magazine whose cover featured a famous photo of Robert Williams standing with Chairman Mao.

Robert Williams was overjoyed to see us in Beijing—we were the first blacks he knew of to take an organized and direct interest in China, and he asserted that it was extremely important for black people to get involved in international affairs separate from America's foreign policy. Of course, there were truckloads of Chinese-influenced Afro Marxists back in the states, and of course some of the Panthers had passed through China, but most of these people came as individuals or as Marxists in small, clandestine, and racially integrated groups. We were the first blacks to enter as an organized body representing a broad grassroots constituency from across the United States.

We spent over an hour talking with Brother Rob as he patiently encouraged us to develop an internationalist viewpoint. What I remember most is Robert Williams telling us about his stay in North Vietnam and how at a state dinner he rose to propose a toast to the Vietnamese people. Brother Rob said the Vietnamese made him sit down by responding that it was they who should be toasting him and the valiant struggle of the Afro-American people.

The North Vietnamese told Robert Williams that the black power struggle greatly helped them understand that the United States could be beaten and that the urban rebellions, particularly in Detroit where the U.S. Army Airborne had to be sent in before "order" could be "restored," had given the Vietnamese the idea to stage the Tet offensive, which was psychologically the major turning point of the Vietnam conflict. The reverberations of the black liberation struggle were felt not only internally but also worldwide. In efforts including the free speech movement, emergent feminism, Vietnam antiwar demonstrations, gay rights and other internal struggles, and work in the international arena our struggle inspired and encouraged a variety of peoples and interest groups who had their own particular battles with oppression and exploitation. These were heady and exciting days of political discussion, analysis, and planning.

At our previous stop in Xian, China, after over a week of inquiries, our delegation had engaged in a major ideological discussion with political theorists of the Chinese Communist Party. I distinctly remember that these particular individuals in their mannerisms, dress, and general physical appearance "looked" different from the majority of the Chinese that we had up to that point encountered. These men may have had "peasant" roots but their current status was cloistered within a circle of folk who "thought" for a living; they were part of the policymaking and implementation apparatus. They frankly stated a line I had never heard before: If the capitalists want to bring on World War III, so be it. Such a war would only hasten capitalism's demise.

These men with the confident-quiet of an armed but not yet exploded bomb calmly ran down their view of progress: Since the 1950s America has been engaged in conflict with Asia and has been steadily losing ground. First came Korea, and there was a stalemate. Then came Vietnam, and America lost. Should America decide to take on China the result would be more than simply another American loss. What would happen would be China's ascendancy. The Chinese had the atomic bomb, there would be no more one-sided nuking of "yellow peoples" as happened in Japan during World War II. Also, the Chinese had constructed underground cities— literally factories, housing, and shelters for not just a handful of select leaders but for masses of Chinese people. They knew that America was not similarly prepared to withstand nuclear war. They were prepared. They were not afraid. They didn't want to have a war, but if it came to that, so be it. Needless to say, we had not been prepared to argue world politics at that level.

For the Chinese, the subsequent disintegration of Soviet Russia, far from reputing communism and the Chinese view, actually was just another wrinkle in the fabric of Eurocentric capitalism's eventual demise. The Chinese had long ago split with the Soviets and saw them as state capitalists who were hopelessly emotionally enmeshed and ideologically intertwined with the Western world. For we black nationalists struggling to conceptualize and actualize some form of a black nation in America, these discussions were eye-opening developments. When we returned to the United States we organized forums and community meetings to report on our trip to China. The general headline we used was "Black Nationalists in Red China." This was my second major interface with Asians.

My third encounter with Asia was the development in 1991 of a partnership with the Chinese American baritone saxophonist and composer Fred Ho. We knew of each other's political work, and we had first met face to face in Houston, Texas, in a meeting arranged by a mutual friend, Baraka Sele, who was then a producer with the Houston International Festival. Both of us were booked to perform at the festival, and Baraka had arranged for us to all go to a dinner together. Fred and I talked. I knew his music from recordings. He had read some of my poetry. We talked that "Yeah, let's get together and do something sometime" talk in which one usually engages acquaintances at festivals and conferences. However, we took it further than wishful talk. We stayed in touch and decided to start working as a duo.

We had two things in common. First, we both had a long history of political involvement and were active as socially committed cultural workers who elevated our political concerns over the economic concerns of making it commercially within the system. Second, we both have a deep love for music and are heavily influenced by black music.

When we got together we were able to work as a true duo rather than as one artist backing up the other. The music was not background for my poems and my poems were not just hooks for Fred to string together saxophone solos. At the same time, Fred and I were not always in total agreement on political and aesthetic matters. We debated each other. Fred remains a Marxist and I, more than ever, am an advocate of socially committed, politically progressive black culture. I no longer consider myself a black nationalist.

Fred and I work together not because of color or because of some trendy concern with multiculturalism or pie in the sky "rainbow coalitionism." We work together because we are politically attuned to opposing the racist/capitalist/sexist status quo. We are searching to develop ideas, institutions, and ourselves as individuals who work to establish egalitarian and just social formations at every level of our existence, emphasizing both the personal one-to-one and the ongoing development of multigenerational organizations that work with young people to help uplift and empower our people and each other.

Our duo, the Afro Asians Arts Dialogue, has performed from Atlanta to Wisconsin to California to Maine and a number of places in between. The majority of our performances are sponsored by Asian student groups and by Third World/minority offices on college campuses. We have yet to be booked by a black student organization. Fred and I talk about why black groups shy away from booking us. The answer is simple: the currents of black struggle are at an all-time low. Our heroes are athletes and entertainers, politicians and academic "public intellectuals," all of whom directly depend on the status quo for their money and status. The bulk of our leadership lives in the big house and dreams of sleeping in the master's bed.

Nationalism is a bankrupt concept. While we strive to become fully integrated into America, the fact of the matter is that the working-class masses of us are more isolated, more exploited, and more hopeless than ever before. The 1990s wave of drug culture, or what we used to call "biological warfare," is nothing new. The "opium wars" in China are a precursor of the inner-city "crack" epidemic. Whether we talk integration into America or separate development in black countries such as those in Africa and the Caribbean, reality has demonstrated that neither option in and of itself is the solution for our people here in America.

We can argue about the causes of our oppression and exploitation, but the effects are real and deadly. Moreover, the major issue to address is our collusion with capitalism and hence our own resultant racism. Do you think Michael Jordan or Tiger Woods could get away with endorsing Nike if the shoes were manufactured in Haiti or Senegal for ridiculously low wages under neoslave conditions? Unfortunately, the answer is yes—if our leadership continues to be apologists for capitalism and mesmerized by glitz.

The truth, I believe, is that we are doing the same thing that white American workers historically have done—we are being bought off by a combination of materialism and isolation. And while we are busy ideologically waving the American flag, capital recognizes no national boundaries. The globalization of economic exploitation by structures such as the multinational corporations, the World Bank, and the most famous of all marauders, the IMF (officially the International Monetary Fund, unofficially the International Mother Fucker!), is the current form of economic exploitation.

Asia will unavoidably be the dominant battlefield of the twenty-first century, especially India—the world's largest English-speaking country—and

China. This is not to say that Africa is insignificant or irrelevant, far from it. Africa will remain a major site of ongoing struggle, and it will remain particularly relevant to the future of black people worldwide precisely because, as a result of disease (particularly AIDS) and famine, and as a legacy of the slave trade, in the twenty-first century Africa will be severely underpopulated. This is an important point to keep in mind. The needs of Africa notwithstanding, I believe that Asia will be the major arena of future North/South, East/West clashes.

Only those of us who are prepared to relate to the whole world will develop and prosper. Everyone else will be left behind to wallow in their own parochialism. For too many of us "integration" has meant, as James Baldwin so prophetically argued, rushing into "a burning house." But the future is not white. The sun will set on Europe, and when the new day dawns, global cooperation will be the order of the day. Now is the time to prepare for that future.

Why do we lie about telling these hard truths? Our leaders lie to us for the benefit of short-term material gain—a salary, proximity to power, a high-ranking career, a lucrative endorsement or consulting contract.

Exploited as both labor and capital, we were money—our physical bodies. If anyone should understand the evils of capitalism, we—as the descendants of enslaved Africans, America's first form of venture capital—should understand.

In contemporary terms, moreover, when we advocate "free enterprise zones," "black capitalism" under the rhetoric and rubric of small business entrepreneurship, or preparing ourselves for "good jobs," we are merely adding another brick in the wall of our people's economic and political disenfranchisement. Business per se is not the problem (buying, selling, and bartering existed long before capitalism). The elevation of an economic bottom line to the top priority of all our endeavors is the problem.

I do not believe that everything in America is wrong, nor do I believe that there is no hope. I do believe that this society is in the midst of a major meltdown and that in the next millennium we will look back on this stage and wonder why we couldn't see the problems for what they actually were. America is imploding. While the United States certainly has been the most militarily powerful country of the past century, military power is no real measure of social well-being.

When we closely examine the social conditions of all people in this society, the conclusion that there are serious problems is obvious. This grand experiment called America was seriously flawed from the beginning, based as it was on the liquidation of Native Americans and the enslavement of Africans, all justified in the name of life, liberty, and the pursuit of (material/economic) happiness. The main reason that people came to and continue to come to America is because of the perception and the opportunity to make fortunes, but all such fortunes are made at the terrible expense of various peoples (mainly, but not exclusively, people of color) worldwide.

The problem is that the center can no longer hold. The world cannot and will not continue to provide over 60 percent of its resources to a country that has far less than 10 percent of its population. There will be a change. The course and results of this change are what is in question.

In the here and now, the solution is for us to open our eyes, travel the world, and begin to find out for ourselves what is going on. The solution is to begin to think and act and live globally. The solution can be found by living harmoniously while putting ethics and not economics in the lead; by emphasizing cultural integrity rather than racial purity; by advocating and maintaining alliances with peoples of color and people of good deeds whomever they may be.

Korean shopkeepers, Vietnamese merchants, Chinese restaurateurs—none of these are our real enemies. Multinational corporations, the U.S. government, academic citadels—none of these are our real friends.

For particularly revealing insights on how America actually works, and for insight into how minorities in high positions don't and can't make a major difference in the economic and political well-being of the masses, read two books: *Diversity in the Power Elite—Have Women and Minorities Reached the Top?* by Richard L. Zweigenhaft and G. William Domhoff, and *Who Rules America Now? A View for the 80's* by G. William Domhoff. Many of us have never faced the truth about the society into which we were born and a society whose existence we accept as the work of "God" rather than the machinations of classes and interest groups often operating out of pure greed and material self-interest. Without serious study, we are not even prepared to argue our beliefs or make accurate analysis of our problems. For far too many of us, the popular media is the sum total of our education and understanding of both world affairs and the realities of American life.

You can believe the ideals, myths, and outright lies if you want to, but I'll take a hard truth over a soft lie any day of the week. The truth is we are knowingly lied to every day of the week by those who have a stake in the status quo. What we really need are leaders who will call into question all of our beliefs and challenge us to address the pressing, very real, and very difficult situations that confront us instead of advocating a mixture of metaphysics and fatalism, a mixture of the traditional "Put it in God's/Jesus' hands" and "There's no way like the American way." If those options are the solution, how is it that after nearly five hundred years of "one nation under God" we have the problems we have today?

The majority of our so-called leaders lie about telling the truth because they are not our leaders but rather are handpicked and specifically groomed judas goats whose main task is to quietly lead us to economic and political slaughter. Regardless of what our leaders believe and what god they pray to, the results of their actions define them for what they are. And that's the truth!

AFRO-ASIAN ARTS:
CATALYSTS, COLLABORATIONS,
AND THE COLTRANE AESTHETIC

Part III features essays that honor, evoke, and expand on the Bandung era in the realm of cultural production and the arts. The African American writer-polemicist Ishmael Reed himself was a major catalyst and connector for Asian American writers. In his terse and humble recounting of how he met and helped Asian American writers such as Frank Chin, Lawson Inada, and Shawn Wong among many others, we are given a rare original account of the origins of modern Asian American literary production. The scholar-activist Cheryl Higashida gives a more detailed analysis of black-Asian female literary production and collaboration. A common theme running through this section is the large debt owed by modern Asian American creativity to African American culture and politics. The Vietnamese American spoken-word artist Thien-bao Thuc Phi describes the impact of black hip hop culture upon working-class urban Asian American youth. Two essays—by Kim Hewitt and Ron Wheeler with David Kaufman—are devoted to black-Asian interactions and inspirations in the martial arts, a cultural territory where Asian dominance both in actuality and in media representation has been uncontested. The ethnomusicologist and master drummer royal hartigan offers a precise and careful guide to Afro-Asian aesthetics in his essay "The American Drum Set." The impact of "Third Worldism" is noted in the unique presence and role of Bill Cole, the ethnomusicologist and "jazz" musician who performs Asian double reeds, interviewed here by Fred Ho.

Ishmael Reed

The Yellow and the Black

I grew up in a city that was largely black and white. Of course, there were ethnic differences, but they were not discussed. For blacks, groups like the Jews, Italians, and Irish were white. To whites, we were black. Ethnic differences were something that happened abroad. This became clearer to me when I traveled to Paris. I was fifteen and attended a world conference where many people were attired in their native dress.

When I arrived in New York, I found that ethnic differences were more obvious than those in Buffalo, New York. One of the reasons was that there was a larger immigrant community: Puerto Rican, Eastern European, and Asian. Living on the Lower East Side, I made friends with Puerto Rican writers and I remember at least one Russian immigrant named Victor, who often visited our apartment.

Carla Blank introduced me to a number of Japanese artists who were living in New York at the time. They included Suzushi Hanayagi, who has performed my work in Japan, her husband, the painter Isamu Kawaii, and the jazz pianist Toshiko Akiyoshi.

I met Frank Chin in 1969 or so, when I published an excerpt from his novel *A Chinese Lady Dies* in my anthology *19 Necromancers from Now*. It was at the party to celebrate the publication of this anthology that the writers who became known as the Four Horsemen of Asian American literature met for the first time: Shawn Wong, Frank Chin, Jeff Chan, and Lawson Inada. Shawn dates their collaboration to this meeting, in an essay printed in Carla Blank's forthcoming book, *Rediscovering America*.

I sent Frank's play *The Year of the Dragon* to Chiz Shultz, one of the producers of *Sesame Street*. I'd met Chiz in 1969 after the publication of my novel *Yellow Back Radio Broke-Down*. Chitz got Frank's play produced at the Public Theater and it was also produced on the Public Broadcasting System.

As editor of *Yardbird* magazine I invited the Four Horsemen to do a special issue. The result was *Yardbird 3*, the Asian American issue, which is now considered a classic work and one of the important documents of the Asian American renaissance. Moreover, I published Shawn Wong's *Homebase* under our imprint Reed and Cannon Publishing. It was the first novel published by an American-born Chinese male. I also was responsible for introducing the Four Horsemen's work to Charles Harris at Howard University Press. He published their *Aiiieeeee! An Anthology of Asian American Writers*.

I met Mei Mei Berssenbrugge in 1974 and published her book *Random Possession*. It was well received by the poet John Ashbury, as well as an important event in Mei Mei's rise as one of America's leading language poets.

We published a number of distinguished Asian American writers in the Yardbird and Y'Bird and Quilt series, including Cyn Zarco and Jessica Hagedorn, and many have received American Book Awards from our organization, the Before Columbus Foundation.

In the early 1990s I produced the video of Genny Lim's "The Only Language She Knows," featuring Genny and directed by M. J. Lee and Carla Blank. The Emmy-award winner Allen Willis was the videographer, and Jon Jang contributed the musical score. This production was included in film festivals in Europe and the United States and exhibited in Japan.

My collaboration with Asian American writers and artists has strengthened my work. I studied Japanese, and the songs I wrote in Japanese were well received by audiences at Tokyo's Blue Note during my one-week gig there with the Conjure band in August of 2003. My song "Tokyo Woman Blues" was performed by Alvin Youngblood Hart, backed up by David Murray, Yosvany Terry, Leo Nocentelli, Billy Bang, Fernando Saunders, Anthony Cox, Robby Ameen, Horacio 'El Negro' Hernandez, Pedro Martinez, and Richard Flores. Fernando Saunders sang my "In an Azabu Café," which I recited in Japanese. This concert was covered by Yuri Kageyama of the Associated Press. In the early 1970s I published Yuri's book of poetry, *Peeling*.

We Asian Americans, African Americans, Native Americans, and Hispanics have formed a coalition that has transformed American literature. This movement has not, however, been recognized by the literary oligarchy, which is still guided by the tastes of those who desire all of us to become Anglo. This view is expressed by the oligarchy's spokesperson Andrew Hacker, who has written the same plea a dozen or so times over the years in the *New York Review of Books*. We refuse to make things easy for them. The multicultural renaissance is recognized everywhere but in our own country. This is the way it's been for jazz musicians, so it's to be expected.

Cheryl Higashida

Not Just a "Special Issue": Gender, Sexuality, and Post-1965 Afro Asian Coalition Building in the *Yardbird Reader* and *This Bridge Called My Back*

n their prologue to the anthology of poetry *Time to Greez! Incantations from the Third World* the editors discuss the need for Third World people to recognize mutual interests, especially in the name of self-representation: "We share common problems of racism, lack of capital and tools; but we share the common beauty of understanding and expressing the rhythm and color of our lives—*for real*."[1] To this end, Third World Communications, "a coalition of Black, Raza, Asian, American Indian, and Native Island people," had formed in 1971 to pool together their resources to publish and distribute the work of ethnic writers. *Time to Greez!* exemplified this effort and celebrated the ability of its contributors to overcome the differences that threatened to divide them: "The 'greez' is a feast—a sharing of our food. This book is a sharing of spirits and a feast of words, music and symbols." On the other hand, coalition building as theorized by Bernice Johnson Reagon assumes a much less celebratory cast: "Coalition work is not work done in your home. Coalition work has to be done in the streets. And it is some of the most dangerous work you can do. . . . You don't get a lot of food in a coalition. You don't get fed a lot in a coalition."[2]

Nonetheless, both Reagon and the editors of *Greez!* perceive the need to build coalitions rather than to advocate separatism, defined by Barbara Smith as "a strategy that often takes a 'to hell with it' stance. . . . Instead of working to challenge the system and to transform it, many separatists wash their hands of it and the system continues on its merry way." Distinguishing separatism from autonomy, Smith explains in an oft-cited passage that "whereas autonomy comes from a position of strength, separatism comes from a position of fear. When we're truly autonomous we can deal with other kinds of people, a multiplicity of issues, and with difference, because we have formed a solid base of strength with those with whom we share identity and/or political commitment."[3]

It is this spirit of coalition building—one that conceptualizes race, gender, and class as interlocking or simultaneous forms of oppression—that characterizes the key U.S. ethnic literary institutions and texts of the 1970s and 1980s. For example, the lesbian journal *Conditions* (1977–1990), one of the few feminist magazines that consistently published work by and about Third World women, was committed to "reflect[ing] the experiences and viewpoints of Third World, working-class, and older women."[4] Notably, this commitment was reflected not only in its content but also in its editorial collective, which in 1982 included Dorothy Allison, Cheryl Clarke, Jewelle Gomez, and Mirtha Quintanales, while Cherríe Moraga served as the journal's office manager.

Within this climate of Third World coalition building, Afro Asian literary collaborations flourished. Especially important to the history, politics, and aesthetics of these collaborations are two texts and their respective publishers: Yardbird Publishing Company's *Yardbird Reader*, volume 3 ("The Asian American Issue," 1974), and Kitchen Table: Women of Color Press' *This Bridge Called My Back: Writings by Radical Women of Color* (1983).[5] Both presses were substantially indebted to the work of African American writer-activists. Yardbird Publishing was founded in 1971 by Ishmael Reed and Al Young; Kitchen Table was largely the work of Barbara Smith, and at the initial meeting in 1980 that Smith organized to do something about publishing, "there were only women of African American and African Caribbean descent in the room."[6] Reed, Young, and Smith realized that people of color would be unheard as long as they did not possess their own media, and as long as the American literary scene remained, in Reed's words, "a white settler's fortress."

Yet the term "black press" is somewhat misleading in the cases of Yardbird and Kitchen Table, insofar as they published and supported all writers of color; indeed, Shawn Wong asserts that it was through institutional support by the black press that many "Asian Americans were exposed to the Black Arts/Black Power movements, rather [than] the other way around."[7] According to the Black Arts poet, jazz critic, and scholar Ron Welburn, Reed "was the driving force behind an effort to have some kind of annual publication a la NEW AMERICAN REVIEW [a digest of fiction, essays, and poetry] and which would take up the slack left by AMISTAD [the two-volume anthology of black writing coedited by Charles Harris and John A. Williams]. . . . Many 'liberal' literary magazines also ran 'special ethnic issues,' after which an ethnic writer was lucky to get into their pages."[8]

To address this dearth of venues for ethnic literature, Reed and other African American writers (including Williams, Welburn, and Clarence Major) had decided to edit a collection of multiethnic work to be called *Dues: An Annual of New Earth Writing*. The editor-in-chief, Welburn, collected two volumes' worth of material, but the project fell through.[9] Its spirit eventually attained material form in the five *Yardbird Readers*, which "contained the work of scores of Asian-Hispanic-Afro- and Euro-American writers."[10] Yardbird and Reed's support of Asian American writers, many of whom were ignored or rejected not only by white America but by other Asian Americans, is emphasized in Frank Chin and Shawn Wong's introduction to the third *Yardbird Reader*: "Yardbird Publishing Cooperative is the first Berkeley-San Francisco based national publication to acknowledge the existence of an Asian American cultural tradition that is not mere mimicry or exotic artifact. We weren't surprised to learn that Blacks were quicker to understand and appreciate the value of Asian American writing than whites" (vi).

Reed had already included an excerpt from Chin's novel, *A Chinese Lady Dies*, in his anthology *19 Necromancers from Now* (1970), and he supported the publication of *Aiiieeeee! An Anthology of Asian American Writers*, which had initially been rejected by white-owned publishing houses on the basis of its being either too, or not properly, ethnic (eventually, Howard University

Press brought it out with their inaugural list of books). Reed also published Wong's first novel, *Homebase,* under the imprint I. Reed Books, after several publishers had turned down what would become an award-winning book (and, for a time, the only novel by a Chinese American in print in America).[11]

Unlike the Yardbird Cooperative, Kitchen Table—the first and in its time the only press founded and directed by women of color—did not initially publish Euro-American writers since its founders saw the need to address first the barriers preventing women of color from publishing during what Barbara Smith called "the era of the 'special issue.' "[12] As Smith further notes: "On the most basic level, Kitchen Table Press began because of our need for autonomy, our need to determine independently both the content and the conditions of our work and to control the words and images that were produced about us. As feminist and lesbian of color writers, we knew that we had no options for getting published except at the mercy or whim of others—in either commercial or alternative publishing, since both are white dominated."[13]

Nonetheless, Kitchen Table privileged coalition building over separatism, choosing from the outset to publish and to serve as a resource network for all women of color. Despite the fact that, as one interviewer put it, "a lot of women ask why Kitchen Table is publishing white women and Japanese women, straying from the works of Black women only," Smith stood by the Press' commitment to "all women of color, of all nationalities, sexual orientations, classes."[14] Smith rightly notes that "This was one of our bravest steps; most people of color have chosen to work in their separate groups when they do media or other projects. We were saying that as women, feminists, and lesbians of color we had experiences and work to do in common, although we also had our differences."[15] As an extension of this logic, Kitchen Table tried to reach all people of color and not only women, since it understood racism and sexism to be interconnected.[16]

Like Yardbird, then, Kitchen Table enabled the work of Asian American writers—in particular, women writers—to be read and heard: in addition to anthologies such as *Bridge* and *Home Girls,* Kitchen Table published Mitsuye Yamada's *Desert Run: Poems and Stories* and Hisaye Yamamoto's *Seventeen Syllables and Other Stories*—the latter of which became the first title that a lesbian feminist press had sold to a major book club—as well as Freedom Organizing Pamphlets including Merle Woo's "Our Common Enemy Our

Common Cause: Freedom Organizing in the Eighties," which was copublished with Audre Lorde's "Apartheid U.S.A." Kitchen Table's commitment to Third World struggles for self-determination is shown in its 1984 publication of *A Comrade Is as Precious as a Rice Seedling*, a book by the Filipina dissident Mila Aguilar, who was imprisoned under the Marcos regime and released in 1986 when her book drew international attention.[17]

In turning to two of the groundbreaking texts of multicultural literature published by Yardbird and Kitchen Table—the aforementioned Asian American issue of the *Yardbird Reader* (1974) and *This Bridge Called My Back* (first published in 1981 by Persephone Press)—I want to focus on the question of how gender and sexuality are central to our understanding of the Afro Asian literary and political coalitions of the 1970s and 1980s. The two collections are distinct and even opposed in their political goals; *Bridge* is explicitly Left in its theorizations of Third World feminism, while the *Reader*'s main concern (as expressed by the editors' statements) is the recovery of literature by and for Asian Americans. Furthermore, *Bridge*'s radical feminism diametrically opposes the *Reader*'s masculine reconstruction of Asian American identity. This male-centered cultural nationalism challenges the racist emasculation by the United States of Asian American men through exclusion acts and antimiscegenation laws resulting in Chinese and Filipino bachelor societies, restrictions on Asian men's economic mobility in America (many of which pushed Asian men into occupations devalued for being "women's work," such as laundering), and pop culture representations of the asexual or homosexual Asian male (Fu Manchu, Charlie Chan). As Frank Chin argues elsewhere, "Chinese-America was rigged to be a race of males going extinct without women."[18] Nonetheless, Asian Americanists have criticized Chin and Wong both separately and together (as coeditors, along with Jeffery Paul Chan and Lawson Fusao Inada, of the *Aiiieeeee!* anthology) for their patriarchal and heteronormative formulations of Asian American identity.[19] On the other hand, *Bridge,* edited by the Chicana feminists Cherríe Moraga and Gloria Anzaldúa, marked a watershed moment in feminist scholarship. Not only did it address sexism and homophobia in communities of color and demonstrate that women's liberation cannot coexist with national oppression, but it did so as one of the first anthologies of multicultural feminism and as one of the first feminist collections comprised primarily by the writing of working-class lesbians of color. While the need to address racism and classism in the U.S. women's movement initially spurred Anzaldúa to create a Third World women's anthology, *Bridge* is ultimately anchored by its "positive affirmation of the commitment of women of color to our *own* feminism" (xxiii).

This gendered division between the two texts breaks down, however, in the course of their engagements with the "dangerous work" of coalition building across lines of race. Because *Bridge* explicitly theorizes such coalition building in ways that are more implicit in the *Reader,* I will begin by discussing *Bridge*—even though it came out seven years after the *Reader*—in order to examine the dialectical relationship between autonomy and coalition as it informs our understanding of identity politics and post-1965 Afro Asian cultural collaborations. In the greater part of this essay I will then argue that the *Reader* initially represents but ultimately cannot sustain a masculinist Asian American cultural nationalism in the course of its Afro Asian (but, more broadly, multicultural) aesthetic experimentations. In particular, this androcentrism is interrogated by two of the *Reader*'s centerpiece texts—Lawson Fusao Inada's long poem "Japanese Geometry," and Act II of Frank Chin's play <u>The Chickencoop Chinaman</u>—as they draw upon the jazz poetics of the Black Arts movement while originating their own symbols and myths of Asian American genius and empowerment.[20]

It is impossible to focus only on Afro Asian collaborations in *Bridge,* for each of its pieces comes out of and speaks to the lives of all women of color— not to mention the fact that *Bridge* was shaped first and foremost by the Chicana feminists Moraga and Anzaldúa. Just as one of the greatest achievements of Kitchen Table Press was its ultimate commitment to all people of color, the significance of *Bridge* has been recognized as its "transformative, coalitional consciousness leading to new alliances."[21] It is this aspect that sets it apart from other women-of-color anthologies, most of which were anchored on a single racial identity.

Barbara Noda's "Lowriding through the Women's Movement" presents one clear example of *Bridge*'s multicultural, feminist ethos. As an elegy for a comrade, Sharon Lew, as well as a larger meditation on the demise of political organizations and political will, Noda's essay recalls the ephemeral days when she and her Asian American, Chicana, and black sisters "discussed the 'colonized' and the 'colonizer' " while "Sharon distributed green tea, Chinese pastries, and Aime Cesaire's *Discourse on Colonialism*" (138). Then, "as the evening wound down we stormed out together—third world sisters—and dragged main with the masses" (138). The male, working-class

Chicano tradition of lowriding, in which Noda and her sisters nonetheless participate as they "[drag] main with the masses," serves as a metaphor for challenging the white, middle-class women's movement (hence the essay's title), male chauvinism in communities of color, and the norms of capitalist America; as Noda ironically speculates some time after her Third World women's group has disbanded, "Maybe we knew something then that we needed to forget in order to live more meaningful lives, when we joined the lowriders in the flagrant pursuit of their destiny" (139). It is precisely this knowledge that she needs to remember as she is then confronted with "the leveled site of the I [International] Hotel" (139), a focal point of Asian American organizing in the 1970s.[22] Concluding with reflections on this former landmark, Noda might seem to address only Asian Americans. However, within the context of the essay, which affirms the multicultural routes of her politicization through its references to Cesaire and lowriding as well as the International Hotel, this image of irrevocable loss—like Sharon's death—speaks to all people of color. It is not just Asian Americans but all of Noda's comrades who define the "us" in her assertion that, in the wake of such loss, "the humanity that had kept us warm and huddled together through makeshift Christmas dinners, internal crises and external warfare had been strained from the air" (139). Noda thus poses the question of how people of color, and Third World women in particular, work through death, whether it be the death of a comrade or a political group or action. In doing so, she explores the dialectic between autonomy, exemplified by Asian American activism around the International Hotel, and interracial solidarity, exemplified by her Third World women's group.

While, in their own ways, all of the *Bridge* pieces address the dialectical relationship between autonomy and interconnectedness, the Combahee River Collective statement (written in 1977 and reprinted in *Bridge*) is especially important as a groundbreaking document within the history of black feminist and woman of color radicalism. Much has been written about this text, but a few of its assertions bear reiteration and further exploration in assessing its contribution to the intertextual and intercultural dialogues within *Bridge*. For this purpose, one of the most striking points made by the Collective concerns its definition of identity politics. Identity politics is now battle-scarred and even, by some accounts, defunct, but when the Collective first articulated its principles in 1977 it was a revolutionary concept. In fact, the founding member Barbara Smith claims that the Collective invented the term, which "had never been quite formulated in the way that we were trying to formulate it, *particularly because we were talking about homophobia, lesbian identity, as well.*"[23] The latter part of this statement is even more radical, centering sexuality as it does within the project of revolutionary struggle. The implications of centering sexuality in this manner are lucidly explained by the Collective member Cheryl Clarke in her *Bridge* essay "Lesbianism: An Act of Resistance," in which she asserts that lesbianism, so long rendered invisible within communities of color, is a form of resistance "that should be championed throughout the world by all the forces struggling for liberation from the same slave master" (128).

This radical centering of sexuality within the Collective's conceptualization of identity politics speaks to its belief that "the most profound and potentially the most radical politics comes directly out of our own identity, as opposed to working to end somebody else's oppression" (212). This definition of identity politics might appear to subscribe to what Patricia Hill Collins calls an additive model of oppression, which ranks categories of identity such that one (like sexuality) is privileged over others.[24] By contrast, the black feminist thought exemplified by the Collective statement asserts the need to develop "integrated analysis and practice based on the fact that the major systems of oppression are interlocking" (210), a corollary being that "although we are feminists and lesbians, we feel solidarity with progressive Black men and do not advocate the fractionalization that white women who are separatists demand" (213).[25] This argument, that identity politics is *constitutively* coalitional, bears repeating precisely because one of the main reasons for its dismissal by the Right and by the Left has been its supposed and real narrowness, its inability or unwillingness to speak beyond its own concerns or to effect systemic transformation.

The third aspect of the Collective statement that I want to underscore is its rooting of identity politics in anti-capitalist and anti-imperialist critique, something else that gets lost in most subsequent formulations of identity politics: "We are socialists because we believe the work must be organized for the collective benefit of those who do the work and create the products, and not for the profit of the bosses. Material resources must be equally distributed among those who create these resources. We are not convinced, however, that a socialist revolution that is not also a feminist and antiracist revolution will guarantee our liberation" (213). To some extent, *Bridge* itself contributes to the downplaying of the Collective's radicalism in this regard.

For example, Moraga's important critique of the Left's narrow view of writing by women of color seems to dichotomize spiritual activism and structural analysis, socialist revolution and feminist/antiracist revolution:

> In writing this conclusion, I fight the myriad voices that live inside me. The voices that stop my pen at every turn of the page. They are the voices that tell me here I should be talking more 'materialistically' about the oppression of women of color, that I should be plotting out a 'strategy' for Third World Revolution. But what I really want to write about is faith. . . .
>
> The materialism in this book lives in the flesh of these women's lives. (xviii)

Yet as Anzaldúa makes clear in "La Prieta," one of her *Bridge* essays, faith and materialism (in either senses of the word implied by Moraga above) are not mutually exclusive. Rather, Anzaldúa theorizes spiritualism (El Mundo Zurdo, the Left-Handed World) in order to enable materialist analysis and strategy by "going deep into the self and . . . expanding out into the world, a simultaneous recreation of the self and a reconstruction of society," one in which "thousands . . . go to bed hungry every night" and "do numbing shitwork eight hours a day each day of their lives" (208).

These three aspects of the Collective statement—that gender and sexuality are central to revolutionary struggle, and that identity politics must be constitutively coalitional and class conscious—are the primary themes of the fourth section of *Bridge*, "Between the Lines: On Culture, Class, and Homophobia," which explores the "difference[s] that we have feared to mention because of our urgent need for solidarity with each other" as well as "the similarities that so often go unrecognized" (106). Strikingly, nearly half of the pieces in this section—four out of nine—take an epistolary form and thus comprise two-thirds of the six "letters" in *Bridge* as a whole. Like Barbara Noda's personal essay, also featured in this section, each letter engages what Hill Collins calls the "creative tension" between "the specificity needed to study the workings of race, class and gender" in the lives of women of color, and "generalizations about these systems created by cross-cultural and transhistorical research" (224).[26] The letter form as it functions in *Bridge* seems to enable this creative tension by marking itself as at once private and public; while each letter is addressed from one woman speaking from a given standpoint to another ("Dear Ma," "Querida Chabela," "Dear Barbara"), it implicitly acknowledges its wider audience by interweaving with its intimate revelations their significance to other women, people of color, and whites. Merle Woo's "Letter to Ma" exemplifies this interweaving of private with public address, of the specificity of an Asian American lesbian's experience with its relevance to other women and the patriarchal norms that constrain their lives: "You gave me, physically, what you never had, but there was a spiritual, emotional legacy you passed down which was reinforced by society: self-contempt because of our race, our sex, our sexuality. For deeply ingrained in me, Ma, there has been that strong, compulsive force to sink into self-contempt, passivity, and despair" (141).

Mirtha Quintanales's letters, "I Come with No Illusions" and "I Paid Very Hard for My Immigrant Ignorance," which are addressed respectively to Isabel Yrigoyen and Barbara Smith, are similarly introspective in their reflections on the relationship between the author, a light-skinned Cuban woman from a middle-class background, and her lover, a working-class white woman. However, like Woo, Quintanales extrapolates from the personal to explore issues of political significance to women and men of all races: interrogating the categories of "women of color" and "Third World women"; critiquing the racism of white and ethnic minority women; combating the tendency to "obscure the issue of class and its relationship to race and ethnicity so important for the understanding of the dilemma" (151); assessing both the need for "separatist spaces" (153) as well as the "pure folly" of thinking that "a small group of Latina or Black or Chinese American lesbians can, on its own, create a feminist revolution" (154). Taken separately and together, the voices of *Bridge* exemplify the dialectics of autonomy and coalition, separatism and interconnectedness, by positing feminist critique at the heart of multiracial, anti-capitalist struggle.

The *Yardbird Reader*, volume 3, extends the largely male-centered Asian American cultural nationalism that Frank Chin and Shawn Wong had articulated in *Aiiieeeee! An Anthology of Asian American Writers*. The *Reader*'s editorial statements and many of its selections assert a militant ethnic identity that "highlights 'unique' cultural traits based on language, history, and values" (357) in order to transform the political consciousness of its audience.[27] For Chin and Wong, the primary terrain on which this struggle to redefine Asian America takes place is the arts—music, film, and especially literature. First and foremost, this issue of the *Reader* positions itself as a tribute to the men who broke ground in Asian American cultural work: "our greatest pioneer" (ix), John Okada, the Japanese American author of *No-No Boy*, a novel about the impact of internment on a young Japanese American man, and James Wong Howe, the Academy Award–winning cinematographer whose passport photograph, a headshot of a young boy immigrating from China, commands our gaze on the *Reader*'s cover. After the table of contents, the first image and text to appear—a photograph of John Okada at his desk and a poem by Lawson Fusao Inada—comprise a dedication to Okada's memory, one made all the more poignant by the editors' disclosure in the introduction that Okada had died only weeks before they had become acquainted with his work, and that his widow had burned his papers in the belief that no one would be interested in them. Together with Howe's passport photograph, the dedication to Okada signifies the urgent need to recover a rich cultural heritage always in danger of being unrecognized or erased by the racist gaze. This recovery is enacted by a multifaceted profile of Howe, the first text to appear after the prefatory section.[28] In commencing with these tributes, the editors reconstruct a history of Asian American cultural work with roots in Chinese American and Japanese American forefathers.

Yet, balancing autonomy and coalition is also at stake in the *Reader*.[29] Even as the editors redefine Asian American culture, the *Reader* is substantially informed by the Black Aesthetic and its Third World internationalism.[30] As the aesthetic counterpart to Black Power, the Black Arts movement involved countering centuries of Eurocentric ideology (decolonizing the mind); developing "a separate symbolism, mythology, critique, and iconology" that emerged from and supported the black revolutionary struggle for self-determination; and protecting black culture from being stolen or exploited by whites.[31] Thus, art was inextricable from political and socioeconomic concerns. The Black Aesthetic was also eminently vernacular and performative, and its different branches—poetry, drama, music, dance—nourished each other. As an example of the Black Aesthetic, Ron Welburn's poem "Boukman in America"—the first text by a black writer to appear in the *Reader*—couples musicality with Third World/diasporic consciousness to critique U.S. cultural imperialism by reinventing the Haitian slave revolt leader as a symbol of its degradation:

> boukman came by
> this way beating
> the breast of a chicken
> as if it were a drum

came by chanting
a hoarse lyric
the prophets recalled
before radios and money.
boukman was arrested
boukman was committed
and niggers just stood,
despising Haiti and forgetting
their galaxy,
and watched.

The poem's alliteration (in particular the hard /b/) and its syntactic repetition produce an incantatory rhythm that evokes Boukman's status as a voodoo priest whose oratory skills instigated a slave revolt in Haiti (what was then San Domingo). However, Boukman is relegated to "beating/the breast of a chicken" and "chanting/a hoarse lyric" in the wake of the triumph of "radios and money"—synechdoches for the culture of consumption. In this age, Boukman's capture does not spark revolution but rather deepens apathy and self-hatred: the /d/ that ends lines 9–11 and 14 juxtaposes the statements that while Boukman was "arrested" and "committed," "niggers just stood" and "watched"; these plosives halt each of these lines, just as revolutionary action is suspended. Through this negative example, Welburn illustrates the need to counter the historical amnesia and consumerism fostered by white American culture.

While incorporating key elements of the Black Aesthetic, such as its jazz poetics, its roots in the aspirations and struggles of the people, and its emphasis on the reciprocity between revolution and art, Asian American writers developed their own forms (Al Robles's "ocean of words"), tropes (cyn. zarco's "parking space in the heart of america"), symbols (Lawson Inada's *shakuhachi*), and myths (Frank Chin's *Chickencoop Chinaman*). In this way, Asian Americans expressed solidarity with African Americans— and rejected what Chin calls "racist love"—while articulating their distinct, complex, and often contradictory relationships to their Asian heritage and the American nation-state. For writers such as Robles and zarco, anti-imperialist critique and the affirmation of Filipino nationhood was analogous to the Black Aesthetic's (sometimes romanticized) recovery and celebration of African roots. For others, such as Inada and Chin, asserting the

Americanness of Asian Americans was a priority in the 1970s, given the perpetually foreign status assigned to them by white America. For these Asian American cultural nationalists, self-determination and nationhood were not goals in the way that they were for the Black Power movement or for Asian American revolutionary nationalists.

Like Welburn's "Boukman," Al Robles's "Rapping with One Million Carabaos in the Dark" exhorts its addressees to decolonize their minds. Most of the poem is presented as an "all-night session" with Robles, Bill Sorro, and other community activists who in the late 1960s and early 1970s fought the eviction of tenants, notably elderly, working-class Filipino men ("manongs"), of San Francisco's International Hotel. Thus, "rapping" uses the everyday speech of Filipino Americans to convey its subject matter and message, which are rooted in the community of manongs who "live, hang, & roam" in Manilatown:

> Bill Sorro: You know, when I go into the poolhalls
> & see my Filipino brothers, I want to say;
> you know, I want to say to them that I know
> how you feel, you know, that I know how
> you think. I want to say to them
> "manong, manong, manong, don't you know?
> You are being fucked." (12–18)

The poem also breaks with Western poetic conventions such as the dramatic lyric or the monologue, which centers on the individual subject of consciousness. Although the poem identifies Bill Sorro as the speaker of lines 12–18, none of the remaining lines are assigned speakers despite the fact that the participants of this rap session are listed in line 2. It could be argued that the rest of the poem is in fact spoken by Sorro, but the unconventional punctuation complicates this reading: while Sorro's lines are demarcated by quotation marks, none of the preceding or following lines are so enclosed. Within this freely conversational "ocean of words" (line 1), it is impossible to distinguish among speakers who share a vision of reclaiming Filipino national identity, as exemplified in their appropriation of "Black is Beautiful": " 'I am brown, I am together, I am beautiful' " (line 19). Thus, Robles creates a collective poetic voice that emerges from the ocean of words and that by the poem's conclusion becomes

a million brown filipino faces
chanting: makibaka, makibaka, makibaka
makibaka, makibaka, makibaka[32]

Meanwhile, the trope of brownness comes to signify both a shared, origi-
nary home ("brown = brown = brown = brown = / fallen coconuts on a cold /
cold winter day") and the future potential for a new, revolutionary consciousness—Brown Power:

Ah, Filipinos
if you only know how brown you are
you would slide down
    from the highest
        mountain top
you would whip out your lava tongue
    & burn up all that white shit
that's keeping your people down.

Two other traits shared by African American and Asian American cultural
nationalism were, unfortunately, misogyny and homophobia, and in most
cases it was the women writers who presented feminine, queer, and/or
feminist perspectives. The poet cyn. zarco's "Pacific Lover" proposes that
their bodies and erotic impulses enable women to envision an alternative to
the emptiness and sterility of "the heart of america." In line 1, the poem's
speaker tells us, "naked i write," and it is the ability to be only "in [her]
skin" that allows her to feel "the waves of the pacific" as "a tongue in
[her] ear" transporting her to the Philippines, while her mother, in a neg-
ligee, can only hear "[her] father snoring." The alienating effects of living
in the United States, epitomized by its urban car culture—"how we must
learn / to automobile / to stickshift / to find a parking space in the heart of
america"—are fought not with the eroticized, linguistic violence that we see
in Robles's poem, but with the sensual dream of returning to a homeland
where the poem's speaker can become a new source of life and community:
"please / bury my body / under a mango tree / feed the fruit / to my
friends."

The possibility for black and yellow solidarity is probed in the Asian
American women's experiences in Hisaye Yamamoto's story "The Brown
House," about a first-generation Japanese-American woman married to a

compulsive gambler.[33] The eponymous gambling den is also a multicultural space that enables the intermingling of "all sorts of people—white, yellow, brown, and Black" (206) in the pursuit of money; even conflicts between people of Asian descent are put aside as Mrs. Wu, the proprietress of the house, tells Mrs. Hattori, "This is America. . . . China and Japan have war, all right, but [she shrugged] it's not our fault" (208). This profit-motivated ethnic tolerance is revised by Mrs. Hattori during a police raid on the brown house, when one of its patrons, an African American man, seeks shelter in the Hattoris's car. Although initially terrified, she altruistically helps him. However, when her husband returns to the car and discovers the man's presence, he angrily reproaches Mrs. Hattori for allowing them to be in such proximity to a *"kurombo"* (a derogatory Japanese word for black people). Mrs. Hattori points out his hypocrisy insofar as he "had no compunctions about that . . . when [he was] inside that house" (209), and their quarrel ends with Mr. Hattori beating her. The story thus links the policing of racial boundaries with patriarchal violence, while situating the possibility for black/yellow solidarity within a Japanese American woman's struggle against both male domination and materialism. Texts like zarco's and Yamamoto's interrogate androcentric and homosocial figurations of both Asian American cultural nationalism and Afro Asian coalition building in the *Reader.*

More surprisingly, this antipatriarchal inquiry extends in different forms through two of the anthology's central texts by writers infamous for reproducing sexist discourses of ethnic identity: Lawson Fusao Inada and Frank Chin. Along with the beginning section on James Wong Howe, Inada's poem "Japanese Geometry" and Act II of Chin's play, *The Chickencoop Chinaman,* are the *Reader*'s longest pieces; respectively, they comprise the middle and end of the collection. The privileging of these works by and about men is symptomatic, I think, of the *Reader*'s androcentrism. Yet these centerpiece texts do not only present further Asian American re-articulations of the Black Aesthetic, but ones that lead to coalition building across lines of gender as well as race. Moreover, Inada reminds us that Afro Asian literary collaborations were not in fact bicultural but multicultural by drawing on the aesthetics and political concerns of American Indian writers and artists, whom Chin and Wong also included in the *Reader.*

As with Robles's "Rapping with One Million Carabaos in the Dark" and zarco's "Pacific Lover," the Black Arts movement's anticolonial poetics infuses the work of Inada, who draws upon the structures, rhythms, and sensibilities of jazz to celebrate its "enduring philosophy—of adaptability, ingenuity, creation," and to reexamine racial and national identity. As Inada writes in his introduction to his jazz poetry in *Legends from Camp*: "The music we [of Fresno's West Side, primarily Asians, blacks, and Latinos] most loved and played and used was Negro music. It was something we could share in common, like a 'lingua franca' in our 'colored' community. And in our distorted reality of aliens and alienation, it even felt like *citizenship*. It seemed so very *American*—'un-foreign,' on 'un-foreign' instruments—and the words it used were *English*. Not 'across town' or 'Hit Parade' English, perhaps, but nevertheless an English that, in its own way, did the job."[34]

In noting that jazz "seemed so very American," Inada capitalizes on the fact that America's first original music is an African American cultural form in order to reclaim the very idea of Americanness for those traditionally at its margins: slaves and the descendants of slaves, the Latinos and Asians of Fresno's West Side who spoke nonstandard ("not 'across town' or 'Hit Parade'") English. In "Japanese Geometry," Inada's jazz poetics explore the "distorted reality of aliens and alienation" produced by the unconstitutional dislocation and imprisonment of Americans of Japanese descent during World War II. A musician as well as a poet, Inada also acts on Larry Neal's assertion apropos of the Black Arts movement that "the poet must become a performer, the way James Brown is a performer—loud, gaudy and racy."[35]

"Japanese Geometry" begins with a few lines from King Pleasure's version of "Parker's Mood" by the jazz saxophonist Charlie "Yardbird" Parker:

When you see me comin
raise your window high
When you see me leavin
baby
hang your head and cry (130)

Despite the fact that the stanza that Inada quotes is about mourning, Pleasure sings it to a swingy, syncopated beat; Inada seems to imply similarly that the pacing of this stanza would be quicker than other parts of the prologue, with their even and large spacing:

Goin to Yreka
Goin to Yreka

Goin to Yreka
Sorry that I
can't take you (130)

Pleasure's version of "Parker's Mood" thus presents the twinned, tragi-comic motifs of the journey and of death—"Going to Kansas City," the original lyric, refers to the Bird's passing, which Pleasure's last stanza describes as a sad but ultimately liberating journey.[36] Drawing on the jazz technique of improvisation, Inada picks up and elaborates upon these motifs in the rest of the poem, which presents the speaker's journey from spiritual death to life as a result of his encounter with an American Indian woman in Yreka, California.

The idea of the journey also evokes the history of Japanese Americans' forced relocation and internment in desert camps across the West. The trauma of the internment continues to haunt the poem's speaker, Lawson, as he travels from Fresno to Yreka. This becomes evident after he meets Mary Ann, a Pit River Indian, and several of her relations at a tavern. When they invite Lawson to their home, he drunkenly revisits childhood memories of the camps and reveals the shame he still carries: "won't nobody pull no shit on me, man, / none of that old time shit, man, / because I'll kill those motherfuckers" (146). The psychic and physical violence of Lawson's experiences in the camps flood his monologue, which climaxes as he recalls the incomprehensible shootings of an elderly Japanese man and of Lawson's dog by soldiers guarding the camp—incidents that symbolize for Lawson the worthlessness of Japanese American life. It is at this moment that Mary Ann's brother-in-law questions the integrity of Lawson's memories, and Lawson beats him with extraordinary savagery, displacing his rage over his disenfranchisement and emasculation by the U.S. military regime onto his unwitting audience: "I'm throbbing and quivering / and pick up the tubular kitchen chair / and bring it down upon him / with all my force, / smash him again and again" (149).

Lawson subsequently flees, terrified, into the cold night, where he falls into a primal struggle between life and death that allows him at last to feel fully the pain of internment:

take me
I can go on
forever in this condition

take me
and freeze and die
with reason enough
take me
with all my life
take me
driven struggling
take me
to find some place . . .
and with all this pain
this everything
slowly
take my head in my hands
and start to cry
whimpering sobbing
slowly at first and then
rushing out of me in great long wails
loud
sobs rushing their own force
gushing aaaaahhhhhh [151–52]

Unlike Lawson's recounting of his time in camp, his interior monologue here relies as much on rhythm and nonverbal sound as on language to communicate his anguish, and it thus draws on a jazz poetics. The repetition of phrases such as "take me" creates a riff that ricochets against the desperate "melody" of the alternating lines, while the "whimpering" and "sobbing" and "great long wails" "rushing their own force / gushing aaaaahhhhhh" evokes a saxophonist like early Coltrane building his emotional shrieks and squawks to a crescendo. Especially in this section, it is the sound of Inada's poetry that conveys its imagery and meaning as much as, if not more than, the denotative and connotative force of the words themselves, for the anguish and confusion that submerge Lawson—just as he falls into a stream during this ordeal—are ultimately beyond the pale of linguistic expression. We can, however, hear the pain of Lawson's existence in the frantic beat of the lines propelled by rhythmic repetitions and punctuated by howls and moans.

Yet this symbolic near-death by drowning ("that part of me / flowing /

relinquished / gone" [152]) is simultaneously a baptism and rebirth that, having plumbed jazz roots in the blues' tragic vision, now accepts the possibilities it extends for communication, transcendence, and healing. In particular, Inada explores the cross-racial dimensions of these possibilities as they are articulated in *Legends from Camp*, where he describes jazz as a "lingua franca" among different ethnic groups. In "Japanese Geometry," jazz and the blues speak specifically to the shared experiences of oppression between Japanese Americans and American Indians. Just as Inada's internment gives rise to his understanding of the blues, such that he has called himself a "campsman"—signifying on the term "bluesman"[37]—it facilitates his sense of solidarity with American Indians, since many of the camps were situated on reservations: "So you might say that it makes sense that the chief camps administrator [Dillon S. Myer] went on to become chief of the Bureau of Indian Affairs, where he 'redeployed' his policy of 'relocation.' Which included, yes, termination" (vi).

Seemingly with a similar idea in mind, Chin and Wong included in the *Reader* the writers Leslie Marmon Silko and Simon Ortiz, and the artist Aaron Yava, all of whom reiterate the shared concerns among black, yellow, and red cultural revolutionaries. Silko makes this clear in her discussion of Yava's sketches of life on the border towns near the Navajo and Pueblo reservations, which include depictions of one Indian man being beaten by police, and another throwing up: "Aaron and I care as much as any Indian people, about the 'Indian self-image' and 'Indian Pride.' But we have been taught to value truth above all else; and these scenes are true, and they must not be hidden. To hide them, is in a sense, denying that these Indian people exist. . . . Denial of ourselves and our own origins is one of the most devastating psychological weapons the Whites have ever found to use against us" (101–3). Like Chin and Wong's introduction, Silko's discussion of Yava's work speaks to the need for artists of color to break with white standards of "truth" that deny life's grotesqueries, often the product of white American modernity. To do so, artists of color cannot rely on the conventions of a "dying culture" that, in Silko's words, has "grown fat from stolen lands, grown monstrous with its barbarism in Asian wars, burning Asian children" (103).

Instead, artists of color must find their own modes of representation, and in "Japanese Geometry" folk songs take their place alongside the jazz aesthetic as Inada probes the bonds between Japanese Americans and American Indians. Recognizing similar ties to their elders—notably, female elders—who keep alive the "old ways," and acknowledging shared struggles over reclaiming their lands, Mary Ann's and Lawson's visions for taking back the land proclaim that *"there is room / for us, for you"* (175), as Mary Ann's "Grandmother Song" tells the "Yellow Man." Similarly, Lawson's "Vision Song" not only insists that *"we must have back again"* the camp sites—*"Topaz and Manzanar, / Tule Lake and Gila"* (172)—but also *"ghettoes, the barrio, / reservations / and plantations— / all these in our hands"* (173). At the end of the poem, Lawson sees himself as a *shakuhachi,* or Japanese bamboo flute, "letting the wind / come in and out of me / naturally, of its own / force and accord, / filling me, around me, / with light and sound" (180). However, Lawson describes the *shakuhachi* as the *"universal* flute" (emphasis added; 180), and indeed this instrument is used to play jazz as well as Japanese folk songs. Once again, Inada portrays music as a "lingua franca" that enables people of different races to "reach / and hold / each other // warm, holding, / strong, holding, / knowing // we will / never / leave this / one who / holds us // knowing, holding / forever" (180–81). In the same vein, Lawson compares Mary Ann to a song in the last line of the poem before the epilogue, which itself is the very song with which the poem began.[38] This music is no longer "purely" jazz but a jazz aesthetic reflecting Asian American and indigenous struggles to reclaim and re-create America.

Furthermore, in Mary Ann, Inada creates a strong female character who critiques Lawson's "bullshitting," masculinist persona, one that typifies the "Chinatown Cowboy" image of Asian American manhood articulated most forcefully by Frank Chin.[39] After Lawson's violent encounter with Mary Ann's brother-in-law, she reproves them both for feeling like they have to prove their manhood, especially through violence, which she significantly links to what Silko called American "barbarism in Asian wars":

> It *always* happens, man.
> People getting hurt, killed . . .
> I seen it all my life.
> And the thing is
> it don't *have* to happen, you know.
> I mean who you gotta
> *prove* yourself to, you know
> I mean do I have to *prove*
> I'm a woman?

I *feel* it. I *know.*

And shit, like Jimmy [Mary Ann's husband], you know,

hell, he didn't

have to go to no Viet Nam, you know.

But I mean he *went,* man.

He *went.*

Jimmy *went* to Viet Nam. (161)

war as the intersectional consequence

Here, the war in Viet Nam is not only an imperialist war, nor is it only fueled by ideologies of gender linking manhood with violence (which is why, even though "he didn't have to go," Jimmy, an American Indian, leaves home to kill Asians and to be killed himself). Additionally, Inada depicts the Viet Nam war as one that is ironically fed by the kind of masculinity privileged within the Asian American movement of the seventies, for Mary Ann associates Lawson's "bullshitting"—the pugilistic attitude that led him to beat her brother-in-law—with her husband's need to prove his manhood by fighting in Viet Nam.[40]

This type of masculinity unites Lawson with "Chinatown Cowboys" such as Tam Lum, the protagonist of Chin's play *The Chickencoop Chinaman,* the second and last act of which concludes the *Reader.*[41] Following this "Chinese American writer film-maker" as he works on a documentary about a black boxer, the play satirically interrogates the origins of and possibilities for Asian American cultural expression. In particular, the play examines the significance of African American culture to the construction of an "authentic" Asian American voice. As I will discuss below, Chin draws on elements of jazz poetics and the long narrative poem from black oral tradition known as the "toast" in order to interrogate an essentialist ontology of race that supports the charge that Asian American cultural forms are merely imitative of African American ones.[42] Furthermore, it is significant that the realization of the Chinese American artist's vision takes the shape of a documentary about a black boxer, since boxing—from Jack Johnson's defeat of the Irishman Tommy Burns in 1908, to Joe Louis's victorious rematch with the German Max Schmeling during the rise of Nazism, and especially in the era of Muhammad Ali—has been a site of racial struggle. In the 1960s, which saw Ali's friendship with Malcolm X, his conversion to the Nation of Islam, his first trip to Africa, and his refusal to serve in the Vietnam War, Ali was a forefather and symbol of Black Power.[43]

Yet critics have argued that *The Chickencoop Chinaman* ultimately depicts the Asian American artist's realization that he cannot base his search for self- and communal affirmation in black cultural nationalism, and the second act would seem to confirm this reading.[44] The play links the Asian American artist's struggle to be seen and heard to the ultimately thwarted search for a father, especially a black one, who will fill the void left by the conspicuous absence/impotence of Chinese fathers, and who will thereby legitimate Tam's art.[45] Even though the subject of Tam's documentary is ostensibly the boxer called Ovaltine Jack Dancer, Tam insists that "it's the Dancer's father, man, Charley Popcorn[,] that's gonna make this movie go" (14)—and, indeed, Popcorn and not Dancer (who is not even a character in the play) generates the dramatic conflict when he turns out to be the owner of a porn house around whom Dancer had entirely fabricated his genealogy. Just as Tam's naive faith in other father figures (including the Lone Ranger) is systematically stripped away, so is his faith in Popcorn. Like the Lone Ranger, Popcorn is unmasked as a "bigot" (although his narrow views of race are much more benign than the Lone Ranger's white supremacy); even more disturbing for Tam, Popcorn asserts, "I ain't *nobody's* father, especially [Dancer's]" (emphasis added; 48), thereby crushing Tam's desire to find a father for Dancer and, metonymically, for himself. It would thus appear that the ideals of African American manhood and Black Power—represented by the black boxing trainer who denies any progeny—cannot sustain the Asian American artist. emasculation

Yet this reading is not altogether borne out either thematically or formally. Thematically, as Josephine Lee argues, "There is a stronger thrust in *Chickencoop Chinaman* toward depicting Asian American men and Black American men as mutually supportive figures whose masculinities complement one another."[46] Although Popcorn refuses to play father to either Dancer or Tam, he revives the legacy of a Chinese elder whom Tam had earlier dismissed with his emasculating description of "an old dishwasher who was afraid of white old ladies peeking at him through the keyhole" while he bathed (16). By contrast, Popcorn's memory of a "fierce, fierce" man whom they nicknamed the "Chinatown Kid" (272) makes this figure as much of a fighter as Dancer or Popcorn himself. Later, this complementary masculinity is restaged when Popcorn carries an unmanned Tam home on his back (after Tam has unsuccessfully tried to punch him for not being

Dancer's father), and then, somewhat inexplicably, Tam ends up carrying Popcorn on his back.

This strange staging symbolizes not only the complementariness of Asian American and African American masculinities but of their cultural work as well, for an undercurrent throughout the play is its anxiety over "making it on the backs of Black people," especially through "faking Blackness" (19). This accusation is expressed most explicitly in Act I through Lee, a "yellow [woman] passing for white" (259).[47] When Tam greets her son, Robbie, with "gimme five," Lee immediately objects: "It's sick of you to make fun of Blacks . . . the way you walk . . . your talk . . . giving five. Who do you think you are?" (13) Her biggest critique on this level, however, is reserved for Tam's Japanese American friend "BlackJap Kenji," so called due to the fact that, as he puts it, "I live with [blacks], I talk like 'em, I dress . . . maybe even eat what they eat" (21). Through Lee, Chin articulates and addresses charges of imitating blackness as a result of—among other things—writing in a polyglot voice that ranges at one point from the accents of "*W. C. Fields to American Midwest, Bible Belt holy roller, etc.*," as Tam's "'*normal' speech jumps between Black and white rhythms and accents*" (6). In having Popcorn carry Tam and then Tam carry Popcorn, Chin visually contests the charge that Asian Americans were "making it on the backs of Black people" or putting on a "goddamned minstrel show" (271).

But this point is made most forcefully by examining Chin's jazz poetics in *The Chickencoop Chinaman*, the richest examples of which are in Act I, scene I, where Tam proclaims, "I AM THE NOTORIOUS ONE AND ONLY CHICKENCOOP CHINAMAN HIMSELF" in an illocutionary act of self-fathering/self-authoring: "I am the result of a pile of pork chop suey thrown up into the chickencoop in the dead of night and the riot of dark birds, night cocks and insomniac nympho hens running after strange food that followed. . . . Born? No! Crashed! Not born. Stamped! Not born! Created! Not born. No more born than the heaven and earth. No more born than nylon or acrylic. For I am a Chinaman! A miracle synthetic!" (7–8). Chin's gleeful, alliterative riffs on hybridization, experimentation, sex, and religion engender a rhythm that smoothly drives as well as percussively punctuates the Chickencoop Chinaman's creation myth.[48] Although spoken with "black" rhythms and accents, this is no more "fake blackness" than fake Chineseness, for Chin throws the whole ontology of race into question. If a Chinaman is a "miracle synthetic," then nothing prevents him from performing blackness any more than from performing Chineseness, and it is in this spirit that Charley Popcorn indirectly refers to Tam and Kenji as "Yellow Negroes" because "it makes ya easier to think about" (274).

This conceptualization of the "Chinaman" is reiterated at the conclusion of Act II when Kenji gives his "toast" mythologizing the Chickencoop Chinaman and his sidekick, BlackJap Kenji, who replace the demeaning figures of the Lone Ranger (Tam's childhood idol/father figure) and Tonto:[49]

Gather round the fire boys, and
I'll tell you how I grew old.
Seeking Helen Keller's smelly love like
Other men seek gold.
I rode with the Chickencoop Chinaman, who
was ornery and cruel,
Notorious for spinnin a fast mean thread
offen life's wooden spool. (290)

Whereas the Lone Ranger vanquishes his opponents with silver bullets, the Chickencoop Chinaman "spin[s] a fast mean thread," as does Kenji himself, using the toast tradition's valorization of verbal skill to construct a heroic Chinese American masculinity. For example, Kenji's allusion to Helen Keller is meant to signify on racist whites by undoing the model minority myth as it is ironically articulated by Tam in Act I: "Helen Keller overcame her handicaps without riot! She overcame her handicaps without looting! She overcame her handicaps without violence! And you Chinks and Japs can too" (11). Helen Keller (whom Tam also calls the "mother of Charlie Chan" [11]) epitomizes the deaf and dumb Asian American object of racist love, an idea that is literalized when Tam's fantasy encounter with the Lone Ranger presents him with a lecherous white paternalist who had "sure wanted [him] a piece of [Helen's] pie" (265).[50] But if, according to this crudely misogynistic logic, Asian American men are reduced to blind and inarticulate women by racist love, Kenji's toast reasserts both their verbal prowess and their masculinity by claiming that it is the "BlackJap" and not the Ranger who will now seek Helen Keller's "smelly love" (which complements Kenji's announcement at the end of the play that he is going to be the father of Lee's baby). It is precisely because the toast links verbal prowess with an affirmation of racialized manhood that Chin reappropriates this form, since it reverses the emasculation and silencing of Asian American men.

The play would thus appear to redeploy African American cultural forms (jazz poetics, the toast) to assert an Asian American aesthetic autonomy that is premised upon masculinity; indeed, Chin, Wong, Inada, and Jeffrey Paul Chan have called Tam "the comic embodiment of Asian-American *manhood*, rooted in neither Asia nor white America."[51] Yet Tam's final monologue surprisingly changes the play's emphasis from envisioning a complementary masculinity between blacks and Asians to interrogating gendered boundaries and hierarchies altogether, something that Chin's critics have missed. Kenji's toast segues into Tam's monologue with the line "Ride with me," which Tam repeats, suggesting that he picks up Kenji's "fast mean thread." However, Tam has receded into the kitchen, where cooking will replace talking, over which Tam has grown weary in the final scene as a result of the hostility his words have generated. As Tam dons a blue apron and sets to chopping green onions, he engages in a different mode of communication that allows him to reach into his past:

TAM The Chinatown Kid would've liked to have seen . . . How do I know what he would've liked? You speak Chinese, Tom?

TOM Some Mandarin.

TAM No, you couldn't talk to him either. Wrong dialect. *It's in the hands, the food. There's conversation for you.* (emphasis added; 289)

In cooking for the others, though, Tam remembers not what his forefather, the Chinatown Kid, "would've liked to have seen," but what his grandmother would have heard as a young girl rolling cigars while her father was working on the transcontinental railroad—namely, the legendary "Iron Moonhunter, that train built by Chinamans who knew they'd never be given passes to ride the rails they laid," and so who "builded themselves a wild engine to take them home" (260–61). Tam relates at the beginning of Act II that, as a boy, he would listen instead to the radio for the latest installment of the Lone Ranger's adventures, which "deafened my ear for trains all [his] boyhood long" (266). However, at the end of the play, Tam tells us to "turn off them radios and listen in the kitchen" to his grandmother's story, which can only be heard by tuning out the dominant discourse and developing her "ear for trains": "Now and then, I feel them old days, children, the way I feel the prowl of the dogs in the night and the bugs in the leaves and the thunder in the Sierra Nevadas however far they are. The way my grandmother had an ear for trains. Listen, children. I gotta go.

Ride Buck Buck Bagaw with me . . . Listen in the kitchen for the Chicken-coop Chinaman slowin on home" (291).

As Tam in this lyrical passage replaces talking with cooking and then with listening he indicates a new way to access Asian American history by reinventing—not romanticizing—"home" as a source of cultural identity. This identity is routed not through the legendary, masculine exploits of the "Chinaman borne, high stepping Iron Moonhunter" (291), but through the domestic/feminine space of the kitchen where the grandmother would listen for the train and tell of how she heard it; significantly, the grandmother's story and her voice become those of Tam's.[52] At the same time, the play does not suggest that the Asian American writer must reject or eschew African American cultural forms, as Elaine Kim argues. Both "Kenji's BlackJap song" and the grandmother's story are counterhegemonic narratives that authorize the hybrid myth of the Chickencoop Chinaman.[53]

When the editors Gloria Anzaldúa and AnaLouise Keating created *This Bridge We Call Home* to commemorate and extend *This Bridge Called My Back,* they included work by men of all colors, by white women, and by transgendered people, and just as Kitchen Table Press had met with objections to its coalitional mission, so did Anzaldúa and Keating. Anzaldúa addresses these objections as follows: "It would have been easier for Ana-Louise [Keating] and me to limit the dialogue to women of color. Many women of color are possessive of *This Bridge Called My Back* and view it as a safe space, as 'home.' But there are no safe spaces."[54] As Anzaldúa continues to point out, the lack of safe spaces has become clearer in post-9/11 America. Yet what some see as a loss of secure national borders has been for others an opportunity to build upon the radicalism of the eras from Bandung through Black Power. For if, as Fred Ho points out, Third World unity is the precursor to today's multiculturalism, much has been lost by way of institutionalization and tokenism in moving from the one to the other.[55] What does it take to replace liberal multiculturalism with a multiculturalism based on anti-imperialist and socialist praxis, and what role can Afro Asian literary coalitions play in effecting this shift?

In posing these questions, I do not want to imply that I can answer them, but in conclusion I will briefly discuss one text that raises some of the possibilities and limitations of Afro Asian and more broadly Third World literary coalitional politics in the post-9/11 era—Amiri Baraka's now infamous poem "Somebody Blew Up America."[56] Middle Eastern, particularly

Islamic, culture was central to the black radicalism of the 1950s and 1960s, as the Nation of Islam grew with the work of Malcolm X, who became an orthodox Sunni Muslim after his post–Nation of Islam pilgrimage to Mecca, and as black nationalists identified with the Palestinian struggle for land and nationhood.[57] In Baraka's response to the 2001 attacks on the World Trade Center, Black/Arab solidarity is expressed by interrogating the rhetoric of the "barbaric / A Rab" (198) who was supposedly behind this inhumanity. Through its anaphoric series of mostly rhetorical questions, the poem enjoins us to consider who profits from this polarizing, racist discourse. Baraka's poem can also be read as implying that the "Somebody" who "Blew Up America" is in fact the homegrown white supremacist terrorism and imperialist violence against all people of color (and Jews). Yet, as much as the range of Baraka's Third World Marxist critique counters the aggressive and amnesiac discourse fueled by the events of 9/11, it works against him insofar as he reaches for some specious or unclear connections ("Who killed the most niggers / Who killed the most Jews / Who killed the most Italians / Who killed the most Irish" [200]). These connections do not provoke the systemic analysis called for by the Combahee River Collective— an analysis that Baraka believes is still needed; rather, they subsume different histories under a generalized conception of imperialism or racism that stokes anger at the expense of critical thought. More compellingly, however, the poem extends the idea of "blowing up" America to America's own crimes against people within and without its borders: the genocide of American Indians, slavery, the occupation of the Philippines, the political persecution of Communists and black radicals, the invasion of Grenada, and the repealing of affirmative action.[58] As Baraka makes clear, such systematic aggression against people of color abroad and at home is what the War on Terror, a war largely directed at the Arab world, serves to cover and justify while bolstering an American empire that benefits the privileged, mostly white, few. Invoking these bases for black/Arab solidarity, "Somebody Blew Up America" belies a multicultural tolerance that the Right has invoked to maintain the myth of American exceptionalism, to sanction state-sponsored violence, and ultimately to obliterate the Other.[59]

The viability of "safe spaces"—(supposedly) homogeneous communities, whether we understand them to comprise a neighborhood, a political group, or a nation—is continually being undermined by U.S. foreign policy. As this happens, the nation-state enlists those who, in the first place, have never been safe to condone and participate in the demonization, exploitation, and murder of people of color around the world. With its anti-imperialist roots and coalitional ethos, Afro Asian political and cultural work at its best provides us with some of the insight into avoiding this zero-sum game.

Notes

1 Janice Mirikitani et al. *Time to Greez! Incantations from the Third World* (San Francisco: Glide Publications/Third World Communications, 1975). Glide Publications was a part of Glide Church, an important multicultural institution headed by the African American minister and community organizer Cecil Williams and the Japanese American poet and choreographer Janice Mirikitani. In 1971, Shawn Wong edited Glide's newsletter, for which he would regularly interview Williams.

2 Bernice Johnson Reagon, "Coalition Politics: Turning the Century" (1981), in *Home Girls: A Black Feminist Anthology*, edited by Barbara Smith (New York: Kitchen Table: Women of Color Press, 1983), 369.

3 Smith, introduction to *Home Girls*, xl–xli.

4 The quotation here is from the *Conditions* submissions statement. *Home Girls: A Black Feminist Anthology* evolved out of *Conditions: Five*. Guest edited by Lorraine Bethel and Barbara Smith, this issue was the first widely distributed collection of black feminist writing in the United States. Although many feminist journals tokenized women-of-color writers, some other feminist magazines that regularly published the work of these writers were the feminist literary magazine *13th Moon*, *IKON: Second Series* (which had special issues titled "Asian Women United" [1988] and "Coast to Coast: National Women Artists of Color" [1992]), *Sinister Wisdom* (a lesbian literary journal edited for several issues by Michelle Cliff and Adrienne Rich), and *Azalea: A Magazine by and for Third World Lesbians*. As Ron Welburn has pointed out to me, other early institutions supporting multicultural literature include the Greenfield Review Press, established by Joseph and Carol Bruchac, and the Society for the Study of the Multi-Ethnic Literature of the United States (MELUS), founded by Katherine Newman, and their respective journals, as well as Ishmael Reed's Before Columbus Foundation. The poet E. G. Burrows organized an important multiethnic writers' workshop at the University of Wisconsin, Stevens Point, in June 1973, which enabled writers such as Ron Welburn, Shawn Wong, Frank Chin, Lawson Fusao Inada, Leslie Marmon Silko, Simon Ortiz, Gary Soto, Ricardo Sanchez, Joseph Bruchac, and Mei-Mei Berssenbrugge, many of whom had not yet published, to meet each other (Ron Welburn, telephone interview by the author, December 31, 2003; Shawn Wong, telephone interview by the author, June 24, 2004).

5 Another signal example of Afro Asian (extra)literary collaboration is Jessica

Hagedorn's performance rock band, the West Coast Gangster Choir, which was formed in 1975 with the sister writers Thulani Davis and Ntozake Shange, and with the help of the jazz trombonist Julian Priester; Hagedorn has said of her group that they were rapping before it became popular (Kay Bonetti, "An Interview with Jessica Hagedorn," *Missouri Review* 18 [1995]: 90–113). I am grateful to Shawn Wong for bringing the Gangster Choir to my attention.

6 Barbara Smith, "A Press of Our Own: Kitchen Table: Women of Color Press," *Frontiers* 10 (1989): 11–13. Other founding members of Kitchen Table were Cherríe Moraga, Hattie Gosset, and Myrna Bain.

7 Shawn Wong, e-mail to the author, February 19, 2004.

8 Ron Welburn, e-mail to the author, June 21, 2004.

9 Ibid. Welburn would teach one of the first multiethnic courses on the East Coast, "Third World American Writers," for which he interviewed Frank Chin on Asian American literature while the latter was preparing to stage *The Year of the Dragon*.

10 "The American Literary Scene as a White Settler's Fortress," *The Art of Literary Publishing: Editors on their Craft*, ed. Bill Henderson (New York: The Pushcart Book Press, 1980), 101. Reed even questioned the tendency of literary wholesalers to refer to the *Reader* as a "minority" publication, given that it had always included Euro-American writers (102); according to Shawn Wong, multiculturalism for Reed was not about excluding anyone, whites included, as long as they were interested in exploring and articulating their identities (Wong, telephone interview by the author, June 24, 2004). For more on Reed's pivotal role in fostering multicultural literature, see his "The American Literary Scene as a White Settler's Fortress," as well as his essay in this volume.

11 Shawn Wong, e-mail to the author, February 19, 2004. As Chin and Wong point out in their introduction to *Yardbird*, white-owned papers also overlooked Asian American writers when it came to reviews. Inada's book of poetry, *Before the War* (1971), the first by an Asian American to be published by a white press, was reviewed by only one major newspaper, the *Seattle Times*, and by only one national magazine, *Black World*.

12 For a discussion of the difficulties that women-of-color writers faced in dealing with mainstream and white women's presses, see "Packing Boxes and Editing Manuscripts: Women of Color in Feminist Publishing," *Sojourner: The Women's Forum* 9 (August 1993): 10–11B.

13 Smith, "A Press of Our Own," 11.

14 Terri L. Jewell, "An Interview with Barbara Smith of Kitchen Table Press: A Voice of International Feminist Literature." *The Bloomsbury Review* (May/June 1990): 13, 29.

15 Smith, "A Press of Our Own," 12.

16 Remarkably, much of this work was done throughout the 1980s by a press situated in Smith's own home with a paid staff numbering three or less (Smith herself received no salary from the Press). In the early 1990s it formed a

Transition Coalition housed at the Union Institute Center for Women, which provided it with greater resources. For more on the Kitchen Table Transition Coalition, see Jaime M. Grant, "Building Community-Based Coalitions from Academe: The Union Institute and the Kitchen Table: Women of Color Press Transition Coalition," *Signs: Journal of Women in Culture and Society* 21 (1996): 1024–33.

17 Kayann Short, "Coming to the Table: The Differential Politics of *This Bridge Called My Back*," in *Eroticism and Containment: Notes form the Flood Plain*, ed. Carol Siegel and Ann Kibbey (New York: New York University Press, 1994), 3–44.

18 Chin, "Confessions of a Chinatown Cowboy," *Bulletin of Concerned Asian Scholars* 4 (1972): 67.

19 As Patricia Chu writes: "Perhaps the most insistent and influential story told about the struggles of Asian American males for authorship is that told by Frank Chin and his [*Aiiieeeee!*] coeditors, Jeffrey [*sic*] Paul Chan, Lawson Fusao Inada, and Shawn Wong" (Chu, *Assimilating Asians: Gendered Strategies of Authorship in Asian America* [Durham, N.C.: Duke University Press, 2000], 64). Elaine Kim critiques the *Aiiieeeee!* editors for their "strident anti-female attitude" (Kim, *Asian American Literature: An Introduction to the Writings and Their Social Context* [Philadelphia: Temple University Press, 1982], 197). Jinqi Ling argues that the *Aiiieeeee!* editors provisionally resolve the contradictions within their cultural nationalism by "problematically us[ing] the trope of 'feminization' of Asian American men as a position from which to attack racism," thereby "prioritiz[ing] a (straight) male gender as a sufficient ground for ethnic solidarity" (Ling, *Narrating Nationalisms: Ideology and Form in Asian American Literature* [New York: Oxford University Press, 1998], 27). Rachel Lee comments on the "rhetorically savvy" nature of Chin's and Chan's prose: "Though they never outright state that the cultural project of Asian American writing is to reinstall male privilege," they effectively argue that "the cultural integrity of the Asian American community is measured by the degree to which Asian American men dominate their literary tradition" (Lee, *The Americas of Asian American Literature: Gendered Fictions of Nation and Transnation* [Princeton, N.J.: Princeton University Press, 1999], 153–54). Frank Chin has borne the brunt of this line of critique; as Josephine Lee observes, "Contemporary Asian American critics tend to be somewhat embarrassed by Frank Chin's angry and misogynistic works" (Lee, *Performing Asian America: Race and Ethnicity on the Contemporary Stage* [Philadelphia: Temple University Press, 1997], 61). Chu asserts that "although Chin does praise some women and attack some men, he seems to identify 'real' accounts of Chinese and Japanese history and culture strongly with affirmations of ethnic male heroism, decency, heterosexuality, and authorship" (*Assimilating Asians*, 67). See also Merle Woo, "Letter to Ma," in *This Bridge Called My Back*; and King-kok Cheung, "The Woman Warrior versus the Chinaman Pacific: Must a Chinese American Critic Choose between

Feminism and Heroism?" in *Conflicts in Feminism*, edited by Marianne Hirsch and Evelyn Fox Keller (New York: Routledge, 1990), 234–51.

20 I spend more time on the *Reader* than on *Bridge* not out of any value judgment but because there is much more critical discussion on *Bridge*, especially with the publication of *This Bridge We Call Home*, whereas the *Reader* has been fairly overlooked even within Asian American literary criticism.

21 AnaLouise Keating, "Charting Pathways, Marking Thresholds . . . A Warning, An Introduction," in *This Bridge We Call Home*, edited by Gloria Anzaldúa and AnaLouise Keating (New York: Routledge, 2002), 6.

22 San Francisco's International Hotel—or "I Hotel"—provided low-income housing for elderly, working-class Filipino men before the building was targeted for demolition in the interests of capitalist "development," which had already led to the razing of key sections of Manilatown. Local activists and students fought to save the I Hotel, a site of Filipino and Chinese American history and community. The hotel was destroyed in 1977.

23 Quoted in Duchess Harris, " 'All of Who I Am in the Same Place': The Combahee River Collective," *Womanist Theory and Research* 2 (fall 1999): 9–21.

24 Patricia Hill Collins, *Black Feminist Thought: Knowledge, Consciousness, and the Politics of Empowerment* (New York: Routledge, 1991).

25 Another way in which the Combahee River Collective's coalitional, nonseparatist approach to identity might have been informed speaks more directly to the issue of Afro Asian connections; the Collective member Margo Okizawa Rey is of Japanese and African American descent. According to Rey, her African American father's working-class background took precedence over her Japanese mother's upper-middle-class upbringing in terms of shaping her identity, but her "early feminist leanings [came] from her [mother]" (quoted in Harris, " 'All of Who I Am in the Same Place,' " 12).

26 Here, Hill Collins refers specifically to a central element of black feminist thought, but I believe that it is applicable more broadly to Third World feminism.

27 On Asian American cultural nationalism, see Lane Ryo Hirabayashi and Marilyn C. Alquizola, "Asian American Studies: Reevaluating for the 1990s," in *The State of Asian America: Activism and Resistance in the 1990s*, edited by Karin Aguilar-San Juan (Boston: South End Press, 1994), 351–64. The cultural nationalism of the *Aiiieeeee!* editors is distinct from the revolutionary nationalism of Left Asian American groups such as I Wor Kuen and the Red Guard Party, which prioritized systemic change, self-determination, and the redistribution of occupied land. See Fred Ho, "Fists for Revolution: The Revolutionary History of I Wor Kuen / League of Revolutionary Struggle," in *Legacy to Liberation: Politics and Culture of Revolutionary Asian Pacific America* edited by Fred Ho et al. (San Francisco: AK Press, 2000), 3–13.

28 The profile includes a timeline and narrative of Howe's life (the latter in his

own words), a description of his prolific work, and an interview with Howe and his wife, the writer Sanora Babb.

29   The difficulty of balancing autonomy and coalition is further evidenced by Chin's conclusion to his preface, the tone of which blends appreciation and authority with anxiety: "The Native Americans in here, Simon Ortiz and Leslie Silko, the blacks in here, everybody in here we think is fine. But sometime through this issue, read something yellow. There's more yellow fiction and poetry in here than most of our people and everybody else has read in a lifetime" (v). Nonetheless, the *Reader* is dedicated not only to John Okada and the Chinese American novelist Louis Chu, but also to Duke Ellington and the novelist William Gardner Smith. And as discussed earlier, both the foreword and the introduction to the *Reader* document the numerous ways in which African American writers and presses have supported Asian Americans.

30   The international dimensions of the Black Aesthetic are probably clearest in its music, as Ron Welburn argues: "The music of the Afro Asian world as a whole is one large musical culture" (Welburn, "The Black Aesthetic Imperative," in *The Black Aesthetic*, edited by Addison Gayle Jr. [New York: Doubleday, 1971], 146). Larry Neal asserts that the Black Aesthetic "encompasses most of the useable elements of Third World culture," in order to pose the question, "whose truth shall we express, that of the oppressed or of the oppressors?" (Neal, "The Black Arts Movement," in Gayle, ed., *The Black Aesthetic*, 274).

31   Neal, "The Black Arts Movement," 27. For more on the Black Arts movement, see also *Black Fire: An Anthology of Afro-American Writing*, edited by LeRoi Jones [Amiri Baraka] and Larry Neal (New York: William Morrow and Company, Inc., 1971).

32   *Makibaka* is the Tagalog word for "fight."

33   Yamamoto would express her own solidarity with African Americans in opposing segregation in her memoir, "A Fire in Fontana," first published in 1985.

34   Inada, *Legends from Camp* (Minneapolis: Coffee House Press, 1992), 57.

35   Larry Neal, "And Shine Swam On," in *Black Fire: An Anthology of Afro-American Writing*, edited by LeRoi Jones [Amiri Baraka] and Larry Neal (New York: William Morrow and Company, Inc., 1971), 655.

36   In the last stanza of "Parker's Mood," Pleasure sings:

> Don't hang your head
> When you see, when you see those six pretty horses pulling me.
> Put a twenty dollar silver-piece on my watchchain,
> Look at the smile on my face,
> And sing a little song
> To let the world know I'm really free.

(*Norton Anthology of African American Literature* [New York: Norton, 1996], 59).

37   For a discussion of Inada's jazz poetics in *Legends from Camp*, see Juliana

Chang's "Time, Jazz, and the Racial Subject," in *Racing and (E)racing Language: Living with the Color of Our Words,* edited by Ellen J. Goldner and Safiya Henderson-Holmes (Syracuse: Syracuse University Press, 2001), 134–54.

38 This symbolism of the *shakuhachi* and the song are analogous to what Maxine Hong Kingston would invoke a year later in *The Woman Warrior* (1975). The book ends by telling about a Chinese poetess, Ts'ai Yen, who introduced the songs of a southern tribe into Han culture, including " 'Eighteen Stanzas for a Barbarian Reed Pipe,' a song that Chinese sing to their own instruments. It translated well" (209). Within this context, the barbarian reed pipe and its song also signify cultural hybridization, although Kingston's own experiments in hybridization, translation, and reinvention would be famously criticized by Frank Chin, who accused her of pandering to white audiences.

39 See for example Chin's "Confessions of a Chinatown Cowboy."

40 The topic of conversation that leads Mary Ann to critique patriarchal violence is the Japanese meaning of Lawson's name, "Mighty Buffalo Samurai" (160). Mary Ann accuses him of "bullshitting" again, not so much because she disbelieves him but because of his implicit valorization of fighting. Before recounting his memories of internment to Mary Ann's family, Lawson has drunkenly imagined himself to be a boxer, "dancing / around [his opponent] ring center, some hapless / Johannsen, writhing white / blubber in slowmotion" (142), and after he beats up Mary Ann's brother-in-law, Lawson returns to this same fantasy to rationalize his actions. It is this form of pugilistic masculinity that Mary Ann critiques.

41 Although the *Reader* features Act II alone, in what follows I discuss the play in its entirety since only by doing so can its commentary on Asian American cultural autonomy be assessed. I use the University of Washington's 1981 edition to refer to Act I, but I use the *Reader* for all references to Act II; hence the erratic-looking pagination. At the same time, because my interest here is on the *Reader*'s articulations of Afro Asian cultural collaborations, and not on Frank Chin per se, the focus of the following discussion remains on Act II, and references to Act I are primarily meant to provide background to and explain the significance of Act II.

42 This anxiety over developing an original Asian American voice was expressed by Chin and the other editors of *Aiiieeeee!* in their introduction to Chinese American and Japanese American literature: "American language, fashions, music, literature, cuisine, graphics, body language, morals, and politics have been strongly influenced by black culture. They have been cultural achievers, in spite of white supremacist culture, whereas Asia America's reputation is an achievement of that white culture—a work of racist art" (7–8).

43 Mike Marqusee writes that as Black Power's ideas of pride and economic and political independence entered black popular consciousness, "Ali became a central point of reference because he had been among the first to articulate the rudiments of Black consciousness to a mass audience" (Marqusee, *Redemption*

Song: Muhammad Ali and the Spirit of the Sixties [London: Verso, 1999], 189; in addition, see this work for more on the role of boxing in articulating race relations).

44 Elaine Kim argues that among the "lessons for Chinese Americans" that the play offers is that "Asian American culture can be found neither by imitating whites nor by imitating Blacks" (*Asian American Literature*, 186), and that Tam ultimately "reject[s] the myth that Asians could be like Blacks," although "he has as yet found nothing to replace the stereotypes and false directions" (187). Jinqui Ling discusses the play's presentation of Chin's "painful recognition of the Asian American artist's problematic dependence on borrowing mythologized histories from African American models in order to force a consideration of the consequence of a vanished Asian American historical referent" (*Narrating Nationalisms*, 82).

45 The linkage between the realization of the Asian American artist's vision and the act of fathering is clear in that Tam's documentary is not only the culmination of his artistic vision, but his paternal legacy to his children, whom he has otherwise abandoned ("I should leave them something. . . . One thing I've done alone, with all my heart" [27]). Furthermore, the documentary is a vehicle for Tam's own search for Jack Dancer's father (who would symbolically father the film and Tam himself). However, the play repeatedly presents the impotence/disavowal of fatherhood. In addition to his thwarted search for Ovaltine Jack Dancer's father, in Act I Tam reveals himself to be a failed father who disavows his responsibilities to the children he has had with his exwife (27); he refuses to act in any fatherly way towards Robbie, the young son of another character who perversely looks up to Tam (16–17); and he unmans one of the play's two Chinese father figures by describing him as "an old dishwasher who was afraid of white old ladies peeking at him through the keyhole" as he bathed (16). Even Tam's great-grandfather, one of the railroad workers usually heralded in Chin's myth of the West, is depicted "broken and frostbit on every finger and toe of him" (291) when he returns home for the last time. It is also telling that Tam's kids' new, "superior" daddy is white (27). One line in particular sums up a central theme of the play: "Chinamans do make lousy fathers. I know. I have one" (23). Yet even as Chinese fathers are most spectacularly impotent, the failure of all fathers—Chinese, white, and black— haunts the play.

46 Lee, *Performing Asian America*, 77.

47 It is thus ironic that Lee, a character who embodies the instability of racial categories, insists on a form of racial purity in assuming that Asian Americans should talk and act "Asian."

48 As one reviewer for *Newsweek* said of the play's language, it "has the beat and brass, the runs and rim-shots of jazz" (quoted in Dorothy Ritsuko McDonald, "Introduction," *The Chickencoop Chinaman and The Year of the Dragon* [Seattle: University of Washington Press, 1981], xv).

49 In Act I: scene ii, Tam prefigures this self-mythologizing when he refers to himself and Kenji in their youth as "BlackJap and Tampax, the Ragmouth—for my fancy yakity yak don't ya know. The Lone Ranger and Tonto of all those hot empty streets" (26). Although I argue that Chin draws on the conventions of the toast tradition, Kenji's poem is not a toast; for one thing, it is only sixteen lines.

50 In Act I, Kenji ironically enacts this emasculation when he *"turns on Helen Keller"* for Tam:

> KENJI (*as Helen Keller*): Aheeeha op eeehoooh too ooh wahyou oooh.
> TAM (*as a Bible Belt preacher*): Yeah, talk to me, Helen! Hallelujah! I hear her talking to me. (10)

51 Frank Chin, Jeffery Paul Chan, Lawson Fusao Inada, and Shawn Wong. *Aiiieeeee! An Anthology of Asian-American Writers* (Garden City, N.J.: Anchor Press/Doubleday, 1975).

52 In their readings of the final scene, Ling, Lee, and Chu ignore or downplay the significance of the grandmother. For Chu, the grandmother does not even register as a presence: "The play closes with a tentative affirmation of the possibilities of fathering, self-fathering, and authoring so polemically explored" (*Assimilating Asians*, 74). Ling and Lee focus on the great-grandfather, the subject of the grandmother's story, rather than on the grandmother herself. Thus, Lee interprets Tam's final lines as "asking us to join in expectantly for the return of the father figure" (*The Americas of Asian American Literature*, 81). Meanwhile, Ling claims that Tam is "on the verge of identifying with his symbolic figure and of (re)possessing his imagined heroic Asian American past" when he "seems to hear, without the mediations of either the Lone Ranger or his grandmother, the sound of a train that recalls the memory of 'grandmaw's pa coming home'" (*Narrating Nationalisms*, 91). However, I argue that the grandmother does mediate the past such that Tam hears it through her ears and voice, and that this is not an insignificant detail that can be overlooked in examining the play's concern with father figures; indeed, quite to the contrary it signals a major shift from the patrilineal to the matrilineal.

53 My reading is thus more optimistic than Kim's, which asserts that Tam "has as yet found nothing to replace the stereotypes and false directions" (*Asian American Literature*, 187).

54 Anzaldúa and Keating, *This Bridge We Call Home*, 3.

55 Fred Ho, e-mail to the author, March 28, 2004. This is not to say that all multiculturalism is liberal or tokenistic. Insofar as its roots are traced to the Yardbird Cooperative and the Before Columbus Foundation, for example, multiculturalism has radically redefined American literature by centering "minority" writers within its tradition.

56 Amiri Baraka, "Somebody Blew Up America," *African American Review* 37 (2003): 198–203. I am grateful to Bill Mullen for suggesting this poem to

address Afro Asian cultural connections in the present. Indeed, theories of identity politics and coalitional praxis would benefit much from analyzing the trajectory of Baraka's career, especially his central role within the Black Arts movement and his later criticism of narrow nationalism in favor of Third World socialism (albeit one that remains committed to the black community and its revolutionary potential). The controversy around Baraka's poem centered on four lines that critics contended were anti-Semitic:

> Who knew the World Trade Center was gonna get bombed
> Who told 4000 Israeli workers at the Twin Towers
> To stay home that day
> Why did Sharon stay away?

While I disagree that the poem is anti-Semitic, my purpose here is not to reprise this debate. For Baraka's response to the charges of anti-Semitism and the demands that he resign from his post as New Jersey's poet laureate, see Amiri Baraka, "I Will Not 'Apologize,' I Will Not 'Resign'!" www.amiribaraka.com/speech100202.html. A defense of the poem comprises the introduction to the special double issue of *African American Review* on Amiri Baraka. See William J. Harris and Aldon Lynn Nielsen, "Somebody Blew Off Baraka," *African American Review* 37 (2003): 183–87. For further background on the controversy and a critical view of Baraka, see Victorino Matus, "Bad Attitude Baraka," *Daily Standard,* October 10, 2002, www.weeklystandard.com/Content/Public/Articles/000/000/001/751zebtv.asp?pg=1.

Among organizations furthering black/Arab solidarity, the Black Radical Congress is key.

57 See Melani McAlister, "One Black Allah: The Middle East in African American Cultural Politics, 1955–1967," *American Quarterly* 51 (1999): 622–56.

58 Baraka also writes of injustices perpetrated by men of other countries, including the Holocaust and the assassinations of Patrice Lumumba and Amilcar Cabral, but in most of these cases, the U.S. had varying degrees of involvement (for example, it is commonly known that the U.S. possessed intelligence about the Holocaust but ignored or suppressed this information until public pressure forced the government to take action).

59 Examples of Bush's opportunistic multiculturalism include his appointment of conservative people of color to his cabinet (a favorite target of Baraka's satire), his courting of Latino/a voters, and his distinguishing between good and extremist Arabs, while eviscerating social services and perpetuating the War on Terror primarily against people of color.

Fred Ho

Bill Cole: African American Musician
of the Asian Double Reeds

This essay is drawn from an interview conducted by the author on February 22, 2002, at Cole's residence in New Rochelle, New York

Bill Cole, an African American "jazz" musician, is unique. He plays traditional Asian double-reed instruments such as the Korean *piri* and *hojok*, the Chinese *sona*, the south Asian *shenai* and *nagaswarm*, a Tibetan trumpet, as well as the Australian aboriginal *digeridoo* and the Ghanaian bamboo flute. But while he plays traditional Asian instruments, he doesn't play traditional Asian music. Instead, he plays "jazz" or African American improvised music using these instruments, much in the same way that African American musicians took European instruments such as the trumpet, saxophone, piano, contrabass violin, clarinet, flute, etc. and reconfigured them to express an African American musical sensibility. While other African American "jazz" musicians have forayed into Asian musical cultures (including Yusef Lateef, Eric Dolphy, and John Coltrane among others), Cole is unique because the Asian double-reed woodwinds are his principal "horns" whereas for others the principal instruments are Western instruments, with the "non-Western" instruments being doubles (the musical term for secondary instruments).

Bill Cole, in his mid-sixties at the time of this writing, is also unique for being among one of the more politically explicit "jazz" musicians of today. He continues to express through his music and song titles a celebration of the African American struggle against oppression and racism. He is author of two musical biographies and analyses of John Coltrane and Miles Davis (newly reprinted by Da Capo Press), long before the current wave of books published on these two giants of African American creative music. Combined with his unique musical persona and his uncompromising political integrity, Cole has also been the subject of much controversy stemming from the calumny and racist vehemence heaped upon him by the reactionary *Dartmouth Review* during his days as a professor of music at Dartmouth College during the 1980s, which was the focus of national media attention. This is hard to believe given Cole's soft-spoken, gentle, and subdued personality; his demeanor is not that of the weird nationalist militant, but much more the mild-mannered, bohemian, vegetarian intellectual-artiste that he actually is.

Cole was born October 11, 1937, in Pittsburgh, Pennsylvania, where he also grew up. His mother was a housewife, and his father was a dentist who also worked for the post office to supplement his income. His father's multiple jobs, typical of most of the black "middle class" of this era, kept him occupied from "7:30 AM to 2 AM" as Bill Cole recalled, which enabled the Cole family to pay for Bill's violin and piano lessons starting at a very young age. It was around the age of three or four that Bill Cole remembers his first interest in music after seeing the opera *Peter and the Wolf.* By his late teens he was playing cello, but his biggest interest was in playing the string bass (contrabass violin) after hearing and watching perform such giants as Charles Mingus, Percy Heath, Doug Watkins, and especially Paul Chambers. Another inspirational artist to the young Cole was the trumpeter/band leader Miles Davis. Cole was an amateur boxer between the ages of eleven and seventeen—a fascination he shared with Miles Davis who also was an avid boxer. But it was the tenor saxophonist John Coltrane who made the greatest musical impact on Bill Cole, who in 1955 heard the Miles Davis band perform live in Pittsburgh where Coltrane was joined by the pianist Red Garland, the bassist Paul Chambers, and the drummer "Philly Joe" Jones.

While Cole was taken by all of the three "jazz" trumpet giants of the era, namely Dizzy Gillespie, Clifford Brown, and Miles Davis, it was Davis who was the most fascinating to the young musician. As Cole explained: "Miles often played against the tempo, he had great creative interpretative ability and he surrounded himself with the most incredible musicians in his band."

By the mid-1950s, the civil rights movement had swept across the United States, and Bill Cole became an activist with CORE (Congress of Racial Equality). The movement brought about a "revelation about the level of racism" in the United States for Cole and many of his generation. Cole entered college in 1956 as a sociology major by day and a music major by night while attending evening school and listening to music performances in bars. Since the time of kindergarten, Bill Cole's teachers were all white except for one black teacher who taught woodshop in high school. Cole attributes his parents as his most consistent role models and for giving him a basic foundation for his life direction.

His immersion in activism and in the vanguard "new music" both occurred during the 1950s and 1960s. Another major music impact that Cole recalls is hearing the pianist Cecil Taylor in 1957 for the first time in a small Greenwich Village club in New York City.

Cole's undergraduate studies would take ten years, owing to his poor grades and lack of money for tuition. By 1967, Cole had married his first wife, and his first child, son Atticus, soon followed. By fall 1970, Cole had entered the Ph.D. program at Wesleyan University. His two faculty advisors in African American music were the multi-woodwindist Ken McIntyre and the visiting artist Clifford Thornton, one of the more radical and socially conscientious musicians of the time and a member of the Harlem branch of the Black Panther Party. Cole recalled that Thornton kept firearms in his apartment. Clifford Thornton would inspire Cole to soon take up the Asian double reeds.

Wesleyan University has for many years had a noted ethnomusicology program, which includes a fabulous collection of traditional instruments from around the world. As Bill Cole tells it, it was from this Wesleyan collection that Clifford Thornton stole a Chinese double-reed *sona* and a Korean double-reed instrument and gave them to Bill Cole, telling him to learn to play them. Cole tells of being attracted to the "human voice-like quality" of the Asian double reeds. He taught himself to play the *sona* and bought the south Asian *shenai* from the House of Musical Traditions, a world music instrument store that had once been in New York's Greenwich Village. Wesleyan brought many visiting master musicians from such places as India, Indonesia, West Africa, China, and Japan, as well as hosting Native American specialists and performers such as David MacAllister and Doogie Mitchell. Cole would later take up additional Asian double reeds such as the Korean *hojok* and the Indian *nagaswarm*.

Bill Cole is very forthright about how he was perceived by other African American musicians for his involvement with Asian instruments. Some considered him a "freak" (he mentions the bassist Wilbur Ware and the cellist Abdul Wadud as examples); while the great saxophonist Sam Rivers were among his more receptive colleagues (Cole met Rivers while Rivers was a second-year visiting artist at Wesleyan). Others who were among his more receptive peers included the poet Jayne Cortez, who often collaborates with musicians, and the late saxophonist-composer Julius Hemphill. It was during Cole's time at Wesleyan that he began building his free improvisation groups who worked without the use of musical notation and instead relied on oral tradition. Cole is also candid about the controversy surrounding him musically both for engaging in free improvisation and for using instruments not conventional to "jazz." Says Cole: "There will always be reactionary types, such as when Louis Armstrong criticized Charlie Parker for not playing dance music."

Following Wesleyan, Cole moved to Walla Walla, Washington, to teach for one semester during spring 1972 as a visiting professor in the Music Department at Whitman College. There he organized an African American music festival and invited the Nigerian musicologist and composer Fela Sowande to be a guest lecturer. Sowande, who was "steeped in the traditional philosophy and lifestyle of West African peoples," was to have a profound impact upon Cole. Sowande introduced him to the concept of "multiple births"—an idea that Cole intuitively understood but that became a reality for him through the influence of Professor Sowande.

As Cole states: "I've never approached playing [Asian instruments] in a traditional way; I express myself as a black person through the human vocal quality of non-tempered double reeds . . . There's so much space between C and C#. I express what I've seen and experienced of racism and hatred against black people." Cole approaches the Asian double reeds as a "black American instrument, the same as black people playing other instruments that originated, say, in Europe; we black Americans express ourselves differently than people who originally developed these instruments."

The singular uniqueness about Bill Cole is his expression of black music on the Korean *piri*, the *hojok*, the Chinese *sona*, and the Tibetan trumpet. In Cole's view, he is playing black music through Asian double reeds. When I asked Cole how Asian audiences have responded to his music, he replied: "With tremendous interest. Asian audiences and instrumentalists can't tell why my sound and desire is so strong."

Cole seeks to reach everybody with his music, but he especially focuses upon the black community. He recently performed at the musician Ahmed Abdullah's Sista's Place in Brooklyn's heavily black Bedford-Stuyvesant neighborhood. He works with the African American instrument-builder Cooper Moore, another performer with a unique approach to music. Just as Harry Partch in the Western European concert music genre performed on self-built instruments, Cooper Moore has African Americanized his performance process.

Cole quotes Fela Sowanade's maxim: "Take what is new and reshape it into a familiar form." Cole bases his music upon the blues, "the cornerstone and building block of black secular music. All of my long works have blues forms." Cole espouses in the arts and in university academic circles the idea of Afrocentrism before it became a buzzword. According to Cole, "Coltrane was a very literate player, but all of his music springs from intuitive knowledge; music is in every aspect of life in African society, from ritual to the most inane recreational music."

Cole's book on Coltrane, the first published book on the late, great tenor saxophone giant, could well be characterized as the first work to provide an "Afrocentric" analysis. Cole's framework and arguments about Coltrane are very controversial among both white and black music critics and scholars. Cole's purpose in writing a book on Coltrane was "to counter the position that Coltrane is a product of Western art and Western instrumental music. To me, Coltrane is an African-descended person in the Western Hemisphere; he was a tremendous rhythmic player. He could play at any tempo—that's his African musical persona, the repetitiveness and ongoing cyclic movement of the interiority of the human body. Coltrane had a pragmatic and intuitive mind. With his high level of skill, he could be so open to his intuitive mind. There are many, many skilled black artists but what made Coltrane so unique is how open he was to his intuitive side."

Cole also notes Coltrane's social consciousness, for which he cites Coltrane's composition "Alabama" dedicated to the four young black girls murdered in a church bombing in Alabama during the early 1960s. "Coltrane couldn't make it ["Alabama"] an up-tempo piece; it wouldn't memorialize the slain children in an effective way."

Coltrane was furthermore, and perhaps most profoundly, a musical radical and revolutionary. As Cole states: "[Coltrane] got away from tonal centers, which he felt were shackles, and crossed over to a realm of music that wasn't fixed." Cole also notes how the late reed virtuoso Eric Dolphy had a tremendous impact upon Coltrane. In Cole's view, it was Dolphy who got Coltrane to move beyond being a consummate "systematic [chord] 'changes' player who mastered arpeggios and scales" to a much freer conception of melody and improvisation. Cole further argues that "Dolphy played fragments and did huge register leaps [unlike the connective playing of improvising on chord changes common to most "jazz" players]. It was in Germany that Dolphy and Coltrane decided to take a trip to India in the early 1960s. 'Trane would become interested in the [south Asian] Shenai in later years."

Cole then notes that "Coltrane was without fear when it came to music. Most musicians fear something different or feel very challenged when it comes to their own music. 'Trane was constantly looking for other influences and instruments to expand his music. He started playing the harp at the end of his life." It was during the semester in Walla Walla that Sam Rivers impacted upon Cole's compositional approach. "Sam would develop these small written parts as springboards for improvisation, getting away from conventional Western harmony." With five students excited about this concept, Cole would begin to develop it into his ideas for ensemble performance.

In fall 1972 Cole went to Massachusetts to teach at Amherst College in both the Black Studies Department and in the Music Department. It was there that he began to experience the pettiness of putrefying academic politics. Cole recounted how the music faculty were "so pissed and hostile" at him for not joining their department, even though he was hired by black studies. However, Cole found his chief support from then-college president William Ward, "who was the only academic administrator with the sensibility beyond anything-Western." Cole submitted a National Endowment for the Arts grant, for which he received $2,500 (which the school then matched) to develop the John Coltrane Memorial World Music Lecture Demonstration Series. In this highly adventurous and innovative program Cole was able to bring to Amherst College and the surrounding five-college community such artists as Sam Rivers, Jayne Cortez, and Warren Smith. It was Clifford Thornton who exposed Cole to the poet Cortez as they had performed together in the late 1960s as part of the militant and radical Black Arts cultural activism.

The Coltrane series brought in master artists from India and West African as well as African American performers. Cole and his young cohorts struggled to raise funds for the series, the success of which had spawned a competing program. Amherst College funded two black students $8,000 to put on a black music conference. According to Cole, however, the two students used half of the money to take their girlfriends on a vacation to Jamaica. This was Cole's first harsh and sobering experience with grant co-optation. The students had in effect stolen money from the grant they were given. When Cole went to the college president to complain about the issue, he was threatened by the two students. The facade of genteel and gracious academia would be ripped away as from this point forward in his academic career Cole would face personal physical threats along with a host of unethical and tawdry events of undermining and attack. Cole minces no words about calling the then-Amherst College black studies chair Asa Davis a "total Tom," who was replaced by radical poet Sonia Sanchez as department head.

Fed up with the rank opportunism of Amherst College, Cole went to Dartmouth College to teach in 1974. Hired by Dartmouth's Music Department, Cole constructed seven new courses, including developing the ethnomusicology program. By 1980, he had become chair of the department—a post that he held until 1983. At Dartmouth Cole implemented a two-track system whereby students could study both Western art music and world music; in addition, he brought the master Ghanaian drummer Adzinyah to teach African drumming and continued the Coltrane lecture demo series. Also during this time Cole published his first book, on his musical hero Miles Davis. Two years later, his Coltrane book was published.

The Dartmouth administration, according to Cole, tried not to grant him tenure, but this move was "politically suicidal" for them because Cole had "strong support from the students." Cole's classes, such as "African Music and Oral Tradition," would attract 90 to 196 students—more than any music class had done before in the history of Dartmouth's Music Department. Cole saw teaching as "theater" and he believed he knew how to "keep students' attention." But he also became a target of administrative and right-wing student scorn, vituperative hatred, and hostility. Cole recounts how certain deans tried to restrict his academic freedom and First Amendment rights for citing in one class Ethel Water's 1920s song lyrics "I'm so blue because I'm black, All the race fellas crave high yellas." These deans told Cole that "you can't talk about these lyrics since they're not in proper English."

Cole has other teaching methods that irked the reactionaries at Dartmouth. For example, he would sing solos as well as give extended monologues/lectures on segregation, oppression, and life in black America—how he wasn't served in restaurants. All of these lectures/stories were poured out by Cole "in a theatrical way." Cole joined student protests in 1979 when two white Dartmouth hockey players dressed as Indians and protestors organized a mascot moratorium in response.

While certain Dartmouth conservatives would be bothered by all the "strangeness" and "weirdness" about Cole and his teaching along with his outspokenness against racism and social oppression, in 1983 the conservative *Dartmouth Review* would begin virulent open attacks upon Cole. He was target of attacks and objections to black, ethnic, and women's and all areas of thought that "were not historically promoted at the institution."

In 1988, four students accosted Cole in his class. Police had to escort these hooligans out so that Cole could continue to teach. The war was on. The *Dartmouth Review* published ongoing anti–Bill Cole pieces in their effort to make him the target of their vicious attacks. In response Cole sued the *DR* for slander—as a national publication, it had an impact on his reputation. A local New Hampshire paper picked up on the *DR* chorus and accused Cole of being "incompetent." Bill Cole's battle with the *DR* took on historic proportions: he became the first and only university professor to take the publication to court. In litigation that ensued for two years, it was a case of a local lawyer (Cole's attorney) versus big-time New York City lawyers for the *DR*. An out of court settlement was eventually reached.

Even after the settlement, however, the worst was still to come. "They really came after me," says Cole. "I was put on their List of Worst Professors. Charges were brought against them by the Committee on Student Responsibility. All of the *Dartmouth Review* students were suspended. They went to court but the judge in New Hampshire said that one of the Committee members had an explicit bias against the *Dartmouth Review* and revoked the suspension." Eventually, the university administration bought out Cole's contract. Says Cole: "I was seen as a problem. I confronted them on the mascot moratorium at the end of the 1970s. At the assembly, I spoke out against sexism and racism, supported affirmative action. They also had problems with me using cuss words in class. I refused to tone it down, my life hasn't been that way. I was totally blackballed."

The national press picked up the story. The conflict between Bill Cole and the *Dartmouth Review* conflict was a feature story on CBS's *Sixty Minutes*. During this time, Cole received many, many threatening letters and phone calls. The notoriety and controversy that resulted from the Dartmouth incident permanently ended his teaching career. Cole has been turned down for numerous positions for which he was far more than qualified, and he has only been able to find short stints in positions such as elementary school music instruction.

Cole is clear that, barring a miracle, his teaching days are finished, and thus he has directed his energies toward greater performing opportunities. He sees his music as "folk music." While he expresses his receptivity to Asians playing traditional instruments in his group, all of his ensembles are African American. Cole believes it is essential that the players "all have a feeling of racial ostracism in America. My band members all share this experience, and a certain expression comes out of that." Cole's current group, Untempered Ensemble (originally formed in 1992), is a "free jazz" African American ensemble featuring Bill Cole (leader, double-reed Asian horns), Warren Smith and son Atticus Cole as percussionists, Joe Daley (tuba and baritone horn), William Parker (acoustic bass), Cooper-Moore (flute and handcrafted instruments) and Sam Furnace (alto sax and flute).[1]

Note

[1]   Sadly, Sam Furnace passed away on January 27, 2004.
Discography: *Seasoning the Greens*, fall 2002, Boxholder Records; *Bill Cole and the Untempered Ensemble, Duets and Solos*, 2 vols., Boxholder Records; *Untempered Ensemble Live in Greenfield Massachusetts*, May 2000, Boxholder Records; Vision Festival 1997 (compiled excerpts from *Seasoning the Greens*); "The Untempered Trio," November 1992; "Everywhere Drums," Jayne Cortez, September 1990; "There It Is," Jayne Cortez, October 1982; "First Cycle," with Sam Rivers and Warren Smith, September 1980; "Unsubmissive Blues," Jayne Cortez, April 1980.

Kim Hewitt

Martial Arts Is Nothing if Not Cool: Speculations on the Intersections between Martial Arts and African American Expressive Culture

I will argue in this essay that there are some similarities between idealized African American cultural aesthetics and idealized training philosophies in the martial arts. While recognizing the complications of generalizing about African American culture and martial arts philosophies, I hope to highlight cultural factors that might account for the appeal of martial arts to African Americans, especially young lower-class black men.

Implicit in my approach are the assumptions that the African diaspora contributed an Africanist presence to African American communities,[1] which culminated in a unique African American expressive style, and that many kinds of martial arts have similar underlying philosophical guidelines. The first assumption manifests in this essay as a loosely defined constellation of aspects of African American culture. I draw on various realms of African American expressive culture—visual, kinesthetic, and musical—and I discuss aesthetic and interactive elements that allow for comparison to martial arts as it is taught, practiced, and idealized. Although each of these expressive realms has its own unique characteristics, they all share the aesthetic value of cool with the martial arts. If this connection makes sense theoretically as we examine African American expressive culture and martial arts, then we may understand the appeal of martial arts to African Americans in the 1960s and 1970s in a new light.

A complete survey of the origins, styles, and philosophies of martial arts worldwide would require at least a volume-length study, as would a survey of how each style is taught in each separate training school (*dojo/dojang*). Therefore, my thoughts remain speculative here, and they are based in a wide-ranging knowledge of various Asian martial arts philosophies and a deep knowledge of a small sample of contemporary martial arts schools and interpretations of their philosophies from both martial arts students and teachers. Although specific philosophies differ among Asian martial arts, most of them share similar principles of training that reflect an underlying traditional philosophy. These training goals and philosophies have been established in well-known martial arts texts, which still serve as guidelines for martial arts schools, teachers, and students. Balancing the martial arts mythology created by these texts and the real-life way in which martial arts schools operate is difficult because the two are so deeply entwined. Adding in the Hollywood representation of martial arts traditions complicates the matter further, but clearly martial arts movies in the 1970s appealed to African Americans and popularized martial arts. Three distinct points in common between African American cultural aesthetics and martial arts philosophies encouraged this initial popularity to grow: martial arts training values self-expression within a defined structure; martial arts strives to promote internal strength and self-respect as well as physical skill; and martial arts schools encourage the student to ground his or her achievement within the martial arts tradition and to create a strong sense of mutual respect between the individual and the martial arts community. These values have parallels in African American expressive culture and can be approached by acknowledging Bruce Lee as a movie star whose films inspired many fans to train.

To state the obvious, martial arts as a tactic of self-defense appeals to individuals historically denied the right to be freely expressive in public space as well as denied the power to defend themselves, including African

RICANdition
your way of thinking
BORICUA

FUERZAS ARMADAS DE LIBERACIÓN NACIONAL

F.A.L.N.

CREATE DETERMINE YOUR DESTINY

© RICANdition is an artist initiative - a C PUERTO RICAN EQUATION Project.
To provoke attention, dialogue, consciousness and activism, we use art and texts on issues concerning our Puerto Rican paradigm.
This is our means of waging struggle toward self-determination.

Bruce Lee appearing as Boricua:
Your Destiny Is in Your Hands
(1995). Bruce Lee postcard.
(Reprinted by permission of
Juan Sanchez)

Americans and other groups excluded from the mainstream by virtue of their ethnicity, socioeconomic status, and age. Without the resources of money or social status, an individual can still achieve self-respect and victory by becoming physically skillful and powerful with the sole resource always available—one's own body. Many forms of martial arts were developed by people denied the use of weapons for self-defense.[2] Linking creative forms of self-defense to the historical circumstances that denied conventional weapons to oppressed people explains one reason why martial arts films and training may have appealed to minorities in the late 1960s and early 1970s. During this time there was a push in the vanguard of the African American community, as well as in other minority communities, to resist the mainstream identities and stereotypes imposed upon them and to embrace self-expression outside of mainstream venues.[3] Minorities in America were actively looking for creative forms of metaphoric self-defense.

Viewed within the context of various innovative cultural uses of the body in art movements during the 1960s and early 1970s to break social conventions, the choice of individuals to grasp onto a highly structured, superficially hierarchical discipline[4] to challenge social conventions seems ironic. During this time period, experimental forms of visual art, dance, and performance attempted to erase all social strictures on the proper use of the body by invoking the Bakhtinian grotesque, intimate, messy body, or, as the dance and theater scholar Sally Banes describes in her chronicle of art in Greenwich Village in the 1960s: "impudent bodily images."[5] In comparison, the contained, controlled, highly disciplined body trained in a martial art, which functions within a structure that values tradition, is quite conservative. The irony deepens considering the attraction of many of these avant-garde movements toward black culture as venue for antibourgeois sentiments and the African American body as "the dancing body, the jazz body, the emotional body, and inevitably, the sexual body."[6] Alternately, in the face of appropriation of the African American body, it makes sense that African Americans might express a more militaristic claim over their own bodies, and choose to embody collective and individual ideals, politically, culturally, and concretely via an art that is an improvisational fighting art. The trained martial arts body is not so much playfully impudent as functionally impudent by virtue of its skill, although it is also capable of poetic and playful movement. Its ability to connect aesthetic performance and fighting skills parallels its ability to link physical training and mental and psychological development. Martial arts of any style present a holistic view of mind/body harmony as a basis of training. Martial arts training ideally transcends mere physical training by creating a warrior mentality in which a person is trained to be physically and psychologically ready to face confrontation fluidly and easily at any moment. This unruffled readiness epitomizes cool in the martial arts.

The fundamental holism of martial arts training is what allows Vijay Prashad to state "Kung Fu gives oppressed young people an immense sense of personal worth and skills for collective struggle."[7] As Miyamoto Musashi, the author of the classic guide to the martial strategy and development of the Japanese sword form of Kendo, *The Book of Five Rings*, promises, "by training you will be able to freely control your own body, conquer men with your body, and with sufficient training you will be able to beat ten men with your spirit."[8] In the 1960s and early 1970s, some radical groups like the Black Panthers trained themselves in martial arts, as did the militant group the Weathermen and some militant feminist groups.[9] Although explicitly training was for health and self-defense, implicitly it helped create solidarity and readiness to face social, and possibly physical, tension.[10]

The growing popularity of martial arts in the African American community can be traced through the appearance of African Americans in martial arts films and dojangs. The Black Karate Federation was founded in 1968, Moses Powell became the first black jujitsu artist to perform for the United Nations (in 1971), and other African Americans earned various martial arts championships and recognition.[11] Although surely only a small percentage of those who saw martial arts films committed to serious training, cinematic martial arts fight scenes and their most popular hero, Bruce Lee, held a widespread fascination because of their depiction of "graceful dirty fighting." The film scholar Stuart Kaminsky points out that "King Fu films" were popular among black urban audiences, especially lower-class audiences, exactly because they eschewed traditional middle-class rules of fighting in favor of fighting to survive. Kaminsky combines the factors of race and class along with a psychological interpretation when he theorizes that "the fantasy resolution for the ghetto kid is not through the law. The fantasy is of being able to right the wrongs of one's personal frustration through one's own limited ability. It is not surprising that films that deal with the skillful handling of wrongs done to one's immediate family (as Kaminski claims Kung Fu films often did in the early 1970s) should be particularly popular among black American youths."[12]

Kaminski further characterizes the typical Kung Fu antagonist as a "small," "downtrodden," but dignified, hero. As the lower-class Chinese antagonist, Bruce Lee fought officials of the Japanese colonial government. As the underdog and nonwhite hero, Bruce Lee conquered oppression. His image still looms large in the cinematic imagination of rebellious youth of all ethnic backgrounds and political persuasions who are entranced by his screen presence. According to Jachinson Chan, in the early 1970s Lee's status as a Chinese American who had been educated in Hong Kong marginalized him as neither fully Chinese in the eyes of many Asian Americans, nor American in the eyes of mainstream America.[13] Lee's ambiguous hybrid American identity accounts for his wide-ranging appeal to nonwhites. His cinematic presence championed the Chinese fight against the oppression of Japan, while also appealing to a diverse audience because of his embodiment of powerful masculinity, which mitigated against the stereotype of Chinese Americans as docile and effeminate.[14] As a Chinese American male hero, Lee provided an image of alternative, nonwhite masculinity for minorities, including African Americans, to counter their exclusion from mainstream masculinity.[15]

As Chan, Kaminski, and Ho remark, both the film narratives and Lee's physicality imbue him with heroic stature as his roles communicate the message that "one's body has the potential to be a lethal weapon."[16] Less scholarship has emphasized the popularity of the African American martial artist Jim Kelly (*Enter the Dragon, Black Belt Jones, Goldfinger*) and his importance to minority fans, as well as the impact of the African American women who displayed fighting skills on screen. Further scholarship in these areas hopefully will be forthcoming.[17] Viewers identified with both Kelly and Lee as cinema protagonists, and possibly also through a vicarious kinesthetic experience of their onscreen fights—a vivid imagined physical participation while viewing that some scholars have noted as a unique dynamic for viewers of martial arts films.[18] Although the slight-statured Lee uses weapons such as *nunchakus* in some scenes, the films emphasize his technical skills, learned though discipline and training, that have culminated in intense determination and an extraordinary harmony of mind, body, and spirit focused for self-defense. The martial arts are first and foremost fighting arts. Lee's primary message is that any individual can use his body as a weapon if he trains hard enough. This message immediately appeals to individuals who have been denied physical and social power historically and on a daily basis.

Lee's physical skill is matched by his adaptation of traditional martial arts into his own unique style, upon which he founded his martial arts school. On the screen Lee displays his own stylistic sensibility, and he commands a highly developed internal strength as well as physical skill ultimately used in the service of others. Lee's trained, fierce, and fluid style emphasizes the visceral experience of an individual reaping the benefits of his dedication to martial arts training. In watching Lee, one realizes that he is as alone and self-reliant as any mythical American self-made man. As he fights he is (seemingly) independent of any help from, or restrictions of, social systems. Lee's skill, style and vitality represent the American dream come true. He achieves victory on his own stylistic terms as he defends himself and his community. The development of individual identity and style is an important aspect of martial arts training, and when we consider that martial arts techniques rely on trained skill rather than brute strength or power, the appeal develops a unique character. For African Americans, the use of the body as an indirect expression of identity and resistance carries historical overtones.

In *Stylin: African American Expressive Culture from Its Beginnings to the Zoot Suit,* Shane White and Graham White chronicle expressions of the "distinctive nature of black kinesics," or embodied manifestations of African American life. Simply put, historically African Americans have used bodily gestures in unique ways to reflect, mediate, and manipulate social interaction. Blacks who were enslaved struggled against the knowledge that not only were their bodies commodities that could be bought, sold, branded, worked, whipped, and used at the whim of slaveowners, but that their status as property also constrained the ways in which they could speak, walk, stand, make eye contact, and present themselves in public.[19] Standing too proudly, walking too confidently, or glancing at the wrong time at the wrong person could result in punishment. Decades after slavery ended, and well into the 1960s, written and unwritten social codes constrained the freedom ~~bodies~~ of African American bodies. Social norms, and too often laws, not only segregated black bodies from white bodies but determined that they must be deferential and servile in public when interacting with whites. In some regions of racial tension the "well-behaved" black body was expected to take up as little public space as possible, both metaphorically and in concrete ways on the street, in public institutions, and in public discourse.

White and White explore the many ways that African Americans historically resisted oppression and bodily constraint. One tactic was to mask all direct emotional and cognitive expression by making their faces and bodies unreadable—a classic martial arts defense strategy promoted by *The Book of Five Rings* with the simple admonition "do not let the enemy see your spirit."[20] Another tactic entailed aestheticizing the body by replacing the constrained body with an expansive body that expressed individuality using style of movement, clothing, language, and dance. The black body was no longer property, work tool, sexual object, or an embodiment of inferior social status. Instead it became beautiful, graceful, adorned, sensual, vital, and defiant. In White and White's words the body became a "political subtext of struggle, a determination to renegotiate the social contract." A structured or tightly coded social system often aims to silence the body,[21] and yet individuals find ways to express their identity and protest in their bodily practices.

The African American body trained in martial arts functions within this genre of bodily practice protesting social constrictions. Trained to fight, the martial artist is able to hide and protect his inner spirit, enabling him to survive confrontation both physically and psychologically as well as subdue his enemies.

For many individuals who study martial arts the desire to be able to physically defend oneself is supplemented by the hunger for inner fortitude. Many martial arts schools encourage individuals to develop more than just physical strength and dexterity, and thus carefully promote self-awareness. The ultimate goal is not mastering physical techniques but rather bringing the mind, body, and spirit into harmony to achieve internal strength. Bruce Lee clarified this position when he claimed that "technical skill is . . . subordinate to psychic training."[22] The common martial arts concept of *chi* or *ki*, for example, refers to the focused integration of physical, mental, and spiritual energies to nurture "intrinsic strength," which transcends mere physical strength.[23] Chi is an internal energy. Intrinsic strength is evidenced by physical fluidity as a martial artist learns to access and direct chi, and by the ability to direct and control one's whole presentation as one moves through space physically and through daily life in a focused, self-composed manner.

Composure is a crucial component of the African American expressive style of cool as seen in several arenas of African American expressive culture, including music and dance. The kinesthetic art of dance provides the best comparison with martial arts because both are motion through space, and a discussion of the Africanist presence in dance illuminates the value of composure in African American aesthetics. As explained by the dance scholar Brenda Dixon Gottschild, several of the characteristics of Africanist dance are startlingly similar to the ideals that martial artists strive to achieve. In referencing the art historian Robert Farris Thompson, Gottschild points out that many Africanist visual arts privilege certain motion concepts and the "aesthetic of the cool." In contrast to European-based dance movements, which emphasize "centeredness, control, linearity, (and) directness," the characteristic Africanist motions are loose and flexible, asymmetrical and polyrhythmic. They encompass power, vitality, drive, and attack, as well as an attitude of composure. Ideally, "cool results from the juxtaposition of detachment with intensity."[24] This aesthetic of cool in dance is parallel to the ideal of composure in the martial arts styles. The ideal motion that a martial artist strives to achieve is both relaxed and focused, executed with full strength and power and yet precise and loose. The ideal attitude is one of inner intensity and calm. Although an accomplished martial artist also knows when to employ linear, direct, centered movements (which are aesthetically European according to Gottschild), the brilliance comes in being flexible enough to move fluidly from one kind of motion to the next as needed and remain composed. The ability to direct and control chi energy means that one can remain detached and relax into the movement because (ideally) the inner strength will fully animate the motion. As mind, body, and spirit harmonize, physical grace and inner strength merge into graceful, effective, fluid execution of one's intention.

A discussion of the aesthetic of cool as developed by African American jazz musicians can further expand our understanding of composure and the particular appeal it has in African American culture. As outlined by the American studies scholar Joel Dinerstein, beginning in the 1930s urban blacks and jazz musicians developed styles of language and presentation that signaled withdrawal from the conflicts of mainstream society and developed into recognizable cultural codes for African Americans. This "cool mask" (which Dinerstein traces through African concepts transformed into African American concepts) entailed a composed exterior that marked "resistance to mainstream social norms and an inner complexity" as a defense against external hostility. Further, as jazz musicians like Lester Young and Dizzy Gillespie developed ways to maintain a controlled presence, they did so while staying relaxed and expressing a sense of "inner spirit." Like martial artists they cultivated "relaxed intensity," which combined "expressive style with public composure." Dinerstein notes that this particular manifestation of the cool aesthetic is "in one sense, composed violence."[25] This musical performance style, indicative of a larger African American aesthetic, parallels the martial arts ideal of relaxed intensity in the face of physical and mental challenges. Martial arts in its ideal form is nothing if not cool.

Martial arts schools often emphasize the value of composure in training as crucial to the ability to fight effectively by relying on inner strength. The instruction of physical techniques coexists with instruction to seek self-knowledge and self-respect, along with the ability to control one's psyche as well as one's body. One of the first emotions a martial arts student learns about is fear (of looking foolish, of failure, of pain, of hurting someone else), but many other emotions follow. One has to become intimately acquainted with a vast array of emotions and learn to function with them in order to train in martial arts and, as Musashi urges samurai warriors, to "develop a steady spirit."[26] Advanced martial artists learn to acknowledge their emotions without letting them control their actions. They remain centered and calm, alert and aware. In *The Art of Peace*, Morihei Ueshiba, the founder of Aikido, encourages students to "leave behind all self-centered thoughts, petty desires, and anger" and develop compassion and wisdom.[27] When he states simply "your spirit is your true shield,"[28] he conveys the idea that physical prowess must be supported by a well-trained psyche in order to become a true martial artist. This philosophy relies on a holistic view of mind and body, and it roots practitioners with a deep sense of self-respect as they learn techniques to enhance both physical and mental control. This control is necessary to execute forms (*katas*) properly and to maintain the calmness necessary to fight an opponent, and it also offers insight into the depth of one's own capacities. Ueshiba reminds his students that ultimately "each one of us is a miniature universe, a living shrine."[29] As one learns self-composure one learns self-respect and active respect for others.[30] The ability to cultivate composure is linked to one's ability to participate in a martial arts dojang and develop a warrior spirit.

self healing and energy first

With self-control and self-respect comes an internal power that exceeds the power of physical force. As Joe Hymans states in *Zen in the Martial Arts*, the goal of a martial artist is to become "so strong inside that he has no need to demonstrate his physical power."[31] Although not directly political, this sense of self-empowerment appeals tremendously to individuals who may have little control over the external factors limiting their options in daily life. One can interpret this kind of self-mastery as diminishing the grip of external factors over the individual, which perhaps becomes the first step toward further activism and power in larger realms. This connection was expressed to me succinctly by a practitioner of the African-Brazilian martial art of capoiera: "First you learn to control your own energy, then you learn to control someone else's."[32] The goal of empowering the individual as the ultimate goal of martial arts training was expressed by Bruce Lee succinctly when he stated: "The true power of our skill is as self-knowledge—the liberation of the self—not as a weapon."[33]

The rudimentary physical techniques gained in the early years of martial arts training eventually blossom as a student develops a sense of style. As one instructor told his students, "First learn the movements, then make them your own."[34] As this happens, the next level of learning begins. Students who began by imitating the motions of others eventually develop their own rhythm and unique kinetic emphasis, and even their own individual breathing and fight sounds. (For example, Bruce Lee's animal sound *kiaps* have often been described as highly individualized). A unique style reflects a deep understanding of technique and a level of skill that allows the student to embellish and improvise as needed or desired.

An exploration of the African American cultural value on individual expression augments an understanding of the intersection of martial arts aesthetics and African American aesthetics. Many forms of African American art encourage individual expression within a structure, such as the chance for a musician to improvise within the structure of jazz, or the opportunity for dancers to make up footwork during the break away or rock step in swing dancing. These moments allow a performer to demonstrate personal style and brilliance, while remaining in the flow of the larger performance. These African-diasporic expressions value a performer whose unique style awes the audience and adds to the lexicon of the art. African American cultural aesthetics value self-expression as a sign of individuality. Style is also valued for its innovative contribution to the community because individual expression strengthens and dignifies the community.[35] When self-expression embraces composure, it reflects the aesthetic of the cool. As detailed in the *Code of the Samurai,* the samurai warrior is at his peak service as a warrior when he maintains an absolute composure in the face of death, the thought of which he must hold in his mind at all times. The achieved coolness is not solely one of composure because the warrior is willing to lose his life at any moment—instead, composure actually enables the warrior to perform his service: "You fulfill the paths of loyalty and familial duty when you keep death in mind."[36] The anthropologist Michael Jackson explores the value of composure as he conveys the value of self-mastery to one African community. He analyzes the community meaning of initiation rituals and healing practices among the Kuranko people. Jackson writes that for the Kuranko the ability to withstand pain is central to the acquisition of self-mastery.

Central to this transition is pain, *dime,* a word that connotes both emotional suffering and physical hurt. The neophyte is encouraged to control his or her *reaction* to suffering. Mastery of one's reaction to pain—standing stock-still, not blinking, not making a sound, not wincing when one is cut—is regarded as the paradigm of all self-mastery. In the Kuranko view it is only when a person learns to discriminate between the action of hurt and his or her reaction to it that he or she gains any measure of control or freedom. *Yiri* (steadiness of body/mind) connotes this detached attitude to an inner state, whether pain, grief, anger, or love. *Kereteye* (bravery) and *kilanbelteye* (fortitude) suggest moral fiber and the ability to withstand the tides of strong emotions. These virtues are all dependent upon the cultivation of an abstract attitude that produces consonance between intentions and actions.[37]

These qualities of emotional and physical self-control are similar to those attempted by martial artists, and are connected to social interactions and self-mastery that, as Jackson notes, are then placed within a community context. When Jackson discusses a Kuranko healer, he claims that "like the exponents of Eastern martial arts, he came to see that the proper exercise of power is not in using it to gain advantage over others but in containing it, holding it under control. Self-mastery in the Kuranko view, is the beginning of social adroitness."[38] For the Kuranko, the ideal of self-mastery functions within a larger context of the individual in relationship to others. Although it would be difficult to connect this Kuranko value directly with African American individuals who train in martial arts, Thompson helps us bridge this gap by reminding us that a general African worldview survived the diaspora and transformed into African American cultural elements. Self-mastery, a form of self-composure, contributes to the aesthetic of cool and always exists in relation to others.

An ethic of self-expression and achievement that serves the community is also often valued in the dojang. Advanced martial artists attempt to develop their own style, while some, like Bruce Lee, attempt a synthesis of different styles to innovate a whole new school of martial arts. Lee created the style of Jeet Kune Do and encouraged his students to bring their own style to their training.[39] In Lee's films, his individuality is only one aspect of his victory, and his dedication to his community also glorifies his fight. The role of community offers another link between martial arts philosophies and the appeal of training to African Americans. Personal growth in traditional martial arts training is often linked to respect for community. A contemporary Korean style, Tukong Moosul, emphasizes "selfless service" or "service without return" as one aspect of a student's training. This philosophy applies within the dojang as each student supports every other student in his or her training, but it also encourages a larger active role within the school and in the larger outside community. Each student helps maintain the dojang and is encouraged to participate in community service projects outside the dojang.

The sense of participation in—and by—the community is also highly valued in African American aesthetics. However, "community" remains a vague concept. Does it mean immediate community, mainstream community, or even audience? The African American aesthetic of interplay between performer and audience, as seen in the call-and-response structure of blues music, lends itself uneasily to parallel with martial arts. Performance is often a low priority for martial artists, as is interplay with spectators who may witness their skill. Sparring can be framed as a form of artistic give and take, but the participation ethic is more applicable to martial arts via a closer look at the role of respect in the dojang. The value placed on the give and take of respect illuminates a philosophy of connectedness between the individual and the tradition of teaching within the dojang that emphasizes mutual respect and is evidenced by community participation.

Almost every form of Asian martial arts predicates a hierarchical system of ranking. The most revered figures of the dojo are usually the masters or grandmasters who founded the school, and who in turn trace the style back to its ancient origins such as the Shaolin temples of China or the original practitioners in Japan. Most martial arts schools display photos of past masters to show reverence for their skill and wisdom. Often martial arts schools will set aside a small altar-like space for incense and other offerings to pay homage to teachers or religious figures who are helpful to the school and the students. The presence of photos and offerings of thanks verifies the importance of lineage and paying homage to ancestoral figures, and it is echoed when instructors encourage students to remain connected to the tradition from which the martial arts teachings originate. This connection is manifested by showing respect for past teachers and the martial arts tradition. No matter how accomplished an individual may become, he or she is taught to always remember that individual accomplishment is not possible without *wisdom of past* the prior wisdom of past teachers and the time and energy they contributed to the community. In turn, in appreciation for the efforts of past and present instructors, each student strives to return as much energy as possible to the tradition. One way of doing this is showing respect within the dojang. Students quickly learn to perform a ritual bow upon entering and leaving the training area as a sign of respect for the school, the tradition, and the special time and effort of past and present students and teachers who comprise the school.

Systems of respect structure martial arts schools and classes. Most schools operate within a structure of formal manners, including ritualized greetings and gestures of respect, such as bowing, which are accorded to all students and all interactions in the dojang. Instructors rank highly within the school and are usually accorded special titles of respect and addressed with formality. Black belt students often teach lower belt students and are accorded titles of respect acknowledging their accomplishments and efforts to help other students. Some schools require all students regardless of belt rank to be addressed with titles of respect like "sir" and "ma'am," and one common teaching is to demonstrate attention, patience, care, and humility when interacting with every student and every instructor. Thus each student, regardless of rank, bows to every other student. This system is on one hand a hierarchical ranking system that acknowledges skill level and lineage, but it also values each student regardless of belt or skill level. What seems to be a hierarchy is based on a system of respect and appreciation for both individual accomplishment and the tradition of wisdom that each student strives to embody, rather than a hierarchy of superior/inferior ranking. Individual accomplishment is lauded, but it exists within a context that acknowledges the significance of community.

equality

It is important to understand these gestures of respect as ways to create community bonds within the dojo. What seems like a hierarchical system is paradoxically democratic in the sense that each individual is valued and respected, no matter the level of his or her learning. Ultimately this system demonstrates respect for the past by acknowledging that each person was once a beginning student, and every accomplishment is gained through the efforts of a community of teachers and students, past and present. Community bonds extend through time, and an individual contributes back to the community not just in concrete efforts of aiding other students and pursuing an active role in the larger community but by giving thanks for the efforts of others. As the founder of Karate-Do, Gichin Funakoshi, stated simply: "Karate begins and ends with courtesy."[40] Although seemingly teaching a hierarchical system, the deeper teaching of most martial arts schools is that one is always involved in a network of participation and mutual respect. For example, instructors are respectful of students, and they often thank students for the attention and effort they bring to class in recognition that it is a return gift for the effort of teaching. This interaction parallels the musical style of call and response and the mutual appreciation exchanged between performer and audience in African American expressive culture. In a more general sense, it echoes the idea that individual achievement becomes meaningful within the context of the community, and that individual and community exist in a relationship of interdependence. One martial arts instructor with ten years of teaching experience encapsulated this idea as "mutuality." When he explains the ritual of bowing to his students he tells them, "we bow to each other because we need each other. Without you, I am not a teacher, without me, you are not students. We exist in a relationship with each other, and our identities depend on one another. Therefore we bow to each other out of respect for this relationship."[41] Herman Kauz, who taught martial arts for twenty-five years before publishing *The Martial Spirit: An Introduction to the Origin, Philosophy, and Psychology of the Martial Arts,* while pointing out the variety that exists in different styles of martial arts also describes a typical class procedure of bowing toward a shrine and the teacher at the beginning of each class and a system in which senior students are shown respect by junior students and vice versa. A senior student who is not aware of and respectful toward the limits and needs of the junior students may be asked to leave class.[42] An ideal senior student has achieved a level of self-composure that enables him or her to continue developing his or her own skill and style while acknowledging and accommodating the limits and needs of others gracefully. Senior students, as well as junior and senior instructors, are expected to serve as role models and elder mentors within the dojang. The ultimate expression of this is the respect they show all members of the school.

Although this ethic of mutual respect and participation does not translate easily into African American expressive traditions, the parallel exists in the African American cultural sense of balancing individualism with connection to ancestors, teachers, elders, and the community that deserves respect. As opposed to the mythical mainstream American value of self-sufficiency, African American cultural ethics recognize that no person succeeds alone, and that no person is truly successful until he or she contributes back to the community. As a parallel, even though Bruce Lee's characters in his films fight for victory using the body alone and in an isolated physical setting, his

[handwritten margin note: dependance of relation-ships]

victories are often within the context of achieving revenge or respect for his community or family. A sense of connection to the community pervades all martial arts schools that strive to convey a firm philosophy of physical and intrinsic strength for one's own enhancement *and* the benefit of others. One can only hope that the martial artist will define achievement as an attainment of inner fortitude employed in the service of mutual respect, and the development of an internal strength so finely tuned that it benefits the larger community without the need for force. Ueshiba claims that "the way of the warrior is to establish harmony,"[43] which is perhaps the ultimate product of a fluid interaction between the individual and his or her community, and the ultimate expression of cool.

The aesthetic of cool, as it appears in Africanist dance and in the styles of jazz musicians and African American expressive culture, reveals one way in which African American expressive culture manifested in the twentieth century. In the late 1960s and early 1970s, as African Americans and other minority individuals sought new ways to carve an identity for themselves, the martial arts of Bruce Lee offered them one alternative to mainstream values and stereotypes of masculinity. When Kung Fu films inspired individuals to train, the philosophies of self-knowledge, inner strength, development of style, and connection to a community found in the dojang offered these individuals a chance to develop a sense of empowerment. The similarities between these philosophies and the valued style of cool found in African American expressive arenas may have further popularized martial arts training for these individuals. Although the disciplined, controlled body trained for martial arts embodies conservative values of an idealized community and wisdom passed from generation to generation, the surface appearance of hierarchy and physical skill give way to deeper achievements of style, physical and psychological composure, self-respect, and participation in community that values mutual respect.

During the 1960s and 1970s, when black youth sought to develop their own styles and identity apart from mainstream stereotypes, oppression, and values, these philosophies appealed to them. Echoing values held by traditional African American communities in some ways, as well as African American expressive culture, the philosophy taught in martial arts schools prepared African Americans to engage in a process of self-growth and self-respect, but it also prepared them to defend themselves physically and psychologically against a larger world dominated by white aesthetics, attitudes, and policies. By offering an arena in which the primary tools were one's body and one's determination to train, martial arts offered opportunities for self-respect and self-expression even to working-class youth whose options were limited. Controlling one's own body and training mind and body together was liberating. The martial arts as a fighting art transcended physical skill alone. The trained, disciplined martial arts body, harmonized with the controlled emotions of a warrior, was a weapon for self-defense and for individual and collective empowerment.

Notes

I'd like to thank Joel Dinerstein and Mansour Bonakdarian for their intellectual support and many conversations that helped nurture these ideas. Many thanks also to the instructors and students of the University of Texas Tukong Moosul Martial Arts Club, without whom I could not have accomplished this project.

1 As Imamu Amiri Baraka pointed out in 1963, it was almost impossible to destroy nonmaterial culture of the individuals brought from Africa and enslaved, and as these elements merged with European-based cultural elements in America, new traditions were born. LeRoi Jones [Imamu Amiri Baraka], *Blues People: Negro Music in White America* (New York: William Morrow & Co., 1963), 16.

2 Some martial arts styles were developed by farmers and peasants, as reflected in the array of weapons used. However, some traditional martial arts forms, such as the Japanese sword form of Kendo, were associated with the noble classes.

3 Why *Asian* martial arts? One obvious answer is that Asian martial arts were most common. The African-based martial art of capoiera remained uncommon in the 1960s and didn't have a counterpart Bruce Lee cinema star to popularize the art. Although capoiera has elements which distinctly demonstrate a black aesthetic, including its dance-like fluidity and the seminal goal of feinting, as well as certain stylistic traits that embody the value of staying cool and the use of African-based Orisha worship as its foundation, in depth discussion of these elements will have to wait for a future essay. As an African-Brazilian martial art, capoiera is unique. Perhaps martial arts training allowed practitioners to escape race, class, and gender in the process of assimilating to a disciplined tradition of bodily practice that emphasizes skill, technique and performance over any biological/physical trait. This assertion is problematic as in reality individuals of color may have faced discrimination even within the martial arts dojang.

4 The way some martial arts are taught and trained even lends itself to describing these particular styles and schools as paramilitary organizations.

5   Sally Banes, *Greenwich Village 1963: Avant-Garde Performance and the Efferves-cent Body* (Durham: Duke University Press, 1993), 189.

6   Banes, 209.

7   Vijay Prashad, *Everybody was Kung Fu Fighting: Afro-Asian Connections and the Myth of Cultural Purity* (Boston: Beacon Press, 2001), 130.

8   Miyamoto Musashi, *The Book of Five Rings*, translated by Victor Harris (Wood-stock, N.Y.: The Overlook Press, 1974), 49. Musashi was a Samurai warrior in Japan, 1584–1645.

9   In a 1970 essay entitled "Self-Defense for Women" several feminist women who trained karate listed its advantages and disadvantages. In the atmosphere of the dojang in which "everyone is to be treated with great respect and humil-ity, regardless of rank," the women were initially handled with extreme polite-ness, verging on invisibility because so many of the male students and even the instructor did not know how to treat them. Eventually, the instructor and other students learned to ignore gender and treat the female students just like male students and expect as much of them, and the women trained equally with the men. They experienced increased health, strength, and self-esteem and felt powerful and liberated as they learned ways to use their bodies which were contrary to the feminine mannerisms they had been taught since childhood, which emphasized quietness, docility and vulnerability. They end by encourag-ing women to develop the mental and physical toughness that karate helped them develop: "women must get strong!" Susan Pascale, Rachel Moon, Leslie B. Tanner, "Self-Defense for Women," in *Sisterhood Is Powerful: An Anthology of Writings from the Women's Movement*, ed. Robin Morgan, (New York: Random House, 1970), 469–477.

10 Prashad, 130–133.

11 Stuart M. Kaminsky, *American Film Genres* (Chicago: Nelson-Hall, 1985), 73–80.

12 Jachinson Chan, *Chinese American Masculinities: From Fu Manchu to Bruce Lee*, (New York: Routledge, 2001), 75.

13 Chan, 77, although Chan concludes that Lee ultimately "exhibits an ambi-sexuality that is characterized by an indeterminate sexual identity" (Chan, 78). There are differing views about the presentation of Lee's sexuality on screen.

14 Although alternative images of sexuality are beyond the scope of this essay, I would like to suggest that Lee's calm, self-determined demeanor may have been welcomed by African Americans, especially men, who had long faced racial stereotypes that depicted them as either overly sexual or childishly and/or comically asexual.

15 Chan, 88.

16 Prashad briefly notes the importance of Jim Kelly in his roles in Bruce Lee's films and in his own films.

17 Anderson, Aaron, "Action in Motion: Kinesthesia in Martial Arts films," *Jump Cut* 42, Dec. 1998: 1–11, 83.

18 Shane White and Graham White, *Stylin: African American Expressive Culture from its Beginnings to the Zoot Suit* (Ithaca: Cornell University Press, 1998), 63–84.

19 Musashi, 53.

20 White and White, 128.

21 Mary Douglas, *Purity and Danger* (London: Routledge & Kegan Paul, 1966).

22 Bruce Lee, *Bruce Lee: Jeet Kune Do: Bruce Lee's Commentaries on the Martial Arts*, (Boston: Charles E. Tuttle Co., Inc., 1997), 342.

23 Peter Urban, *The Karate Dojo: Traditions and Tales of A Martial Art* (Rutland, VT: Charles E. Tuttle Co., 1967), 47.

24 Brenda Dixon Gottschild, *Digging the Africanist Presence in American Performance* (Westport: Greenwood Press, 1996), 11–19. Gottschild is careful to explain that her use of the word detachment does not indicate disinterestedness. She uses it to describe a "philosophical" stance that is *not* aloof and yet remains able to execute complex artistry with calmness.

25 Joel Dinerstein, "Lester Young and the Birth of the Cool," in *Signifyin(g), Sanctifyin' & Slam Dunking: A Reader in African American Expressive Culture*, Gena Dagel Caponi, ed. (Amherst: University of Massachusetts Press, 1999), 239–276.

26 Musashi, 54.

27 Morihei Ueshiba, *The Art of Peace* (Boston: Shambala, 1992), 16.

28 Ueshiba, 98

29 Ueshiba, 112.

30 A correlation I hope to develop further in a future essay is the similarity between martial arts concepts of self-respect and respect for others via the development of internal strength and the African-derived concept of cool, which art historian Robert Farris Thompson delineates as an important part of Yoruban art and religion that have transformed into aspects of African American culture. Described as the confidence and calmness to cope with all kinds of situations as well as a generous and respectful relationship with others, according to Thompson, coolness is considered a valued part of character within Yoruban culture. Robert Farris Thompson, *Flash of the Spirit: African and Afro-American Art and Philosophy* (New York: Random House, 1983), 13–17. Thanks also to Joel Dinerstein for many conversations that have helped to fertilize this idea.

31 Joe Hymans, *Zen and the Martial Arts* (New York: Bantam Books, 1982), 133.

32 Capoiera student, Raleigh, North Carolina, August 2001.

33 Lee, 31.

34 Buddy Sustan, University of Texas Tukong Moosul Club, Austin, Texas, spring 1998.

35 Gena Dagel Caponi, "Introduction: The Case for an African American Aesthetic," in *Signifyin(g), Sanctifyin', and Slam Dunking: A Reader in African American Expressive Culture* (Amherst: University of Massachusetts Press, 1999), 5–

6. See also Ben Sidran, *Black Talk* (New York: Holt, Rinehart &Winston, 1971) for a recognition that black culture prizes individual expression and the exploration of this aesthetic during the 1960s in African American music.

36 Thomas Cleary, *Code of the Samurai: A Modern Translation of the Bushido Sho-shinsu* (Boston: Tuttle Publishing, 1999), 4. The Samurai fulfilled the warrior role in a highly structured class system and a culture which valued fulfilling duty to one's family and ancestors in 1600s Japan. *The Code of the Samurai* was originally written by Taira Shigesuke.

37 Michael Jackson, *Paths Toward a Clearing: Radical Empiricism and Ethnographic Inquiry* (Bloomington: Indiana University Press, 1989), 41.

38 Jackson, 24.

39 Lee said "martial arts means honestly expressing yourself" (Lee, 349) and asserted that Jeet Kune Do was "the absence of a system of stereotyped techniques" (Lee, 342).

40 Funakoshi, 32.

41 James Espy, martial arts instructor, Austin, Texas, February 7, 2004.

42 Herman Kauz, *The Martial Spirit: An Introduction to the Origin, Philosophy, and Psychology of the Martial Arts* (Woodstock, N.Y.: The Overlook Press, 1977), 32–33.

43 Ueshiba, 103.

royal hartigan with Fred Ho

The American Drum Set:
Black Musicians and Chinese Opera
along the Mississippi River

T he drum set is a twentieth-century American instrument whose historical development has largely
been the result of African American creativity. It
stands today as one of the most widely played, recognized,
and powerful instruments used on the global stage.

The trap drum set emerged in the late 1890s, when single percussionists were forced for economic and logistical
reasons to operate a multitude of instruments. Snare and
bass drums of the concert and marching bands in New
Orleans provided a foundation to which, from 1900 to
1930, other accessories or "trappings"—hence the name
traps—were added. This diverse sound palette enabled percussionists to accompany films, theater, and other stage
shows and dances. Additions included whistles, cowbells,
tympani, chimes, marimba, bells, bird calls, and many
other instruments. Early drummers, in their search for
new sounds, also adopted the instruments they heard

played by Chinese immigrants in urban areas in the late nineteenth and early twentieth centuries, like the small Chinese cymbal (*bo*), large gong (*da luo*), woodblock (*ban*), varied pitch temple blocks (*mu-yu*), and the first tom-tom (*bangu*), usually a thick painted pigskin drumhead tacked onto a red painted wooden shell and suspended on a folding carriage stand.

Between the seventeenth and nineteenth centuries, when the use of musical instruments, especially drums (which could be used for communication and revolt as well as for spiritual remembrances and affirmation), were forbidden on the part of enslaved Africans in the United States, African American people used their bodies as instruments. The coordinated interdependence of multiple percussive instrumental voices in a composite statement is found in the "pattin' juba" hand clapping and foot stomps of African American peoples throughout the South.[1] Juba is a clapping play similar to the "hambone" patting and movements that many Americans learned in the 1950s and 1960s.

While the drum set is relatively "new," it has a spiritual heritage traceable to the ancient drum orchestras of West Africa, especially in the coastal rain forest region from present-day Cote d'Ivoire through Ghana, Togo, and Benin to Nigeria, where drumming is highly diversified into variously pitched and timbred drums, bells, and rattles. In these areas there is a master drummer who directs the dynamic interplay of song, dance, and drumming with conversational dialogue (calls and responses). An ensemble of distinct personal drum voices, each with its own pitch range, timbre, and rhythm specified by tradition, repertoire, and occasion of performance comes together to make a composite statement. This dynamic living force creates a space for the "gods to descend," for people to connect with each other, with nature, with life, and with themselves. The interplay of coordinated independent voices characterizes the function, sound, and feel of the drum set practitioner in the African American "jazz" tradition and West African drum ensembles.

During the post-slavery era, African Americans sought employment and economic self-activity in many areas, including as professional musicians performing in various recreational venues, theaters, traveling shows, and aboard steamships that traversed the Mississippi River and visited port cities from New Orleans to Chicago. It was during the late nineteenth and early twentieth century that the hybrid instrument, the drum set, was created and shaped into its basic form, still in use today, of bass and snare drums, tom-toms, high-hat cymbals, and ride and crash cymbals.

Since the immigration to the Americas of large numbers of Chinese during the mid to late 1800s, Chinatowns took root primarily in Hawaii, on the West Coast, and in cities such as New York. By the beginning of the twentieth century, a highly active and extensive Chinese opera touring circuit had been established in Chinese communities extending from Vancouver, Canada, along the West Coast, to Central and South America, to the Caribbean (notably Havana), and on into New York City. In Chinese theater, percussion figures prominently with an array of gongs, cymbals, drums, clappers, and woodblocks that accentuate, highlight, and drive the stage drama. In the aesthetics of Chinese opera, a stage performer must be well versed in singing, acting, and movement (with martial arts–like acrobatics and specific physical movements and hand gestures). The repertoire of Chinese opera is a collection of well-known traditional scenes and stories with all-too-familiar plots, characters and story lines, and verses. Chinese opera audiences know the stories, lines, and lyrics by heart. What makes a particular performance fresh and enjoyable are the virtuosic performances. Typically, a Chinese opera actor-performer never asks, "What is my line?" but rather, "What are my beats?" referring to the percussion rhythms to which they follow and use as a springboard for their particular individual performance.

In 1904, the World's Fair took place in New Orleans where it featured "exotic" exhibits from around the world, including Asia, Polynesia, and the Philippines. Chinese opera was an especially popular and well-attended exhibition in the 1904 World's Fair. During the late nineteenth century and the early twentieth, a small population of Chinese had resettled to Mississippi and other southern states, where they were brought in as a short-lived experiment to replace African labor after the formal ban on slavery in the United States. The more enterprising and successful of these Chinese laborers began small service and mercantile businesses. Historians have documented the contact between the Chinese and African Americans during this period, with events of both conflict and cooperation (including mixed marriages).[2]

It is surmised that African American drummers, fascinated by the sounds and role of drums and percussion in Chinese music, especially in opera and theater performances, found a way to incorporate both the instrumentation and setup of the multiple-percussion arrangement of the Chinese opera percussion ensemble into the drum set. This effort was seen as a way to broaden the sonic percussion palette as well as to economize and reconfigure an array of percussion played by multiple performers into a "single" instrument (the drum set) played by one musician. This was especially practical and efficient for steamboat musicians who were greatly limited by space. Where once several percussionists played a single percussion instrument, with the drum set one player using all four limbs in coordination could play multiple percussion.

Much of the early research in the historical development of the drum set is drawn from Theodore Dennis Brown's exhaustive dissertation *A History and Analysis of Jazz Drumming to 1942*, as well as from the oral interviews conducted by royal hartigan of many drummers.[3] Several components of the African American drum set have connections to Chinese percussion. The wood block was an important element in the ragtime and later New Orleans drum sound. This instrument, which is a hollow oblong chamber of wood with slits for sound projection, was widely used by drummers (in many sizes and shapes) well into the 1940s. With its various sizes and tones, it can be seen as a descendant of African slit-log drums, although Theodore Dennis Brown groups the wood block with the Chinese tom-tom and Chinese cymbal as instruments with an Asian heritage. Wei-hua Zhang, a Chinese ethnomusicologist, has stated that the wood blocks and temple blocks she has seen in this country, the same as those used in the early drum set, are similar and perhaps traceable to hollow wooden blocks played with a stick in China. These blocks are of varying sizes and pitches and are used during prayer in Chinese Buddhist temples. Zhang also relates that the general onomatopoeaic name for the sound of Chinese drums is *don-don*, which parallels the sound and name for the tom-tom (the general name for snareless drums, such as tom-toms, obviously has a wide and international derivation).[4]

Another Chinese ethnomusicologist, Wu Wen-guang, has noted that wood blocks (*bang-zi*), temple blocks (*mu-yu*), tom-toms (*tang-gu*), cymbals (*nao bo*), and large and small gongs (*da luo* and *xiao luo*, respectively), used in the early years of drum sets, are all found in Chinese theater performances and in Buddhist temple prayer rituals. A continuous bass drum-cymbal pattern in quarter notes is also used as a Chinese folk parade rhythm. Wu has identified a common African American ride cymbal beat—a quarter note followed by two eighth-triplets separated by a triple-eighth rest—as similar to a rhythm found in Chinese drama. He has also described two small hand-held cymbals, sounding on alternate beats.[5] The inclusion of wood block, tom-tom, temple block and Chinese cymbals in the early drum set indicates that jazz drummers heard and were attracted to the sounds of Chinese instruments.

There are many similarities between not only the physical characteristics of Chinese percussion with aspects of the African American drum set, but also in the manner in which individual components are played. For example, the Chinese double hand cymbals (the *nao bo*) are played by striking up and down (vertically) as opposed to the Western hand-held crash cymbals played striking against each other ("crashing") side to side (horizontally). The high-hat in the drum set is composed of two small cymbals suspended on a pole carriage and played by a foot pedal, clanging vertically. The high-hat, like the *nao bo,* can be "choked" to create a tightened, nonringing metal accented sound.

Brown points out that the nineteenth-century immigration of large numbers of Chinese people to the United States, and the music that in their new home remained a part of their festivities—including opera, theater, and parades, influenced American jazz musicians.[6] He also points out that wooden slit drums, Chinese cymbals and tom-toms are commonly used in Chinese theater productions and are traceable to the Ch'ing dynasty (1644–1911). The sounds of these instruments were adopted by African American jazz musicians, as well as by their white counterparts. In stage and steamboat shows, dance hall revues, and cabarets African American drummers had to utilize a variety of sound effects and percussive techniques in a manner similar to that performed by the Chinese percussionists. Chinese percussion instruments used in Chinese theater functioned as a unit to portray dramatic action, parallel to that of jazz drummer reflecting the dramatic action of soloists or dancers. African American drummers studied and borrowed these instruments, the particular instrumental construction and combination, and the narrative role of Chinese theater percussion, which then became incorporated into the hybrid drum set and subsequently expanded the role, scope, and power of American vernacular music across the globe.

Notes

1 Bessie Jones and Bess Lomax Hawes, *Step It Down: Games, Plays, Songs, and Stories from the Afro-American Heritage* (Athens: University of Georgia Press, 1972), 37–40.

2 See, for example, James W. Loewen, *The Mississippi Chinese: Between Black and White* (Prospect Heights, Ill.: Waveland Press, 1988).

3 Theodore Dennis Brown, "A History and Analysis of Jazz Drumming to 1942" (Ph.D. dissertation, University of Michigan, 1976); royal hartigan, "Blood Drum Spirit: Drum Languages of West Africa, African-America, Native America, Central Java and South India" (Ph.D. dissertation, Wesleyan University, 1986; part 3, chapter 6, "The Evolution of the Drum Set in the African-American Tradition").

4 Oral communication between hartigan and Kwadzo Donclar and Kobena Adzenyah, 1986.

5 Oral communication between hartigan and Wei-hua Zhang, 1986.

6 Oral communication between hartigan and Wen-guang, 1986.

Ron Wheeler with David Kaufman

Is Kung Fu Racist?

People used to speak of the United States as a melting pot, as a place where ethnic and cultural differences were refined so that we could all come out as just plain Americans. We now live in an age where this image from the era of heavy industry seems a bit outdated. This is probably just as well, as it was always a bit hard for racial minorities to melt into the general population. We have not found a fitting metaphor for our new multiracial society, but it would have to be one that would describe both our diversity and our ability to draw on other peoples' cultures. The sad truth is, of course, that we do not have a new image for the identity of the new America because, in part, we have not yet achieved it, although we are on our way. Nonetheless, one example of the possibilities and difficulties of this new understanding is my experience as an African American in the Chinese martial arts.

I don't want to indulge in the popular game of comparative suffering. The history of chattel slavery and segregation is well known and doesn't have to be repeated here. The Chinese, too, had a difficult time in the United States. In the late 1800s, many of the Chinese who settled in this country were brought in as a form of cheap labor and were separated from their families. A good number of these workers had a high degree of martial arts skill, and because most came from southern China, near Canton, it is safe to assume that southern systems were primarily taught. As the Chinese population began to grow in the United States, small communities sprang up on the West Coast and the violent nature of the times drove the Chinese to defend themselves.

Violence, segregation, and a certain ethnic pride kept the Chinese Americans somewhat insulated, so when African Americans began to get interested in self-defense in the 1960s (influenced in part by urbanization and in part by the galvanizing model of the civil rights and Black Power movements), they did not find a ready welcome in the Chinese martial arts. Many African American men took up the Japanese systems because, unlike most Chinese teachers who wanted to hide their art from the *lo fan* ("foreign devil"), many Japanese teachers welcomed outsiders as a way to keep their art alive and growing. Although on the East Coast Jow Ca Sifu Dean Chin of Washington, D.C., and Fu Jow Pai Sifu Eng Wai Hong of New York were among the first Chinese instructors to teach kung fu (also spelled gung-fu) to non-Asians, it is a well-known fact that the few Chinese teachers willing to instruct non-Asians taught a watered-down version of their style while teaching the true art to their fellow countrymen.

Matters eventually improved. The 1970s, which brought the movies of Bruce Lee and the show *Kung-Fu,* saw an unsurpassing and important growth in martial arts interest—in particular, in Chinese gung-fu. Instructors like Dean Chin, the late Ark Wong (who was noted for his mastery in both the Five Animal/Five Family styles), and others began openly instructing African Americans, even now blacks seem to make up the majority of the students found in these schools. Many of the early black pioneers, like Dennis Brown (a top student of Tien Shan Pai Sifu Willy Lin), Chuck Jeffries (also a student of Willy Lin and a successful martial arts actor), and Paul Atkins (a senior instructor under Dean Chin and one of the few people to be taught Jow Ga's Iron Palm by Sifu Chin), made it possible for those like myself to study authentic gung-fu, but it was still much harder than it needed to be.

As an African American I am no stranger to racism. But I was surprised to find it both subtly and not so subtly exhibited in the martial arts. I can remember one of my instructors telling me that a lot of the Chinese in Washington's Chinatown did not like blacks and would refer to us as *hop gois* (black ghosts). Of course, there are mitigating factors here. In the 1800s few Chinese had ever seen a black person, and in order to describe these "strange" people of color, they merely amended the term they used for white folk. It was not meant as an insult or as a derogatory name. Even today, there are many people in remote parts of China who have never seen a black person. In 1982, Dennis Brown of the Shaolin Wu-Shu Academy was the only African American to be invited to study contemporary Wu-Shu by the Chinese government. On his return to the United States, he told me that his Chinese instructors constantly referred to him as "Coffee." This was the only way they could think of to describe what to them was completely new: the color of his black skin.

In the United States, however, the novelty of black skin must surely have worn off for the Chinese. African Americans want to study gung-fu, not some watered-down version of the art. Perhaps it was a different kind of prejudice that made instructors reluctant to teach the real thing to their black students. Perhaps most Chinese masters felt that blacks would never be as good as Asian martial artists. The opposite has turned out to be the case, however. Now, depending on the region, many non-Asian and, in particular, African American artists are rising through the ranks quickly and effectively.

What is it that makes African Americans just as good (if not better than) their Asian counterparts? Strange as it may sound, I believe that it is the importance of dance and rhythm in black culture that gives African Americans a predisposition for gung-fu. My own master understood this. When I was about to take my test for the Small Controlling Tiger form, Sifu Chin asked me if I could dance. Dance? Sifu repeated the question. I answered yes. I knew how to dance. Was I any good? Yes, I told him, I guessed I was. He was not interested in my guesses: was I good or not? So I had to reply that I was a very good dancer. "Good," Sifu said, "then you will have no problem doing gung-fu." I must have looked at Sifu Chin as if I thought he was crazy, because he began to explain himself. He told me that all Chinese martial arts are based on rhythm, and that they stress the continuity of movement and are performed in dance-like patterns. Sifu Chin's point explains the success of African American martial artists. But that is not to say that blacks are only good at forms. In 1979 at the first World Kuo Shu tournament in Taipei, Taiwan, Sifu Chin's team—comprised entirely of African Americans—did remarkably well.

The success of African Americans in the Chinese martial arts is bound to continue, and the number of blacks learning gung-fu will only increase. This does not mean that the established styles will be adulterated. Gung-fu need not pass through the melting pot to become part of a featureless, generic amalgam. My experience shows me that African Americans have earned a place for themselves in the traditional Chinese martial arts community where they are helping to maintain its vitality. They want to and can do well; they only need to be treated with respect and as equal partners in what has become a shared inheritance.

Thien-bao Thuc Phi

Yellow Lines:
Asian Americans and Hip Hop

t's telling that I begin this essay wondering if I have the right to write it. I'm neither a professional journalist nor a distant academic with a degree in ethnomusicology. But then again I'm also not really a hip hopper because I don't practice one of the four officially acknowledged elements of hip hop[1] (unless you count hip hop–influenced spoken word, in which case I've been holding it down for the past eleven years). I'm not some middle- to upper-class suburban Asian kid who loved hip hop for rebellion's sake, nor am I an Asian who learned to love hip hop in college because he bought "Midnight Marauders" and fell in love with it as he danced to *Electric Relaxation* while smoking bud. Instead, I am a straight-up ghetto-raised hip hop fan. I was never a hustler or a street kid or a banger, but rather a ghetto nerd who grew up in hip hop—and I didn't necessarily always like it. Still, what right do I have to write this? An Asian kid who is neither a hip hopper nor an academic?

This very late and probably outdated essay is concerned with Asian Americans and hip hop, and despite my insecurities I have to explore the intersections of two different social groups that I love dearly. First is Asian America, that fragmented, fluid, beautiful, painful, powerful, and confused/confusing nation that gives my center its gravity, a people whose culture and history are ignored or dismissed by the mainstream as well as progressives and radicals of all colors, even as they covet Asian food and women. Second is hip hop,[2] that complicated, fluid, contradictory, beautiful, and commoditized culture whose music and icons have gone global. It is an art form that voices experiences and concerns from communities held down by police brutality, drug epidemics, class oppression, and other forms of systematic racism; a beautiful, uplifting, complicated culture and music that is identified primarily with African Americans,[3] originated in a country whose race politics are still rigidly black and white—and don't get it twisted, the African American community is not to blame for this, but rather a white supremacist power structure that continues to oppress African Americans and does not want to deal with any other issues concerning communities of color, unless they can use us for their own benefit.

This essay is not meant to be a definitive academic statement about what is and what is not Asian American, hip hop, or Asian American hip hop. Instead it is meant to be a conversation starter, an exploration of many difficult issues presented with an alternative perspective not often seen in either mainstream or so-called alternative media: an Asian American perspective that doesn't pander to anyone.

Race

Other than white people African Americans are the most visible race in America, and Asian Americans are the most invisible. Part of this invisibility is rooted in a lack of knowledge and awareness of Asian American history and issues, an ignorance that we, as well as non-Asians, carry. Consequently we, and non-Asians, fail to identify Asian Americans as people of color, or fail to understand the specific ways in which we have and still do suffer from racism. Everyone constantly talks about the black-white divide in speaking about race. Sometimes people throw in the words Latino or Hispanic for some flavor, and if they remember to mention Native Americans at all, most people will concur that they are oppressed racially. However, it is entirely possible that one can be considered by most people in this country to be a progressive or radical *without knowing or mentioning a thing about Asian American history or issues.* In James Loewen's national best-seller *Lies My Teacher Told Me,* nowhere does he mention the complete lack of Asian American history in classrooms and education. In his introduction, he states that "African American, Native American, and Latino students view history with a special dislike." No disagreement there, but he uses this pronouncement to insinuate that people of color do not like history classes because there is nothing about their history or culture reflected in their education—and he excludes Asian Americans from that racism. In a later chapter, he states: "Caste minority children—Native Americans, African Americans, and Hispanics—do worse in all subjects, compared to white or Asian American children, but the gap is largest in social studies. That is because the way American history is taught particularly alienates students of color and children from impoverished families."[4]

By lumping Asian Americans in with whites, Loewen insinuates that *education* Asian Americans are learning what they need in American history as opposed to other people of color, and that Asian American children do not suffer disproportionately from class oppression based on race. This is especially problematic because his book does not talk about Japanese American internment, Chinese American workers on the railroad and in gold mines, plantation workers in Hawaii, the extreme poverty and lack of access to education for Southeast Asians, the past (and present) exploitation of Asian Indian and Filipino workforces, or any other of the many ignored facets of Asian American history. In the book there is a single picture and a short statement about sweatshops in Chinatown. And although Loewen does devote part of one of his chapters to the war in Vietnam, it is presented as a foreign dynamic and not a domestic one: common enough, that the most visible issues regarding Asians are the ones that concern us in Asia, not America.

This is not a plea to make the case that one group is more oppressed than another. But in the case of Asian Americans, who are often incorrectly lumped in with whites, it can be challenging to even engage in dialogue or action against white supremacy: *What do you people have to complain about? Aren't you better off than the others? Haven't we whites been good to you?*

In this sense, hip hop mirrors mainstream and progressive culture: you don't have to know a thing about Asian American history or issues to be engaged in hip hop culture or lifestyle. At its heart, hip hop is an Afrocentric culture. You have to at least have *some* semblance of knowledge regarding African American history and culture in order to be truly hip hop. In order to understand and appreciate the vocabulary, references, and music you must be familiar with the culture. If you drop the names Diallo, Farrakhan, and Mumia in your rhymes,[5] most hip hoppers will know who and what you're talking about. What if you try to drop Vincent Chin, David Wong, Thung Phetakoune, Thien Minh Ly, Richard Aoki, and Bill and Yuri Kochiyama in your lyrics?[6] Who the hell is going to know what you're talking about? Most Asian Americans wouldn't know these names, let alone anyone else. Back when Ice Cube's "Black Korea" came out,[7] I encountered far more hip hop fans of various races, including Asians, who understood, sympathized, and defended his diatribe than ones who considered the Korean perspective or even empathized with Koreans. This is especially problematic because the larger mainstream press as well as academics also effectively silenced the viewpoints and dynamics of Koreans and Asians in Los Angeles. As Ishmael Reed states in his essay "An Outsider in Koreatown," "Thousands of black and Asian American businesses were destroyed by a minority of blacks, whites, and Hispanics, who have been described by some talented tenth intellectuals and academics, safely ensconced on college campuses, as 'warriors' participating in an 'uprising.'"[8] The mainstream press was able to distract the national consciousness away from issues of white racism, police brutality, economic devastation, and institutional oppression by hyping the tensions between blacks and Koreans.

Racial ignorance is rampant. If Asian Americans had as much access to popular culture and hip hop, I'm sure we would be saying all kinds of ignorant racist shit about black people and each other. We've all internalized racist stereotypes about different races and ourselves. I'm not arguing that blacks are inherently more racist or powerful than Asians or anyone else. I'm mentioning these things to point out the way that white supremacy, as a system, both encourages and reinforces racial ignorance, hatred, and objectification.

We don't need to be oppositional to African Americans and hip hop culture; rather, I think the above points illustrate a lack of understanding and knowledge about Asian Americans in American society in general. And if we don't stick up for ourselves, if we don't actively seek to center ourselves and place our own culture and histories at the center, who will?

To become hip hop as it stands today is to move away from having Asian America at our center, which in a way is the antithesis of hip hop. As Maanav Thakore, a longtime struggling underground hip hop artist, said to me in a recent conversation: "As an Asian American trying to make it in hip hop, I had to know how to move between worlds in order to be accepted. I could talk about being a young man of color, but some of the things relating specifically to my Asian heritage—I had to leave some of that at the door, because heads weren't really feeling it."

This is not to insinuate that Asian Americans can't be hip hop, but if we want to be true participants and proponents of hip hop then we must re-define it, to respect hip hop and ourselves. We must revolutionize the way we conceive and practice hip hop so that Asian America is at the center of it. And again, that doesn't mean that we have to be separate or oppositional or racist toward African Americans, but it does mean that we have to be equal in the exchange.

This is easier said than done. Just because you incorporate Asian and/or Asian American cultural elements into your work doesn't mean that you're automatically going to produce quality work, or even interesting work, or that your own people will appreciate you. You need the skills to prove it: nobody's gonna care if your rhyme scheme has been influenced by the *luc-bat* form of Vietnamese lyric poetry if you sound wack. And there is such a thing as self-exotification: if you approach Asian culture in a superficial manner and lose touch with your own Asian American community, you run the risk of performing in front of white audiences drawn by your "authen-ticity." Or, if you're really out of touch, maybe you'll be so slick that the only people who can appreciate the genius of your work are upper-middle-class college-educated white "rebels."

Signifying

Signifying is a powerful thing. At the time of this writing Eminem is really, really big—and whether or not Slim Shady's sexist, homophobic ass wants to claim that his race doesn't matter, the reality is that we don't exist in a vacuum. Eminem may not wish to call attention to his race, but that won't stop the rest of America and the world from seeing him as a white boy, and it won't stop white America from favoring him, as abrasive as he may seem, over African American MCs and other MCs of color.

Seeing an Asian American face up on stage, on an album, or in a music video is a very powerful thing—especially since the American consciousness rarely sees Asian American people in the media at all, and especially not together. There are tokens who pop up now and then, but rarely do you see a positive representation of *community* rather than *individuals*. Whether or not we have the privilege of having an education that urges the deconstruction of race, class, etc., Asian kids are going to consume and gravitate toward pop culture—or at least they will encounter and interact with it before they are taught not to. It is tremendously important to see Asians on stage, Asians who can be successful and skilled on the mic, who can move a party and rock a body at a show. There is a hunger for representation, a hunger to see a reflection of us on stage, to open up opportunities and become visible in hip hop. The Philadelphia-based Asian hip hop crew the Mountain Brothers have acknowledged this dynamic in several interviews and on their Web site: "This is music that makes . . . yellows say 'finally.' . . ."

But is simply being an MC or DJ who just "happens to be Asian" really enough?

This kind of essentialist thinking is pretty common among artists of various fields and races—a belief that art and aesthetics are ultimately race-less, cultureless, and apolitical. Asian Americans can't afford to be that naive, and this gets complicated when we talk about hip hop. On one hand, there is an ideal that hip hop is a meritocracy: it doesn't matter who you are, what race you are, or your gender, as long as you have skills. On the other hand, hip hop is a cultural force that is informed, shaped, and dominated primarily by African American men, and mainstream hip hop has been commodifed by largely white record-label executives who either don't know how to, or don't want to, market Asian Americans. At least nowadays there is a relatively heightened awareness about the history of white people ripping off black music.[9] How then can we pretend that our culture and race should have or has no impact or impression on hip hop or ourselves?

In a black and white country, one must choose being either black or white or risk being invisible. For me, seeing Asian American faces together at hip hop events is fairly new: there have been token faces here and there throughout the history of hip hop, but how will the hip hop nation, as it is today, react to entire groups of Asian Americans being together and united in hip hop? This is not to say that African Americans have not been receptive or accepting of Asian Americans in hip hop, and that they don't have the right to be suspicious of perceived outsiders: African Americans have had their culture swindled, condescended to, debased, and dismissed throughout history. I remember a discussion regarding race that I took part in when I was seventeen years old, when a slightly older black guy said that whenever he saw some white kid or Asian kid trying to sag the pants, twist caps, and get down with hip hop, he asked why did we have to come and steal a culture that his people created?

As much as African Americans are suspicious of outsiders and rightly question whether or not Asian Americans appropriate hip hop, we Asian Americans should also be cautious about all non-Asian peoples' approach (or lack of it) toward Asian American issues, and we should also ask if hip hop appropriates Asian culture. And of course we, as Asian Americans, need to ask ourselves whether we dismiss or ignore our own Asian American issues and culture in order to "get over."

Asian American history and issues continue to be ignored or dismissed. Asian culture has historically been ripped off, appropriated, objectified, condescended to, and manipulated by various cultural forces—and it still is. As Dennis Kim/Denizen Kane of I Was Born With Two Tongues/Typical Cats states: "I don't think there's any people on this continent who experience such a unique blend of total commodification and total invisibility. All peoples have their story, and it's not about comparing your oppression. I'm talking about total consumer awareness: eat what I eat, wear what I wear, get my shit tattooed on you. All kinds of shit. It can get even deeper, to where you can marry my sister, you can order her off the Internet. But as opposed to knowing who I am, or who she is, or what we need, or what we want, nobody knows."[10]

Mirroring the larger white mainstream culture, some practitioners of hip hop have borrowed liberally from Asian culture, or have borrowed from the white mainstream's appropriation of Asian culture. The group 2 Live Crew sampled the Vietnamese woman from *Full Metal Jacket* saying "me love you long time." Rappers sport kanji tattoos, sample Asian music, wear Asian clothes, brag about being accepted in Japan, brag about all the Japanese women they've slept with, admit fetishes for Asian women, and put Asian models in their videos. Though martial arts seldom gets credited, you can clearly see how Hong Kong action flicks of the 1970s have influenced break dancing—most of those flairs, leg sweeps, and other insane acrobatic maneuvers were done in *Shaolin Temple* by *wu shu* experts, including a teenage

Jet Li (it was his first movie). Martial arts films, especially Bruce Lee movies, were tremendously popular in urban areas. Nelson George, in his book *Hip Hop America*, explains that Bruce Lee and martial arts flicks provided a "nonwhite, non-Western template for fighting superiority."[11] He goes on to suggest that the in-your-face attitude and aggression found in hip hop is partially rooted in the influx of martial arts films in urban communities, which is an exciting view of populist cross-cultural influence.

Everyone from Digable Planets to Mystikal to the Wu-Tang Clan have referenced kung fu flicks in their rhymes.[12] The old-school title "grand-master," as in Grandmaster Flash and Grandmaster Caz, is also taken from martial arts films—the title of someone who has mastered a martial arts form or technique or is the ultimate practitioner of it. Four well-known women in hip hop, none of them Asian, got dressed up as deadly venoms (a homage to the kung fu classic 5 *Deadly Venoms*) for a Sprite commercial.

But are all of these references and appropriations of Asian culture done out of respect or even racial consciousness? Admittedly, the icons, symbols, and references to and of Asian culture in hip hop have been signifiers that are easily identifiable and digested by the mainstream. When people talk about how Foxy Brown is half Filipino, it's because of her "exotic" good looks and not because of any skills she may or may not have—one of her albums is called *Chyna Doll*, even though she's half Filipino not Chinese.[13] Asian culture and symbols have been used in hip hop much as the mainstream would use them, to suggest an aura of otherness, fetishism, or mystery. These stereotypes can manifest as racist caricature, from the unknown white rapper Frozen Explosion's faking of an Asian accent in his song *Iwo Jima*, to the two times Wyclef has used skits clowning Asians, to Ice Cube threatening to "go down to the corner store and beat the Jap up" (*Horny Lil' Devil*), to Cam'ron (*Shanghai*), Cella Dwellas (*Land of the Lost*), and Foxy Brown (*I Shot Ya Remix*) using the word "chink"—and I'm not talking about saying "chinky-eyed,"[14] I'm talking about using the word "chink" in reference to Asian people.

African Americans are *not* the originators of neo-orientalism, and I do not mean to condemn all of hip hop and African Americans for the actions of a few. We have to understand that these elements have a lot more to do with the way the larger mainstream (white) culture portrays and markets Asian people—that's where the majority of non-Asians get information about us. The rappers mentioned above, and also the numerous mainstream rappers who have used the term "chinky-eyed," kicked racist rhymes about Asians and pretty much got away with it. This illustrates the predominantly white record companies and white listening public's hypocrisy—they are not going to deal with race unless they have to or unless they can get something out of it. While we shouldn't excuse the insensitivity shown by some rappers, it helps to understand the root. It goes both ways—in Asia and America, you will encounter Asians whose preconceived notions of African Americans are shaped by racist and/or fantasy representations put forth by the predominantly white mainstream: for example, Asian men who feel they can throw around the word "nigga" and take on a racist exaggeration of black manhood to replace the demasculinization placed on them by white supremacy; Asian women who sexualize black men and use their relationships with black men to validate their racial consciousness. But I think it's worth noting that, when talking about both mainstream and hip hop cultures and the many intersections within, we can't just plug in Asian people and assume they have the same power, influence, and exposure as white people.

Obviously, various elements of culture are going to meld and fuse, whether we like them to or not. And there is already a long history of Asian American and African American cultural influences and collaborations.[15] There is no inherent harm in learning or appreciating different cultures, as long as it is done respectfully—and as long as we can openly and constructively criticize when we feel that our culture is getting played.

At the same time, we need to recenter ourselves. Asian Americans have been expected to recenter and learn about other people in order to "be down." It's about time we asked people to learn about us in order to get down. We need to signify for, and to, ourselves and our community. I'm not asking for every Asian American hip hopper to rhyme solely about kung fu, rice, import cars, or Wen Ho Lee.[16] Neither am I suggesting that we aspire to get jiggy in music videos with scantily clad Lucy Liu look-alikes handing out backrubs.[17] Hip hop contains the opportunity to communicate and convey signifiers and ideologies through art. It contains the opportunity to represent ourselves, our stories, and our people. In hip hop is the power and sensibility to educate and uplift our communities.

For example, the Filipino Bay Area/L.A. rapper Kiwi rhymes: "I flip like a page in *Source* magazine / to page 13 / Ad for an overpriced pair of GAP jeans / Made by some twelve year old in the Philippines / Makin' 5 cents a day / Makes no sense to say / the least."[18] It may be that some people aren't going to be feeling us if we do so. But part of the role of the trailblazer is to take risks, to go forward even if that means some people are not going to follow you. Even if people don't recognize the name or reference, drop it and make people curious. I remember reading an interview with Chuck D in which he was talking about one of his rhymes from "Rebel without a Pause": "Hard—my calling card / recorded and ordered—supporter of Chesimard."[19] Chuck D said that, at the time, he knew that most people would have no idea that he was referring to Joanne Chesimard (more popularly known as Assata Shakur), a black nationalist who was accused of killing a cop in New Jersey. Chuck D said he wanted people to hear the name and look her up in the library. Some Asian American hip hop artists are signifying: the Mountain Brothers have a track called 5 *Elements*, with five MC's representing the five elements of Tao alchemy. The hip hop duo Kontrast (New York) have a track in which they retell a Filipino myth. The aspiring artist Jamez attempts to combine hip hop with Korean music.

Asian Americans have the opportunity to name drop or make references that may not be readily recognizable to the majority of people, Asian or otherwise. However, Asian Americans have the added challenge of pan-ethnicity: How do we signify to a culture that is already so richly varied and complicated? Especially since there is a lack of education on what, say, a Hmong American has in common with a South Asian American. But this is both an advantage and a disadvantage: it is a disadvantage because we are already divided and confused within the definition of what it is to be Asian American; it is an advantage because we have the power to shape it.

Language

The various words and slang used to signify in hip hop are enormous and regional—a lot of slang is localized, transmitted to different parts of the country through hip hop music and culture. Just because you're hip hop doesn't mean that you will automatically know what *off the heazy* or *bremelo* means.[20] You may be able to derive meaning from context, but the point is that you will often hear vocabulary that is not commonly used in your area until it is popularized by hip hop. The code number 187 is what police use for homicides in L.A., yet everyone in hip hop has learned what it means even if they're not from the West Coast.

Similarly, you can create a very unique form of regional sensibility by using languages that are not English. Latino/as have had the ability to signify in Spanish while still being able to be seen as hip hop. Big Pun, the Beatnuts, Fat Joe, Kid Frost and the Latin Alliance, and others have combined language, music, and culture to create an undeniable identity in hip hop.

Asian Americans have not. Asians in Asia use their languages to rhyme, but Asian Americans have not heretofore visibly used Asian languages in their rhymes—certainly not to the same extent that Latino/as have used Spanish. They also have a shared language, whereas "Asian American" is an umbrella term that incorporates many different languages, most of which are completely different from each other—for example, Vietnamese is completely different from Hmong, which is completely different from Punjabi, which is completely different from Cantonese, which is a dialect that is different from Mandarin. Although different Latino/as will speak different dialects, it has not stopped them from rhyming in their distinct dialects of Spanish. two separate worlds in lang.

Some may argue why Asian Americans should rhyme in anything other than English. After all, for many of us English is our primary language. But this is dodging what is at the heart of the matter: assimilationism and white supremacy has had a history of attempting, with various degrees of success, to wipe out native languages, especially those of people of color and the indigenous. Language is culture, it's a code in which we speak to our own people: if you want to understand, you have to learn it.

Hip hop is its own ever-changing dialect, you have to be born into it or learn it in order to be fluent, just like any other language. Hip hop dialects were created out of necessity, a coded language used to signify and communicate culture, with a rich heritage that taps into resistance and signifying against the dominant racist culture.

The closest that Asian Americans have to such a dynamic is pidgin English—usually a mix of English and an Asian language. Hawaiian pidgin is particularly interesting, given its mix of several Asian and indigenous languages with English.[21] It is also interesting given that it was a language formed out of necessity during the plantation days in Hawaii when Asian workers were being exploited.[22] But even then, will mainland Asian Americans understand Hawaiian pidgin? Maybe one answer is that we use words and phrases and hope everyone else catches up. Like I insinuated above, you have to learn or figure out what *for sheezy my neezy* means. Maybe I don't understand Tagalog, Japanese, Korean, Cantonese, Thai, etc. But if you drop some rhymes using those languages, maybe I'll get curious and try to figure it out.

As for musical language, Asian Americans also have what can be seen as a disadvantage. Part of hip hop's musical language is sampling—whether it be an avant-garde artist flipping a sample at twice the speed and backward or Puffy ripping off an entire song. Although hip hop artists of various colors sample from a wide variety of musical palettes, African Americans have the ability to reach back and sample/reimagine songs from an enormous culture of African American music—everything from jazz to rock to R&B. Outkast's song "Rosa Parks" incorporates a jook-joint breakdown featuring a harmonica, representing for the Dirty South. In "Me, Myself and I," De La Soul and Prince Paul sampled Funkadelic's "(Not Just) Knee Deep."

Although sampling in hip hop is not without its critics, it's a powerful mode of expression—taking a rhythm or melody from an old tune, maybe not immediately recognizable but striking a cord in you nonetheless. Hip hop revolutionized the way the world looked at music through sampling—using threads of music to conjure moods or signify while at the same time reinventing music. Paying tribute to past African American music while moving on to something new. And, at its best, making young heads curious about their peoples' musical past and encouraging them to seek it out.

While there have been Asian recording artists in America, we don't have an American musical culture that we are popularly credited with creating. So it's not possible for us to signify for each other and others as Americans of color using sampling in the same way that African Americans have. Of course, we can sample Asian music from Asia, but Asian Americans come from an incredibly diverse set of cultural origins, each with its own unique musical traditions and forms. And since racism toward Asians in America includes the racial stereotype that we are all foreigners, many Asians in America feel the need to disassociate themselves from Asian culture in order to seem more "American." The power to signify with musical sampling is not going to be as great for us as it is for African Americans, at least not yet.

But the term Asian American is a political and social construct anyway, and maybe in order to create a uniquely Asian American musical form we need to start melding different Asian musical forms together—if we're going to be a pan-Asian people, let's make some pan-Asian music.

Gender Roles

Let's make something clear: *sexism and patriarchy are not unique to hip hop or men of color.*[23] This doesn't justify or excuse the use of these forms, but we have to realize that gender roles and sexism are social dynamics that pervade all aspects of life all over the globe. Here, I want to explore these issues specifically as they appear in hip hop.

I don't want to imply that Asian Americans or other people of color should strive to fit in to the "dominant" culture's idea of what a man is and what a woman is. But I think it's important to talk about what those racialized roles are, how we sometimes play into them, and how they are forced upon us.

A strong and resilient aspect of commercial hip hop is the expression and exploitation of black hypermasculinity—both the trading and the subversion of the fear and fascination of the taboos associated with black male sexuality that have been heaped upon black men since slavery. We've all heard the stereotype of black men with huge cocks: "Once she goes black, she never goes back." Though this may seem like a "positive stereotype," it makes Black men out to be abnormal sexual monsters. The role of black women is often portrayed as either adversarial or complementary to the men: gold diggers, 'hoes, chickenheads, fellow thug, etc. Asian sexuality is racialized differently in America: Asian men are seen as domineering yet boring sexists with small cocks, and Asian women are seen as exotic sexual trophies who will do anything to get with a non-Asian man.

When I asked the various Asian American women and men involved in hip hop about their perceptions of the gendered ways that they and other Asians were treated in hip hop by non-Asians, the common sentiments were that Asian women are not taken seriously and are objectified and fetishized, and that Asian men are ignored, dismissed, or treated with suspicion. Both genders also said that they felt underestimated, or were seen as a novelty at best. "Asian American men have been de-masculinized across the board," states Maanav Thakore. "The stereotype of the Asian man contradicts the accepted image of manhood in hip hop culture."[24] Theresa Vu, a

Bay Area MC who performs in a duo known as Magnetic North, was once mistaken for a sound engineer when she took the stage.

This is not surprising. Even if we remove white people from the equation, there are very few honest, constructive, and informed interactions between people of color and the indigenous in this country—we have to receive our information about each other elsewhere. Usually that information is handed down to us from the racist white supremacist mainstream, or from people of all colors who have a superficial or even prejudiced perception of their own people's culture. As this relates to hip hop, I want to explore gender issues with the knowledge that black masculinity is an element at the hip hop center (note: I said *an* element, not *the only* element), and how various outside influences work on our notions, understandings, and reactions to gender.

The only time that Asian men are even remotely seen as masculine in American culture is through martial arts. Back in the day, martial arts flicks presented Bruce Lee and other Asian males as nonwhites superior to white men in combat, much as black men in boxing have become popularly believed to be superior to whites: and with the growing popularity of Jet Li, Jackie Chan, and the fight choreography of Yuen Wo Ping in the United States,[25] there seems to be a resurgence of the Asian man as nonwhite hero image.

However, the notion that Asian men are masculine because of martial arts needs to be qualified as different from the masculinity of black men, because the popularly believed sexual prowess and endowments of black men are essentialized; that is, there is the racist belief that black men are just more inherently sexually masculine and driven—a belief rooted in racist propaganda about black rapists that has been used to demonize and fetishize black men throughout history.[26] Asian men's proficiency in martial arts, while also carrying essentialist elements (how many of us were asked as children if we knew karate?), is seen as a learned skill: sure we're good at it, but black men and white dudes can learn how to kick ass too, and in many ways it's seen as an improvement, because not only can they learn martial arts but they are supposedly bigger and stronger than Asian guys. If Americans can make a film about martial arts or martial arts cultures without any Asians in it, they will. Wesley Snipes, Chuck Norris, Jean-Claude Van Damme and others have had sustained careers in entertainment, knocking the tar out of Asian stuntmen and villains in action flicks.

Some elements of martial arts, as discussed above, have been readily borrowed by hip hoppers. In terms of gender, it is one of the few times that Asian men are visible or recognized in mainstream hip hop: examples include Jeru the Damaja's friends and foes in his music video "You Played Yourself" that was influenced by Hong Kong action flicks, and the various references to Asian male martial artists by many different hip hoppers (including Ghostface Killa's hyperbolic boast that Bruce Lee was his teacher on *Supreme Clientele*). In an interview with Craig Smith, the Mountain Brothers revealed that a major label executive wanted to market them by getting them to perform onstage wearing karate outfits and wielding gongs.

In hip hop, there is a certain level of invisibility around Asian American men; of the four elements, the discipline that has the most visible concentration of Asian Americans is DJing or turntablism. In Eric K. Arnold's story about Bay Area hip hop in the November 2001 issue of *The Source*, he namedrops Mix Master Mike and twice mentions turntablists in general, but the majority of the piece is about MCs even though the Bay Area has a lot of amazing turntablists, many of them Asian.

There is also a difference in the way that MCs and DJs are marketed. You would think that with the incredible number of talented Asian American DJs out there, even mainstream hip hop magazines and record labels would notice. But the press coverage on Asian American DJs has been relatively minimal, and many of the Asian American DJs are on smaller independent labels. Nothing wrong with that, and it may even be the choice of some of these DJs to be loyal to a smaller label and stay underground to counter mainstream hip hop's more glossy lifestyle. But we also have to question whether marketability has anything to do with it, and why Asian American MCs get even less attention. "As MCs, Asians are not as marketable and don't yet have the kind of credibility they need to get major love," states Kiwi. "The record execs, A&RS or whatever, they are looking for someone who in the end will make them money."[27] Part of the reason why we have seen relatively more Asian American DJs than MCs is the fact that DJs are regarded as being behind the scenes and are acknowledged for their musical skills, whereas MCs are given attention not just for lyrical skill but for their image and personality. While a DJ may speak with his or her hands, an MC has the option of actually putting his or her thoughts and issues into concrete words and rhymes. The Houston-based MC and poet ASIA Continental concurs: "I don't think that, right now, there is any lack of Asian/Asian Pacific American MC's out there . . . The Entertainment Industry, right now, does not see a market for Asian/Asian Pacific American Music Artists."[28]

Asian women have opportunities to be visible in hip hop, but that's not necessarily a good thing: like in the mainstream culture, Asian women are objectified and fetishized but not expected to speak their minds. You'll see Asian female models and backup dancers, but they are usually voiceless: tokens at best, objectified at worst. Asian and Asian American women are not expected to have skills or have anything to contribute to hip hop except for their bodies. "Back when I used to battle a lot, people would automatically assume that I was gonna lose," Theresa Vu states. "People will be hesitant to respect you, because Asians aren't believed to have any street cred—the stereotype of Asian women as engineers, middle class, etc. clash with the hip hop norm. You have to go up there and earn respect with your skills."[29]

Some may argue that all races of women are objectified and/or not taken seriously in hip hop. But seen racially, Asian women's gender issues are uniquely shaped by their race. In the 20 *Questions* section of the December/January 1997 issue of *Vibe* magazine, a writer asks, "Considering that . . . Ghostface [Killa] was checking for a sister who was 'half Hawaiian with a touch of Chinese,' and Rakim's girl 'almost looked Korean, but European,' you think maybe, just maybe, folks are still colorstruck?" You could add Nelly's line, "I got a chick rolling up, half-Black and Asian" in *E.I.*, and Icarus claiming "I got a Japanese chick with my dick in her hand" on Redman's *Malpractice* album. The writers of *ego trip* note that Dana Dane talked about sexing up a Japanese woman waaaay back in 1987's *Dana Dane with Fame*, impersonating her by saying "choy yoi yoi yoi yoooiii!" (and as the writers of *ego trip* suggest, I don't speak Japanese but I'm pretty sure that's not really Japanese). And, of course, there is Puffy's infamous lines about "Asian women that'll change my linen / after I done blazed and hit 'em," in 2001's *Diddy*. I always hated Puffy.

It's important to reemphasize here that men of color in hip hop aren't the only perpetrators of racist sexism toward Asian women. Take Puff Daddy's song quoted above: when he was called on it, at least he apologized and released the single with the racist, sexist lines removed. While I still hate Puffy for it, take his actions and compare them to the Bloodhound Gang's dismissal of Asian Americans protesting their song "Yellow Fever," which contained such lyrics as:

I told her every Soon Yi needs a little Woody / She said for all the tea in China my vagina's not free / But my love will linger longer than the Ming Dynasty / I said I needed her to do and her to do my laundry / I knew she needed a way to stay legally within the country / She was made in Taiwan I said I'm O.K. with that / Just promise me you'll never try to eat my cat / Chinky chinky bang bang I love you / Chinky chinky bang bang I know you love me too . . .

Cause I ride my slant-eyed slope like a brand new Kawasaki / Oh me chinky she's so kinky got me hot like Nagasaki / Burnin' up like Napalm burstin' like an A-bomb / I think I got that jungle fever but I caught it in 'Nam / She's like an oriental rug cause I lay her where I please / Then I blindfold her with dental floss and get down on her knees / I'm a diving Kamikaze eating out Chinese / First I'll have the poo-poo platter then some tuna sushi / She'll be screaming like Godzilla and kickin' like Jackie Chan / I'll get her redder than China wetter than the Sea of Japan / Like the Chinese New Year she's gonna see fireworks / Now be a good chinky and press Jimmy's shirts

Even with such blatantly racist, sexist (not to mention tone deaf, stupid, and wack) lyrics, this all-white-and-one-black-man band received relatively no negative press, and the protests organized by Asian American women and men against the Bloodhound Gang remained unheard and dismissed. In a *Rolling Stone* interview, the lead singer Jimmy Pop dismissed the protests by saying the song was okay since they had an Asian American female fan who advised them to say "fuck you" to the "chinks."[30] When I and some other Asian Americans invaded Bloodhound Gang's chatrooms to start a discussion, we found many white people and a few Asian women who fiercely defended the group's "sense of humor" and "freedom of speech." In an interview, Jimmy Pop stated, "The whole song is about how I want to bang an Asian chick. In my own way, I'm saying that I like Asian chicks." When asked how he felt about the reactions to the song, the bassist Jared said, "I want to tell them to go fuck themselves."[31]

In organized protests against these derogations in the Twin Cities, numerous white men and women, and also a few Asian men and women, yelled derogative comments and tried to start fights with us protestors. The (white male) producer of the concert came to one of our organizational meetings and claimed that he was not racist, since his fiancé was an Asian woman. The sole man of color in the Bloodhound Gang came out to talk to some fans during the protest, and talked to two women who were part of our protests (one Asian American woman, one African American woman). In the conversation, he said he could see how the song was sexist, but refused to acknowledge that it was racist. I guess racist sexism toward Asian women is okay as long as white people are the ones doing it.

fetish

Asian women are presented by the mainstream as being closer to the standard of white beauty than are black women, and there is the historically loaded racial stereotype of Asian women being more submissive. Both views represent widespread orientalist racist gender stereotypes based on the desire of white men. These stereotypes are in turn taught to, and internalized by, the rest of us. It is a racialized standard of beauty that teaches all of us that Asian women are "exotic" trophies. The growing number of African American men with Asian women has caused some tension between black women and Asian women; even here in the Twin Cities I've had personal, on-the-downlow conversations with black and Asian women about this topic, and there are some clubs in town where the tensions are thick enough to cut with a knife. I've been told which clubs have patrons that welcome Asian women and don't welcome Asian men, and which clubs that Asian women should avoid attending if they don't want any trouble from black women. There have been fights, verbal abuse, and misunderstandings on all sides. There have been no reports or academic theses or bandana-wearing radicals speaking up about this issue—rather, it is on the everyday personal. In the middle of this often confusing interpersonal maze are the racialized gender roles that white people have forced us into, the roles that we sometimes play, play ourselves out in, and are forced upon us: super-sexualized yet animalistic black man, super-sexualized yet disposable black woman, super-sexualized yet submissive Asian woman, and non-sexy yet domineering Asian man.

All women and men deserve to be met on their own terms. The question is how do we get there, and how do we get there with our respect for one another intact? Will Asian men feel the need to overcompensate for their demasculinization by adopting played out chauvinist ideals and sexual boasting, and feel the need to compete with non-Asian men? Are we going to start fights in order to counter the stereotype of us being "soft"? Will Asian women internalize a racial dislike toward Asian males as sexually inferior to non-Asian men, hook up with men who are popularly believed to be more attractive or superior to Asian men, and feel the need to compete with non-Asian women in order to get over?

The Next Level

Sometime ago I was in Manhattan's Chinatown in a music shop. A white European lady with a thick accent asked a Chinese American clerk for some suggestions. "I want authentic music," she said, "traditional music, none of the modern stuff." The clerk shrugged and said he couldn't help her, he just listened to the pop stuff. I myself was looking for Utada Hikaru, Coco Lee, and some other pop music in Asian languages I can't understand. In fact, a lot of Southeast Asians, specifically Hmong kids but even a ghetto Viet like myself, are listening to Korean, Japanese, and Chinese pop and hip hop (even if we can't understand the words) as well as ethnic specific music. When I ask some of the Hmong youth I work with why they listen to Asian music in languages they can't understand, the common answer I get is a shrug, they like it, the singer (male or female) is cute, and it's Asian.

Life is complicated. Authenticity, if handled a certain way, can be just as alluring to the white mainstream as colorblindness, and just as alienating to our own people. I'm not saying it's hopeless or even preferable that we turn from our own people: on the contrary, we need to see how we can reach our people and be accountable in our own communities. The only way we can do that without playing ourselves and our own people is by centering ourselves, so that Asian America occupies our center. That means that we can't afford to be snooty and diss others for listening to bubblegum pop Asian music or apolitical music, because in doing so we cut off a large part of our community.

I don't want to downplay how empowering it is to simply see Asian American artists rock the crowd or listen to their art. Personally, I get strength from seeing not just the faces on the stage but the faces in the crowd: I think Asian Americans are still, generally speaking, riddled with self hate and inferiority complexes toward whites and blacks. Maybe I'm relieved that Asian American faces are at least more welcoming toward each other in these scenes than they used to be, and that there seems to be a sense of family; not long ago, if I saw another Asian and tried to talk to him or her, I would get the ice grill of a token whose territory is being stepped on.

It is a comfort to see Asians rocking for other Asians, and Asians interacting and supporting each other in hip hop: the P.A.C.I.F.I.C.S. have one of the most energetic and engaging live shows I've ever seen, period; Denizen Kane possesses an incredibly intricate, melodic flow that the world at large may not have heard yet but won't be able to ignore; I play the Mountain Brother's "Community" track to my students; I rock mix tapes by Roli Rho and listen to cuts by Kuttin Kandi and Invisbl Skratch Piklz; I listen to the strange and original flow of Lyrics Born; I see Asian b-girls and b-boys like Asia One and Eternal Illusions and graf writers and visual artists like Phloe doing their thing; I hear communities buzzing about Kiwi, Bambu, Himalayan Project, Karmacy, Jupiterdisciples, and Nomi; I see Tou Saiko Lee perform with his grandmother, fusing hip hop–inflected spoken word with traditional Hmong chanting; I see Robert Karimi as a show stopper of hip hop punk sensibilities with DJs D Double and Yellowfist anchoring his incredibly kinetic performances; I think "The Emperor's Main Course in Cantonese" by Kid Koala is a work of genius; I listen to the flows, hip hop poems, singing, and beatboxing of Taiyo Takeda, Geologic, Vidya Rao, Golda Sargento, and Paul Kim—and in all of this I see the future. While I'm writing this and you're reading this, there is probably some Asian in your area on the mic, on the wheels, poppin and lockin and bombing—just killing it. Maybe they haven't made the pages of *The Source* or *Vibe* yet (and maybe they don't want to) but they're trying to do their thing and make a name for themselves. Find them, support them, argue with them, politic with them.

I love being Asian American, and I love hip hop. Recognize that I talk about a lot of negative elements in this article. It's meant to be critical, not condemning. If you love something, you must criticize it fairly.

Though many will try to romanticize hip hop and what it means, we have to remember that hip hop began in parks and at parties, with DJs "borrowing" from the city's power supply through the lightposts. Hip hop emerged not as an overt political statement but because it *had* to exist. It became a voice and culture for the disenfranchised, and a lot of the disenfranchised wanted to entertain and be entertained, to express themselves, and to party: hey, even activists got to party, got to enjoy each other's company and dance together after a hard day's work, right?

Asian American hip hop will evolve and emerge naturally, if we do it together. Hopefully Asian Americans in hip hop will encompass a diverse set of ideologies, expressions, and forms. We can do this. We can create quality hip hop, our own flavor, so we are seen as innovators and everyone else has to catch up with us. One of us should have been able to say that we came up with that beat for *Oochie Wally* (not the lyrics though) or the beat for *Get Yr Freak On* first, because it was our innovation and because we were applying the love and knowledge and some of the musical traditions and musical qualities of the language of our culture to create something that is hip hop yet uniquely our own, without using our culture merely to make a buck because we know of non-Asian people's fascination with us. Signify for us, not for others, and if they follow or catch up, fine. But we occupy the center, we know the flavor is ours, we know it couldn't have happened without us.

Easier said than done? Yes. Necessary? Absolutely.

So what do we need to do? Make sure we keep up the ownership of our expression. We need to center ourselves and start taking some risks and accountability. We have to realize that we can only go forward and innovate if we do it together: support Asian American artists while still being critical; recognize the importance and innovations while asking if we can do more or add our own flavor; respect personal expression while knowing that all we got is ourselves and the only ones who will really do it for us is us; know that we are possible, and that we can always do better.

Challenging? Yes. But we're not going to be alone. We're gonna be together on it, on stage and in the audience. We need to have faith that we're gonna get there, that we're gonna grow, and learn, and change ourselves and others. So keep on keeping on. I'll be here—listening, thinking, feeling, watching, speaking, and dancing.

Notes

In addition to the books and articles cited in this essay, there were other sources of information and inspiration that were invaluable to me, including lectures (like Trisha Rose's presentation at Macalester College on the globalization of hip hop), concerts, the www.ohhla.com online hip hop lyrics archive, and late-night talks, CDs, mix tapes, contact information, arguments, phone conversations, edits, and e-mails with the following people who were gracious enough to share their time and thoughts with me: Oliver Wang, Dan Diggity, Theresa Vu, Juliana Pegues, D'Lo, DJ Kuttin' Kandi, Giles Li, Doug Kearney, Dennis Kim, Fred Ho, KP, Kublai Kwon, Ed Bok Lee, Michelle Myers, Jane Kim, Kiwi, Bambu, Vijay Pendakur, ASIA Continental, Julie Hwang, Helen Yum, Fran Hwang, Diaspora Flow (Chamindika and Pradeepa), Phloe, Taiyo

Takeda, Elson Trinidad, James Choi, BIONIC, Catzie, Art Concordia, Maanav Thakore, Jason Bayani, Jona Mercado, Sarah Chang, Michelle Won, Ellen Guidone, and the table of young brothers that I met at Pho Ca Dao who jumped in on the conversation I was having with some friends. Thanks also to Key Kool, who sent me "Kozmonautz"!

1 Namely, the MC, the DJ, break dancing, and graffiti art.

2 It is important to understand that hip hop is not just about rap music: hip hop is a culture made up of different languages, music, traditions, art forms, etc.

3 Many would also say that Chicanos, especially Puerto Ricans in South Bronx and Uptown New York City, were also there in the beginning. It's hard to know whether any Asians were there, since usually, as a race, Asians are so easily subsumed or ignored.

4 James Loewen, *Lies My Teacher Told Me* (New York: Touchstone, 1995), 12, 301.

5 Amadou Diallo, an unarmed black man shot forty-one times and killed by New York police; the Honorable Minister Louis Farrakhan, leader of the Nation of Islam; Mumia Abu-Jamal, a black journalist wrongfully incarcerated, placed on death row, and blamed for the death of a police officer in Philadelphia.

6 Vincent Chin was killed in Detroit in 1982 in a hate crime by two white men who paid a fine but did not spend a single day in jail; David Wong, without benefit of a language translator fluent in his dialect, was wrongfully accused of murdering a fellow inmate by self-interested fellow prisoners, though Wong was nowhere near the scene of the crime when it happened; Thung Phetakoune is a sixty-two-year-old Laotian American man killed in a hate crime in New Hampshire in 2001; Thien Minh Ly is a Vietnamese American murdered in a hate crime in 1996 in Tustin, California; Richard Aoki is one of the founding members of the Black Panther Party; Bill and Yuri Kochiyama are two of Asian America's most beloved radical activists.

7 "Everytime I wanna go get a fuckin brew / I gotta go down to the store with the two / oriental one-penny countin motherfuckers / that make a nigga mad enough to cause a little ruckus / Thinkin every brother in the world's out to take / So they watch every damn move that I make / They hope I don't pull out a gat and try to rob / they funky little store, but bitch, I got a job / Yo yo, check it out / So don't follow me, up and down your market / Or your little chop suey ass'll be a target of the nationwide boycott / Juice with the people, that's what the boy got / So pay respect to the black fist / or we'll burn your store, right down to a crisp / And then we'll see ya! Cause you can't turn the ghetto—into Black Korea."

8 Ishmael Reed, "An Outsider in Koreatown," in *Airing Dirty Laundry* (Reading, Mass.: Addison Wesley, 1993), 82.

9 Even Eminem raps, in *Without Me*, "I'm the worst thing since Elvis Presley / to do Black music . . ." But again, I emphasize this is *relatively* speaking. I've met plenty of fools who say that hip hop is raceless.

10 Quoted in Mosi Reeves, "Citizen Kim: Korean American MC Denizen Kane

Makes the Transition from Chicago to Oakland, Spoken Word to Hip-Hop," *San Francisco Bay Guardian*, November, 2002.

11 George, *Hip Hop America*, 105.

12 A few examples include "Like the invincible Master Asia, a true warrior," Doodlebug from Digable Planets speaking of the *Swordsman* movie series from Hong Kong; "Kicking like Brandon," Mystikal referring to Brandon Lee, Bruce Lee's son; and I would need an entire dictionary to catalogue all of the martial arts references the Wu uses, let alone the references used by other rappers pertaining to kung fu/martial arts.

13 China Doll is a derogative orientalist term applied to Asian women, Chinese or not, that usually implies sexual objectification, exotification, and otherness.

14 This term is popularly used in hip hop by everyone from Mos Def to Method Man. It refers to eyes getting smaller from smoking too much weed. And yes, it's racist.

15 See Vijay Prashad's *Everybody Was Kung Fu Fighting* (Boston: Beacon Press, 2002).

16 Wen Ho Lee is the Chinese American nuclear scientist wrongfully accused of selling secret information to China; he was incarcerated for a year before the charges against him were dropped. As people of color and the indigenous in this country know, we're guilty until proven innocent.

17 Lucy Liu is a Chinese American actress and interracial girlfriend icon du jour.

18 See the song "Portraits of Son Rising" on his album, *Writes of Passage*.

19 You'll have to take my word for this interview; I read it in high school and can't find it now, but I remember what it said.

20 If you don't know, and if you really must know, go to http://www.faqs.org/faqs/music/hip-hop/dictionary/part1/.

21 For some popular representations of pidgin, see the poetry and prose of Lois-Ann Yamanaka and Kayo Hatta's film *Picture Bride*.

22 Read Ronald Takaki's *Stranger from A Different Shore* (New York: Penguin, 1989). If you're Asian American and you haven't read this yet, what is wrong with you? Yeah yeah, it's not perfect, but neither are you. So read it.

23 Let me say that one more time: sexism and patriarchy are not unique to hip hop or men of color.

24 Maanav Thakore, personal e-mail correspondence, November 2004.

25 Yuen is the fight choreographer for, among many Hong Kong films, as well as *The Matrix* and *Crouching Tiger, Hidden Dragon*.

26 This was racist propaganda used to frighten whites and justify racist crimes against blacks. In reality, white slaveowners were raping black women daily.

27 Kiwi, personal e-mail correspondence, November 2004

28 ASIA Continental, personal e-mail correspondence, November 2004.

29 Theresa Vu, personal e-mail correspondence, November 2004.

30 Rollingstone.com, May 9, 2000.

31 Ibid.

AFRO/ASIA EXPRESSIVE WRITING

Part IV features an eclectic array of creative writing expressing Afro Asian interaction ranging from the personal to the political. The veteran African American poets Everett Hoagland and Kalamu Ya Salaam offer unique testaments to radical Asian politics and honor the Bandung legacy and spirit. The anti-imperialist and radical fire continues with today's younger generation in the works of the Filipina activist Maya Santos and of the Korean American Ishle Yi Park—a rising Def Jam spoken word/poetry performance star. The Japanese American writer David Mura and the African American writer Alexs Pate explore Afro Asian mutually held stereotypes as well as struggle through common dialogue in their poignant and humorous performance text. The Chinese American JoYin Shih explores her self-identity in a story of her friendship with an African American girl named Chyna.

David Mura and Alexs Pate

Secret Colors and the Possibilities of Coalition: An African American–Asian American Collaboration

I am a Sansei (third-generation Japanese American) writer; my best friend, Alexs Pate, is an African American writer. Both of us live in the Twin Cities. Around 1989 or so, Alexs and I first got to know each other on a long car ride to a reading we were giving at Winona State University. I don't recall exactly what we talked about on that trip but we got along well, and at the reading we gave our writings seemed to complement each other. Both of our bodies of work centered on the issues of race and identity and on the ways our lives and communities were marginalized by mainstream culture. We both wrote out of a sense of trying to retrieve and restore parts of the American experience that had not yet been put into literature or recognized as essential to an understanding of America. On the drive back home, I'm sure we spoke about the alienation we sometimes felt as writers of color in Minnesota, a place whose self-image is still defined by Garrison Keillor's

Lake Wobegone (the place where all women are strong, the men good looking, and the children above average—and, I always add, everyone's white). We probably also talked about sports, one of the other topics besides literature that always seems to come up in our conversations.

Over the next few years the two of us became better friends. When the *Miss Saigon* controversy hit and I began to have arguments with white friends over the issues of race in new and more antagonistic ways, Alexs was a source of comfort and understanding, and he helped guide me through a difficult period when I left a number of white friendships behind. He understood immediately why the casting of the British actor Jonathan Pryce as a Eurasian bothered me, as well as why I objected to the stereotypical portrayals in that musical. And, on a deeper level, he understood the pain and anger I was feeling at my white friends' inability to critique their own thinking about race and their refusal to entertain the idea that their aesthetic views could be tainted by racist assumptions. At the same time, Alexs helped me understand that race work is long and arduous, and because of that one needs to guard against burnout and letting the bitterness and rage cut too close and raw. I didn't need to fight every single battle all at once; I needed to take care of myself and prepare myself for the long haul.

As our friendship grew, we began to talk about working together on a collaborative piece; we both had done one-man performance pieces and a two-man piece seemed a logical next step for us both. And then the Rodney King decision came out and L.A. erupted in a violence that bewildered and scared many, and, to many others, seemed the logical consequence of a local and national systemic practice of racism. At any rate, beyond the obvious issues about the police and the court system surrounding the events in L.A., Alexs and I were struck by the images of violence between the African Americans and Korean Americans there. It was as if the only time the media would ever consider the relationship between these two groups was when they were shooting at and fighting each other.

Alexs and I both understood that the conflicts between the Korean Americans and African Americans, while very real, were also being used to mask the more prevalent and more powerful system of white racism. We also saw that the subtleties of the interactions between the two communities were being reduced to the image of the Korean storeowners with their guns and the African American looters. We knew that there needed to be alternative images to the ones provided by and repeated over and over by the media, and we knew that we needed to stop talking about working together and actually get down to creating a piece. We reasoned that if we simply presented on stage the two of us, an African American and an Asian American, as friends, that such a statement would be in its own small way revolutionary.

So we started with the idea of a piece that would explore the friendship between the two of us, and at the same time examine our lives as men of color and the relationship between the communities we were a part of—African Americans and Asian Americans. In the process, we would look at the various ways the culture and our communities defined identity—from stereotypes in the media to community-based identities (which are often generalized idealizations or based on essentialist notions) to the actual day-to-day realities of the two main performers and writers. We particularly wanted to contrast the ways African Americans and Asian Americans formed their image of each other with the ongoing dialogue between the two performers.

As we began to explore the notion of identity and engage in our dialogue we also started creating autobiographical sketches of our lives, so that the audience would have to grapple with the particulars of our experience and personalities—particulars that the culture has ignored or kept mute. At the heart of these autobiographical sketches were certain transformative moments when we had had to grapple with what it means to be a man of color in American society. These moments often involved a painful self-recognition—the realization of our own internal racism or the ways in which we have harmed others and ourselves or the knowledge that the rage we hold inside is somehow killing us. Through these moments we wanted to explore the possibilities of change and questioning, of understanding in greater depth the complexities of race and class and sexuality, and of how each of us fits in with the changes going on now in our culture.

Given the fact that both Alexs and I were used to working in multiple genres, the writing used in the piece tumbled out in various modes—poetry, fiction, dialogues, monologues, creative nonfiction, and conversation. We moved back and forth between generalized or fictional characters and our autobiographical selves, exploring connections, discontinuities, and contradictions between the two realms. The writing was to be presented live on stage and on videotape, at times with musical accompaniment. We would also use slides, some from personal or family photographs, some from historical photographs or popular culture. There were also video montages and film clips (rap videos, TV shows, clips from the Rodney King video and the Sun Ja Du/Latasha Harlins trial, and Hollywood films such as *Year of the Dragon* and Melvin Van Peebles *Sweet Sweetback's Baadassss Song*). Specially created video animation ranged from an image of a huge police boot kicking to an image of a hand unfolding a child. Through switching from various literary modes and through the use of various media, we wanted to provide some sense of the cultural background out of which our work appears, and to attack and question that background. In creating the show we worked in collaboration with a multicultural group of incredibly talented artists: the jazz musician and composer Douglass Ewart (African American); the video artist Me-k Ando (Korean American); the animator Alison Morse (European American); the visual artist and set designer Tom Rose (European American); and the director Ralph Remington (African American).

We performed the piece in several venues: at the University of Minnesota, at the Southern Theater for the Walker Art Center in Minneapolis, at a convention of grant-makers in San Francisco; and at the Painted Bride art center in Philadelphia. At each of the performances we received standing ovations, and at some of them we had lively discussions afterward. Particularly in Minnesota, we brought together a significant audience of both African Americans and Asian Americans, and in this way I think we helped start a cultural dialogue that has now extended into the next generation of African American and Asian American artists in our area. In our post-performance discussions we were sometimes asked about our intentions in writing the piece. One of the ways we answered this was by saying that we wrote the piece thinking about how an African American and Asian American audience would react to it. In part this meant that we wanted to both accurately portray various aspects of our communities and, at the same time, critique our communities. By implication, we were saying that while we were happy to have whites in the audience the piece was not intended primarily for them. A colleague who brought a mainly white class from the University of Minnesota said several of the white students were put off or bewildered by the piece, and he surmised that this was in part because it was probably the first one they had seen where whiteness had been placed at the margins rather than the center.

As we intended, the piece does include and comment on the events in L.A. surrounding the Rodney King beating and court decision; in a way, however, this background serves as a springboard to more personal and introspective examinations of the issues of race and identity. Though Alexs and I were trying to do justice to the ways that our communities in general tend to view each other, we also wanted to particularize and critique those views. Especially noteworthy is the dialogue between Alexs and myself about the course of our friendship. In part, it presents, if the audience is willing to see it, a map of how racial boundaries can be crossed.

In the piece, in recalling an initial meeting before we became friends, Alexs comments: "i remember being conscious of trying to impress him. david was not an asian then. i saw a white man, i think his asian self was unformed. . . . so much of him was still connected to his white strivings. yes the effort to be accepted to give yourself over to the oppressor's education, unabashedly and unapologetically, scares me. It created a distance between us I wasn't sure could be bridged." One way of glossing this passage is, of course, the ways that many Asians take up the role of honorary white person, of refusing to see race as a central issue to their identity or to the ways our society functions.

Over the course of the dialogue, I go over how my increasing racial consciousness brought about arguments with white friends about *Miss Saigon* and other racial issues. In the process, I discovered a growing sense of rage and alienation from white mainstream society, and as a result I broke off my friendships with a number of white friends and began to develop relationships not just with Asian Americans but with other people of color. Alexs then notes how something had changed both in me and in his perceptions of me:

ALEXS: it was easy to open myself to him
    perhaps not at the beginning
    but from the moment david showed himself to me
    his self-confidence wavering
    his knowledge of self in question
    and asked how i dealt with the effects of racism
    how could I know how to respond
    i had met too many young asian students
    in high schools through the midwest who were
    clearly confused by the difference between
    what they were told about race
    and what they felt

there was a young woman in long prairie
who told me that she was traumatized by
the upcoming prom because she was sure
the boy who asked her just wanted to go with her
because she was exotic
no one around her seemed to understand
but i did, the outlaw understood
we must find a way
those of us who feel marginal
to love each other
not some bullshit we are the world singalong
but really come to see the way
we are taught to hate who we are. . . .

Alexs goes on to discuss the possibilities of friendship between the races:

> I am always surprised when I hear a black man talk about his friend so and so
> who is white. I immediately wonder about the nature of that relationship. i
> can't help it. how does a black man born in these united states learn to love a
> white man? how is this possible? i'm not talking about that 'gettin' over'
> bullshit. but really? every time i start feeling buddy buddy with a white guy i
> find myself saying to him, "you know. I've never had a white man as a friend.
> I don't think it's possible for me right now. I'm too goddamned angry."
>
> Most white motherfuckas back right the fuck on off. But one dude actually
> said, "well, i want to be the first." and you know what, he was bullshitting me.
> Yeah, they do that shit too. we all be kind of bullshitting each other don't we.
> Anyway he didn't mean it. I don't think i ever saw that motherfucka again.

Many white audience members interpreted this last statement by Alexs
as proclaiming racial separatism. Even some of Alexs's white female friends
failed to notice that he says that he hasn't had a white *man* as a friend. But
Alexs—and I—knew this wasn't a statement of separatism. Indeed, taken in
the context of our dialogue, it's clear he's talking about something more or
other than skin color. After all, he states that when he first met me he saw a
"white man," despite my outward appearance as an Asian American. Somewhere in the process of our getting to know each other and in my own
transformations I changed enough so that he no longer saw a "white man."

The implication is that if I could make these changes and alter my own sense of identity, a friendship between us was possible and, further, that white men could also make these changes. But, as Alexs points out, white men don't want to make these changes. They don't want to give up their privileges. The burden of the failed friendships is not with Alexs, as those—including a local critic—who charged "racial separatism" maintained, but with whites who want to uphold the racial status quo.

At the end of our dialogue, Alexs talks about how our friendship has taught him both how to make connections beyond his own community and how there's a need, within race work, to heal on the inside rather than simply directing one's focus on the very real injustices in the society around us. So much of our discussions on race come out of the intellectual and extroverted and self-righteous sides of ourselves; we wanted to make a space for feeling, for introspection, for private conversation, for doubt and questioning and uncertainty. I'd like to feel that with our performance piece, which we titled *Secret Colors*, we were able to do a little of that.

Alexs has since said that one result of our friendship is that he began to realize that retiring some of his anger was better for him and for the people close to him. Part of the reason for this was that I developed anger; the development of my anger allowed him to give some of it to me or to let some of his go, because there were now two people fighting on the same issue. He could thus feel more comfortable and relaxed; he could sit back and watch me fight for a while. "And you're a much better fighter in some ways because you're coming from the left side," he added. "Like a southpaw. They're looking at me and you can coldcock 'em."

Conversely, when I am in Alexs's presence I don't feel like the irrational angry Asian American who is too difficult to consider hiring for a faculty position or inviting to a writer's conference. I'm simply myself, accepted for who I am. Safe, calm.

What I hope both African Americans and Asian Americans come away with after viewing our work is the possibilities of coalition—of how much stronger we can be if we can find ways of communicating and working together.

Secret Colors was not the end of my collaboration with Alexs. A few years later we were in New York making a film, *Slowly, This,* which started out focusing on our performance piece and eventually came to focus more on *coalition on* *an individual* *level* our friendship and the conversations between us (the film aired as part of the PBS series *Alive TV*). Each day Alexs and I would travel from our hotel to the apartment of our director, Arthur Jaffa, and discuss what we were going to do in the film. Inevitably our conversations centered not just on race but on the differences and similarities in our perspectives.

For instance, on one particular afternoon Alexs mentioned how earlier in the day he and I were trying to hail a cab outside our hotel. No cab came by for a few minutes.

"So you said, 'Let's go up the street and get a cab,'" Alexs said, looking at me. "And it's like, Well, okay. But I stand here. Because if I'm in front of a hotel, I'm gonna get a cab. Right then, I was feeling like an outlaw. And you know, I've dressed but you start to say, Fuck it. I don't give a shit. Yes, I'll look just like that brother over there who is going to take you down. And it's your job to figure out that I'm not a outlaw and he might be."

I pointed out that that's something I've had to learn about and keep on learning. I recalled the time I was in a bar with Alexs and three other black artists—a director, a performance artist, and a writer—and all of them were talking and joking about being picked up by the police, most often because of DWB—driving while black. These were all college-educated, award-winning artists, one of whom had written for the *Cosby Show*, and yet they spoke of their experiences with the police as something they expected, as almost a rite of passage. And they joked about these experiences.

That, I said, is something as a middle-class Asian American man I've never had to go through.

"You suffered suburban alienation," said Alexs, "being the odd person out in your school. But you didn't suffer the way I suffered. Which is what black . . ."

A. J., our director, spoke up: "I think we as black people often are saying that we want to take the victimization . . ."

I interrupted him: "But you know, my transition has led me to a point that when a black person says something like that, I don't go, 'Yes, but . . .'"

Alexs murmured "right" and nodded. I went on.

"And then the conversation can go on. It's when you go, 'Yes, but . . .' that you get into an argument. When a person does that, that 'Yes, but . . .' it's part of their resistance to really seeing what life is like for black people in this country. All the while they think they're being rational or intellectually precise, and they do not see it as part of their denial. And they do not see that's the point at which the conversation shuts down, precisely because their remark says, 'I'm not really interested in listening to you, I'm not willing to entertain as a real possibility my own ignorance and blindness; in the end there's nothing you can say to me I haven't considered.'"

"In order for the conversation to flow onward, all you have to do is just go, 'yeah.' And it's so hard for people to do that, that right there—that 'yes, but . . .'—is the wall that a lot of white people can't get over. They think, 'Oh, I'm really on your side, I'm just making this intellectual quibble'—when in fact it's really this huge denial of your experience as a black person."

During this conversation I asked Alexs if in our friendship and in our working together it made a difference that I was Asian American and not black or white.

"You couldn't be white," Alexs replied, "because I wouldn't be this close to you if you were white. It makes a difference because you're still engaged in a struggle. If you were black and doing this, I don't think it would be all that more significant. I think finding anyone who is at once an oppositional force and who is trying to be healthy and who is trying also to tell the truth, that's a pretty powerful potent mixture that you don't see much of. The key accent is on the word "healthy." It's about me also learning to trust, to trust someone who's not black.

"Again, it's about realizing that part of the shame and part of the struggle of black people is our inability to empathize and our inability to understand other people's struggles . . . Now black people naturally have that quality to empathize and understand, but it is always snuffed by the conditions of our society. So for me to make that step across that line and for you to be willing and appropriately matched—in a way that we can actually do this—that's why I keep saying, to me that's drama. We don't need to go very far to find it. It's right there. Because we both represent people who are nationalistic in their hearts, and who both believe they're better.

"You see I think black people believe they're better than everyone else, just like the Japanese do. We are the saviors, that's what black people say in the hood. We will save white people. We are their humanity. And it could be true, but the way things are now, we can never do that, because we are either fighting ourselves or fighting them or being too angry to lead, and then when we are confronted with people who are struggling, who are trying to find their own identity, we don't know how to make connections with them, and we end up hating them. We wind up looking at them as different from us—even though it's the same thing.

"But it's easier for us to connect, you and I. We live in a more abstract world. You don't own a grocery store, and I don't live down the block in the neighborhood. I'm not going to your house and place of business and constantly feeling, why isn't this mine, why aren't I giving my money to a black person . . ."

I pointed out that Alexs could feel that way because of my literary successes or because my parents lived in an upper-middle-class neighborhood and I grew up in a white suburb.

"That's true," Alexs said. "However, metaphorically, it is about my journey, not about yours. And for you, it's about your journey, and not about mine. It's about developing levels of support and a relationship. You see, metaphorically, if black people spent more time dealing with themselves, dealing with their shame and pain, then we'd be in a different place. And the fact that there are other people of color who may have a better time in the society doesn't necessarily mean that they are your enemy or that you can't empathize with them. That coalition and relationship is one way to subvert a system that is naturally and systematically aligned against you. The only way to work against that systemic aberration turning everything against you is to make a coalition with others in the process."

I pointed out that you have to work at the process, you can't look at it as static: "You can't say, 'They are there, and I'm here, and neither of us is ever going to move.' Of course each of us may be who we are today because of the ways society has formed and affected us. But we all have a choice—and that other person also has a choice—to move. You have to recognize that . . ."

"And you have to see your stake in motivating choice," said Alexs. "You have to see that movement, that coalition, as part of having a stake in your own survival. . . ."

I finished his sentence: "That it's in your own self-interest to help that person move, for both of you to move."

That movement—across the lines of color, across the lines of identity, across the barriers within and without—is what our collaborative work, our *Secret Colors*, is all about. It's work we continue to do, through the performances and talks we give together, through our writings, and through our friendship—a friendship whose possibilities America has yet to recognize but must and will.

SECRET COLORS

A performance piece by David Mura and Alexs Pate

This performance piece was created in January 1994 by David Mura and Alexs Pate in colloboration with the musician-composer Douglass Ewart, the video artist Me-K Ando, the animator Alison Morse, the set designer Tom Rose, and the director Ralph Remington. Mura and Pate perform the piece, and each wrote the sections in which they speak.

[Start with video I—Segregation/Camps. David plays piano at end of video; lights up on Alexs]

1 THE OUTLAW HAD A FATHER—Alexs

my father drove a truck
was not an outlaw
believed he belonged
but didn't know where
carved his comfort
into the couch in the living room
from there he suffered the
silent struggle of that
invisible army of men who
always tried to do right
he wanted to do right
he was responsible
a hard, cracked hand worker
who died for me
so that i may speak what
he never did
and he never did
not to me
never once did he
curse you or
anyone
never one was it against
he never complained
about Jews or niggers or
japs or anybody
and he loved my mother
as if she had been made

of rice paper
but when a black face
appeared on ed sullivan
or scored a touchdown
he would make sure we all
stopped what we were doing "gwen, he'd say, come in here
and see this. there's a colored man
on lawrence welk"
and this was how i learned
to love black people
this and the dunbar and hughes
my mother plied me with
and from my father's slow love
a love hardly spoken
was how i learned of
tragedy
how he could die so
unmeasured, so unknown
there are no black men who are
heroes if my father
isn't
and if there are no heroes
it isn't so bad
being an outlaw

[Live piano fades to music cassette 1—On the Midwestern Front]

2 LONG KONG RADIO (I)—David

[On the Midwestern Front fades when David is set up as D.J.; lights up on David]

Long: [Whispers.] You out there? Are you listening? You with me, love?
[Screams.] Well, welcome to KONG—Kong radio. K-O-N-G.
As in Hong Kong or Viet Cong or King Kong or Long Kong.
That's me, Long Kong, and I've got it for you. And for you and for you.
Tonight I'm as Long as Long Duc Dong or Long John Silver
or our own Supreme Court Justice, Mr. Oreo, Clarence Thomas.
[Southern accent] Oh, I ain't, I ain't, I ain't gonna play the coolie no more.
[Asian accent] Honey, I'm the new Jason Scott Rhee, I'm your rice paddy
lover.
Okay, okay, okay, this is Uncle Kong, without his bong,

holding on to his schlong,

waiting for the Gong. I said waiting for the Gong—[Gong]

Thank you Marvin. What do you expect with a white engineer?

He can't tell time, can't work the dial, it's all made by Orientals.

I'll get you a Seiko for Christmas, Marvin.

Maybe then you can be on time.

Well, well, well,

it's the witching hour, just turned twelve,

and in the deep blue of midnight,

when the censors are out of sight,

when I'm feeling hot and tight,

and everything's all right,

I'm ready to roll,

and I don't mean egg roll, baby,

I mean, to get down, go down, rock and roll

lose control, do the bump and grind, the nasty, nasty,

so let me blast you with my love juice,

and my instruments of Oriental delight,

all through the night.

In other words, I get to the talk about sex,

dirty sex, clean sex, hexed sex, Tex Mex sex, and my favorite of all,

Gook to gook sex, something you don't see enough of these days,

if you ask Uncle Kong.

Anyway, you know I was thinking the other day

about how, despite all the Kung Fu fooey and the chop sockey movies,

despite all the screaming yellow monkeys storming G.I.'s out in the Pacific

or the jungles of Vietnam,

Asians are not frightening.

Oh, we can be funny. All you have to do is speak with an Asian accent.—

Ask not what your countly can do for you, ask what you can do—somewhere
    over the lainbow,

Jordan dlives into rane, fakes light, fakes reft, dlibberus behind his back,

reaps, and it's a fingerloll, what a pray, what a pray, what a pray—

But can we be frightening?

I mean think about an Asian you know having sex—Mao, Charlie Chan, Mrs.
    Rivingston—

you remember her—But Mista Eddie's father, Eddie's sheets have funny stain
    on them—

I mean, take any Asian, Pat Morita, Tojo, Bruce Lee, Tina Carerre,
and try to imagine them having sex? Is it frightening? No, it's funny.
It's a simple equation: Whites—Frightening. Asians—Funny.
Okay, Tina Carerre, it's something else.
But Tojo or Ho or Mao slipping in the old egg roll?
Hilarious.
But take a white person like that. I mean, imagine Margaret Thatcher having
    an orgasm?
As Count Dracula would say, Oooh, that's scary kids.
Or imagine Ross Perot coming toward you with an erection.
I mean I would rather face a hoard of wild dogs or swim in the Hudson
or become Manuel Noriega's dermatologist
than have to watch Dan Quayle and Marilyn doing it doggy style.
It's like the advertisement for the Fly. Be afraid. Be very afraid.
Of course, if we begin to stray from heterosexual displays,
well, who knows how to read that? Sab Shimono and James Shigeta?
Joan Chen and Nancy Kwan? The Golden Girls as dykes? Howard Cosell and
    Tony Randall?
Okay, the last one's still scary. Of course, not as scary as homosexuality
in the Asian American community, is it? So scary it doesn't exist.
Of course, I could be gay as the Frisco Bay, couldn't I? You wouldn't know.
This is radio, you can't even see me, I could be playing the Crying Game on
    you, and you, and you.
Cause I'm the shaman without shame, shapeshiftin's my game, and Kong is
    my name,
so don't go running baby, just keep guessing maybe, and anyway, I see
it's time for the quarter after news of color update—Ahem!
"Women and people of color compose 65 percent of the work force, white
    males 35 percent.
White males, though, hold 95 percent of the top management jobs.
Ow! Ow! Ow! Ow!—What's that?
Oh I just keep smacking my head against the glass ceiling.
O, do I detect a conspiracy here? Oh say it ain't so, Toto. Say it ain't so.
Oh, I do believe in America. I do believe in America. I do believe in
    America . . .
What Marvin? The decision was what? What? Oh man. Oh man."

[Cassette 2—In Los Angeles; followed by Cassette 3—Ice Cube.
Videotape II—Allison video of Rodney King]

3 BLUES FOR RODNEY KING

and forgive us how we show our love (for rodney king)
—David and Alexs

they kicked his ass good
hauled him out of his car
stunned his inhuman mass
juiced him, lit him up
like a black light in a room
full of marijuana smoke
and they danced their batons
all over his body
an' every time he flinched
he gained more control
he willed them forth
My head hurts.
It's filled with sirens and red flashes. Gashes. Slashes. Ashes.
My head burns. Flakes settle on my eyelids. Eye lash. And lash. And lash.
[Look at back of hands.] What's this stuff? Skin? The most important thing in
   your life.
It keeps the outside out. The inside in. It tells you where the world ends and you
   begin.
Whether the air is cool or hot. Whether you're clothed or not.
It's not like a jacket you can take off. It's not the wrong size. And if it is you can't
   return it.
My skull lies inside my skin. My skull is a muzzle. I nuzzle. I sin. [Move to Alexs]
Who wants a share of this skin? To stroke, to rub, to lick, to suck?
Who's got the prize? Whose eyes? Whose halcyon days do we walk besides?
"swing harder"
he must have pleaded
"put more into it
you can do better than that
what are you anyway?
some weak-kneed lackey?
some underpaid soldier?"
where is your outrage/
they will want my blood
don't hold back
i can take it
i am not a man like you

i am wild, unspecified, a demon
and you can prove that
with your kindness
and your just love
which expresses itself
sweetly in the muted thuds
which leave the marks of passion on my skin
[From prone position.] *I felt a butterfly land on my skin. I slapped it and slapped it.*
Whacked and whacked it. It fluttered. Rose.
Huge, immense. It glowed. Rising like an apparition out of my skin.
Huge wings. Beady eyes. Or was it huge claws. Or paws. A face like an ape. King Kong.
Yes, that's it, it was King Kong. And I was beating him. And I thought he was dead.
But he kept on rising. I jolted him
with 5,000 volts. He slumped. He rose. I kept on beating him.
I was itching in my skin. My skin was damp from sweat. My muscles ached.
I leapt in. It was wonderful. It felt like sex. Like sin. I had to have it.
he must have wooed them in this way
made them powerless to his will

pleasure to his ruby whispers which beckoned
in war for they gave in
and embraced him
Shit, it was only a butterfly. Only an ape. Only a man. I was just doing a job, doing
a job.
So sue me, sue me. I've got the power, I've got the hour. [Get up, stand still.]
Stop speeding on me, stop getting to your knees, stop bleeding my dreams with your
buzzin bees.
The cities on fire, and you've got these tires. Light 'em with gas and have a blast.
Burn it to ash.
I've got the burn it baby, blues. The fire next time in Baldwin's line. Over the line.
Gotta get mine.
We're doing time, things ain't fine. Here, it comes. Here it comes, here it comes. The
end,
the end of this rhyme.

[Allison video ends; music fades. Video 3—Sun Ja Du]

4 MONOLOGUE: MY MOTHER AND THE L.A. RIOTS—David

I'm sitting in this Japanese restaurant with my parents, in Chicago,
and instead of talking about shopping or golf or tennis,
my mother for once is talking about something serious:

She can't understand why there's people in L.A. tearing things down.
Now you must understand, as much as I am intellectual, a writer, an artist,
as much as I have all the politically correct far left wacko socialist leanings—
I really don't—repeat really don't—want to talk about this with my mother.
Because I know what will happen: I will talk, I will explain things,
and then, she'll repeat her question as if she hasn't heard a word:
[Turn to right] "Why did they burn down their own neighborhood? David,
they don't have any grocery stores now, they can't buy food nearby.
I know you say they're angry. But what good does that do?
And look at those men who pulled the white truck driver from his truck and
    threw bricks at him?
Isn't that the same thing as Rodney King?"
And I begin to explain again, and again she interrupts, and so I ask,
[Look at her] "Do you really want to know my answer, Ma, or is this a rhetorical
    question?"
only I try to phrase it so bitterly ironical,
because I don't, repeat, I don't want to get into it with my mother.
I mean really, I should just shut up and eat my dinner, which my father, of
    course, is paying for.
[Stand up] And so I just gave up. [Start up Video 4—Rodney King]
Now I know, I know. I could have told her two black men and two black
    women
who drove down to Compton and saved that white truck driver.
Or I could have told about Sun Ja Du and Latasha Harlins,
how the judge's sentence said to the black community—Fuck you.
A black life ain't worth shit. We've got to protect the Koreans and their
    property.
(Course, once the riots went down, you know where the police made their
    stand? Not at the Korean
stores. No way. The cops were down at the malls of Alexander Haagan, a white
    political patron.)
[Back to table] Or I could have said to her: Mom, do you think only black people
    riot?
Do you think Japanese Americans don't do things like that?
But what about the riots at Heart Mountain, Ma? What about Tule Lake?
What about the time two thousand Japanese Americans went on a rampage in
    Manzanar,
wanted to tear the whole place down, and the guards opened up at them with
    machine guns,

killed this Issei man. That man, he was just Rodney King.

And the good Japanese Americans?

They were burning down their prison, they had nowhere else to go either.

And that's what happened in L.A., Mom. That's what happens when you keep people in cages.

Only you don't see it. Just like you didn't see how miserable I was all through high school,

how depressed, how I hated myself, how I hated being Japanese American,

how I hated *feeling* this pressure all the time to get A's and be a good model citizen,

and all the time inside I felt like a gook, a fucking gook, Ma,

and you don't want to see it, you don't want to see anybody else's pain.

It's all that goddamn Nisei see no evil, speak no evil, hear no evil, let's be monkeys bullshit.

Ma, when are you going to wake up? When are you going to wake up? [Cut Video 4—Rodney King]

[Turn to audience.] Oh, sorry. I guess I'm straying a bit, aren't I?

Anyway, what does it matter? What does it matter? My mother doesn't know this.

And even if she did, she'd still vote Republican.

And every time a homey sees a Japanese woman driving by in her Lincoln or Prelude,

it won't mean jack shit that she's Jap not Korean.

All he'll see is someone who got theirs before him.

Someone living off his back. Who just came yesterday.

[Get up] And if one of those homeys sees me? Well, he'll think the same thing.

What the fuck does he care I'm telling you this story? [Look at Alexs. Blow out candle.]

[Lights up on Alexs; music cassette 2A—James Brown]

5 HISTORY—Alexs

naw, this is the point see, here we are, poor motherfuckin black folks. ain't got a goddamned thing. no square business, we ain't got shit. seems like we never had shit. and what shit we had somebody was always trying to take it from us.

back in the day, the jewish people owned the stores around here. some black folks too, but mostly they was jewish. i came up goin down to ben's to get bread and shit like that. didn't have to take no money neither. only had to sign in the book. ben knew my ass too. he'd see me comin in the door and he'd wave his hand at me, his big fuckin head would stretch wide when he smiled. i remember that motherfucka. just like yesterday.

see that's what i don't understand. i mean, what the fuck happened? one day ben was behind his counter smiling and adding up the numbers in the black and white composition book and the next day we was watching that store go up in flames. same kind of shit as now.

one day the jews was friends to black people, the next day we was runnin them out of our motherfuckin neighborhoods. everybody was saying shit like, yeah, now we can have our own shit. everybody was so tired of givin their money to the white man. so they said they was gonna own their own businesses in the inner city and shit. okay, that sounds hype and i thought, damn right. this is our motherfucking neighborhood. and since we never had shit no way, maybe this was the way we could get a piece of the action. damn right.

but shit, home, you know what happened. you know the story. drugs and crime. the malls, the 80s and all that me me me shit. buppies. black folks that got a little taste of the life out there never came the fuck back. no shit. something out there drags black folks out and they never come back.

if you got a friend or somebody in your family say, and they tell you they goin somewhere like to college or some shit like that, forget it. if you stand back here waiting for them, you be a stupid motherfucka because, shit, they ain't comin back.

then you look up and the stores in the hood got these koreans in them. damn. what the fuck happened. first there was one or two. then, suddenly everywhere you look there was stores owned by those people. how did that shit happen? that's what the fuck I want to know. they don't know shit about us. about our struggles.

you go in there and they act like you a goddamn criminal. following you all around the goddamn place.

then you get this crazy boy driving like a bat out of hell running from the man, pissin them off in the process, course just being black is enough to piss off the man you know,   .

anyway, so they're pissed and he's just driving,

and you know what happened then, they caught his black ass and whipped him like a mad hog. i know what i'm talking about too. when i was a boy i saw a bunch of men do the same thing to a hog that bust out of the hog pen. on my grandfather's farm they ate crazy animals like that.

that's what they did to rodney king. ate his ass alive. then they got the nerve to say that just because he was twitchin from those licks they was givin him, they got the nerve to say he was still fightin them. he wasn't fightin no more than that hog was. he was just still breathing. they ate his ass anyway.

and wouldn't you know that there would be some nosy ass white man with a television camera nearby. if that don't beat all. caught the whole fucking thing on tape.

when I saw that shit, i said, okay, so they got these motherfuckers dead to the rights. they shit was wide open, clear as day, those motherfuckas kicked hi ass.

so when the jury said not guilty, and shit, man, what the fuck does that mean? what does that say? we ain't never had shit, look like never gonna have shit and they don't even recognize that we ain't mad hogs. shit. who wouldn't be pissed off?

then you go to the fuckin store to get six pack and you look in the face of another sonofabitch who act like you got some kind of fuckin disease or something and you want to kick his ass. course you know it ain't right. it ain't right. but fuck it. shit. we never had shit no way. . . .

6 MY FATHER—David

There were times my father sat at the dinner table
and shouted he was going to take me out to the garage
and smack me with a two by four.
To his credit he never actually did this.
Which is not to say he never hit me.
But with his fist, only his fist.
I used to dream of hitting him back, only
I knew that was impossible, I'd
start hitting him
and then he would hit back, it would hurt, I'd become afraid
and I would stop
and he would keep hitting me
and I'd hurt even more,
I'd become even more afraid.
It was better just to take it. To not fight back.
After all he only did this on special occasions. Perhaps once, twice a year.
And I still keep wondering—Is it really that important?
Only when I got to therapy did my therapist ask:
Where was your mother?
My mother was in the Heart Mountain internment camp.
Which she never spoke about.
Which she claims she was too young to remember.
"You think too much of yourself, David," she used to say.
Did she mean I had a swelled head?
Or that I was too preoccupied with my sorrows?

The sorrows of young Mura?

It rhymes with the Sorrows of Young Werther.

Only, of course, I'm not Goethe.

I'm not some dead white fucking European male.

Even though all my life

I wanted to be one.

Did my father want me to be one?

"I never wanted you to have this chip on your shoulder," he says.

"To always be on the lookout for racism."

Jesus. Fuck this whining. Fuck this bitching and moaning.

Fuck it. Fuck it. Fuck it. What the fuck do I have to complain about?

After all, would I rather be black?

Still, there are times, I'm sitting on some committee for diversity,

or some board of an arts organization

or at some dinner party,

or talking with a white friend,

and they'll say something that makes me want to scream,

Fuck you. Fuck you. Fuck you. Fuck you.

Only I don't.

Because then they wouldn't let me on the committee,

they wouldn't let me on the board,

they wouldn't let me eat their dinner,

they wouldn't let me be their friend,

because if I

screamed, Fuck you. Fuck you. Fuck you, whitey!

Or even simply said, "That's just racist bullshit." Or "That's your racism
    talking."

they would strike back, they would say I hate them, say I'm filled with bile

full of resentment and scorn, I'm uncontrolled, radical, politically correct,

and I would stop hitting back,

and they would keep hitting me,

and I'd hurt even more,

I'd be even more afraid,

I'd be even more

alone. I'd be the shitty little victim I've always felt myself to be.

I get back at my father by writing about him in books.

By talking about him on stage.

He never talks about it.

It's a game of pretend we play. *No harm done. No foul.*

It's the way we maintain our relationship.

It's the way he puts the past in the past, so that nothing can change.

I simply couldn't bear it if our relationship changed. If we actually became
   intimate.

It would be too embarrassing.

I get back at white people by writing about them.

They pretend not to notice. Just another friendly game.

Where was my father?

He was in the Jerome Arkansas internment camp.

Why didn't the Nisei fight back?

They were afraid. Very afraid.

7 THE OUTLAW COMES TO KNOW HIMSELF—Alexs

[Music cassette 4—heartbeat]

have you ever
in an instant
been jolted by an intense fear?
have you been somewhere
maybe in your car
on the freeway
i94 maybe and been electrified
by an instant trembling of dread?
i have
and it has brought me here
actually i was on 94
mindless, speeding through
traffic eyes focused on the road just
ahead disappearing
under the hood of my car
and suddenly i was full of terror
sweating, shaking
suddenly i realized that i was not going
anywhere
i was fleeing
i was a fugitive
i was running from you
i understand you've been looking for me
and that haunted me
at first i didn't know why

and that haunted me too
but it finally came to me
on that day
in the car
i killed someone
murdered someone
in this life or the last
a conscious crime
or dream
but i did it
and now i understand why
i always freeze when
the doorbell rings
why i stare police in the eye
(a practiced deception)
why i reveal as little as possible
why i can't watch richard kimble
search for the one armed man
anymore
why
it just makes me mad
that he won't simply turn around
and tell those motherfuckas
"i did not kill my wife"
is there no justice?
but kimble knew there was no justice
and i think he was afraid he'd
confess
just like me
(kill a man)
i could confess to you right now
the bombing at the world trade center
all of the slain police
all the robberies
all the abductions
all the rapes
all the murders
i did it.
i mean i'm a black man

i am an outlaw
by law
i could have done it
when that policeman died
was shot
like a paper target
pinned on a bale of hay
my life became tenuous
less solid
more abstract
my picture rode in squad cars
and was distributed
from memory
everywhere
i was everywhere
and the police wanted
me for questioning
or because i knew someone
or because my jacket's blue
or because my brake lights
weren't working
or something
but they were looking for me
and you know i couldn't wait
until they found me
i knew they would
i would have gladly surrendered
just to relieve the pressure
i'm here now aren't i?
but i waited, often in darkness
at night [Video 5—Melvin Van Peebles]
as the mississippi mud
falls from my face
i have to still my shudders
remind myself that no one is
after
me no one wants me
and in the moon's black
i cower

try to remember what i've done
who i've hurt
to make them pursue me so
relentlessly
i am the murderer
i am the rapist
i must be
why else would i feel their sour
breath on my neck
but i am growing tired of the run
want my picture to instead be enshrined
celebrated
known for its brilliance and strength
so you might know the lines given to me by my mother
as they differ from those given to me by my father
but we are so far from that
i am the outlaw always
even to myself
i frighten myself
because i will help you
demonize me
like marion barry
or iron mike tyson
or michael jackson
or clarence thomas
i will take that toke
i will touch you
torture you
i will
because it doesn't matter
what i do
i am not luke perry
on the cover of Vanity Fair
with a gun in his sexy hand
posing
i am not the Duke teaching
boys the details of cowboy styling
the subtle relationship between
being white and being right

even if you are jesse james
people will march down
small town streets
high school band horns blowing a
canopy
over a celebration of murder and
robbery: jesse was the ultimate
outlaw and they celebrate him
but me i can't breathe wrong or
poof, i'm the demon
i'm just an extension of my lineage
nat turner, jack johnson, and richard pryor or just
that brother sittin over there:
outlaws
but not the celebration kind
nosirree, the hangin kind
oh yes, oh yes
i had to learn the distinctions
between outlaws
turner to be hung
bush to be president
tyson to be prisoner
stallone to be star
i had to learn to feel like an
outlaw
which is not done overnight

8 OUT OF WHITENESS (I)—David and Alexs

[Video 6—Rambo]

David: What was it like for me growing up in an all-white suburb?
Raised by parents who wished to escape the internment camps?
Well, I used to think it was a compliment when a white friend said to me,
"I think of you David just like a white person."
As for blacks, well, I was all for civil rights,
all for the black students at my college who took over the library, all for Martin
    Luther King Jr.,
but in the end, my thinking wasn't very different from most white liberals—
somehow blacks were vaguely other, a bit scary, angry;
somehow they made me feel—I don't know—guilty, self-conscious.

So, up until about six years ago, almost all of my friends were white.

And then, well, things began to change. I became someone I never expected myself to be—

"Oh Jesus, you mean I'm not white? What the fuck? Oh Jesus. My god. My god. Oh Jesus."

—Okay, it wasn't quite like that. I mean, I wasn't having an orgasm or anything.

It's more like my friend Garrett Hongo says, "For thirty some years, David thought he was white. Now he's become more Asian American than thou."

—How did my white friends react to my change?

"Oh Jesus, you mean you're not white? What the fuck? O Jesus. My god. My god. Oh Jesus."

Well, actually, it was a little more restrained. [Sit.]

Alexs: *david and i first met at this restaurant, Cafe Latte . . . i remember being conscious of trying to impress him. david was not an asian then. i saw a white man, i think his asian self was unformed.*

he was already an intellectual. i could tell that.

he was not like me

who had learned and forgotten everything i'd ever learned,

had lost my will to develop scholarly anything . . . wanted only to make my own ideas . . .

and he was into marx at the time. i could tell.

so much of him was still connected to his white strivings. yes the effort to be accepted to give yourself over to the oppressor's education, unabashedly and unapologetically scares me.

It created a distance between us I wasn't sure could be bridged.

[Video 7—Line Animation]

David: Do you see that? That line? You don't see it? You don't? Really?

To tell you the truth, I don't see it either. But I know it's there.

It's the line that separates us Asian Americans from other people of color.

The line that tells us we're special, we're not like them, we can make it, we don't get angry,

we got brains, culture, we're quiet, hardworking, good upstanding citizens—

[To Alexs] WE ARE NOT OUTLAWS. NOSIREE, WE ARE NOT OUTLAWS.

Of course, if you pass that line—or if they change that line, as they did for the Japanese Americans during World War II, well, who knows what can happen?

It's a funny thing about race. Everything thinks it's just about skin color.

But I had lots of white friends who loved me, and read my work and supported
   my work,
and the whole issue of race never came up. Never came up.
They probably thought they could look at me and not even think about color.
Of course, I didn't want them to think about color either.
And then, then came Miss Saigon, and the whole controversy about casting a
   white guy,
Jonathan Pryce, as a Eurasian. And when I found out all the Asian American
   actors in New York
were protesting this, I found myself saying,
"I'm sick and tired of white guys playing Asians,
of Peter Sellers and Warner Oland as Charlie Chan.
You can't do it with blacks anymore, but you can still do it with Asians."
Only, only, my best friend, Mark, who was white, didn't agree.
"David, isn't color-blind casting what we're striving for?
Isn't art trying to get into other people's skin? Isn't that what we have
   imagination for?"
"Mark, Why is it everyone gets so upset when a white actor may be denied a
   role?"
"What about every time an Asian American actor
tries out for a part that says 'lawyer' or 'doctor' and is turned down
or doesn't even get to try out for the part?"
[Folded arms] "But David, reverse discrimination isn't the answer."
And then I could hear this whisper, from my friend, from my past, from all my
   education—"Quality, excellence, quality, excellence, the best and the
   brightest always make it to the top"—which meant, there were no Asian
   Americans who could cut it.
And the more I thought about that, the more pissed I got.
That old gook in whiteface routine—that's not art, that's not imagination,
   that's not democracy,
man, that's humiliating, fucking humiliating.

Alexs: *David is moving closer to his community.*
i think i am moving farther away from mine
but i came from the bowels of a culture
so thick with beauty and pain and power
that only government-paid white people
have the privilege of even passing
through it, a place where you
could go miles, pass hundreds of people

on the streets and never see a white face
he is still learning
his struggle involves creating distance between him and white
people
and i'm trying to stretch out
i feel like i've been where he's going

David: After months and months of arguing with my best friend Mark,
over race, over whiteness, over Miss Saigon, I finally said—
"I need to know that you see I know more about race than you,
that we don't start here on an equal ground."
—He couldn't accept that. And that, that was the end of our friendship.
A little later, I write an article about losing white friends. In *Mother Jones*.
And I describe my breakup with my white friend Mark,
and a lot of his friends—whom I thought were my friends—are really pissed,
and they start wondering if I've become a separatist, if I can't have white
     friends any longer,
and they accuse me of violating Mark's *privacy, of grandiosity and pettiness,*
and I began feeling crazy, and paranoid, and I wonder if they're right,
Did I betray them? How? Why? Why *was I* throwing away a friendship of ten
     years?
I mean, *what the fuck happened here?*
All I wanted was for my best friend to understand why I hated Miss Saigon.
What did I do wrong? Was my mother right, Do I really think too much of
     myself?
Have I suddenly acquired that chip on my shoulder my father didn't want me
     to possess?
I've got it, don't I? That chip? That too-eager readiness to take offense?
And shouldn't I be at least a bit more ironical here [wave a finger]
about this sob story of crossing the color line? All this hand wringing? [act out]
I mean, I can imagine other people of color going, well, welcome to the club
     asshole.
Where have you been? What you got to complain about? Some of us never,
     ever get to be
honorary whiteboys. [Video 8—Best Friend Clip—again, again] Besides, as
     everyone knows from my *Portrait* interview—
—When my wife saw that, she said, "Did you have to look so guilty?"
—Anyway, the only people I felt comfortable talking to about all this
were people of color. Like this black writer I knew, Alexs Pate.
I feel like I'm going crazy Alexs. [Look at audience as if Alexs]

I mean, it's not like I'm having this conversation just with Mark.
Everyone finds out Mark and I are having this fight,
and then one of my other white friends asks me what it's all about,
and when I tell that friend, and he or she doesn't get it,
I end up fighting with them,
and even if they do get it, even if they agree with me on Miss Saigon,
they can't see why Mark and I can't be friends any longer,
they think it's all about personality,
and then I begin thinking I can't be friends with them either.
I mean each of them only has to have this argument with me,
and I've got to have the argument with almost every single white friend I've
    got.

*constant
racial just.*

Alexs: *it was easy to open myself to him*
perhaps not at the beginning
but from the moment david showed himself to me
his self-confidence wavering
his knowledge of self in question
and asked how i dealt with the effects of racism
how could I know how to respond
i had met too many young asian students
in high schools through the midwest who were
clearly confused by the difference between
what they were told about race
and what they felt
there was a young woman in long prairie
who told me that she was traumatized by
the upcoming prom because she was sure
the boy who asked her just wanted to go with her
because she was exotic
no one around her seemed to understand
but i did, the outlaw understood
we must find a way
those of us who feel marginal
to love each other
not some bullshit we are the world singalong
but really come to see the way
we are taught to hate who we are

[Look at Alexs]

David: But Alexs, what I wanted to know was something else.

That it wasn't my fault.

That it wasn't my fault I was losing all my white friends.

God, it seemed as if you could be on more cordial terms with them than me.

I was becoming the angry man of color, not you.

So where did that leave me?

I didn't know you that well, I didn't know how good friends we were,

and if you ended up thinking I was an asshole

or that my troubles with my white friends were because of my personality

and not race [Stand, look at audience]

then what the fuck was I doing?

Alexs: *In my book, a friend, real friendship, overrides nearly everything. A person can't be your friend unless they know and accept who you are.*

you know the way black people bullshit. we say shit all the time that we don't mean. seriously. we're trained to be that way. i mean really, nearly every black person i know who has a job or who belongs to some kind of organization or something has been over to some white person's house for dinner or with them for drinks and thought, what the fuck am i doing here? "these people don't really want to know me." but we go anyway because we wouldn't get anywhere, no job promotions, no raises, grants, nothing if we couldn't every now and then, be sociable with white people. and when we're there we're liable to say anything. lie like a motherfucka. i know i've done it. we'll say shit that makes it sound like we're friends but really, you know, it's the old okey doke. it's bullshit. i was out of town once, up in bemidji minnesota, over this one dudes house for sunday brunch and he was trippin' over this golf match that was on tv. like what was i supposed to say. "Oh yeah, I guess I can see how this is exciting." that's bullshit. michael jordan and the bulls were on cbs. what the fuck are you doing? there's basketball on. but i stayed and ate their food and made small talk as we watched white men play golf. cool. i liked the guy well enough. but friends?

friends. i've come to believe that it takes a special kind of white man to be my friend. haven't met one yet. i'm talking about a motherfucka who is willing to let all his privilege shit go. because i can't deal with that. i don't want to be in a relationship where i have to prove shit about me. i just am.

I am always surprised when I hear a black man talk about his friend so and so who is white. I immediately wonder about the nature of that relationship. i can't help it. how does a black man born in these united states learn to love a white man? how is this possible? i'm not talking about that 'gettin' over' bullshit. but really? every time i start feeling buddy buddy with a white guy i find myself saying to him, "you know. I've never had a white man as a friend. I don't think it's possible for me right now. I'm too goddamned angry."

Most white motherfuckas back right the fuck on off. But one dude actually said, "well, i want to be the first." and you know what, he was bullshitting me. Yeah, they do that shit too. we all be kind of bullshitting each other don't we. Anyway he didn't mean it. I don't think i ever saw that motherfucka again.

David: BUT ALEXS, [Turn to audience] what I wanted to know was something else.

Intermission

19 OUT OF WHITENESS (II)—David and Alexs

[No Music]

[David sits] **David:** I remember this dinner Alexs and I had together at Chez Bananas. I was going over and over the end of my friendship with Mark and my white friends,
and I suddenly realized Alexs understood more about what I was going through than Susie.
I think that was when I thought we might become friends.
And it wasn't just the advice he was giving me.
I suddenly understood that what I had seen as this barely controlled anger in him
was actually restraint, a great human effort of self-control and spiritual survival and grace,
And I saw that given his life and the life of African Americans,
the fact that he wasn't going around putting a gun to white people's heads
was in itself a minor miracle.
That the way I'd been looking at him, my surprise at how psychologically astute he was,
well, it was simply racist. I'd been looking at him through racist eyes.
I'd been looking at all blacks with racist eyes. And if I was doing that,
and I'm a person of color, well, everything I'd ever believed about race had to change.

Alexs: *That's when you became an outlaw. That was when you had to let go of the people who stood between you and yourself.*

David: [Move toward Alexs] But how can I be an outlaw? I'm an Asian American, I studied hard in school, I haven't been in jail—well, once for an unpaid parking fine. I mean, some part of me's still going, I'm respectable, aren't I? Aren't I? Aren't I?

Alexs: *It's too late, man. It's already happened. I've heard the whispers. You've already crossed the line. You've betrayed them. Nothing angers white men more than betrayal.*

David: Yeah, maybe I'm no longer the sexless Charlie Chan eunuch. Now I'm the devious sex-crazed Fu Manchu. Or some brand-new stereotype, like the gook who wouldn't shut up. [A beat.] Or maybe they think I'm just your sidekick.

Alexs: *but you know it's not like that. i think watching you deal with your white friends, and the fact you didn't deceive them, and you discovered your need to express your identity as some sort of whole thing is something that i never valued for myself, it seemed way too painful to hold any value for me, you see, for me it's been about crash and burn, that's the only way i know black men to be, anybody that was like that was buying into the system, but as time passes i'm beginning to see some value in that, an integrated peace.*

David: So you actually learned something from me?

Alexs: *Yeah, I guess I have.*

Kalamu ya Salaam

We Don't Stand a Chinaman's Chance Unless We Create a Revolution: There's a New World Coming

To Fred Ho and all others in the world who are not afraid of the future

Chance, like the lottery, is dependent on the universe
What the conditions of the competition are
How many of us competing and whose pullin the numbers
Look at the world, my people, where we draw our borders
Determines who we are, defines our social status as a people
If we stop at the Atlantic & Pacific
We could just dumbly call all ourselves Americans
If we start at Canada
Then for certain we are deep in the South,
Down below the real Mason-Dixon line
If we start at Mexico & work our way north
Then most of us are just
Non-Spanish speaking, dark-skinned gringos
But if we go back into ourselves, into our souls
Our history and the reality of our befores
Then there is something greater than geography
That defines us

I am a political creature
Praxis, ideology put into practice
Defines a major part of me
I am also an individual particle of my people
My roots, blood and genealogy
Defines another part of me
But more than politics and biology combined
I am a human being, a creature defined
By the character and quality of my social
Relationships
Who I am, is very much
The way I relate to people, both my race & others
Is whether I lie about my realities
Or struggle to tell the truth
Is whether I want to get over by bullshiting
Or want to develop by facing & changing my reality
So what is a lie versus
What is the truth?
A lie is when we knowingly say the opposite of what
We are, were and strive to become
The truth is simply what is
Our problem is not just telling lies
But also being able to recognize lies
We've been lied to for so long
Believed lies for so long in the past that
Today we don't know the truth
How can we honestly know who we are
If we don't truthfully know who we were
Truth looks strange to us, sounds
Weird, even corny or square, is a foreign language
Certainly painful and discomforting, the truth is
A hard lesson to swallow when we've been
Filled up with lies, our bowels blocked by
Government cheese & our arteries hardened
By imbibing consumer prescribed drugs
You don't know it
But you don't really know anything

If all you know is what you have been
Taught in school combined with the limited
Education you get from media distortions of world
Realities
If you think dope in our lives is bad now,
That crack houses exemplify moral decay,
That we need to get back to the past
Then what do you think of opium dens
And native Americans besotted by alcohol
Chemical warfare
Is nothing new, especially in this nation of junkies
Where the twin drugs of tobacco & alcohol rule the roost
Consider this a gentle wake up call:
We don't stand a chinaman's chance
Of creating a better & more beautiful future
If we don't make a revolution
You don't stand a chinaman's chance
Is what people used to say to define hopelessness
You don't stand a chinaman's chance
Used to be a definition of a loser
But after Mao & crew did their do
A chinaman's chance got so good
That nobody played that number anymore
Regardless of the problems and perplexities
Of China's current state at least they got a chance,
A future & the whole world recognizes that
What about us, my people
Do we stand a chinaman's chance,
We, the underdogs in a horse race
The ice cubes trying to stand the heat of hell
The fifth wheel on a tricycle
Buying bus tickets to cross the ocean
Worshippers without a god
We who can't stand to reign
Will continue to suffer a million to one
Odds of redemption
Unless we create

A revolution
Plant the seed, raise the tree
Dig, we made America into a democracy
Now we must re-create this whole country
Into a multicultural community where all peoples
Can live & be their natural selves
Can live their traditions & carve out a future
Can call on their ancestors & give birth to healthy children
Can learn what they don't know & teach everything they do
Can honor the earth & respect the sacredness
Of all living beings
There will be no bright future for us
Unless we create & seize control of our lives
Consume no more than we produce &
Produce all we need to consume
Unless we define progress in terms
Of the quality of relationships &
Measure wealth by the status of the poor
No future until we consciously empower women &
Proudly display a healthy respect for diversity
No tomorrows unless we shut down
The hegemony of cave culture & reinstitute social circles,
Bring back the vision of the tepee, the hut &
Other architectural & social structures that avoid
The dominance of the box & straight line
Nothing will grow unless we merge
With the other rather than thinking separate is equal
We can only greet the dawn with smiles
By doing for self & sharing with all
By building marketplaces at the crossroads
Rather than forts on the frontiers
By learning the literature of the world
Rather than imposing a canon of monoculture
A true revolution
Motivated by the force of love
Sustained by the generosity of spirit
Is ultimately victorious not because it conquers

But rather because it endures
Outlasts exploitation & overcomes oppression
A revolution, a revolution
A revolution of the human
Body & soul, mind & consciousness,
A decisive change, after which
Nothing can ever be the same
Change is the external truth
Everything that exists becomes
Something other than what it now is
Some people think that ugly gon last forever
That whites will always rise to the top &
Revolution is impossible, i.e., that is the
Flat earth school of foolish thought
Those same people think
We don't stand a chinaman's chance
To create a revolution—you wanna bet
Whether through evolution or
Revolution, things have got to change
We, like all humans, will evolve or die
Regardless of what we think & do
We will either renew ourselves or
Become extinct
There is a new world coming
There will be a revolution
In our lifetime
The only question is where we gon' be standing
What we gon' be doing
Who we gon' be loving
When it comes!

Lisa Yun

El Chino

El Chino!
You dance alone in a maelstrom of well-heeled couples,
the tango, danzón, salsa, merengue, mambo, cúmbia,
chachacha, guaracha on a midsummer night at Lincoln
    Center Plaza.
The singer shouts and you raise your hands:

    el mundo se va a acabar
    el mundo se va a acabar
    aprovéche y pónte a guarachar

Dance, old man, dance!
Your chest shines with the sweat
of memory, running rivers down your brown skin
down your moving waist and swiveling hips
down the strength of your sex
still alive still alive you say it!
You dance the unpolished dance of the soil

of making love on leaves and
burning sugar fields:
chino man, your song is long, descendant
of proud men from farm lands
brought in chains to Cuba in 1847
to break bones on cane,
only to die
under the harsh gaze of a New World sun.
Your songs of rebellion, imprisonment, and suicide
cheated the Spaniard
who paid 500 pesos for a live chinaman
estimated life span—eight years.
Chino, know that your son
boarded a boat and crossed the Pacific
with the savings of a village
to find your bones and bring them back,
only to find nothing.
Unable to return, the son repeats the deaths
Of fathers, uncles, brothers,
distant and unremembered.
You, shouting Spanish and Chinese,
chanting the names—Lee, Lau, Liu, Yee, Yang, Chu, Chan, Wong, Fung!
Chino, you so old, so strange, we barely know you!
You, singing your *son* in a strange uptown place
of ballet, opera, symphony, and summer dancing,
disturbing the peace with
your story, shouting your name

    HOY REPRESENTO EL PASADO!

You are alive
the center of the world,
sweating oceans of the Atlantic and Pacific,
stomping your feet, jerking your hips,
lifting your face to the sky.
Tangled gray hairs escape your straw hat,
your faded shirt and raggy pants are
dignified, your mouth open, lined and defiant:

aprovéche y pónte a guarachar!

a proud ritual
under bright Lincoln Center lights
and a $10 ticket to dance in the plaza.
Sing Chino, Sing!
Of your ancestors long ago, packed on ships
coolie and slave, African, Chinese, Indian, brown-skinned pobres
to Cuba, Peru, Jamaica, Trinidad, Guyana, las Americas.
Your language labored under another tongue,
you cut cane under the overseer's eyes, and
loaded guano, bird-dropping fertilizer?
its poisonous fumes killed you within a year,
while men waited for loads in the harbor
dining under umbrellas
held aloft by silent boys.
Old man,
clench your hands and praise Chango and San-Fan-Con!
Let us remember the leaves and shells as they were,
let us remember how you chanted
run, run from the overseer
run, run from the overseer

ay húyanle, húyanle, húyanle al mayoral

how you worked the land in faith and despair
how you swept the leaves aside,
making love with Juanika in the sugar fields and in the sand
hearing the peasant music of criollos and drums of Africans,
how you carried the gold ring of your mother,
her last advice—carry your name:

el cariño que te tengo
yo no lo puedo negar

Dance, dance old man
at 63rd Street under the stars
Sing your *son*, sing your sex, sing your family name

EL CHINO

still alive still alive
Sing it!

Note

The italicized lyrics are from the Cuban *sons* and other music about dancing,
love, peasant *guajiro* life, folktales, and the plantation legacy. Songs include: "El
Mundo" by Johnny Almendra y Los Jovenes del Barrio from *Evolucionando,*
1996 (performed outdoors at Lincoln Center Plaza July 9, 1998); "Veinte
Años" by Maria Teresa Vera; "De Camino a La Vereda" by Ibrahim Ferrer; and
"Chan Chan" by Francisco Repilado (Compay Segundo) of *Buena Vista Social
Club,* 1997. References to midsummer Lincoln Center refer to the annual
outdoor summer festival of Latin dancing held at the center's plaza, where
people are admitted inside the velvet ropes if they pay the fee. Thousands cannot pay the fee but, nevertheless, exuberantly dance outside the main arena.
"You, singing your *son*" refers to two meanings, in Spanish and in English. In
Spanish, the term refers to the Cuban *son*, the popular dance music that arose
from nineteenth-century Afro-Cuban rhythms. The story of the son who jour-
neyed to Cuba to claim his father's bones is about my great-uncle. He searched
unsuccessfully for my great-great-grandfather's burial site in Cuba, which remains hidden to this day. The history of the poem is based on the saga of
the Chinese coolies and my great-great-grandfather from Guangdong, China.
They were abducted, tricked, and taken by force onto European and American
ships and sold in the Americas from the 1840s to the 1870s. In Cuba and Peru
a quarter million Chinese coolies were sold, with the majority dying within
eight years of arrival. Chango and San-Fan-Con refer to African and Chinese
gods, both gods of war and protection present in Cuban rituals today.

Ishle Park

Samchun in the Grocery Store

Last night, I slipped over ice and wet black snow
into the quiet mouth of a grocery on East 3rd and Ave. B.,
shocked by the pockmarked face of my uncle
behind the counter: *Aigu, Eesulah,* he said, with broad sweep
of arm, *take anything,* in this store that wasn't his.
Eyes scanning Entemanns crumb cakes, cereal boxes,
I wander a labyrinth of stacked aisles,
smell of orange yam meat roasting dark
and sweet at the sight of my samchun: dirty blue cap,
chipped front tooth, crescent moon eyes spilling light
over his rough beach of brown skin
This samchun, who taught me to crack warm walnuts
open with teeth; back cracked from hauling fish store crate
and fruit carton, spine held stiff with a thick leather safety
     belt,
My samchun, hands exploding knife into fist
telling my dad: if you ever hit her mother again

I chop off both your hands, like this
My samchun after 26 years just recently blessed
with a fat-cheeked granddaughter whose Yi family
earlobes turn up like little buttons
As I reminisce a customer enters, grabs a Hershey bar,
a Heineken, pack of Lucky Strike cigarettes,
asks how much is this? What? How much? Speak English!
1.19 . . . 1.19 . . . 1.19 dick, I hiss from behind the stack of potato chips
lemonade chills my palms as I watch a bruised mask
eclipse samchun's face as he swallows the spit insults,
the perennial chink, the speak-English bullshit,
clicked trigger and bullet: I imagine him falling,
snapped neck under cigarette shelves; I imagine him fallen,
crushed flower at the altar of jagged Korean
store windows after Sa-I-Gu, white picket signs,
white arm bands of 1992, Latasha Harlins,
Soon Ja Du, thick innocent blood
pooling on both sides of the counter . . .
Somewhere, La India streams out an open car window
and samchun rubs his temples. The customer slaps
silver change on the counter and leaves, solitude freezes
the bodega immobile on this corner trimmed with icicles and wet black
    snow.
Suddenly I know why my love is a clenched fist,
Why I can only love like this. Scent of burnt yams thicken the air,
Samchun bags my Countrytime lemonade, tells me to watch it.
We, in here, hug over the dividing counter, we hug as if our lives depend on
    it.

Maya Almachar Santos

Self-Rebolusyon, April 1998

Glass cases preserving aged elements from the
    contamination of human touch
We, the diseased are eliminated from our own attempt to
    control the evolution of time
The decreasing value of life in relation to duration of breath
Ironically, we return to the challenge of notoriety/an
    opportunity/a threshold
broken at an exponentially increasing rate
Alarming satisfaction for the greatest number/utopia
Equivalent to recognition of singular symbol of self
destruction
Survival destruction
Survival destruction
Self
Destruct
Moth eaten within my ribcage/a holy membrane/a
    vestibule in molecular opposites

A niche of balance and a social construct:
I leave, a heathen heals, brethren deals anotha deck,
sistren takes a step only to kneel once again
Down from the egotistical throne with humility transcend
The imperial manipulated evolution of time
Survival of self inter est
To put the phenomenal mind to rest in pieces
As we release this air between our lips
Which don't mean shit these days
The stars I gaze for something esoteric/searchin for anotha atmosyrical
    dimension
Like Coltrane's ascension easing tension not to mention reflection and
    action
Pedagogy of oppression word life be Friere's middle passage to liberation
Like love beyond mere relation you see, you gotta break it up in sections
Create your own rendition
With love, faith humility, and hope,
sons and daughters, can I get it on the one?

Ikalat mo na
Peace, pass it on

Ikalat mo na
Like Gil Scott-Heron, we gotta work for peace
Cuz peace ain't comin this way
The paradox of stray bullets aimed at our people and you mental if
    you pull it
The disparity of solidarity, the popularity of false charity, the rarity of
    sincerity and the cause
"our people . . . cannot hung around por you!!!"
stagnant static instability
walkin around in a daze as if more bounce will set us free
our pinay bodies!
Cuz you know we got ability and then some
To move the masses with agility like our rising sun
Rotatin 360 degrees flippin our flag to unknown seasons
Like our kindred spirits be the epitome of all reasons
To resist we must persist

Like my Lolo death march in the Bataan
His soul the definition of naasahan

Nayon saan ang rebolusyon?
An doon sa pera or sa sariling katawan?
Kung sabi niya, 'sino ka?'

Anak ng bayan
Sige' na, sige' na
Kalayaan
Kasi mamabuhay ang katipunan
Demokratikung Pilipino movement
Raise up yo fist and laban
Cuz this be the continuation
Our breath the duration
Like the incessant path to liberation
To escape existential situations
Bob Marley called it "redemption song"
Kinda like, "ang bayan kong pilipinas,"
I press pause and ask the annihilating question,
"what happened to our world war II veterans?"
survival destruction
survival destruction
survival destruction
self
rebolusyon

Nayon saan ang rebolusyon?
An doon sa pera or sa sariling katawan?
Kung sabi niya, 'sino ka?'

Anak ng bayan
Sige' na, sige' na
Kalayaan
Kasi mamabuhay ang katipunan
Demokratikung Pilipino movement

Now, where is the revolution
Is it in the money or in your own body?

If they ask you, "who are you?"
Child of the people
Lets go, lets go
freedom
because the atipunan
Demokratikung pilipino movement
Will live on.

*translations in tagalog:
Ikalat mo na:* pass it around now
naasahan: trustworthy
laban: fight
ang bayan kong Pilipinas: my country/people the Philippines.
rebolusyon: revolution

JoYin C Shih

Chyna and Me

Mr. Zeigler, my third grade teacher, had just ordered me to stand in front of the class along with Lillian. I stumbled up the aisle toward the front of the room, exposed and framed by the green chalkboard. Turning on my heel, I faced the rest of the class, all thirty-eight kids sitting in their rows, shades of skin varied like a box of mixed white to dark chocolates.

"Go on," Mr. Z encouraged, "Talk in your language so that the rest of the class can hear a bit of culture." I stared at his sincere request, trying to pick out meanness akin to the all-too-familiar peer taunting "Chinese, Japanese, Dirty knees . . ." but there was none. The Ziggy doll that Mr. Z. kept on his desk smiled its dumb "I'm a nice guy, you gotta love me . . . or at least feel sorry for me" smile, as I bit my lip, wanting to be a good student, and Lillian, who was a good student, hung her head. Our similar long, black hair hung at our faces like limp curtains pulled back for a sorry show. I heard Lillian's breath heave in and stutter up into a high-pitched sob. *Oh no you don't,* I remember thinking, *don't you dare cry, you little ninny.* But, of course, the breathing quickened into juts of snot and tears and I fixed my gaze on our elder accusingly. "Mr. Ziegler," I was ashamed at the waver in my own voice, "Lillian is Korean and I'm Chinese . . . and besides, she's adopted."

The teacher cleared his throat and quickly ushered us back to our seats with a herding gesture of his arms. "Mmm, well, why don't you write a report about what it's like to be Chinese."

Over recess time, I produced two sentences:

Chinese is hard work. I eat rice and play the piano everyday and kids think I am weird.

On the bus ride home from school, Griff, my spelling bee rival, advised me, "You oughtta tell your parents on Z. If he ever asked anyone in class to stand up and tell 'im what it's like to be black, my Daddy'd raise hell."

"It'd be the talk of the PTA, for sure," his little sister agreed.

That evening, though, my mother shrugged her shoulders, "He didn't mean any harm. He isn't *racist,*" she emphasized the word as if it were too terrible to assign anyone, let alone my teacher. "They just don't understand. Besides, you should be ashamed that you can't speak more Chinese." I tucked away the blame into my own pocket, the rights and reasons of anger jostled and messed. It began a collection of frustration and misled feelings of discrimination.

Four or five times a year, my father would drive my mother, older brother, and me to visit his sister, *Goo-goo,* in New York City. On the playgrounds of West 125th St., I befriended a black girl with shiny cheeks and hair twisted into fun sculptures tipped on the ends with plastic, candy-colored barrettes. Her mother called her Chyna, like fine China, her precious baby girl. Ironically, Chyna had a toughness she had donned from having three older brothers and two pit bulls at home. When a kid on the playground teased that her mother had shaped her hair like alien antennae, she spat back, "At least my momma does more'n' wails on me, you silly nigger," and a deft, Afro-aimed wad of gum hurtled from her mouth with more precision than any ten-year-old I knew had, including my much-idolized older brother. The antagonist, pissed and a bit shamed for the jab, started cussing up a slew of insults, but I was still struck by Chyna's casual, "you silly nigger." The latter word being what plowed me down: Nigger. It was a no-no word from where

I was living in Maryland, among the mixed black and white who consciously and carefully dwelt on the fine line of the Progressive North and the Ignorant South. It was worse than saying any of the four-letter curse words that I only dared to spell out when I was really mad. The early lyrics of rap hadn't reached my ears yet and "reclamation" was only a word in the spelling bee. This girl has balls, I thought, or the equivalent of what a nine-year-old me would think.

I tried to punch the same line a few days later on my brother during a squabble, "You silly Chink," to which my father bawled and slapped out of me any rebellious inclination to try that line again. I got a lengthy lecture about how unfair he was treated in the workplace; that his hard work and high education would still be passed over when promotions came around. Even now, I can't say the word "Chink" without wincing. It just doesn't sound empowering or provoke the same admiration that I felt for Chyna's words.

My teenage years were spent in a mall-centered town of northern New Jersey, where the high school was attended by only a handful of minorities. I permed my jet-black hair and then sprayed gallons of "Sun In" bleach onto it, while flipping through a *Vogue* in which Iman and Naomi Campbell were the only tokens. I didn't yet know there was such a thing as Asian fever (an exclusive desire for Asian women), and, to be quite honest, when the idea was first introduced to me I welcomed it as pretty fine praise and affirmation until my later college years taught me to examine the twisted undercurrents. I didn't have a single Asian friend during high school, and when my public speaking/debate team visited with schools that were populated with East and South Asian students, I eyed the cliques with uncertainty and unease. I had bought into believing the stereotypes of my background. Academic success meant nerd. Playing the piano was discipline and "good" in a bad, uncool way. Quiet and polite was socially inept and passive. The unease also came from the development that much of my identity was dependent on being different. I had internalized the defenses so much that it worried me to be racially similar. I looked at the photos of streets in Beijing, crammed with bicycle traffic, black eyes, and black hair, and I was secretly scared that I would get lost in the multitudes if I were to be transported there, to "people of my own kind."

Even when I had attended Saturday Chinese school in Maryland, I felt like an imposter. "Grace is already on the fifth level in her piano studies and Jenny is at the top of her math class and won the science award." Mothers would compare us like prize pigs at a farm auction. I clung to my mother and hung my head at her approving nods toward the other specimens of blue-ribbon children. With my piano skills *Fur Elise* stuttered out like a mangled musicbox, and my school grades were high, but unremarkably so. It made me angry that such competitiveness was laced in the Chinese community, but that heads turned with tight lips from social injustice. I remember hearing the women speak of the Ivy League colleges that their children applied to. Some universities were limiting the number of Asian students that could be accepted, almost a reverse affirmative action. It was strange to me that the issue was spoken of as though this were a great compliment to how many good students there were with yellow skin. I didn't want to be part of a community that could wag its head with a modest smile at such discrimination.

It was the "outsider" complex that drove my adolescent experience toward the punk rock and goth scenes, arenas that were not only Eurocentric but to the degree that plaster-white complexions and British accents were the desired ideal. It must have been at a hardcore club when I encountered my first Nazi skinhead. He was a big, rangy fellow, whose pants still hung to his ass despite the stringy suspenders. The skinhead, whom I'll call Nick, toted a thick and slightly crooked swastika on his forearm. Throughout the first two sets of identically angry bands I noticed that Nick kept jutting his chin my way, and whenever he leapt into the mosh pit, he always jostled his way out a bit closer to the corner I was standing in. Wary of his lumbering advancement, I checked around to be sure of my own troop of vampyric comrades backing me. I cupped my hand to Moshe, my mohawked friend who insisted on the nickname "Mosh." "There might be trouble," I remarked, being seriously sixteen and thinking of the pepper spray that I had in my purse, which was left on the bar across the crowd of ruckus. Mosh chuckled, "Nah, that's Big Nick. I went to grade school with him. He's not really into it." "It" being Nazi; being for this New Jersey kid like any other club that you might join and outgrow—the Mouseketeers, for example. (I don't mean to imply with this one example that all Nazi skinheads are so flimsy in their beliefs, but the ones I have met in the Northeast have more often than not turned out to be middle-class kids who haven't had the same beaten-in, outright racism that is passed on like a bad gene from generation to generation as it is in more rural parts of the country, where white sheets are not a Jerry Springer joke.)

After one bellowed-out lyric, Nick gives a hardy kick in the center of the pit and jumps out next to me. He grunts, wipes his red forehead (razor burn?), and grins down at me with a set of steel-aligned teeth. "What's your name?" he hollers down through the guitar solo blare.

"JOYIN!"

"What?!" It's not just the noise level, I'm used to spelling out my name and saying it at least three times slow, as if leading my listener through a first reader's book.

"JOO-YINN."

Big Nick shakes his head, "I'll just call you JOY, okay? Can I get you a drink, Joy?"

For once, the name isn't the issue that annoys me. It's that this jackass with the most offensive hate message scrawled into his flesh is hitting on me. I'm fuming and I know that in this club, with the amps spewing out repetitive lyrics about a blind society, there was no way that I could administer my finely tuned, debate club tactics and try to make sense of what was going on in Big Nick's cerebellum. So I just yelled and pointed at the swastika, "NAZI!"

"Yeah!" Big Nick smiled back and saluted as if I were praising his Popeye muscles.

I pointed to myself, "CHINESE!" (Me, Jane. You, Fuckhead.)

"I LIKE CHINESE." I think he meant food, because I doubt that he mingled in the Chinese Cultural Center much.

I pointed to myself again, almost out of sheer mockery, "MINORITY."

He got the point and quickly blinked his eyes at me and shook his head, "BUT YOU'RE A MODEL MINORITY!"

Those two words stunned me more than the time Chyna ranted out the word "nigger," but it was an altogether different shock. It took something that sounded like praise and invoked a shame in me, while Chyna had taken a word that had a history of shame and invoked a connection, a proud one, albeit teasing. I felt like a scandal, like someone "passing" into a social privilege that I did not want yet could not deny.

It was just a couple of years later when I packed my bags, found an apartment in Harlem, and grabbed out desperately at the words to fit my anger in college. The first movements of identification were not clearly pursued. At a quick and skeptical glance, the Asian clubs at the university still seemed academic, social, or Christian. They seemed to lack the intensity and anger that the African American groups had. Again, I bought the stereotype. Everywhere I turned I felt boxed in, even by the boys and men who pursued me because of my Asianness. I felt that they were looking at my black hair and almond-shaped eyes for something exotic, something far beyond the New Jersey home that I really came from. I remember that a Caucasian hallmate once explained to me the subsets of Asian Women: "You've got your dowdy girls who shrink away from you in the elevator, and will blush all the while they help you with the lab report. There are the Gucci girls, usually Korean or Japanese, who are a real expensive date. They have twenty pairs of black shoes and usually stick with their own, anyhow. Then there's the Joy Luck Club, who are the best bets for dates because they're sick of their domineering Chinese fathers." (I've recently heard that this person moved to Korea and is a rather popular television celebrity there.)

I don't mean to say that I assimilated into the black Harlem community; I couldn't and wasn't quite pretentious enough to believe that I could. I was attending Columbia University, one of the best and most-privileged colleges in the nation, but out of some illusion of self-preservation I had decided to live off campus, a few blocks higher into Harlem yet still at the safe edge of its perimeters.

Black culture meant strength to me. I made my way down the street from the bodegas and African cafés to the literature classes of Baldwin and Achebe. At the university I envied the hip, independent black women whom I befriended on campus. Through my eyes they were soulful, strong, and spoke their minds, like my childhood friend Chyna. I saw African American students wearing colorful garb, growing their dreds, beating their drums, and saying "This is who I am." My feet itched to the sounds of hip hop and the lyrics seemed to match my own heated sentiments. But when I looked around for my Asian brothers and sisters, I saw them donning khakis and polos, assimilating for good jobs.

"Asian Americans are known for their success in business, education, and emphasis on family values. What is there to be angry about? It's a compliment." My mother still tries to convince me. I resented it, though, as many kids, not just minorities, with privileges resent their handed-down sweaters of ease that blanket personal struggles and hardships. I yearned for the ferocity of black anger, the right to that obvious and unifying spirit. The ability to protest was far more appealing and righteous to me than the polite assimilation of the Asian American community.

Coming to terms with my ethnicity relied heavily on breaching the gap that I had set up between myself and other Asians. On campus, I finally became close friends with other Asian women. The first comforts were simple. "Isn't it nice to eat together?" we grinned at each other, gnawing on our cold soy-chicken feet. "No one to make faces at us." At our dinner table, though, our familiar issues came forth with the platters of familiar food. We compared notes on childhoods (we all wince at the echoes of the teasing "dirty knees" song), adolescence (how many of us permed and bleached our hair?), and the present. I found myself with symptoms of my own sort of yellow fever, seeking out black-haired, sleek-eyed comrades to claim as my "sistas."

After years of shifting layers of identity I embrace my Chinese heritage. Yet I still question the issues of discomfort and discrimination and acknowledge the ever-changing relations in the cultures around me. From the African American community I gained a sense of right to empower and to protest. From the Asian American community I gained a sense of affirmation and sharing of experiences. Living among and as part of the urban collage, I enjoy the motley group of cultures and recognize the struggles of each group and individual, but, most importantly, I am able to look in the mirror and recognize my own.

Everett Hoagland

All That

For Fred Ho and for us all

Shuttles in the rocking loom of history.—ROBERT HAYDEN

here you are
just as surely as all
arabian
barbary
spanish
native american
mustangs
are of asian origin you

are here in karmic world music
with bass clef lapels large
as plane wings your trademark
red silk zoot suit—spun
as much from ananse's akan
trickster webs of sonic yarn
as from mandarin moth larvae—

is all that

just as surely as ancient giant
chinese merchant ships with four-square
sails big & red as sunset plied the indian

ocean just as surely as indians traded with east

africans who traded with arabs
who traded in african slaves
in the name of the one the merciful just
as surely as hulled middle passage
floating hells with holds full
of iron-collared captives branded "black

devils" were named *mercy* & everything
between *angel* & *zong* oceanic weaves
logged cross-
stichings mapped the patterned kente warp
& woof of moaned american music just

as surely as communal rum-brown afro-
cuban hands life-lined like cured tobacco
leaves freely drum whatever ogun & shango
congas mambos sambas they damn
well please africans indians chinese mix

it up in trinidad steel pan bands that play
paisley raindrops pinging corrugated tin
balafon rooftops on plum fluted trade
winds swishing hushes in palm trees

from beached coconuts washed up by measure-
less water refrains of singing seas'
deep sounding whales'
songs that buoyed net numbers of hope-
ful chinese laborers who over-

came the choke-holds of quiet money's
dead calm pacific migrant ships
their hands cradling stern urns of ancestors'
dust & empty heirloom blue willow ginger jars
full of silent music just

as your own old new borrowed blue
strong suit baritones liberation suites based
on the red bordered story quilt "internationale"
an outfit of twelve-bar blood-dyed fabric
cut from history's misogynist sweat shop's

whole-nine-yards of child labor magic
"oriental" rugs woven with all the overtones under-
tones of pan-people music
hued variously as a multimedia

ho-mao-chou-nehru-nkrumah-nyerre-fidel

frock made into today's big red *mien ow*
(you wear with a clef sign clasp pin
fashioned from a browning
photo moment's clipper shipped west/east
east/west gold trans-

continental railroad tie-spike)
of woven straight black hair
from scourged "coolies" cut off
pigtails in burned down china towns of america's
white lies & yellowing declaration
yet here you are dust-

jacketed with fly-away lapels being zoot-
winged victory brass flame saxophon dragon
suits you pressed as you want to be in your all-
american ever-new prez-era ever-hip as all
that ongoing junket in a jazz junk

ark that has gone
around & around
& comes out
here

CONTRIBUTORS

ELIZABETH ESCH, assistant professor of history at Barnard, specializes in twentieth-century U.S. history and American studies. She received her Ph.D. from New York University in 2004 with a dissertation entitled "Fordtown: Managing Race and Nation in the American Empire, 1925–45." She joined the Barnard faculty in 2007.

DIANE C. FUJINO is an associate professor of Asian American studies at the University of California, Santa Barbara. She is the author of *Heartbeat of Struggle: The Revolutionary Life of Yuri Kochiyama.*

ROYAL HARTIGAN began tap dancing at the age of three and then added piano, drums, and world music to his art. He is an artist who is committed to radical change on plantation earth toward justice for all the world's peoples.

KIM HEWITT is an assistant professor of American Studies at Empire State College, New York. She is the author of *Mutilating the Body: Identity in Blood and Ink*, which explores the meaning of body modification. Her interest in the body in popular culture leads her to investigate issues of race and expressive culture, while her interest in the mind/body connection has led her to research mental health and altered states of consciousness.

CHERYL HIGASHIDA is an assistant professor of English at the University of Colorado, Boulder, where she works on multicultural literature of the Left from the 1930s through the Cold War, focusing on African American and Asian American writers. She is a member of the Los Angeles–based Labor/Community Strategy Center, a multiracial, anti-imperialist "think tank/act tank."

FRED HO is a Chinese American baritone saxophonist, composer, writer, producer, veteran revolutionary socialist activist, and leader of the Afro Asian Music Ensemble.

EVERETT HOAGLAND came of age as a poet and had the first national publications of his poetry during the Black Arts movement. He is professor emeritus at the University of Massachusetts, Dartmouth. From 1994 to 1998 he was the poet laureate of historic New Bedford, where he has lived and been an activist for thirty-two years.

ROBIN D. G. KELLEY is a professor of American studies and ethnicity at the University of Southern California. He is the author of several books, including *Hammer and Hoe: Alabama Communists during the Great Depression* (1990), *Race Rebels: Culture, Politics and the Black Working Class* (1994), and most recently, *Freedom Dreams: The Black Radical Imagination* (2002). He is currently completing a biography of the pianist/composer Thelonius Monk.

MAO ZEDONG was Chairman of the Communist Party of China, a poet and revolutionary theoretician, organizer, and one of the giants of contemporary world history.

BILL V. MULLEN is a professor of English and the director of American studies at Purdue University. He is author of *Afro-Orientalism* (2004) and *Popular Fronts: Chicago and African American Cultural Politics, 1935–1946* (1999). He is coeditor, with Jim Smethurst, of *Left of the Color Line: Race, Radicalism, and Modern Literature of the United States* (2003) and, with Cathryn Watson, of *W. E. B. Du Bois on Asia: Crossing the World Color Line* (2005).

DAVID MURA has written two memoirs: *Where the Body Meets Memory: An Odyssey of Race, Sexuality and Identity* (1996) and *Turning Japanese: Memoirs of a Sansei*, which won a 1991 Josephine Miles Book Award from the Oakland PEN and was listed in the *New York Times* notable books of the year. Mura's third and most recent book of poetry is *Angels for the Burning* (2004). His second book of poetry, *The Colors of Desire* (1995) won the Carl Sandburg Literary Award from the Friends of the Chicago Public Library; and his first, *After We Lost Our Way*, won the 1989 National Poetry Series Contest. His book of critical essays, *Song for Uncle Tom, Tonto & Mr. Moto: Poetry & Identity*, was published by the University of Michigan Press in its Poets on Poetry series in 2002. The performance piece *Secret Colors* premiered at the Walker Art Center in Minneapolis in 1994 and has been presented at various other venues throughout the country. A film adaptation of this piece, *Slowly, This*, was broadcast in the PBS series *Alive TV* in July/August 1995. Mura has also been featured on the Bill Moyers PBS series *The Language of Life*.

ISHLE PARK is a writer.

ALEXS PATE'S fifth and most recent novel, *West of Rehoboth*, was published in 2001. His debut novel, *Losing Absalom*, was awarded best first novel by the Black Caucus of the American Library Association and a 1994 Minnesota Book Award for best fiction. *Finding Makeba*, his second novel, tells the story of a father and daughter who overcame the struggles of a disintegrating family to find each other; it was listed as a family classic and one of the five novels every black woman should have on her bookshelf in the December 1999 issue of *Essence Magazine*. In 1997 Pate wrote and published the novel *Amistad*, commissioned by Steven Spielberg's Dreamworks/SKG and based on the screenplay by David Franzoni, which became a *New York Times* best-seller. Pate's fourth novel, *Multicultiboho Sideshow*, was published in 1999.

THIEN-BAO THUC PHI is a Vietnamese American spoken-word artist based in the Twin Cities. Born in Saigon, he is the youngest son of two mixed-blood Chinese and Vietnamese parents who raised him in the Phillips neighborhood of South Minneapolis as a Vietnamese boy in the hood. A graduate of Macalester College and a retired pizza delivery boy, Bao has performed at numerous venues and schools locally and nationally, from the Nuyorican Poet's Café to the University of California, Berkeley. He has twice won the Minnesota Grand Poetry Slam, and he also won two poetry slams at the Nuyorican Poet's Café in New York. He remains the only Vietnamese American man to have appeared on HBO's Russell Simmons Presents Def Poetry, and the National Poetry Slam Individual Finalists Stage, where he placed sixth overall out of over 250 national slam poets.

ISHMAEL REED is the author of numerous novels, including *Mumbo Jumbo, Japanese by Spring*, and *The Terrible Twos*, and the editor of numerous anthologies. He is also one of the editors of the influential *Yardbird Anthology*. He resides in Oakland, California.

KALAMU YA SALAAM was born in 1947 in New Orleans. He is a professional editor, writer, moviemaker, educator, producer, and arts administrator, and is cofounder (with Kysha Brown) of Runagate Multimedia publishing company. He is the founder and director of the Neo-Griot Workshop, a New Orleans–based black writers workshop and is the moderator of e-drum, an electronic mailing list of over sixteen hundred black writers and diverse supporters of literature. He is codirector of Students at the Center, a writing program in the New Orleans public schools. His latest books are the anthologies *From a Bend in the River: 100 New Orleans Poets* (1998) and *360°: A Revolution of Black Poets* (1998). Salaam's latest spoken-word CD is *My Story, My Song*. He is the recipient of a 1999 Senior Literature Fellowship from the Fine Arts Work Center in Provincetown, Massachusetts. His latest movies include *He's On His Way*, a documentary about jazz funerals. *The Magic of JuJu*, a book-length appreciation of the Black Arts movement is forthcoming.

MAYA ALMACHAR SANTOS is a Filipina American poet/artist born and raised in the south end of Seattle, Washington. She began writing in 1995 and went on to organize open mics in school. In 1997, she became a founding member of isangmahal arts kollective—artists in residence of the Northwest Asian American Theater. Isangmahal, meaning "one love" in Tagalog, is a collective of Filipino poets, artists, dancers, and musicians who aim to subvert cultural genocide through their art and, more importantly, one love. Santos graduated in 1999 from Washington State University with a bachelor's degree in architecture.

JOYIN SHIH is currently living in New York City. Her previous works of fiction and nonfiction have appeared in the *San Francisco Bay Guardian* and *Mixer Magazine*, as well as in numerous online zines. In her continuing essays, Shih continues to examine the fetish of race as a personal study.

RON WHEELER is a veteran African American martial arts champion. He was a member of the touring cast of Fred Ho's martial arts/music/theater show *Voice of the Dragon*.

DANIEL WIDENER is an assistant professor of history at the University of California, San Diego.

LISA YUN is an associate professor of history at the State University of New York, Binghamton.

colonialism: African American view of, 61–70, 81 n. 23; in China, 155–56; Chinese "coolie" labor and, 34, 42–45; in Cuba, 31–32, 38–41; Korean war and, 62–70; Revolutionary Action Movement fight against, 114–17

Color Curtain, The, 5

Coltrane, John, 256–58, 260–64

Combahee River Collective, 226–28, 246, 250 n. 25

Committee against Jim Crow in Military Service and Training, 56

Committee for a Unified Newark, 133

Committee for the Defense of the Foreign Born, 74

Committee to Defend Negro Leadership, 74

communism: black revolutionaries and, 97–148; opposition to Korean War and, 61, 72–77, 81 n. 22

Communist Labor Party (CLP), 121, 130–32, 146

Communist League, 120–21

Communist Manifesto, The, 97

Communist Party (Marxist-Leninist) (CP-ML): Black Arts movement and, 140–41; evolution of, 131–32

Communist Party USA (CPUSA): China and, 156–59; Japanese Americans and, 166–69, 189 n. 3, 190 nn. 8–9; Maoism and, 102–7

Communist Workers Party (CWP), 147, 148 n. 6

community: interracial friendship and, 323–52; martial arts and role of, 277–81

Comrade Is as Precious as a Rice Seedling, A, 224

Conditions, 221, 247 n. 4

Congress of African Peoples (CAP), 133–36, 142–46, 162

Congress of Racial Equality (CORE), 107–8, 258

Conjure Band, 219

Continua, Lotta, 120

"cool" aesthetic, 265–81, 283 n. 30

coolie labor: contract purchases by, 46–49; decline in Cuba of, 47–50; East Indians as coolies, 35–36; in Haiti, 36–38; history in Americas of, 32–36; human costs of, 41–45; kidnapping and decoying for procurement of, 44–45; legal status of, 46–47; as slavery, 31–32, 41, 45–50; survival rates for, 41–42; trafficking statistics for, 41–45, 53 n. 44; violence against, 43–46

Cors (ship), 43

Cortez, Jayne, 259, 262

Council on African Affairs, 64, 74

Coup, The (hip hop group), 97–98

Cox, Anthony, 219

Criminal Justice Codification, Revision & Reform Act, 145

Crouch, Stanley, 7

Crusader, 106–7, 110, 137, 208

Cruse, Harold: Black Arts movement and, 180–82; communism and influence of, 111, 147; Revolutionary Action Movement and, 103, 107–8, 114, 117

Cuba: China and revolution in, 103–7; Chinese coolie labor in, 32–34, 36–38; Chinese diaspora in, 30–50; sugar production in, 37–38

Cuba Commission Report, The, 33–34, 45

Cubic Air laws, 28

cultural institution, cultural institutions: Afro-Asian coalitions and, 2–16, 221–47; Asian-American cultural nationalism and, 224, 229–47, 250 n. 27; hip hop as, 295–96, 316 n. 2; martial arts as, 265–81; multiethnic collaborations and, 323–53; racial identity and, 200–214

Cultural Revolution, 122–24; African

American art and influence of, 137–46

Cumings, Bruce, 81 n. 22

Daily People's World, 65, 74
Daily Worker, 106
Dana Dane (rapper), 310
dance, 272–81, 293–94, 362
Daniels, Stan, 110
Dartmouth College, 257, 262–64
Davis, Ben, 72
Davis, Judy, 139
Davis, Miles, 257–58, 262
Davis, Thulani, 247 n. 5
Deacons for Defense and Justice, 105
DeBerry, Clifton, 118
Debs, Eugene, 171
December 12th movement, 9–10
De La Soul (rap group), 306
Deng Xiaoping, 146, 207
Denizen Kane (hip hop musician), 314
de Quesada, Gonzalo, 30
Desert Run, 223
developing countries, 62
Dewey, Thomas, 57
Diallo, Amadou, 298, 316 n. 5
Diddy (rapper), 310
Digable Planets, 302, 317 n. 12
"Dig It" (song), 97–98
Dinerstein, Joel, 273
Dinkins, David, 22
Diversity in the Power Elite—Have Women and Minorities Reached the Top?, 213
DJing, 309
Dodge Revolutionary Union Movement (DRUM), 109, 119–21, 161–62
dojo, 276–81
Dolphy, Eric, 77, 256, 261
Domhoff, G. William, 213
Do the Right Thing, 21–22
"Double Victory" campaign, 71, 85 n. 62
Douglas, Aaron, 64, 74

Dower, John, 62
draft evasion and resistance: by African Americans, 56–60, 75–77; by Japanese Americans, 167–69
Dreams (ship), 43
drum set, 285–89
Du Bois, W. E. B., 3–5, 15, 139, 147; in China, 98–99, 157; on economic conditions of African Americans, 24; in Ghana, 104–5; on Korean War and military racism, 64, 74
Dues, 222
Dunayevskaya, Raya, 118
Dupierris, Marcial, 40
Dutch East Indies, 35

East, The (community school), 162
Ebony, 65
economic conditions: for African Americans, 24, 26–28, 57–60; Afro-Asian unity and challenge of, 212–14; for Asian Americans, 24–25, 28–29; in postwar United States, 70–71
education levels, 27–28
ego trip (rap), 310
E.I. (rap), 310
"Eisenhower Blues," 71
Elbaum, Max, 148 n. 6
Ellington, Duke, 251 n. 29
Eminem, 299, 316 n. 9
Empresa de Colonización, 40
Epton, Bill, 102
Esch, Betsy, 97–148
Esquire, 116
essentialist black fundamentalism, 7
Ethiopians in the Greco-Roman Experience, 3
ethnic cultural institutions: coalition building among, 221–47, 247 n. 4; martial arts and, 269–81
ethnic studies programs, 159–64, 174–76
Evans, Arthur, 108

Library of Congress
Cataloging-in-Publication Data

Afro Asia : revolutionary political
and cultural connections between
African Americans and Asian Americans /
edited by Fred Ho and Bill V. Mullen.
p. cm.

ISBN 978-0-8223-4258-8 (cloth : alk. paper) —
ISBN 978-0-8223-4281-6 (pbk. : alk. paper)

1. African Americans—Relations with Asian Americans.

2. African Americans—Politics and government—20th century.

3. Asian Americans—Politics and government—20th century.

4. African Americans—Intellectual life—20th century.

5. Asian Americans—Intellectual life—20th century.

6. United States—Race relations

I. Ho, Fred Wei-han.
II. Mullen, Bill, 1959–
E185.615.A5934 2008
305.8'95073—dc22
2007044906